In 1909, former Memphis mayor James H. Malone led a project to procure portraits of all the city's former mayors to hang in the newly built City Hall. Because there was no existing portrait of Marcus Winchester, one was painted by S. D. Rogers of Walter Gray's Studio in Memphis. Today, the portrait is on display with others in the Hall of Mayors in the lobby of Memphis City Hall at 125 Main Street.

TOWNMANIA
MARCUS WINCHESTER
AND THE MAKING OF
MEMPHIS

R. Scott Williams

Also by R. Scott Williams

The Accidental Fame and Lack of Fortune
of West Tennessee's David Crockett

An Odd Book:
How the First Modern Pop Culture Reporter Conquered New York

The Forgotten Adventures of Richard Halliburton:
A High-Flying Life from Tennessee to Timbuktu

In memory of Barbara Trefren Mayer
who loved her home on the fourth Chickasaw bluff.

Copyright ©2025 R. Scott Williams

All rights reserved.
No part of this book may be reproduced, stored in a retrieval system, or transmitted in any form or by any means—electronic, mechanical, photocopying, recording, or otherwise—without the prior written permission of the publisher, except in the case of brief quotations embodied in critical articles or reviews.

First edition

Softcover ISBN: 978-0-9986997-5-2
Hardcover ISBN: 978-0-9986997-7-6
E-book ISBN: 978-0-9986997-6-9

Library of Congress Control Number: 2025916759

Cover design by Tom Martin
Edited by Jennifer Wildes Hunter
Printed in the United States of America

For information, contact:
R. Scott Williams
Union City, Tennessee
rscottwilliamsemail@gmail.com

rscottwilliams.info

Author's Note:
This is a work of nonfiction. Every reasonable effort has been made to verify the facts and events described. Any errors or omissions are unintentional.

"I am satisfied the effects of townmania will not last always, and perhaps not long."
—James Winchester to John Overton, November 22, 1818

"There is an astonishing rage at the present day for the establishment of new towns. Does a man possess a tract of land convenient to river navigation? If he be a man of enterprise, he starts the plan of a town—lays off his land into lots, and expects to make his fortune by selling out."
—*Richmond Enquirer*, 1818

"There was never a member of any community more esteemed while he lived, or more honored at his death, than Major Marcus B. Winchester, the most graceful, courtly, elegant gentleman that ever appeared upon Main Street, and the 'dress proclaimed the man.'"
—*Memphis Daily Appeal*, January 16, 1871

Contents

Introduction: Going to Memphis
In the beginning
1

Part One
Chapter One: All American Boy
The Winchester family settles in Tennessee
7

Chapter Two: Baby Let's Play House
Construction of James Winchester's Cragfont, John Overton's Travellers Rest, and Andrew Jackson's Hermitage
17

Chapter Three: We the People
Marcus's father, James Winchester, fights in the War of 1812
25

Chapter Four: Good Morning Baltimore
Marcus's grandfather, William Winchester, founds Westminster, Maryland
31

Chapter Five: Trouble, Heartaches & Sadness
James Winchester's military reputation destroyed
39

Chapter Six: Big River
History of the fourth Chickasaw bluff
51

Chapter Seven: Hello Memphis
John Overton purchases the John Rice tract
61

Part Two

Chapter Eight: Chickasaw Special
Marcus Winchester with Andrew Jackson at The Jackson Purchase
65

Chapter Nine: Memphis Blues
Andrew Jackson sends Marcus Winchester to the bluff
73

Chapter Ten: Walking in Memphis
Marcus Winchester and William Lawrence arrive and begin surveying the bluff
81

Chapter Eleven: Changes Comin' On
Marcus Winchester takes care of business in Memphis
89

Chapter Twelve: Considering a Move to Memphis
John Overton advertises the new town on the east bank of the Mississippi River
101

Chapter Thirteen: That's How I Got to Memphis
The new town of Memphis begins to grow under Marcus Winchester's leadership
105

Chapter Fourteen: Memphis Bound Blues
Marcus Winchester befriends Isaac Rawlings, David Crockett, and Frances Wright
125

Chapter Fifteen: Anywhere But Memphis
Death and disease come to the city on the bluff
147

Part Three

Chapter Sixteen: Tired of Being Alone
Marcus Winchester marries Amarante Loiselle, a free woman of color from St. Louis
165

Chapter Seventeen: I am Somebody
The battle over slavery
181

Chapter Eighteen: Soul Man
Racism impacts the Marcus Winchester family
201

Chapter Nineteen: Memphis in the Meantime
Culture, hospitality, and community development come to Memphis
213

Chapter Twenty: Memphis Money
Marcus Winchester and the fight for Memphis's first bank
231

Chapter Twenty-one: Born Under a Bad Sign
Marcus Winchester loses it all
253

Chapter Twenty-two: Love and Happiness
Marcus Winchester marries Lucy McLean
275

Chapter Twenty-three: Berry Rides Again
Marcus Winchester attempts a comeback
283

Chapter Twenty-four: From Graceland to the Promised Land
Marcus Winchester dies with his harness on
297

Chapter Twenty-five: Trying to Live My Life Without You
Lucy Winchester becomes a celebrity
305

Chapter Twenty-six: I Forgot to Remember to Forget
*Marcus Winchester, Isaac Rawlings, and other
early founders of Memphis are forgotten*
311

Acknowledgment
326

Appendix One: About the Chapter Titles
328

Appendix Two: Winchester Cemetery Records
334

Bibliography
346

Index
356

Unless otherwise noted, text in direct quotes has been replicated as it was originally written, retaining errors, obsolete and variant spellings, and other inconsistencies.

Both "Black" and "White" are capitalized when referring to racial identities to acknowledge each as a distinct cultural and historical group and to provide consistency in punctuation.

"Native American" is used when referring to the Indigenous peoples of what is now the United States. While no single term is universally preferred, "Native American" is widely recognized in historical and academic writing and encompasses the many distinct tribes and nations with their own identities, histories, and cultures.

JAMES T. MIX. THEODORE MIX.

JAS. T. MIX & BRO.,
CARRIAGE
REPOSITORY,
MAIN STREET,
Memphis, Tenn.

EVERY DESCRIPTION OF

CARRIAGES MADE TO ORDER

WE have now on hand, and are constantly receiving a large and well selected assortment of

CARRIAGES

OF OUR OWN MANUFACTORY,

Together with others from the best manufactories in the United States consisting of

Coaches,   **Buggies,**
  Barouches,   **Goslin Buggies,**
    Rockaways,   **Express Wagons,**
      Phætons,   **Travelers "**
Harness,   **Whips, Mats,**
  Cabs,   **Childrens' Gigs,**
    Hobbies,   **Velocipedes, &c.**

For style, beauty, durability and cheapness, our carriages cannot be excelled in any other establishment in the Union. Persons in want are invited to examine our stock.

From Rainey's Memphis City Directory, 1855/56

Introduction: Going to Memphis

In the beginning

On the episode of the game show *Jeopardy!* that aired on Christmas Day 2024, the final clue came from the category "U.S. Place Names." As the contestants held their breath, host Ken Jennings read the clue: "A trio including Andrew Jackson founded this city with a name that evokes a great city of the ancient world." Among the contestants was returning champion Laura Faddah, who was in second place heading into Final Jeopardy. To guarantee her spot in the Tournament of Champions, she needed a fifth consecutive win. The clue proved to be a perfect Christmas gift—Faddah is a native of Memphis, Tennessee, so she confidently answered correctly and secured her victory.

John Overton, James Winchester, and Andrew Jackson have been recorded in the annals of history as the trio of founders of Memphis, Tennessee. However, Winchester and Jackson had only small financial investments in Memphis; Jackson, who likely never even visited, only had his investment for a short time. Overton was the financial mastermind behind the land deal, and all three saw it as nothing more than that—a way to make a profit, then get out. Only one man—really just a boy at the time—Marcus Brutus Winchester, envisioned it as a community where thousands would one day live, work, and play.

In the summer of 1851, Marcus Winchester was answering questions of his own, but this was no game show. He was testifying in the case of *The Mayor and Aldermen of South Memphis v. Wardlow Howard and Joseph Kent*, a case concerning the intentions of the original proprietors for use of the riverfront, or promenade, as they called it.

Winchester was born on May 28, 1796—four days before Tennessee became a state—so, like the state, he was fifty-five at the time. Life on the Mississippi

River was not conducive to longevity, so Winchester was among the oldest residents in the county and one of the few original settlers still living at the time.

After reading the transcripts from that day, James H. Malone, Memphis mayor from 1906 to 1910, proclaimed, "The intelligence of Maj. Winchester cannot be better illustrated than his capacity in cleancut English to recite the early history of Memphis."[1]

Those who met Winchester frequently described him using adjectives such as sophisticated, polished, well-dressed, and handsome. Early historian James Davis wrote that during Winchester's time as a prisoner of war, he "attracted a great deal of attention for the remarkable beauty of his features and figure."[2] Davis added that English tourists who met young Winchester wrote letters home that were "lavish in their praise for the "little Yankee Major.""[3] Writer Frances Trollope claimed Winchester was "the only gentleman west of the Appalachians," while her friend Frances Wright described him as "a pleasing, gentlemanlike man" who seemed "strangely misplaced in a little town on the Mississippi."[4]

All eyes were on him in the courtroom in 1851 as he cleared his throat and began:

> I settled in Memphis, then known as the Chickasaw Bluff, in the year 1819, I believe in the month of May as one of the agents of the proprietors of the John Rice 5,000-acre grant. The town of Memphis was laid off in that year. The surveys may not have all been completed until the latter part of that year or the spring of the following year. The engraved plan marked X with the name of E. S. Todd written thereon was made under the direction of the Proprietors and published in the year 1820. I believe it to be a mainly correct plan of the town as then laid off.[5]

Everyone in the courtroom that day knew Marcus Winchester was the true founder of Memphis. As one writer put it in 1855, "As a citizen of Memphis, there is no person living so closely identified with its interests and prosperity, and the history of one could not be written without the other."[6]

As the son of Brigadier General James Winchester, Marcus grew up among the privileged and wealthy early Americans at Cragfont, one of the first mansions on the Tennessee frontier. He was sent east for his education where he lived with his father's notable family in Baltimore, Maryland. As a teenager, Winchester left school and joined his father as an unofficial aide-de-camp serving in the War of 1812. He was captured, along with his father, in a conflict that resulted in the greatest number of Americans killed in a single battle during that war. Winchester watched as the reputation of his father, who had been a hero in the Revolutionary War, was tarnished beyond repair.

At just twenty-two, Marcus Winchester was there during a pivotal moment in the settlement of West Tennessee. In 1818, he joined Isaac Shelby and Andrew Jackson at the negotiation and signing of a treaty with the Chickasaw Nation that came to be known as the Jackson Purchase. This historic agreement opened approximately eight million acres of land—spanning present-day West Tennessee and Southwest Kentucky—for American settlement. It also marked a significant step in westward expansion. Long before the treaty, a portion of that land had already been titled to James Winchester, Andrew Jackson, and one of Jackson's closest friends and political allies, John Overton. Overton would become one of Winchester's biggest mentors, although frequently the two did not see eye to eye.

Immediately after the treaty was signed, the proprietors, as they were called, sent Marcus Winchester to create a town on the fourth Chickasaw bluff that could be divided into lots and resold at a profit. It was a task he could have quickly completed then returned to Nashville, near where his parents lived, or to Baltimore, where he had been educated and where his extended family resided. He could also have moved to New Orleans, where his father often conducted business and other family members had settled. Instead, he chose to make Memphis home for the rest of his life. Young Winchester found himself living among a rugged yet enterprising mix of flatboat crewmen, Native Americans, fur trappers, and traders—all eking out a living on the bluff that his father, Brigadier General James Winchester, soon named Memphis.

In addition to helping lay out the streets and greenspaces—some of which remain in their original locations today—Marcus created the first map of Memphis and sold the city's first lots. He was selected as the first mayor, opened the first store, facilitated the first bank, handled the construction of the first courthouse and jail, and was the first postmaster. Knowing transportation was key to the growth of any city, Winchester championed the first ferry that crossed the Mississippi River on a regular basis, the first major roads east and west, and the first train tracks that were laid in the Midsouth. It was also Winchester the people of early Memphis could thank when the first pages of *The Memphis Advocate and Western District Intelligence*, the town's first newspaper, rolled off the press.

Applying a combination of creativity, diplomacy, and strong business acumen, Winchester guided the transformation of a sparsely populated outpost on the Mississippi River into a thriving commercial hub. Driven by the cotton industry, his little town then became one of the most important cities in the American South.

Through it all, he had to manage the complicated relationships that formed between those of different races including Native Americans, enslaved and free Black individuals, White enslavers, and abolitionists. His father, an early Tennessee settler, was an Indian fighter, and Marcus's uncle had been murdered and scalped. Marcus Winchester conducted business on the bluff with Native Americans and, by all accounts, showed respect for their culture. However, he also owned several ferries used in Memphis during the Cherokee Trail of Tears and other forced relocations, where Native American men, women, and children were displaced and transported west against their will.

Winchester also had to navigate the complicated relationships between Black and White individuals that existed in the earliest years of slavery in the South. Although he was raised on a plantation where the enslaved were forced to work both inside and outside the house—and he was an enslaver himself—he assisted other enslavers in navigating the legal system to free many enslaved men, women, and children. He also ran one of the few banks that the enslaved could use to save money to purchase their freedom or that of their loved ones. Race became especially personal for Winchester when he married Amarante Loiselle, a woman of mixed race from a land-owning free family in St. Louis. Together, they had eight children. The racism directed at him and his family culminated in the passage of a city ordinance that stated no White man could "keep a colored wife." This forced them to live outside the city limits of the town he had founded and faithfully served. The animosity he experienced because of his marriage to a free woman of color is especially ironic today, considering recent discoveries by his descendants: it is likely that Winchester was the great-great-grandson of Gideon Gibson Sr., a free Black landowner from North Carolina.

Great personal and professional losses in Winchester's later years were met with resilience and tenacity. He experienced the deaths of many close friends, a beloved daughter, and his wife, Amarante. Then, politics cost him his job as postmaster. He owned a significant amount of land in Memphis and across the river in Arkansas, but then lost it all in the bursting of the real estate bubble following the Panic of 1837.

With his second wife, Lucy, at his side, Winchester started over founding the Hopefield Real Estate Company, serving as a Tennessee State Legislator, and working to bring a railroad to Memphis. The story of Marcus Winchester embodies the profound dualities that defined the early Antebellum South. He fought for liberty and freedom when very little of either existed for women or free and enslaved Black individuals. He bravely chose to live life as a settler of the fourth Chickasaw bluff then worked to turn it into a transportation powerhouse. He had a front row seat during the Jackson-era fight over how the country would be governed—limited federal government and greater state sovereignty or an active federal government to promote economic development and modernization.

Winchester was the first Memphian to advocate for safe and reliable ferry service, the construction of wharfs to accommodate all types of boats along the riverfront, and the development of roads to facilitate the transport of goods and people into Memphis. He also laid the foundation for the city's first railroads.

Today, the Greater Memphis Chamber of Commerce proclaims Memphis is the "Supply Chain Capital of the World," a testament to the city's success in the "river, rail, road, and runway" sectors. As the home of FedEx Corporation, Memphis boasts the busiest cargo airport in the nation and the second busiest in the world, trailing only Hong Kong International Airport. The city is also the third busiest trucking corridor in the United States and, thanks to the Mississippi River, ranks as the fifth largest inland port. Railroads continue to play a vital role, with Memphis standing out as one of the few places in the country where five major freight rail companies converge. The seeds of that success were planted by Marcus Winchester.

When he died on November 2, 1856, at age sixty, his obituaries included words like *charitable*, *warm*, *sympathizing*, and *chivalrous*. Although, the comment he likely would have appreciated the most acknowledged he was working right up until the very end. The reporter wrote, "he died with his harness on."[7]

After his death, Winchester was buried in the cemetery on land he had donated to the city, then was quickly forgotten. It seems that his more progressive views on race and equality found little favor in the decades that followed. Around 1892, the city stables were unceremoniously built atop his unmarked grave.

In the words of the late historian James Roper: "Perhaps Memphis and Tennessee owe him a bit more than has been acknowledged."[8] Hopefully, this biography will, in a small way, help acknowledge the debt those of us who love Memphis owe Marcus Winchester.

Introduction Endnotes

1. James H. Malone, "History of Early Land Grants for Public Purposes in Memphis," *Commercial Appeal*, March 21, 1915.
2. James D. Davis, *History of Memphis* (Memphis: Hite, Crumpton & Kelly, 1873), 2.
3. Davis, *History of Memphis*, 2.
4. Alice J. G. Perkins and Theresa Wolfson, *Frances Wright, Free Enquirer: The Study of a Temperament* (New York: Harper & Brothers, 1939), 144.
5. Marcus Winchester, *Deposition*, September 15, 1851, *The Mayor and Aldermen of South Memphis v. Wardlow Howard and Joseph Kent*, Benjamin L. Hooks Central Library, Memphis and Shelby County Room.
6. E. R. Marlett and W. H. Rainey, *Rainey's Memphis City Directory, 1855* (Memphis: D.O. Dooley & Co., 1855), 27.
7. "Death of Major Winchester of New Orleans," *New Orleans Times-Picayune*, November 11, 1856.
8. James E. Roper, "Marcus Winchester and the Earliest Years of Memphis," *Tennessee Historical Quarterly* 21, no. 4 (1962): 351.

CAR FACTORY.

A. STREET & CO.,
(Successors to Phelon, Street & Co.,)

Poplar st., bet. Main & Second sts.,

are prepared to build all descriptions of

RAIL ROAD CARS,

including **PASSENGER CARS.** Also,

WAGONS, CARTS, WHEELBARROWS, PLOWS, &C.

All kinds of WROUGHT IRON WORK done promptly.
We solicit a share of public patronage. Encourage Home Manufacture.

TERMS CASH OR CITY GUARANTY.

E. F. RISK,
Wholesale and retail dealer in

STOVES, GRATES, SHEET-IRON, WIRE RIVETS,
Castings, Copper, &c. Manufacturer of plain and Japanned

TIN WARE,

COPPER AND SHEET-IRON WARE, &C,

EAST SIDE OF MAIN ST., BETWEEN MADISON & MONROE.

Next door to Grosvenor's Furniture Rooms,

MEMPHIS, TENNESSEE.

☞ Jobbing, of every description, promptly attended to. ☜

C. C. MAYDWELL'S

MARBLE WORKS,

CORNER OF SECOND AND JEFFERSON STS.,

MEMPHIS, TENN.

Keeps constantly on hand

MONUMENTS, TOMBS, HEAD AND FOOT STONES

Also, Building work done at the shortest notice.

From Rainey's Memphis City Directory, 1855/56

Part One

Chapter One: All American Boy

The Winchester family settles in Tennessee

One freezing morning in late January 1813, Marcus Winchester awoke on his first day as a teenage prisoner of war. Then just seventeen, he was likely held in Beauport, a small village on the outskirts of Quebec, Canada. While others in captivity experienced nightmarish conditions in freezing prisons and offshore on crowded, rat-infested ships, he was kept in a private home and given advantages reserved for only a few. Early Tennessee writer James Davis wrote a book published sixty years after the war in which he summarized young Winchester's time in Canada as an opportunity to impress the locals:

> [Marcus] attracted a great deal of attention, for the remarkable beauty of his features and figure, his gentlemanly and soldier-like bearing, and, above all, his astonishing intelligence, though a beardless boy. He met with many English tourists there, who conceived for him a strong attachment, particularly the female portion of them; and in their letters home, some of which were published, ridiculing and scandalizing the American people generally, and her military men particularly, were lavish in their praise of the 'little Yankee Major.'[1]

Just a few weeks before the battle, the "Little Yankee Major" had been safe with his father's family in Maryland where he had been sent for an education. His then sixty-one-year-old father, Brigadier General James Winchester, sent for his son believing service as his aide-de-camp was a logical next step in his eldest son's journey to manhood. Military service ran in the family. James and his two brothers, William David Winchester and George Washington Winchester, served in the Revolutionary War. Their father, William Winchester, fought in the French and Indian War and supported the Revolution in many ways from his home in Maryland.

James Winchester knew having Marcus at his side would provide an opportunity to personally instill the attributes he thought were needed to inspire patriotic passion and bravery in a third-generation aristocratic American.

James Winchester's own military service as a young man during the Revolutionary War had been notable. From research by Emma Shelton, it is known that in the months leading up to the war, the Winchester family provided financial support and served in leadership roles in various projects and initiatives with the aim of an independent America. James was appointed to serve in a group called the "Committee of Observation" and given the role of gathering signatures and keeping an eye on the local citizenry to ensure the embargo of British goods.[2]

James and his brothers, William and George, signed up to fight the British on the battlefield. While William eventually resigned and returned home before seeing action, James and George were both part of historic battles.

Letters exchanged during that time show the family was close, and the brothers were greatly missed by their family in Maryland. In a letter to James, his father fretted about the fate of George. He wrote:

> I have received two Sundry Letters from him the last dated at Charleston where he arrived the 6th of April. Well, I have had no acct from him since. . . . but as Charleston has fallen into the hands of the enemy, if he is Alive I expect he is a prisoner also. These are hard times for us in Our Old age.[3]

James Winchester was wounded twice, and then on August 22, 1777, he was captured by the British on Staten Island. He received a letter from his father that illustrated how much he was missed at home: "As for your Mother she is well at present but Never hears your name mentioned but tears Drop from her eyes."[4]

Winchester was held for two years before being released as part of a prisoner of war exchange. He then returned to battle serving as a lieutenant under General Nathanael Greene, the widely respected general and military strategist. James Winchester's name can be found listed among the seventeen thousand young American and French soldiers present when British General Charles Cornwallis surrendered his eight thousand soldiers to General George Washington at Yorktown on October 19, 1781. That victory effectively ended all chances of

British success in the Revolutionary War. America was now the land of the free.

James Winchester and his brother, George, were among the first officers initiated into the Society of the Cincinnati.[5] The organization was named after the ancient Roman hero Lucius Quinctius Cincinnatus. Rome faced a serious threat from enemies in 458 BCE when Cincinnatus was appointed dictator to deal with the crisis. He quickly organized the Roman army, defeated the invaders, and then willingly gave up his power, returning to his farm. For young American men like the Winchester brothers, Cincinnatus symbolized the virtue of selfless service to their young country, but also the opportunity to find success once they returned home.

After an impressive military career, thirty-three-year-old James Winchester was discharged in the winter of 1785. He and his younger brother, George, would prove that America was not only the land of the free—it was also the home of the brave.

They left their family's comfortable Tidewater plantation and timber-framed home, White's Level, near Baltimore, Maryland and headed out to carve out a new life beyond the Allegheny Mountains. The brothers' destination was an area called the Mero District in present-day Middle Tennessee. Part of North Carolina at the time, it was a dangerous, unsettled part of the country that had been officially established in 1788. The name Mero was chosen to honor Esteban Rodríguez Miró, the Spanish governor of Louisiana, in hopes he would persuade Spain to reopen the Mississippi River to American traders. One wonders if spelling his name incorrectly contributed to the failure of that effort.

When North Carolina elected to give up all the land that is now Tennessee in 1790, the Mero District became part of the Southwest Territory. The territory's leaders, including its first and only governor, William Blount, quickly began lobbying for it to become a state.

Early settlers in the Southwest Territory had to deal with isolation, sickness, frequent conflicts with Native Americans, and a long list of other challenges that came with attempting to tame a wilderness and turn it into someplace families could survive and communities could grow. Many who attempted it either died or gave up and returned home. In spite of the challenges, it seems it was exactly what the Winchester brothers needed, as they thrived in their new environment.

The Winchesters were not the only settlers making a home in the territory that would later become Tennessee. John Overton was launching his career in the Mero District, with no indication yet of the remarkable success he would eventually achieve. Through his life working as a planter, lawyer, judge, and real estate developer, Overton would become one of the wealthiest and most influential men in Tennessee.

Overton was born to James and Mary Waller Overton on April 9, 1766. Along with eleven children and numerous enslaved men and women, they made their home on Elk Creek in Louisa County, Virginia. When he was born, John Overton grew up in a large family. He had three older sisters—Ann, Molly, and Elizabeth—and several older brothers, including James, Thomas, and Waller; another brother had died in infancy. The younger children in the family were two brothers, Samuel and William, and a sister, Sarah.

John Overton was too young to fight in the revolution, but his father and older brothers served, leaving young John home with his mother to help care for his sisters. As a young man, he developed a love for books that stayed with him throughout his life. While teaching school as a teenager, Overton used the money he earned to purchase textbooks to teach himself the basics of law.

At the age of twenty, Overton decided to pursue a career as a lawyer. He followed brothers Waller and James to Mercer County, Kentucky, where he and James boarded at the home of a widowed distant relative, Elizabeth Lewis Robards. It is doubtful the measured and ambitious John Overton anticipated his moving into the Robards home would lead to his involvement in a troubled marriage and a love triangle that would one day become a national scandal.

Living with the Widow Robards was her son, Lewis, and his wife, the former Rachel Donelson. Despite the family's respected status on the frontier and their residence being one of the finest stone houses in the region, the household was troubled by the tumultuous marriage of Robards's son and daughter-in-law.

Overton later wrote that soon after he arrived, he noticed tension between the young couple and was informed by his brother that the relationship had been strained for quite some time. As Overton observed, one of the other boarders, Peyton Short, showed Rachel Robards "perhaps a little more than ordinary politeness."[6] After finding his wife talking with Short on the porch one afternoon, Lewis Robards exploded in another of his many fits of rage and demanded his wife leave their home and never return. It was not their first major fight, but this time, he wrote to Rachel's mother telling her to come get her daughter because the marriage was over. The actual timeline and details of what happened next are impossible to know for certain. With the passage of time and the many stories shared in the media once the issue became part of an election, the truth is murky at best.

Rachel's brother, Samuel Donelson, picked her up and took her back home about ten miles from Nashville. Soon, a new boarder, twenty-one-year-old Andrew Jackson, arrived and began staying from time to time with the Donelson family. Jackson, also a young lawyer like John Overton, had been admitted to the bar in 1787 and was working as a public prosecutor in the new Mero District.

John Overton moved further west to be closer to Nashville and began boarding at the Donelson home as well. Later, when he was part of those working behind the scenes to get Jackson elected president, the details around Jackson's marriage to Rachel became a major campaign issue. To clarify, Overton wrote:

> In the winter of 1788-1789, I was determined to fix my residence in Tennessee. Mrs. Robards entreated me to vie my exertions to get her son and daughter-in-law to live together again. I took the occasion to converse with Captain Robards on the subject. He assured me that his suspicions were unfounded, that he wished to live with his wife, and requested that I use my exertions to restore harmony. . . . I had frequent conversations with Rachel Robards on the subject of living happily with her husband. She assured me that no effort should be wanting on her part. It was agreed that Captain Robards and his wife were to live at Mrs. Donaldson's—they reunited sometime in 1789. . . . Not many months elapsed before Robards became jealous of Jackson.[7]

Overton remembered after Lewis Robards became jealous of Andrew Jackson, he was angry and abusive and threatened him. "Jackson told him he had not bodily strength to fight him," wrote Overton years later. "At the same time telling him that if he insisted on fighting, he would give him satisfaction."[8] Jackson moved out of the Donelson home, but that did nothing to slow Robards growing jealousy. Just a few months later, Robards returned to Kentucky, leaving his wife behind for good.

It was during this time Overton and Jackson developed a personal and professional friendship that would influence the legislation of Tennessee and the direction of national politics for decades to come. The personality and temperament of each man complimented the other. Both were certainly self-made and ambitious, but where Jackson was impulsive, fiery, and full of passion, Overton was intentional, measured, and judicious. If Jackson was the heart of the friendship, Overton was the brains.

According to the story that would be shared by Overton and the Jackson camp nearly forty years later, Rachel Donelson had been abandoned. She and Jackson had been told in 1791 that Robards had been granted a divorce. With her abusive marriage finally over and much to the surprise of their friends and family, Rachel Donelson Robards became Rachel Jackson in a wedding that took place in Natchez, Mississippi. Several years after the two became husband and wife, John Overton was reviewing some documents in Nashville and discovered that the divorce had never actually been finalized. Once he took steps to make sure it was, the Jacksons were married once again in 1794.

Meanwhile, James Winchester and his brother, George, were making themselves at home at nearby Bledsoe's Creek, approximately thirty-five miles northeast of present-day Nashville. During the next decade, both Winchester brothers influenced the business, law, and politics of the entire Southwest Territory. By all accounts, they were popular and well thought of among their friends, neighbors, and others in the territory.

A notebook the brothers shared during the Revolutionary War and in their first years in what would become Tennessee includes notes they made when surveying Sumner County and others in the region. The notebook also includes a "grocery list" of items the brothers needed on the frontier that was likely sent to them by family in Maryland. It included extracts and syringes, gum Arabic, opium, and medicine. An accounting of goods dated September 1, 1785, includes "2 servants" along with the names Jabo and Polly Cruse, who were likely enslaved. Other items found on the list are iron, harness, shoe leather, ammunition, scales and weights, axes, and "one set desk furniture."[9]

The Winchester brothers built a sawmill, distillery, and several other businesses on Bledsoe's Creek. To protect themselves against attacks from Native Americans, they also built a fort they christened Fort Tuckahoe, leaving little question about their ambition. In that time, the word Tuckahoe was a slang reference for aristocratic, wealthy, and landowning settlers from the eastern tidewater regions of Virginia who were part of the plantation society. The term was sometimes used to contrast these elites with the "Cohee" settlers from western Virginia, who were often of Scotch-Irish or German descent and more likely to be farmers or tradespeople.

The idea of personal honor, duty, and military leadership was also deeply rooted in the Tuckahoe mentality. Serving in the military, or at least supporting military efforts through resources and political influence, was expected of gentlemen of the Tuckahoe class like the Winchesters. Patriotism and devotion to one's land, community, and social order was central to their identity. James Winchester's military experience and enthusiastic willingness to serve made him an obvious choice for an appointment to Brigadier General of the local militia. His primary charge was to protect settlers from the Native American attacks that were breaking out with increasing frequency in the territory.

Those attempting to carve out a life there had to live—and sometimes die— with raids and small battles by members of tribes including Cherokee, Chickasaw, Choctaw, Creek, and Seminole. There were various treaties and agreements with the leaders of the tribes not to encroach on Native American land. However, for some White settlers, the desire for land on which to make their fortune took precedence over all else—even the lives of their friends and family.

Not only were they among the first settlers, the Winchester brothers can also be counted among the first to use the river to get the products they grew and manufactured in present-day Middle Tennessee to market in New Orleans. Early settler William Martin, who lived with them at Fort Tuckahoe for a while, wrote about the building of the Winchester brothers' first flatboat.

A flatboat was a rectangular, flat-bottomed boat that came in various sizes, depending on the goods they were intended to carry. Some flatboats, were as small as four feet by sixteen feet, while larger ones, known as Mississippi Broadhorns, could be as large as twenty feet by one hundred feet or more. Most were discarded once the pilots reached their destination.

To construct his first flatboat, Winchester hired Ellick Moore, a large man with the unforgettable attribute of having "monstrous big jaws and fore-teeth in the shape of grinders."[10] When the boat was completed, it was loaded with goods by the Winchester brothers, William Martin, and their enslaved men. They navigated the loaded flatboat up the Cumberland River then down the Mississippi River to New Orleans. It was likely unloaded along Tchoupitoulas Street where the New Orleans convention center can be found today. Once they completed their business, they had to sell or discard the flatboat since it was impossible to get it back up the river. Typically, flatboats were then torn apart and the wood used to construct buildings or as sidewalks. "Kaintucks," as flatboat men were often called, typically spent a few days in the city spending some of their hard-earned cash before returning home over land. Martin remembered:

> We were nearly the first that ever went down from the country, and all were unacquainted with the business. Nevertheless, we arrived there safely. The return march—800 miles, and more than half through Indian country—was the worst of all.... We were absent almost six months.[11]

James Winchester was also making a name for himself as a leader in the territory with those in the nation's capital. President George Washington appointed him to one of five positions on the Legislative Council, and Governor William Blount enlisted his help in conducting a census of the settlers inhabiting the territory with an eye toward statehood. The Northwest Ordinance of 1787 set the number of free residents for territories to become states at 60,000, so Winchester and others got to work counting their neighbors.

The notebook mentioned earlier also includes notes from that census. At the top of the first page of that section was written in James Winchester's handwriting, "Enumeration of the inhabitants of the Territory of the United States South of the Ohio taken between the 15th day of September and the 15th day of November 1795." The notes made by Winchester include a list of the counties in the territory with one column for slaves and one for free residents. Known as the Three-Fifths Compromise, each slave was recorded, but only counted as three-fifths of a person. Any Native Americans living in the territory were not counted at all.

The census to which Winchester contributed proved that there were enough residents to form a legislature and write a state constitution. Tennessee was admitted to the Union on June 1, 1796, as the sixteenth state and the first created from a federal territory. While proponents of statehood for Tennessee rejoiced at the milestone, Winchester had more to celebrate than the birth of a new state. His firstborn son, Marcus Brutus Winchester, had arrived just four days earlier.

James Winchester was selected as the state senator representing Sumner County for the first state legislature and was unanimously chosen as speaker. Unfortunately, George Winchester—who had been just as ambitious and successful as his brother—would not be around to celebrate the birth of Tennessee or meet his nephew. Two years earlier, while serving as justice of the peace, he left his home at Bledsoe's Creek headed to a meeting of the Sumner County quarterly court. As he neared Gallatin, at the junction of present-day Hartsville and Scottsville Pikes, he was ambushed by a group of Native Americans, scalped, and murdered. In later years, it would be noted that George Winchester was the next-to-last White man killed by Native Americans in Sumner County, Tennessee. The last was Robert Peyton, who was killed while checking on his cattle in 1795 less than a mile from James Winchester's fort.

The morning after George Winchester's death, a party of fifty members of the militia attempted to hunt down those who had murdered him, but the attackers had vanished. Joseph Bishop, one of their neighbors, wrote of George in his journal: "His death was much lamented by his fellow-citizens. I knew him to be an estimable man, and know that the public sustained a loss which was seriously felt in those days. I joined the company that followed the Indians after they had murdered him, but we never could overtake them."[12] William Martin, who had accompanied George to New Orleans on one of the first flatboats, wrote, "George was a superior man in every way to James."[13] James Winchester likely would have agreed. He remembered, "On this unhappy occasion, I rather attended to my own feelings as a man and a brother, than to my duty as a soldier and an officer."[14] Though George never married or had children of his own, his memory lived on thanks to his brother. In 1823, when James Winchester welcomed the birth of his youngest son, he honored his late brother by naming him George Washington Winchester.

The deaths of George Winchester and Robert Peyton marked an important milestone for Tennessee, as the terror that had kept some settlers from migrating west was slowly evaporating. As the fear eased, the settlers flowed west.

Chapter One Endnotes

1. James D. Davis, *History of Memphis* (Memphis: Hite, Crumpton & Kelly, 1973), 72.
2. Emma Shelton, *William Winchester, 1711-1790* (Westminster, MD: Historical Society of Carroll County, Maryland, 1993), 42.
3. Shelton, *William Winchester*, 43.
4. Shelton, *William Winchester*, 43.
5. Walter Durham, *James Winchester: Tennessee Pioneer* (Gallatin: Sumner County Library Board, 1979), 10.
6. Marquis James, *The Life of Andrew Jackson* (New York: Bobbs-Merrill, 1938), 52.
7. Paul Clements, *Chronicles of the Cumberland Settlements, 1779-1796* (Nashville: Private Printing, Jennifer and William Frist Foundation, 2012), 302.
8. Clements, *Chronicles 302*.
9. *Winchester Revolutionary War Account Book, 1779-1804*, Lot 205, Case Antiques Auctions & Appraisals, January 27, 2018.
10. Durham, *James Winchester*, 18.
11. Clements, *Chronicles*, 306.
12. John W. Gray, *The Life of Joseph Bishop* (Nashville: self-published, 1858), 128.
13. Clements, *Chronicles*, 306.
14. Clements, *Chronicles*, 306.

THE MEMPHIS APPEAL.

PUBLISHED DAILY, TRI-WEEKLY AND WEEKLY,

BY

JNO. R. M'CLANAHAN, LEONIDUS TROUSDALE, WILLIAM M. HUTTON, BENJAMIN F. DILL,

UNDER THE STYLE AND FIRM OF

McCLANAHAN, HUTTON & Co.,

EDITORS AND PROPRIETORS.

Terms of Subscription:

DAILY, IN ADVANCE, (per annum)..........................$10 00
TRI-WEEKLY, "   "   " 5 00
WEEKLY,   "   "   " 3 00

The Weekly Appeal is the

LARGEST WEEKLY PAPER

in the South-West. Principal circulation in Tennessee, Mississippi, Arkansas, Texas, Louisiana, Florida, Alabama, Georgia, South Carolina, North Carolina, Virginia, Kentucky, California, Missouri, Illinois and Indiana.

Owing to its immense circulation in the above mentioned States, it offers a medium for advertising unsurpassed by any other paper in the South-West.

Rates of Advertising:

☞ All advertisements on which the number of insertions is not marked, will be inserted 1 month only, and charged accordingly.

☞ All Legal and Transient Advertisements will be charged by the insertion.

For 1 Square of 10 lines or less, one insertion,....................$1 00
For each additional insertion of same,............................. 50

From Rainey's Memphis City Directory, 1855/56

Chapter Two: Baby Let's Play House

*Construction of James Winchester's Cragfont,
John Overton's Travellers Rest, and
Andrew Jackson's Hermitage*

Four years after his brother's death, James Winchester embarked on an ambitious project of constructing a house befitting his growing stature as one of the most important leaders in the young state. The Winchester mansion, Cragfont, was begun in 1798 and completed in 1802. It sat high on a hill, offering sweeping views of the Tennessee countryside. With craftsmen recruited from Maryland at his side, Winchester meticulously oversaw the construction of every detail of his new home. Winchester brought his Maryland taste in architecture to Tennessee. The ell, or wing extension, at Cragfont was centered at the rear of the house as more commonly found in the homes of Virginia and Maryland. The house also featured a large stone chimney on each side.

The estate became a symbol of Winchester's prosperity and social standing and was noted as a home where visitors enjoyed the highest degree of hospitality. Beyond its aesthetic appeal, Cragfont became a bustling center of social and political activity in Middle Tennessee, serving as a venue for many meetings, dinners, and events each year.

Meanwhile, John Overton acquired 320 acres forty-five miles southwest of Cragfont where he would construct his own status symbol. The land, purchased by Overton in 1796, had originally been granted to David Maxwell as a reward for his service in the Revolutionary War. As construction began on his new home, workers discovered it had originally been the site of a Native American village and sacred burial ground. Undeterred by the discovery, Overton proceeded and initially gave his plantation the name "Golgotha," the Aramaic word for "place of the skull." Golgotha is mentioned in the Bible as the site where Jesus was crucified.

The two-story Federal-style house, built by both free and enslaved laborers, was constructed of wood and brick and sat on a stone foundation. It featured glass windows and large fireplaces with brick chimneys. The initial part of Overton's new home was completed in 1799, and wisely, the name was soon changed from Golgotha to Travellers Rest. It was a name the still-single Overton chose to reflect the peace and quiet he found in his home after long days traveling as a circuit judge. He continued to acquire more of the surrounding land, and by the time of his death, it included more than two thousand acres.

Andrew and Rachel Jackson were beginning their own ambitious project approximately fifteen miles northeast of Travellers Rest. In 1804, Jackson purchased a 640-acre plantation that he and Rachel developed into the property known as the Hermitage. Like Winchester's Cragfont, the Hermitage was intended to reflect Jackson's growing prominence in Tennessee. The original structure was a modest log cabin, but as Jackson's influence and wealth increased, he commissioned the construction of a grand Federal-style mansion that was completed in 1821.

The Hermitage became a hub for Jackson's political supporters and acquaintances—along with the occasional adversary. Like Jackson, The Hermitage came to embody the frontier spirit of men and women mastering their environment and, despite often modest beginnings, taking their place among the eastern elites in national influence.

James Winchester continued to grow his many business investments, land holdings, and the size of his family. Relationships were different on the frontier, and survival often took priority over formality. It had taken a while for Winchester to begin his family, and it would take even longer for him to legally marry Susannah Black, his common law wife and the mother of his children.

Susannah, who later went by Susan, had arrived at Bledsoe's Lick—a natural salt lick—from South Carolina in the late 1780s, traveling with her mother, Mariah Susan Gibson Black, and her brothers, George Gabriel Black and John Black Jr. Her father, John Black, died during the family's journey to Tennessee at age fifty-six. They were headed to a piece of land that had belonged to Susan's late maternal grandfather, Jordan Gibson. Gibson received a North Carolina land grant of 640 acres located on the north side of Bledsoe's Creek on April 17, 1786.

There are no recorded references, so it remains unclear how much the family was aware of the race of their ancestors. Evidence recently uncovered by descendants of the family suggests that Jordan Gibson was likely the son of a free

Black man, Gideon Gibson Sr., and the brother of prominent South Carolina landowner Gideon Gibson Jr. Born in Boston to a free Black family, the elder Gibson married a White woman, Mary Anne Browne. In 1731, the family and their enslaved individuals relocated from Virginia, where the couple had initially settled, to South Carolina. One of their new neighbors reportedly complained that "several colored men and their white wives had moved into the area." Colonial Governor Robert Johnson met with Gideon Gibson Jr. to evaluate the group and to determine if they should be accepted into their community. He decided in the affirmative:

> I have had them before me in Council and upon Examination find that they are not Negroes nor Slaves but Free people, That the Father of them here is named Gideon Gibson and his Father was also free, I have been informed by a person who has lived in Virginia that this Gibson has lived there Several Years in good Repute and by his papers that he has produced before me that his transactions there have been very regular, That he has for several years paid Taxes for two tracts of Land and had several Negroes of his own, That he is a Carpenter by Trade and is come hither for the support of his Family.[1]

In spite of his mixed-race heritage, Gideon Gibson Jr., became a wealthy land owner and an enslaver himself in South Carolina. One of America's founding fathers, Henry Laurens, had the Gibsons in mind as he grappled with the concept of slavery. He wrote to a friend, "Gideon Gibson escaped the penalties of the negro law by producing upon comparison more red and white in his face than could be discovered in the faces of half the descendants of the French refugees in our House Assembly.... the children of this same Gideon, having passed through another stage of whitewash were of fairer complexion than their prosecutor George Gabriel."[2]

George Gabriel, to whom Laurens referred, was George Gabriel Powell, who took a leading role in a battle against Gideon Gibson Jr. and a group known as the Regulators. The Regulator movement was a grassroots effort by South Carolina colonists protesting the corrupt practices of colonial officials. Seeking fairer representation, the Regulators challenged the colonial government's authority. On July 25, 1767, Gibson led a group of Regulators in a confrontation with constables near Marrs Bluff on the Pee Dee River. Reports in the *South Carolina Gazette* depicted Gibson and his fellow Regulators unfavorably, referring to them as a mixed group of "Mulattos, Mustees, and Free Negroes."

In reality, Gibson and the other Regulators were colonists intent on improving their communities through reform. The Regulators intensified their resistance to the colonial government, with Gibson continuing to lead protests for reform, which ultimately culminated in the Battle of Alamance in 1771. In this battle, colonial forces defeated the Regulators, ending the movement but leaving a lasting impact on early American resistance efforts.

If, as Laurens suggested, brothers Gideon Gibson Jr. and Jordan Gibson "passed through another stage of whitewash," then Jordan's granddaughter, Susan Black, had passed through two more. No known references describe her as anything other than White.

When Susan Black's grandfather settled on the north side of Bledsoe's Creek, he was already in his early to mid-70s. Gibson did not get to enjoy his new home for long. On January 17, 1788, Gibson, who was around eighty at the time, departed the fort of John Morgan, on the west side of Bledsoe's Creek, with Charles Morgan. The two were headed to the home of William Hall's mother-in-law. When they were near Hall's cabin, the two men were ambushed by Native Americans. Gibson was shot and killed instantly, and although he too was injured, Morgan attempted to get away. William Hall wrote about what happened next:

> Morgan was pursued by two Indians. He was troubled with asthma, and when weary and closely pursued, would tree. The Indians shot at him once or twice, but missed. Finally, as he turned a fence corner less than 300 yards from James Harrison's house, he was shot in the back, scalped, then another shot entered his shoulder. Several persons stationed at Mrs. Hall's ran out, and William Martin, William Ridley and I searched for the bodies. We found Gibson dead, scalped, and stripped, and Morgan badly wounded. . . . George Winchester, who had some knowledge of surgery learned in the Army, attended Morgan who survived 14 days. Winchester often attended the wounded, always without pay, and when necessary, would sometimes go by night to see his patients - so anxious did he feel for their recovery.[3]

Susan Black surely knew the story of her grandfather's death and likely saw the Winchester brothers as protectors and caregivers of all the settlers living around Bledsoe's Creek. Many Native Americans were not giving up the land on which they lived and hunted without a fight. Susan Winchester later wrote of losing a friend, Elizabeth Steele, who was traveling on horseback from Greenfield to Morgan's Station with a group of men. They were ambushed, and Steele was thrown from her horse. Susan Winchester wrote, "The Indians attempted to stab her, she seized the blade of the knife in her hands, by which they were severely cut. She seized them by the hair. They finally killed her by repeated stabs. When the body was found, hair was still in her clenched hands."[4]

For a young woman living in unsettled territory, surrounded by the constant threat of Native American attacks on her friends and family, the importance of securing a mate on which she could depend was clear. Fortunately, James Winchester was ready to settle down. For Susan Black, he offered shelter, financial stability, and the instant respect that came with becoming part of a respected family. In 1793, Black, then in her mid-teens, gave birth to her first child, Maria Eliza, with the forty-one-year-old Winchester. Despite their significant age difference, their union ultimately proved beneficial for both.

It seems Winchester, starting his family late in life, was determined to make up for lost time. After Maria, their first son, Marcus Brutus, was born in 1796. Cynthia was born in 1799 but died as an infant. Selima arrived in 1800, followed by Betsey Ann "Caroline" in 1802, Lucilius in 1803, Almira in 1805, and Napoleon in 1806. In 1809, Louisa Orville was born along with her twin, Malvina, who died at birth. Valerius Publicola arrived in 1810, Helen Marr in 1812, and James Martin in 1816. The youngest, named after his late uncle, George Washington, was born in 1822.

On the early Tennessee frontier, couples who lacked easy access to courthouses or clergy often lived as husband and wife without completing a formal ceremony. By 1803 Winchester's fortune and political stature had grown to the point that he evidently wished to eliminate any question about inheritance. That year, he persuaded the General Assembly to pass a private act that changed the surname of his first four children—Maria, Marcus, Selima, and Betsey—from Black to Winchester and declared them "capable of inheriting as if born in lawful wedlock." A second act in 1807 did the same for Lucilius, Almira, and Napoleon.

Whether Winchester ever formally legalized his union with Susan Black remains uncertain, though they were clearly regarded as husband and wife. In her 1851 War of 1812 pension application, she stated that she "was married to the said James Winchester sometime in the winter or early spring of 1792," yet searches of surviving marriage records in Sumner, Davidson, Robertson, and Wilson Counties have yielded no documentation. Nevertheless, Winchester consistently referred to Susan as his wife in deeds, letters, and his 1826 will, and their partnership appears to have been both legitimate and contented. Winchester was certainly fortunate to find a partner who could manage a large home, a plantation with many enslaved men and women, and a growing family.

As the eighteenth century turned into the nineteenth, in addition to the construction of Cragfont, Winchester shifted some of his focus five miles south.

In partnership with William Cage, he purchased one hundred fifty acres on the bank of the Cumberland River in 1799 for a town named Cairo. Businesses there eventually included a cotton gin, woolen mill, boatyard, gristmill, and a large brick warehouse.

Historian Walter T. Durham spent years exploring records and journals of the businesses of Winchester and Cage. Their records provide a good example of the various business transactions that were taking place regularly in the communities that were springing up along the rivers and tributaries of the South where once there had been only wilderness:

> There were transactions listed to "Cotton Account," "Horse Account," "Negro Account," "Boat Account," "Tobacco Account" and "Bonds and Notes." All these activities reflected trading activity, usually both buying and selling.... One of the oldest documents of the Winchester and Cage partnership is a Bill of Sale for Negro Frank dated February 18, 1809 by which George Hallum of Wilson County did sell unto Winchester and Cage merchants of the county of Sumner ... one Negro man about seventeen years of age named Frank.[5]

James Winchester also continued his business relationships with family in both Baltimore and New Orleans. Some of the merchandise James resold in Cairo had been shipped to him by his brother, William, from Baltimore, making its way overland by horse-drawn wagons.

Winchester's New Orleans business was mostly done through his son-in-law, the husband of oldest daughter, Maria Eliza. Her husband, James Waller Breedlove, was a veteran of the War of 1812 and a close friend of Andrew Jackson. James and Maria moved to New Orleans in 1818 and, through the years, had four children who survived to adulthood.

Breedlove found great success as a commission merchant. He received goods, often agricultural products like cotton, tobacco, and sugar, from producers or planters. He then stored, marketed, and resold those goods, keeping a percentage of the sale. To be successful in this business, men like Breedlove had to develop skills in the new business sectors of shipping logistics, warehousing, and transportation over river and sea.

In later years, Breedlove was appointed collector of the Port of New Orleans by President Andrew Jackson, then was president of the Atchafalaya Bank. From 1829 to 1831, he served as the Mexican vice-consul in New Orleans and became a close friend of Stephen F. Austin—now known as the Father of Texas.

In a letter to Austin from New Orleans dated November 30, 1829, Breedlove captured the hunger for expansion that existed in the country.

> I have shown your letter to several of my friends who are interested in Texas and they have advised me very Strongly to have it published, this I have declined doing, as you had [not] expressed such a wish. Your letter has shed light on the subject of the Colonization Laws and regulations. which many persons stood in need of and to such persons I have taken pleasure in reading it. I shall feel under much obligation to you when I receive the promised translation of all the Laws on that subject as it will afford me the means of giving such information as is almost daily asked of me, as the representative of the Mexican Government in this City. The impression is rapidly spreading that the United States are now negotiating for the purchase of Texas it may be without foundation, but it has already had the effect to cause many to look in that direction for a future residence.[6]

Chapter Two Endnotes

1. Minutes of House of Burgesses, 1730–35, box 2, bundle 9: S.C. 9, Parish Transcripts, New York Historic Society, quoted in Winthrop D. Jordan, *White over Black: American Attitudes Toward the Negro, 1550–1812* (Chapel Hill: University of North Carolina Press, 1968), 172.
2. David Duncan Wallace, *The Life of Henry Laurens* (New York: G. P. Putnam's Sons, 1915), 454.
3. Paul Clements, *Chronicles of the Cumberland Settlements, 1779–1796* (Nashville: Private Printing, The Foundation of Jennifer and William Frist and Paul Clements, 2012), 274.
4. Clements, *Chronicles*, 395.
5. Walter Durham, *James Winchester: Tennessee Pioneer* (Gallatin: Sumner County Library Board, 1979), 95.
6. Eugene C. Barker, ed., *Annual Report of the American Historical Association for the Year 1919: The Austin Papers* (Washington, DC: Government Printing Office, 1924), vol. 1, pt. 2, 294–95.

BLUFF CITY ARMORY.

 BLUFF CITY ARMORY.

A. WEISGERBER,

Manufacturer of

RIFLES,

Guns &  Pistols,

WITH THE

LATEST IMPROVEMENTS

NO. 8, COURT STREET,

MEMPHIS, TENNESSEE.

REPAIRING:

SPORTING APPARATUS,

PUT IN PERFECT ORDER.

From Rainey's Memphis City Directory, 1855/56

Chapter Three: We the People

Marcus's father, James Winchester, fights in the War of 1812

Marcus Winchester's father, James, held numerous professional roles, including businessman, politician, land speculator, farmer, and "Indian fighter," to name a few. But one that he seemed to take slightly more pride in than others was veteran of the Revolutionary War. Although the end of the war had taken place decades earlier, Winchester was eager to show the world he was still made of the right stuff. However, in spite of his experience on the battlefield and intense pride in the United States of America, he was not ready for what was to come in 1812. For that matter, neither was the United States of America.

As one historian put it, "the United States swaggered into the War of 1812 like a Kansas farm boy entering his first saloon. And like that same innocent, wretchedly gagging down his first drink, the new nation was totally unprepared for the raw impact of all-out war."[1]

The reason for entering "the second war for independence" while woefully unprepared was complicated. Economics certainly played a role. Both France and Britain had imposed trade restrictions on the United States during the Napoleonic Wars. Both countries interfered with American trade, and the British practice of stopping American ships for "inspection" rubbed salt in the wound.

American pride and honor were also a motivating factor. For some time, the British had begun capturing American sailors and forcing them to serve in the British navy. The offspring of the generation that fought for and won the nation's independence from Britain had a strong sense of national pride and a need to establish and defend American dignity. Watching Britain drag American soldiers onto British ships and hold them captive was not the freedom for which their parents and grandparents had fought.

In 1807, the captain of the American ship *Chesapeake* was fired upon by the British ship *Leopold* after refusing to allow the British to board. Three Americans were killed and eighteen were wounded. In a speech to Congress on June 1, 1812, President James Madison said, "we behold our seafaring citizens still the daily victims of lawless violence, committed on the great common and highway of nations, even within sight of the country which owes them protection."[2] Tennesseans leading the young state strongly agreed. Marcus Winchester, who was in Maryland receiving an education with his male Winchester cousins, likely heard a great deal from his father about the situation whenever he was home. James Winchester was passionate about defending American pride, and even held a meeting in Nashville where his friend, John Overton, delivered a speech calling the attack on the *Chesapeake* "an act of war." Tennessee Senator George W. Campbell and another contemporary of Winchester believed America should "relieve its lost character, by washing off the stains on its honor in the blood of its enemies."[3]

James Winchester's appetite for war was clear in a letter he wrote to Andrew Jackson: "Peace is always desirable, when it can be maintained on honorable terms. But war, dear General, with all its evils are preferable to the present state of things in these United States."[4]

The British also armed and provided supplies to their Native American allies. Settlers had already decided they were entitled to the land, and the British support and arming of Native Americans who tried to keep them off it was enough justification for many to go to war. A group of young, ambitious politicians in the United States known as the War Hawks was especially vocal. Led by men like Henry Clay, John C. Calhoun, and Felix Grundy, they adopted the rallying cry "Free Trade and Sailor's Rights" and exerted significant influence in Congress. They pushed for aggressive policies against the British and ultimately played a crucial role in pushing the United States into war. In early 1813, Kentucky Congressman Henry Clay ended a speech encouraging the war with a variation of the cry. Today, a reader can almost see him gripping the side of the podium with one hand while waving the other in the air as he loudly proclaimed, "With the aid of Providence, we must come out crowned with success; but if we fail, let us fail like men, lash ourselves to our gallant tars, and expire together in one common struggle, fighting for 'Seamen's Rights and Free Trade.'"[5]

As early historian and president of the Tennessee Historical Society Albigence W. Putnam put it, many Americans were ready to fight and possibly die for their new republic:

> Old warriors champed the bit and pawed the earth when they heard the drum of war and saw their country's flag unfurled;

aged citizens were fired with the enthusiasm of youth, or would teach their juniors that patriotism could not die—that in old age they would resent and punish insults, and defend the rights of the country.[6]

Strongly opposing the war were members of the Federalist Party. They criticized President James Madison's administration for pursuing war with Britain as passionately as the War Hawks championed it. Much of their argument was that a war would negatively impact the economy in the Northeast where trade with Britain was essential. Federalists, like Alexander Hamilton and John Q. Adams, were in favor of seeking diplomatic solutions instead of rushing to war.

A vote took place on June 18, 1812. Because of the differing opinions caused primarily by these regional interests in the United States at that time, the resolution of war was passed only by a narrow margin and after much debate. In the House of Representatives, the vote was 79 in favor of war and 49 against. In the Senate, the vote was 19 in favor and 13 against. The War Hawks had gotten their way, and they expected a quick victory that would inspire great patriotic pride at having "the country's honor restored in the eyes of the world." Unfortunately, they were wrong.

Richard W. Stewart, former chief historian of the U.S. Army Center of Military History summed up the early challenges of the war. He wrote:

> Much of the story of the War of 1812 is about the unpreparedness of America's Army and Navy at the conflict's outset, and the enormous difficulties the new nation faced in raising troops, finding competent officers, and supplying its forces. Most of America's military leaders were inexperienced and performed poorly, particularly in the first two years of war. Only gradually did better leaders rise to the top to command the more disciplined and well-trained units that America eventually fielded.[7]

Even before the official declaration of war, the Army Act of January 4, 1812, empowered President James Madison to nominate two major generals and five additional brigadier generals—and James Winchester wanted in. According to his biographer, Walter T. Durham, Winchester was anxious to take up arms and join the fight. He was already eagerly recruiting and training volunteers in his role in the Tennessee state militia. Simultaneously, he was asking associates with connections in Washington to encourage President James Madison to appoint him as a brigadier general in the regular Army.

The militia and regular army in the United States at the time were different.

The militia was made up of part-time civilian soldiers who had little training and were managed by each state. They served for shorter periods of time and lacked proper equipment. In states like Kentucky and Tennessee, the militia was made up of frontiersmen, usually farmers, who focused on protecting the settlers against Native American attacks. Members of the militia were key in facilitating expansion further into Tennessee onto Native American land.

On the other hand, the regular army consisted of professional soldiers under federal command. Primarily from the northeastern states, they had better training, served for longer periods, and had access to standardized equipment and rations provided by the government. While both were used during the war, the militia was often less reliable due to lack of supplies—including food and clothing—and limited training.

When James Winchester finally received his much-desired commission of brigadier general, he was assigned an administrative role in Lexington, Kentucky, primarily focused on recruiting. While disappointed he would not be leading men into battle, it appears he took on his new role with great enthusiasm. He wrote to one of his subordinates, "Recruiting, like all other business, requires vigorous industry, perseverance, and address: and those therefore who most diligently employ these necessary qualifications, are generally found to meet with the most perfect success."[8] All indications are that in that role he was considered a strong leader and served as a respected mentor to his many direct reports.

James Winchester's biographer, Durham, suggests that around this time Winchester likely spent a few days at Cragfont, where he persuaded his wife, Susan, to let their son, Marcus, accompany him into battle as his aide-de-camp. While the record offers no way to know for certain, it would be understandable if she had been reluctant to agree. She likely did not expect her sixty-year-old husband to march off to war with their eldest son, leaving her with a large plantation, multiple businesses, and eight—soon to be nine—children to raise alone.

According to one account, as soon as he received the order from his father, Marcus headed straight from Baltimore to Lexington, Kentucky, where he joined his father and others as they traveled to Fort Defiance in Ohio.[9] It is unknown if Marcus was enthusiastic about his father's plan to provide a front-row seat to the horrors of war for his eldest son. Either way, the experiences he encountered in war would prove starkly different from the life he had known in Baltimore.

Chapter Three Endnotes

1. John R. Elting, *Amateurs, to Arms!: A Military History of the War of 1812* (Boston: Da Capo Press, 1995), 3.
2. James Madison, "Message to Congress, June 1, 1812," in *The Writings of James Madison*, ed. Gaillard Hunt (New York: G.P. Putnam's Sons, 1901), 161.
3. William A. Walker, "Martial Sons: Tennessee Enthusiasm for the War of 1812," *Tennessee Historical Quarterly* 20, no. 1 (1961): 31.
4. *Nashville Clarion*, April 7, 1812; John M. Harrell, "James Winchester," *Tennessee Historical Quarterly* 18, no. 3 (1959): 311.
5. Paul A. Gilje, "'Free Trade and Sailors' Rights': The Rhetoric of the War of 1812," *Journal of the Early Republic* 30, no. 1 (2010): 23.
6. Albigence Waldo Putnam, *History of Middle Tennessee* (Nashville: A. A. Stitt, Southern Methodist Publishing House, 1859), 597.
7. John R. Maass, *Defending a New Nation, 1783-1811* (Washington, D.C.: Center of Military History, 2023), 5.
8. Roger H. Durham, *James Winchester: Tennessee Pioneer* (Gallatin, TN: Sumner County Library Board, 1979), 114.
9. Memphis City Directory, "Maj. M.B. Winchester," (Memphis: D.O. Dooley & Company, 1855), 3.

LARGEST PRINTING AND PUBLISHING HOUSE
IN THE SOUTH-WEST.

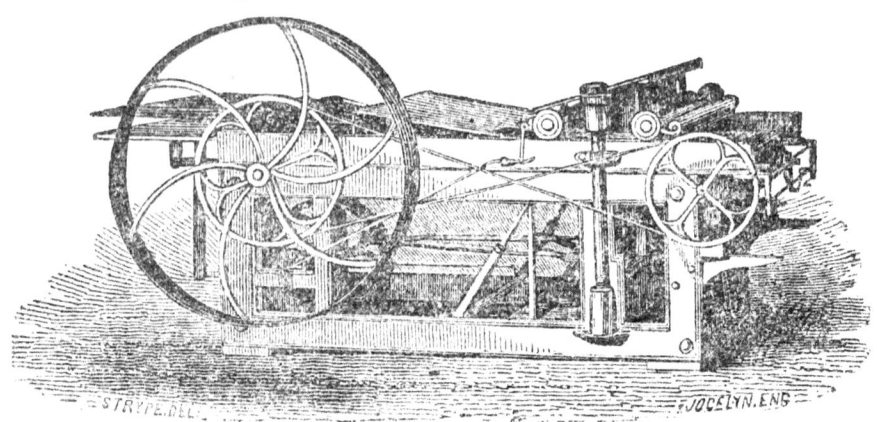

Memphis Eagle & Enquirer
JOB PRINTING HOUSE,
No. 225 Main Street,
OPPOSITE ODD FELLOWS' HALL.

This old and permanent establishment is now under the superintendence of J. B. MOSELEY, who has been connected with the office for the last eighteen years. Its great facilities for executing work in the most elegant style and with the greatest expedition, has been recently greatly increased by the introduction of one of Ruggles' celebrated Presses, which, in addition to the mammoth Hoe—the Adams and the Foster Poster Press, enables it to execute with more promptness and elegance, contracts for PLAIN, FANCY AND ORNAMENTAL

Book and Job Printing.

Attached to this Mammoth Establishment is a complete

BOOK BINDERY,

And BLANK BOOK MANUFACTORY. Orders for Bill Heads, Blank Books, &c., will be ruled to any given pattern, with neatness and despatch.

STOCKDELL, PRYOR & GRAY,
PROPRIETORS

From Rainey's Memphis City Directory, 1855/56

Chapter Four: Good Morning Baltimore

*Marcus's grandfather, William Winchester,
founds Westminster, Maryland*

William Winchester, father of James Winchester and grandfather of Marcus Winchester, was born in the Westminster section of London on December 22, 1711, to James Winchester and his wife, Janet. According to stories passed down through the generations, before his early death at age forty, James Winchester of London had worked as a locksmith.[1]

A few months before William was born in London, Parliament passed the New Churches in London and Westminster Act of 1710, partially in response to the collapse of the roof of an aging church. The act commissioned the building of fifty churches in the cities of London and Westminster to serve the needs of the exploding population. Small congregations of worshipers were filling up Presbyterian, Quaker, Congregationalist, and Baptist chapels around London. The Tories, members of a political party that supported the monarchy and the Church of England, had returned to power and had resolved to strengthen the Church of England by building magnificent places of worship. This was intended to draw the people away from the "dissenting churches" that opposed royal interference in religious matters.

It was a fitting time and place for the birth of William Winchester who, after settling in America as an indentured servant, would be responsible for founding the town of Westminster, Maryland. As a young boy, he would have experienced a bustling hub of activity. The city was overflowing with migrants from the countryside seeking economic opportunities from the industrial and commercial expansion that was taking place. The result was overcrowded living conditions, poor sanitation, and a lack of infrastructure. Construction sites dotted Westminster, disrupting daily life of its residents with constant noise of hammers, saws, and carts hauling construction materials through its narrow streets.

Williams's parents, James and Janet Winchester, died in 1730 of plague, leaving young William an orphan. In January 1731, then twenty years old and already a skilled surveyor, William signed up as an indentured servant and immigrated to the Province of Maryland. The patriarch of the Winchester family in America arrived a dirty, hungry immigrant in Annapolis on March 6, 1731, aboard the *Hume*. While he had only a little education, the ability to survey land made him a valuable commodity in a new country ready to be measured and divided.

He completed his obligatory years of service working as an overseer on George Buchanan's plantation, then continued working for Buchanan for several more years. William Winchester perfected many of the skills used to carve out a place to live in the wilderness that he would later pass along to his sons.

In 1744, Winchester was able to purchase his own land in Baltimore County, that he christened "Winchester's Lot." Two years later, thirty-six-year-old Winchester married twenty-year-old Lydia Richards, a daughter of his neighbor, Edward Richards.

Marcus Winchester's father, James, born on February 6, 1752, was named after his grandfather. He had two older siblings, Catherine and William Jr. His parents would go on to have seven more children, bringing the total to ten—four girls and six boys. They would need all the hands they could get as William Winchester continued to acquire and develop land, a critical part of colonial expansion. The process was different for young William than it would become for his sons after the Revolutionary War. Land ownership was controlled by the British Crown and colonial governments at the time. Each colony followed its own procedures based on royal charters and land grants. When William Winchester wanted to acquire his own piece of property, he began by petitioning colonial authorities, such as the governor or a proprietary lord, for the right to claim a specific piece of land. In colonies like Virginia and Maryland, the headright system was commonly used, granting settlers land based on the number of people they brought to the colony and whether they were family members, servants, or enslaved.

Once settlers received permission to claim land, a surveyor was sent to measure the property's boundaries, a crucial step in the process. Following the survey, settlers paid fees or "quitrents" to the colonial government or the Crown to formalize their claim. These payments were sometimes steep, making land acquisition easier for wealthier settlers, while less affluent settlers, like William Winchester, often struggled to gather the resources, or they had to rely on wealthier patrons for loans. After the necessary fees were paid, a land patent was issued, granting the settler legal ownership of the property. This patent was a formal document, often signed by the colonial governor, providing proof of ownership and describing the land's exact boundaries.

Documents show Winchester continued to acquire land and added to Winchester's Lot with properties that had names like Corbin's Forest, Loveall's Prospect, and Friendship Completed. One property, White's Level, was substantial enough that Winchester had to sell a portion of Winchester's Lot to afford it.

The poor indentured servant had come a long way from the dirty and crowded streets of London. Researcher Emma Shelton, who conducted extensive studies on Baltimore County land records, noticed that by this time, Winchester had begun referring to himself as a "yeoman" in his land transactions. "What confidence in himself this appellation evokes," she wrote. "On the English social ladder, a yeoman belonged to the class of freeholding farmers ranked below the gentry. The city boy was now a man established among his peers as a land owner and a farmer."[2] Shelton's research also shows that Winchester became one of the earliest major land speculators. In the years prior to 1774, he patented more than two thousand acres around Baltimore and present-day Carroll County.

William Winchester can also be credited with beginning the family legacy of town development, and one day his footsteps would be followed by his descendants who founded Cairo and Memphis in Tennessee and Hopefield and West Memphis in Arkansas.

In 1764, William Winchester laid out a town on sixteen acres of land known as White's Level, situated along the main road leading to Baltimore. The first recorded sale of the town's forty-five lots occurred on October 10, 1765. Drawing on memories of his youth—and perhaps in memory of his late parents—Winchester chose to name the settlement Westminster, a nod to his English roots. Located approximately thirty-six miles northwest of present-day Baltimore, Westminster would gain greater significance in 1837, when the newly formed Carroll County designated it as the county seat. The original courthouse, constructed soon after, still stands at the intersection of Willis and Court Streets. Remarkably, it continues to serve its original function, with legal cases tried there to this day.

When Winchester came to America, he had nothing. By the end of his life, he had raised a large family, cultivated several successful plantations, and even established an entire town. When he died on September 2, 1790, at age seventy-eight, he was buried at the Westminster Cemetery on land he had donated. His wife, Lydia, lived another eighteen years on their Tidewater plantation along with the three of her younger children who never married. James Winchester and his brother George were already living in Tennessee, while their brother, William Jr., was making a name for himself in Baltimore as a judge, justice of the peace, and banker.

William Winchester Jr. was one of the original directors of the Bank of Baltimore and, in 1804, became the first president of the Union Bank of Maryland. The brothers remained close as indicated by William and his wife, Mary "Maria" Parks Winchester, naming their first-born son James in 1772. William and Mary had twelve children, with Marcus Winchester's closest cousins in age being Charles who was born the year before he was, and Lycurgus, who was born the year after. When Marcus was sent to Baltimore for an education, he likely stayed at the home of his Uncle William and Aunt Mary.

William Jr. wrote to James about Marcus after returning home to Baltimore in late August 1810 after a few weeks of rest and relaxation. He had been, as he put it, "bracing up his earthly tabernacle" at York Sulphur Springs. The summer resort was patronized by a wealthy clientele primarily from Philadelphia and Baltimore. While many inns and hotels claim "George Washington Slept Here," the first president and his wife really did sleep at York Sulphur Springs when they visited in summer 1799, a few months before George Washington died. At York, wealthy patrons, like the Winchesters, enjoyed outdoor sports, games, and other activities during the day and fancy balls and parties in the evenings. William Jr.'s letter to his brother, James, reveals that Marcus spent a significant amount of time with his uncle. James must have expressed hope that William Jr. was helping Marcus develop plans for his future career.

> I have often pressed Marcus to say what he intended or wished as a profession for life but never could prevail on him to say. I shew him your letter and told him he ought to write you on that subject, which I expect he will do shortly—It is my opinion that his application and attention to what he undertakes, would qualify him for any situation he might make choice of, but I have always thought it a primary object for a youth to choose for himself.[3]

While the specific details of the education of young Marcus Winchester are unknown, he likely received his education from a private Baltimore school or from a tutor in his aunt and uncle's home alongside his cousins.

In a letter written to his brother, David, James Winchester expressed worry for Marcus's health:

> I've have had the pleasure to receive your two letters of the 13th and 20th of Nov., the former gave us the first information concerning our son Marcus since he left Nashville, and being then in a bad state

of health, we were very uneasy on his account, fearing he might be laid up on the way and unable to write to us. We have rec'd a letter from him dated from Louisville the 27th of November, where he had been nine days waiting for a passage, at length got on board the S B Tennessee and was to depart the day he wrote to me, the rivers being high, he probably reached Memphis in four or five days after his departure from Louisville. I am told by some of my family that Marcus entertains apprehensions of a breast complaint. . . . The old stock of the Winchesters were remarkable for large round chests and sound lungs and so is our Mother's family.[4]

In the same letter, James Winchester also shared his opinion on the importace of sports, especially for those, like Marcus, attending school in large cities:

I have long thought it a disadvantage to go to school in large cities where there is not room to exercise as much as is necessary to form robust constitutions and where manual labor is not practised. The Athletic games should be encouraged, particularly those which require great exertion of the hands and arms. All kinds of ball plays are advantages to persons while growing; they require great exertions of the hands and arms as well as the feet. It would be well if all seminaries for the education of youth to have capacious parks for the boys to exercise in where they could play Bandy, Wicket, townball, long bullets, etc.[5]

In the early 1800s, young Americans played a variety of games that reflected their English heritage while helping develop their own traditions. On frozen ponds, players enjoyed bandy, using curved sticks to drive a ball across the ice. Wicket, a simplified form of cricket with a long, flat bat and a low wicket, was popular in New England, while town ball—an early bat-and-ball game in which runners could be put out by a thrown ball—was common across the frontier. In long bullets, participants threw a heavy ball along a road or field, competing to see who could throw the farthest.

Schools and private tutors were more focused on education than sports. They offered classes in reading, writing, and arithmetic. Other subjects that were considered crucial to the education of a young American gentleman included those offered by the Baltimore Academy that opened in 1796. They advertised lessons in geography, philosophy, and history, along with what would have been especially beneficial to Marcus Winchester in the coming years—navigation and surveying.

Another part of young Winchester's education in business occurred organically because of his presence in a bustling center of commerce, transportation, and national politics. His family was influential, and as his uncle William was one of the leading bankers of the day, Marcus was exposed to some aspects of the business of running a city.

Another visitor during the time just before Marcus left Baltimore, John Melish, noted more than eighty "well-dressed men" at a local tavern. He attributed their presence to the fact that Baltimore was "the great thoroughfare between the northern and southern states; and the number of people passing to and fro, in business and pleasure is immense."[6] Although any memories written by Marcus of his years in Baltimore are lost to history, a little of what he may have experienced can be learned from the memories shared by others. One visitor observed:

> The houses in Baltimore are mostly built of brick, and many of them are elegant . . . the town exhibited a very handsome appearance and the country abounded in villas, gardens and well-cultivated fields. . . . the town included a number of churches, a court house, a jail, three market houses, a poor-house, the Exchange, a theater, assembly rooms and a library which contained a very excellent collection of books. . . . the streets of Baltimore were kept very clean.[7]

Marcus's surroundings may have influenced his early interest in a legal career. At one point, James Winchester sought a tutor to instruct his son in the basics of law. In 1814, George Washington Campbell, former secretary of the treasury under James Madison, resigned from his post and returned to Tennessee. Before that, Campbell had served as one of the first justices on the Tennessee Supreme Court and was elected to the U.S. Senate in 1811, where he became a vocal advocate for war with Great Britain. In May 1815, he responded to what appears to have been a letter from James Winchester inquiring about a place for Marcus to study law. Campbell stated that he was willing to "take young men for law study at $75 a year." Whether Marcus pursued this opportunity remains unclear, but later in life, he wrote that he had ultimately decided to "give up a law career for that of a merchant."

Marcus Winchester would one day stand on the fourth Chickasaw bluff where he could count as many as seventy flatboats waiting between Paddy's Hen and Chickens and President's Island to unload produce or other goods in Memphis. One early Memphian remembered, "These boats were manned by rude, athletic, uncultivated Western men, who, when a large number of their boats would tie up for the night at the mouth of the Wolf, would make the night hideous."[8]

It is impossible to know whether Marcus Winchester ever compared the uncultivated flatboat pilots to the well-dressed men he had observed in Baltimore's taverns or if he reflected on the life he might have led in that city. Nevertheless, the knowledge he gained during his time in the bustling port of Baltimore undoubtedly shaped his vision for the early development of Memphis.

Chapter Four Endnotes

1. Emma Shelton, *William Winchester, 1711-1790* (Westminster, MD: Historical Society of Carroll County, Maryland, 1993), 9.
2. Shelton, *Winchester*, 25.
3. William Winchester to James Winchester, August 25, 1810, *Correspondence*, The Gilder Lehrman Institute of American History, GLC06997.13, accessed through Adam Matthew, *American History, 1493-1945*.
4. Louis Farrell, *Descendants of William Winchester* (Washington, D.C.: Self-published, 1933), 51.
5. Farrell, *Descendants of William Winchester*, 51.
6. Raphael Semmes, *Baltimore as Seen by Visitors, 1783-1860* (Baltimore: Maryland Historical Society, 1953), 38.
7. Semmes, *Baltimore*, 38.
8. Judge Q. K. Underwood, "Address," *Old Folks Record*, no. 12 (September 1875): 532.

APIUN HOUSE,

RECENTLY UNITED STATES HOTEL,
CORNER OF ADAMS AND MAIN STREETS,
MEMPHIS, TENN.

The undersigned, in changing the name of this house, would respectfully inform the public, that he has also made other important changes in the building, by re-modeling the whole, in the most modern style, and building a large addition to the former house, in which he has a splendid Dining Room, equal to any in the city, and a large and elegant Barber Shop, with which is connected an elegant set of Bath Rooms, so that persons stopping at this house may always find those conveniences of health and luxury at hand.

The whole house has been but recently fitted up with entire New Furniture, and is now in complete order; and having superior Cooks and the best waiters in the country, the proprietor pledges himself that this House shall not be surpassed by any Hotel in the city.

J. J. WORSHAM,
Proprietor.

From Rainey's Memphis City Directory, 1855/56

Chapter Five: Trouble, Heartaches & Sadness

James Winchester's military reputation destroyed

Family connections in Washington City, Maryland, and Tennessee allowed Marcus Winchester to witness firsthand some significant social and political moments in early American history. For most, these were events that were only read about in newspapers at the time, or in history books in years to come. He also witnessed some of the ugly aspects of early nineteenth-century politics and learned the skills needed to navigate public relations on a national scale.

Brigadier General William Hull provided a prime example for young Winchester of how a man's reputation could easily be destroyed. Like Marcus's father, James Winchester, Hull was an aging, but respected, veteran of the Revolutionary War. He had studied law under John Q. Adams and practiced in Massachusetts. Hull served as a major general commanding in the Massachusetts militia and was commissioned as the first governor of the Michigan Territory and an Indian agent by President Thomas Jefferson. By the first decade of the nineteenth century, the old solider was nearly sixty years old, overweight, and recovering from a stroke. That did not dissuade President James Madison from selecting him as one of the newly appointed brigadier generals leading up to the War of 1812.

It would be Hull who would lead the first major offensive of the war—an invasion of present-day Ontario, Canada. Some naively believed that capturing the British territory would weaken their power in North America and compel them to withdraw from any further conflict. Additionally, Hull believed that Canadian settlers would join the American cause once "freed from British rule." Hull led his U.S. forces across the Canadian border on July 12, 1812, planning to take the British post of Fort Malden at Amherstburg, Ontario. To say he failed would be an understatement. Hull decided there was no way to take the fort, so he and his men quickly retreated back to Fort Detroit.

British Major General Isaac Brock and his troops, along with Tecumseh and his Native American warriors, tricked Hull into thinking they had more men than they had and gathered around the fort in a dramatic display of threat. By their mere presence and without firing a shot, they intimidated Hull into surrendering Fort Detroit. Its loss to the British was a public relations disaster for the United States. It also gave the British a base to increase their presence in the Michigan Territory and convinced more Native Americans they could actually win in a battle against Americans. It was a major embarrassment for the United States, destroyed Hull's reputation, and nearly cost him his life. The list of charges he faced afterward included cowardice, neglect of duty, and conduct unbecoming an officer. Although he was court-martialed and actually sentenced to death, Hull was ultimately pardoned due to his Revolutionary War service.

Despite the striking parallels between William Hull and James Winchester, no evidence suggests that James Winchester—or Marcus, for that matter—viewed Hull's fate as a cautionary tale, though they would have been wise to do so. Especially since James Winchester had something Hull did not—a nemesis in the form of William Henry Harrison.

Harrison was the son of Benjamin Harrison, a governor of Virginia, one of the signers of the Declaration of Independence, and a close friend of George Washington. William Henry Harrison's mother, Ann Carter, was the daughter of Robert "King" Carter, a prominent colonial American landowner and politician in Virginia during the eighteenth century. Known as "King" Carter due to his wealth and influence, he played a significant role in Virginia's political and economic landscape, primarily around the Tidewater region. In naming the first fort they constructed "Tuckahoe," the Winchester brothers signaled their aspiration to emulate prominent families such as the Harrisons and Carters.

The Carter family, much like the Harrisons, wielded significant influence in both American politics and society. In addition to significant family connections, William Henry Harrison also developed a reputation as a strong military commander. He began his service in 1791 as an ensign in the First Infantry of the Regular Army and later served as aide-de-camp to Major General Anthony Wayne at the Battle of Fallen Timbers. Wayne led two thousand men of the Legion of the United States, along with Choctaw and Chickasaw scouts and members of the Kentucky militia, against the Northwest Confederacy in Ohio. Their victory led to the Treaty of Greenville which created the opportunity for occupation of the Northwest Territory. Harrison's experience extended beyond the battlefield as well; he held various political roles, including secretary of the

Northwest Territory and its first delegate to Congress. He also played a key role in the division of the Northwest and Indiana Territories, and in 1801 he assumed the governorship of the Indiana Territory.

At the end of his term as governor in 1811, an opportunity presented itself in which Harrison's reputation as a military commander would be even more firmly established. The U.S. government's aggressive land acquisition policies from Native Americans had alarmed Chief Tecumseh, who had been primarily responsible for Brigadier General William Hull's recent calamity.

Tecumseh, along with his brother Tenskwatawa, also known as "the Prophet," established Prophetstown, a pivotal Native American village close to the Tippecanoe River, near present-day Lafayette, Indiana. It served as a political and military center for Native Americans who were opposed to White expansion. Tecumseh and the Prophet proposed a united confederacy made up of members of all Native American tribes to fight against the settlement of Whites on their land and preservation of their traditional way of life.

Harrison mobilized around eleven hundred troops and marched to confront Tecumseh and the Prophet at Prophetstown. On November 6, 1811, Harrison was preparing to hold a council with the Native Americans the following day. Instead, the Prophet launched a surprise attack with around six hundred warriors in the pre-dawn hours. The American soldiers were caught unprepared. However, under Harrison's military leadership, they managed to withstand two hours of intense combat. As Harrison later reported to Washington, "Such of the men as were awake, or easily awakened, seized their arms and took their stations; others, which were more tardy, had to contend with the enemy in the doors of their tents."[1] As dawn approached, Harrison ordered a counterattack, forcing the Native Americans into retreat. The next day, the soldiers advanced on Prophetstown, destroyed the food that had been stored for the winter, and burned the village to the ground.

The battle and subsequent publicity branded Harrison a hero, resulting in the nickname "Tippecanoe." The Senate and House of Representatives of Kentucky passed a resolution that stated, "Resolved that in the late campaign against the Indians upon the Wabash, Governor William Henry Harrison has behaved like a hero, a patriot and a general; and that for his cool, deliberate, skillful and gallant behavior in the battle of Tippecanoe, he well deserves the warmest thanks from his country and the nation."[2]

Public acknowledgement for his leadership would prove long-lasting and contributed to Harrison winning the presidency decades later with the campaign slogan "Tippecanoe and Tyler, Too."

Where others saw William Hull's defeat and the loss of Fort Detroit as an embarrassing loss, both William Henry Harrison and James Winchester saw an opportunity. With the new rank of brigadier general, Winchester was prepared to lead an army of soldiers and volunteers—primarily from Kentucky—in the effort to retake Fort Detroit. Harrison, however, argued that he should be the one to lead the soldiers into battle because he had just been promoted to the rank of major general in the Kentucky militia, and most of those serving were Kentuckians. At thirty-nine years old, Harrison had another advantage over sixty-one-year-old Winchester—youth.

The stage was set for the two men to become bitter rivals. Both attempted to use their influence and connections in Washington, D.C., and neither had any intention of serving under the other. As Durham noted:

> Both were determined to serve their country. However, both also had strong personal ambitions, and it was there that the conflict arose. Winchester would have been satisfied to lead a brigade, but Harrison had to have an entire army. And he would let nothing stand in his way, as Winchester presently discovered.[3]

Ultimately, Harrison would command the army of the Northwest Territory with Winchester second in command. In addition to their rivalry over leadership, their very different styles also contributed to a source of tension between the two men. Harrison was known for his cautious approach to warfare. He favored defensive tactics and careful planning, while Winchester was more aggressive and more likely to take offensive action.

While Harrison was popular among the men of the militia, Winchester struggled to earn their respect. Despite a privileged upbringing in the east, Harrison managed to connect with even the most rugged frontiersmen on their level. Winchester had spent more than twenty-five years as a settler and "Indian hunter" in Tennessee, yet he failed to "have the common touch among the backwoodsmen."[4] That failure would become even more pronounced as he led his army of starving, untrained members of the Kentucky militia, with Marcus at his side, toward Canada to retake Fort Detroit. One soldier wrote, "General Winchester being a stranger and having the appearance of a supercilious officer, he was generally disliked. His assuming the command almost occasioned a mutiny in the camp."[5]

Some of the men openly showed their disdain for Winchester, and a few even played jokes on him. At one point, a story spread that a log over the area the men used as a latrine was sawed nearly in half so it would snap, and Winchester would fall into human waste. While that likely did not happen, it illustrates the great dislike the men had for their commander. Winchester later claimed Harrison held up supplies for the starving soldiers in order to make him even more unpopular.

Marcus Winchester witnessed what he surely saw as a great injustice taking place against his father. First-hand observations of young Winchester at the time are limited, but one newspaper editor referred to him as a "sprightly boy of eighteen or nineteen who assists in writing."[6] Clues that Marcus performed administrative and clerical duties can also be found in his father's archive of documents from the war that include his notes and signatures.

Marcus Winchester sent a letter to his older sister, Maria Winchester Breedlove, dated November 9, 1812, from Camp Miami Number Two near Fort Winchester. In the letter, he included a hand-drawn map on which he traced the route they traveled through Ohio knowing "yourself and the family would be very grateful in knowing our route."[7] He also reported to his sister that he and their father were in good health.

If they were in good health, they were in the minority. By January 1813, the nearly frozen, starving men being led by Winchester made it to the Maumee River Rapids. Harrison had instructed Winchester to hold his position there. When Winchester received word that an American settlement at nearby Frenchtown, present-day Monroe, Michigan, was being attacked by a small army of British and Native Americans, he ignored that command. Winchester sent Marcus and nearly half the troops under his command with Colonel William Lewis to cross the frozen River Raisin to help the Americans. That would prove to be a fatal mistake. While Lewis and the men were initially victorious, the real battle had not yet begun. James Winchester was thrilled by Lewis's victory and moved the rest of the army into Frenchtown to rest and wait.

Harrison sent a message to Winchester ordering him to prepare for further combat and letting Winchester know he was sending the requested provisions and three companies of troops as reinforcements. Winchester was later accused of being slow to prepare as well as he should have for another attack. A small group of soldiers informed Winchester the British were preparing to invade immediately, but they would later claim he waved them off and ignored their report. If so, it was a foolish mistake that would have disastrous results.

While the men were settled in and camping throughout Frenchtown, James and Marcus Winchester were staying south of town in a home on the bank of the River Raisin built by early-French explorer Francois Navarre, the first European to settle in the area.

As the sun rose on the morning of January 22, 1813, British commander Colonel Henry Procter and Native American Chief Roundhead led the second attack against surprised soldiers resting in Frenchtown. As the battle began, James Winchester awoke to the sound of gunfire. He and Marcus hurried into town where James attempted to rally his disorganized troops and prepare a defense, but it was too late. The American forces were surrounded and being butchered.

With casualties mounting by the minute, Winchester ordered a surrender to prevent further deaths. Stripped of his uniform by Chief Roundhead, he would have to live with the humiliating story that he was captured in his nightshirt. It was made worse by a British newspaper cartoon that showed Winchester nearly naked, captured by Native Americans, and mocked by Procter, British soldiers, and Native American warriors.

Under the terms of the surrender, Winchester later claimed Procter agreed that the sixty or so sick and injured prisoners who were unable to travel to Fort Malden would be cared for until they could be transported to a prisoner of war prison or ship. Procter claimed that was untrue. Whether there was a verbal agreement in place or not cannot be proven. What is known is that few of those injured men would survive to return to their homes.

After the British departed with their American prisoners, including James and Marcus Winchester, a group of Native Americans returned to torture and murder all the wounded, scalping many of them alive. They set fire to the buildings where wounded soldiers were being held, and those who could not escape could be heard screaming as they were burned alive. Soldier Elias Darnell wrote:

> My feeble powers cannot describe the dismal senses exhibited. I saw my fellow soldiers naked and wounded, crawling out of the houses to avoid being consumed in the flames. Some that had not been able to turn themselves on their beds for four days, through fear of being burned to death, arose and walked out and about through the yard. . . . A number, unable to get out, miserably perished in the unrelenting flames of the houses, kindled by the more unrelenting savages.[8]

In total, more than five hundred men were killed, ninety were injured, and four hundred were captured. It was the deadliest battle ever fought in Michigan and is remembered as the battle with the highest number of Americans killed in a single engagement during the War of 1812. News of the River Raisin Massacre, as it came to be called, spread around the country and added even more fuel to the fire of the War Hawks resolve to continue the war. Years before "Remember the Alamo" was heard on the battlefields where Texans were fighting for independence from Mexico, soldiers fighting in the War of 1812 shouted "Remember the Raisin."

Marcus Winchester was held prisoner with the others who had been captured, but most likely was released after a month with other prisoners. He returned to his family at Cragfont in Tennessee where it appears he stayed until the war was over.

On October 5, 1813, while James Winchester was still a prisoner of war in Quebec, Harrison led the army that defeated Procter's troops along the Thames River in Upper Canada. As shouts of "Remember the Raisin" could be heard from Colonel Richard Johnson's Kentucky Mounted Volunteers, Procter's defenses were shattered and Americans would once again celebrate a major victory over the British. Harrison's star shined even brighter while Winchester was now cast as a villain.

General James Winchester went on the defensive almost immediately. A letter he wrote to the secretary of war from Fort Malden, where he was initially held, would eventually make its way to newspapers back home in Tennessee. He wrote, "However unfortunate may seem to be the affair yesterday I am flattered by a belief, that no material error is chargeable upon myself, and that still less censure is deserved by the troops I had the honor of Commanding."[9]

Harrison was equally as quick to blame Winchester for the disastrous results. He publicly pointed out that when Winchester sent soldiers to answer the call for help from Frenchtown, he did so against orders. And once the first battle had been won, he declared Winchester should have anticipated a counterattack and begun planning immediately rather than wait for reinforcements.

His humiliation at the Battle of the River Raisin would be a shadow Winchester would live under for the rest of his life. While he was not officially court-martialed for his actions, like Hull had been, he faced censure and a loss of confidence. Later, Winchester served in the Battle of Fort Meigs in May 1813. American forces, again under the command of Harrison, defended the fort against a British and Native American attack. Although the fort was defended, Winchester's leadership and some of his decisions during the battle were once again criticized, and he once again faced public scrutiny.

After the war, Winchester returned to his family at Cragfont hoping perhaps time would help ease the damage to his national reputation. To his great aggravation, in the fall of 1818 Kentucky state senator Robert B. McAfee published *History of the Late War in the Western Country*, in which he was critical of Winchester.

About the Battle of River Raisin, McAfee wrote, "a disaster so calamitous would necessarily excite much discussion with respect to its cause."[10] And he made it clear where he thought the cause was found. Harrison's only mistake, he wrote, was trusting Winchester:

> If Harrison committed an error, it appears to me that it consisted in allowing too great a latitude of discretion to general Winchester.

His responsibility for the conduct of the army, his accurate knowledge of the country, his experience in Indian warfare and knowledge of the caution it required, all entitled him to control, in the most positive manner, the movements of General Winchester's command.[11]

It is relevant to note that one of McAfee's biggest contributors to his research was actually Harrison himself. In response, Winchester sought a ghostwriter to help him write his own narrative of what happened at the River Raisin to defend his honor. Through friends John Overton and Andrew Jackson, he made the acquaintance of writer Charles Cassedy. Cassedy had served Overton as an administrative assistant and had done some clerical work for Jackson.

After a series of interviews and researching the battle, Cassedy hid away in a house in Nashville and wrote a series of letters "from Winchester" to be published in various newspapers. On July 8, 1817, the first article appeared in the *Nashville Clarion*. It was signed James Winchester and patriotically dated July 4, 1817. It began:

> A work, purporting to be a *History of the late war in the Western Country*, in which my name is mentioned with some asperity, and perhaps some injustice has lately made its appearance in this part of the world. Had not this production some claim to attention of posterity, I could suffer that part of it which has relation to the disasters of the left wing of the north western army to pass without observation. I could reply upon future historians, to judge of, and record dispassionately those events ... but under existing circumstances, silence would be criminal.[12]

Of course, the articles defended each of Winchester's decisions in the battle and accused Harrison of failure to provide much-requested supplies and reinforcements that were so desperately needed. Winchester pointed out that it was foolish to assume the troops at Frenchtown were unprepared for battle, considering they were deep in enemy territory. There would be seven more articles in the series, and they were later combined into a book titled *Historical details having relation to the campaign of the north-western army, under Generals Harrison and Winchester, during the winter of 1812-13: together with some particulars relating to the surrender of Fort Bowyer, &c.* Although attributed to Winchester, the book was compiled and written by Cassedy. The original title page was even hand written by the author.

Cassedy, a heavy drinker who struggled to find work, became a frequent guest at Cragfont and continued to press Winchester for more freelance writing assignments long after the General had decided it was time to move on.

Cassedy wrote to Winchester's daughter Maria Winchester Breedlove in 1838, twelve years after her father's death, requesting the use of an oil painting she owned that had been painted by the early American portrait artist Ralph E. W. Earl. He was married to Andrew and Rachel Jackson's niece and painted portraits of many in Jackson's circle including the Overtons, Breedloves, and Winchesters. After an introduction to the artist by Andrew Jackson, James Winchester became one of the first Tennesseans Earl painted. Jackson suggested he would be glad to see Earl "gratify a little family pride and promote the fine arts."[13] After completing James Winchester's portrait, Earl painted Winchester's wife, Susan, and their daughter, Selima Winchester Robeson.

Cassedy wanted to have a steel engraving produced of the painting of James Winchester that would be used for the frontispiece of the biography he was writing, *Military Biographical Memoirs of General James Winchester*.

The General's old nemesis, William Henry Harrison, was running for president at that time, and Cassedy knew there would be renewed interest in the topic of his military career. In the letter, he assured Breedlove the book would be "perfectly satisfactory to his family and friends and equally astounding to his enemies who rest in peace on the false assumption that the darkness of the tomb has silenced the voice of historical truths and justice forever."[14] The biography was never published.

The War of 1812 ended with the signing of the Treaty of Ghent on December 24, 1814, in Ghent, Belgium, between the United States and Great Britain, formally ending the war. The news was slow to reach America, however. Andrew Jackson's victory at the Battle of New Orleans in January 1815 occurred after the treaty was signed but before news reached New Orleans. This battle invigorated American morale, cemented Andrew Jackson's status as a military hero, and played a pivotal role in propelling his political ascent. Americans were eager to celebrate, but more significantly, they were ready to embrace the expansion of the western frontier for settlement.

President James Monroe went on a victory tour through New England and received thunderous applause at every stop. In Boston, after a crowd of 40,000 loudly cheered for both the president and the strength of the nation, a Federalist newspaper dubbed it "the era of good feelings."

James Winchester was certainly not left with "good feelings" after the war, although with the passage of time, his bravery and willingness to serve came to be appreciated. In 1857, an old friend of the family, John Carr, wrote of Winchester's military service:

He was taken prisoner by the British and Indians at the unfortunate battle of the River Raisin, and was carried to Quebec, where he remained a prisoner during the following winter. A great deal has been said about that disastrous affair, and General Winchester has been severely criticized; but I do not believe any person in a similar situation could have done better than he did under his circumstances.... I knew him long and well; and I do not hesitate to say that I believe he was a persecuted man.[15]

Historian John Hibbett DeWitt was passionate about Tennessee history and served as president of the Tennessee Historical Society for nearly a quarter century. In 1915, he wrote an article in the *Tennessee Historical Magazine* in which he defended James Winchester:

While he showed no lack of courage, he was the victim of misfortune and defeat. The writers of history have shown scant willingness to do him justice, if not a desire to cast obloquy upon his name. The rivalries and jealousies among the leaders resulted to his disadvantage, and he had to endure the inevitable blame which attaches to a general who leads his army to disaster and surrender, although they are beyond his control.[16]

The reputations of others from Winchester's home state would fare much better after the war. Tennesseans played a major role, and it changed the trajectory of the lives and careers of many of those who survived. Marcus Winchester knew and worked with many of them. Tom Kanon, considered the foremost expert in the War of 1812, wrote:

[For] Tennessee at least, the period between 1812 and 1815 proved to be a watershed moment in its young development. Personalities such as Andrew Jackson and William Carroll (as well as iconic figures Sam Houston and David Crockett) proved their mettle on the battlefields and advanced their political careers by way of the popularity their martial activities generated ... and while the expansionist tendencies of the United States provided an opportunity to extend southern slavery, the War of 1812 (via the Creek War of 1813-14) also set the pattern for the eventual removal of the Indians east of the Mississippi River.[17]

In Marcus Winchester's post-war life and career, it appears he chose diplomacy over warfare and regional politics over the national stage. Unlike his uncles and cousins in Baltimore and New Orleans, he carved out a life among the "rude, athletic, uncultivated Western men" rather than captains of business and industry. When faced with conflict, he used charm and charisma as a weapon and applied his skills as a talented mediator rather than a fighter. The war also provided him with two important tools. First, the relationships forged during his time serving as his father's aide put young Winchester squarely on a path that would take him to Memphis. Second, although he was never officially commissioned into the militia—or the military of any kind—the boy who Canadian newspapers had dubbed "the Little Yankee Major," was referred to as "Major Winchester" for the rest of his life.

Chapter Five Endnotes

1. Bob Kriebel, "Battle of Tippecanoe through Harrison, Indians' Eyes," Journal & Courier (Lafayette, IN), accessed March 24, 2024.
2. *The Palladium*, "State Legislature on Jan. 15, 1812," January 15, 1812, 3.
3. *Palladium*, "State Legislature," 119.
4. James E. Roper, "Marcus Winchester and the Earliest Years of Memphis," *Tennessee Historical Quarterly* 21, no. 4 (1962): 327.
5. Elias Darnell, *Massacre on the River Raisin* (Leonaur: United Kingdom, 2013), 97.
6. Thomas Smith to W. W. Worsley, November 7, 1812, State Historical Society of Wisconsin Library, Draper MSS, Kentucky Papers, 5CC69.
7. Marcus Winchester, *Map of Ohio and Letter from Marcus Winchester to His Sister* [map], The Gilder Lehrman Institute of American History, GLC06997.18, available through Adam Matthew, *American History, 1493-1945* (Marlborough, UK).
8. Winchester Map, Lehrman Institute, 118.
9. *Pittsburgh Weekly Gazette* (Pittsburgh, PA), March 12, 1813, 2.
10. Robert B. McAfee, *History of the Late War in the Western Country* (Bowling Green, OH: Historical Publications Company, 1919; originally published 1816), 248.
11. McAfee, *History of the Late War*, 255.
12. John Winchester, *The Clarion and Tennessee State Gazette*, July 8, 1817, 2.
13. Walter Durham, *James Winchester: Tennessee Pioneer* (Gallatin: Sumner County Library Board, 1979), 245.
14. Charles Cassedy to Maria Breedlove regarding a biography of her father, James Winchester, *Correspondence*, The Gilder Lehrman Institute of American History, GLC06997.77, accessed through Adam Matthew, *American History, 1493-1945* (Marlborough, UK).
15. John Carr, *Early Times in Middle Tennessee* (Nashville: E. Carr, by E. Stevenson & F. A. Owens, 1857), 62.
16. John H. DeWitt, "General James Winchester, 1752-1826," *Tennessee Historical Magazine* 1, no. 2 (1915): 87.
17. Tom Kanon, *Tennesseans at War, 1812-1815* (Tuscaloosa: University of Alabama Press, 2014), 2.

WHIPPLE, M'CULLOUGH & CO.,
FLOORING AND LUMBER DEALERS,
NO. 124,
Madison st., near the Bayou,
MEMPHIS, TENN.

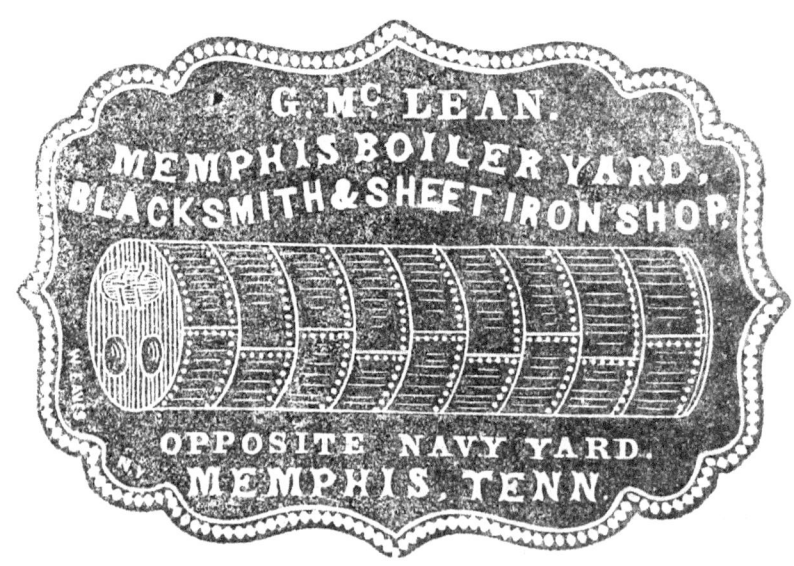

KEEPS ALWAYS ON HAND
SECOND HAND BOILERS
which he will sell at very low prices. Also, keeps constantly
FIRE PROOF BRICK, TILE AND FIRE CLAY.

From Rainey's Memphis City Directory, 1855/56

Chapter Six: Big River

History of the fourth Chickasaw bluff

The location of the fourth Chickasaw bluff, high above the Mississippi River flood plain, kept those living there safer from flooding, a common occurrence along the Mississippi River. And being able to watch the river from fifty feet or more in the air meant those keeping watch could quickly spot potential enemies. The fourth bluff in particular also provided the easiest access from the river due to small islands of mud that slowed the current and a shelf of sandstone that provided a place to more easily dock a canoe or flatboat to load or unload supplies.

In spite of the river moving like a snake through the middle of the country, the four bluffs can still be found between present-day Fulton and Memphis, close to where they are today. The first Chickasaw bluff is the site of Fort Pillow Historic State Park in Lauderdale County. The small community of Randoph is located at the second bluff. The third can be found within Meeman-Shelby Forest State Park, and Memphis is on the fourth Chickasaw bluff.

In 1818, Marcus Winchester stood on that bluff, felt the breeze coming off the river, and recognized great potential. He was not the first. If you could turn the clock back to around 10,000 B.C.E. and visit the bluffs, you might discover a group of Paleo-Indians whose ancestors had followed big game as the glaciers melted. It took time for these early settlers to develop into societies recognizable today as Native American tribes. Archaeologists believe that the formation of substantial, organized communities on the bluffs began during the Late Woodland period, around 500 C.E., with groups known as Mound Builders. Their villages contained large earthen mounds used for religious, burial, or defensive purposes, often constructed on high cliffs. At one time, as many as seven mounds were located on the fourth bluff at what is now Chickasaw Heritage State Park. Today, two mounds remain.

Travel ahead to 1500 C.E. and ten miles south of those mounds, and you would find an example of a tribe of the late Mississippian Culture. They depended on farming for much of their food, mainly growing what came to be called the Three Sisters—corn, beans, and squash. These were the first real farmers, clearing large fields using stone axes and fire, then working the soil by hand digging with sticks, hoes made of stone, and large animal bones. They created mound-like structures by piling up the soil in these fields. The village nearest the fourth Chickasaw bluff included a town square, athletic fields, and houses made of wood and dried clay with thatch roofs. It was abandoned around 1500 C.E. The village was given the name Chucalissa—which is "abandoned house" in the Choctaw language—by archaeologist Charles H. Nash after it was rediscovered in the late 1930s.

To witness the first European visitors, you would need to advance the clock by nearly half a century. It would be fascinating to see the Spanish explorer Hernando de Soto push aside thick grass and cane to catch his first glimpse of the Mississippi River from somewhere near the fourth Chickasaw bluff. The sheer power and magnitude of the water rushing south must have left him in awe. He called it the River of the Holy Ghost—a fitting name, as he would die on its banks just a year later, and his body sunk to the bottom.

De Soto's presence can also be seen as a metaphor for what was to come. In his relentless search for riches to take back to Spain, his army—like other European explorers—murdered, raped, pillaged, and kidnapped Native Americans. Even more devastating, they brought with them deadly diseases, which would prove to be the most destructive weapon of all. It is estimated that European arrival in 1492 led to fifty-six million deaths of Native Americans by disease by 1600.[1]

Those who survived banded into tribes like the Chickasaw who populated the bluffs in the late seventeenth and eighteenth century. While there were no more than seven thousand by 1700, they became an important factor to consider for the Spanish, French, and English who began harvesting the valuable resources available along the river. The Chickasaw called it the "Misha Sipokni," translating to "Beyond Age River" or "Ancient Father of Waters," reflecting the river's importance in their culture. Most of the invaders would not have the same respect for the Mississippi River. As one old saying goes, "The Spanish came to find gold, the French came to find fur, and the English came to find God."

Slightly more than one thousand years after De Soto, French Jesuit priest Jacques Marquette and philosophy-student-turned-fur-trader Louis Joliet stopped at the fourth Chickasaw bluff while exploring and mapping the path of the river so the best locations could be selected for trading posts. In 1673, they reported they were "kindly received" by the Native Americans there. Their trip also confirmed that it was possible to travel from the Great Lakes all the way to the Gulf of Mexico by water. Soon came a four-thousand-mile network of French trading posts that exploited the natural resources along the river for the next century and a half. Marquette's map, published in 1681, included the "Mitchisipi Highlands" and shows the first, second, and fourth Chickasaw bluffs.

Advance the clock just one more year, and you would find the French officer René-Robert Cavelier, Sieur de La Salle, exploring the Mississippi River with a large party traveling by canoe. He called the river the Colbert, in honor of Jean-Baptiste Colbert, secretary of state for the French navy under King Louis XIV. The expedition stopped at one of the bluffs—most likely the second, at present-day Franklin, Tennessee, just below the mouth of the Hatchie River—so La Salle and his men could hunt.

When a member of his party, Pierre Prudhomme, failed to return to camp, La Salle ordered a simple structure built to shelter the group while they searched for their lost comrade and continued exploring the river. It was assumed that Prudhomme had been captured by the Chickasaw, who were known to detain outsiders who landed on the bluffs, march them to their village, and—after great pomp and ceremony—return them unharmed to the place they were captured.

Prudhomme, however, was not taken by the Chickasaw; he had simply gotten lost. He returned ten days later to find that the first European-built structure in West Tennessee had been named in his honor—Fort Prudhomme.

Visit the bluff in 1739, and you might encounter Jean-Baptiste Le Moyne de Bienville, the governor of Louisiana and founder of New Orleans. He chose the site to build a fort as a base camp for his campaign to eradicate the Chickasaw and claim the entire region for France. His army included twelve hundred French troops and another twenty-four hundred Black soldiers and Native American allies from other tribes. At that time, the Chickasaw, then allies of the British, lived primarily around present-day Tupelo, Mississippi, but frequently hunted on their land in West Tennessee.

On August 15, 1739—Assumption Day—Bienville dedicated Fort Assumption, situated near the east end of what is now the Memphis–Arkansas Bridge at Chickasaw Heritage Park. Bienville's forces were unable to achieve victory due to the Chickasaw's strong resistance and their strategic advantage of being on home turf. The campaign was further hampered by sickness, logistical challenges, and insufficient support from his own government back home in France. Bienville abandoned his efforts and retreated.

Isaac Roberts arrived at the bluff in December 1786 with work to do. As deputy surveyor of North Carolina's western district, he was responsible for surveying five thousand acres recently purchased by John Rice. Just three years earlier, North Carolina had opened a land office in Hillsboro to redeem specie certificates, a promise to pay the bearer a specified amount, issued during the Revolutionary War for supplies. John Armstrong, appointed as entry taker, oversaw land transactions at a rate of ten pounds in specie—money in the form of gold or silver coins—per hundred acres. This offering included all of present-day Tennessee, except for the Military District and Cherokee-held land in the southeastern corner of the state.

To facilitate land distribution, the territory was divided into three districts. The Eastern District encompassed the land between Greene County and the Cumberland Mountains. The Middle District stretched from the Cumberland Mountains to the Tennessee River. The Western District, where the tract of John Rice was located, extended from the Tennessee River to the Mississippi River, despite being claimed by the Chickasaw Nation.

Roberts completed the survey, and the final registration of the grant was recorded on August 14, 1789. Nearly thirty years would pass before Marcus Winchester made his first visit.

A year after Roberts's survey was registered, a visitor to the bluff might have encountered Lieutenant Governor Manuel Gayoso de Lemos. A respected and multilingual diplomat, Gayoso, governor of the Natchez District, recognized the bluff's strategic importance. By the mid-1790s, he was tasked with securing the area for Spain, assisted by Indian agent Benjamin Fooy.

A native of Holland, Fooy had earned a reputation as a swashbuckling river hero among the Spanish. In May 1782, he negotiated with river pirates to secure the release of the Spanish commander's wife in St. Louis. Later, he established a small settlement on the fourth Chickasaw bluff, only to be expelled by the United States government in 1797. Undeterred, he relocated directly across the river, where he founded Camp de la Esperanza or Camp of Hope.

It was also a camp of love. Fooy functioned as a judge, of sorts, even marrying couples from the bluff in his home. One early settler recalled seeing the ferry and boats with musicians lit by torches crossing the river from time to time for weddings.[2]

It was not love Gayoso was after. In a letter to his wife on May 31, 1795, the Spanish governor wrote, "Yesterday I passed from my post of Esperanza over to the Chicacha Bluffs, where I now write. I hoisted the King's flag and saluted it in the most brilliant manner from the flotilla and the battery. It being St. Ferdinand's day (the name of my prince), I gave the post that name."[3]

While the exact location of Fort San Fernando de las Barrancas is unknown, it was located somewhere along the Wolf River near where Front Street intersects A.W. Willis Avenue today. What is known is that it was a horrible place for a fort. Because of the surrounding swamps and low-lying land, malaria and yellow fever were a constant issue, and the mortality rate for soldiers assigned to the fort was high. The hot temperature and crushing humidity also made summers unbearable, and to make matters worse, the fort had been located in a spot prone to flooding. Historian James Roper observed, "It was a hardship post, its small jail usually full of brawling soldiers and sailors, its fevers unrelenting ... there was no lime for making mortar, hence no ovens for making bread. Insubordination was a way of life."[4]

Fortunately for them, they were not on the bluff for long. In the 1795 Treaty of San Lorenzo—also known as Pinckney's Treaty—Spain granted the United States free navigation of the Mississippi River, the right to deposit goods duty-free in New Orleans, and recognized the southern U.S. boundary as running along the 31st parallel. Spain also agreed to withdraw from forts north of this line, like Fort San Fernando de las Barrancas, and promised not to support Native American attacks against settlers. The fort was destroyed, and most of the Spaniards withdrew across the Mississippi River. Some of the squatters who had built shacks and settled near the fort to take advantage of trading with soldiers and Native Americans chose to stay. A few were still there to welcome and share stories of the past with early settlers like Marcus Winchester.

Francis Baily, a then 21-year-old wealthy Englishman with an appetite for adventure, docked at the bluff two decades before Winchester. He wrote of about five or six "half-Indian" families and recorded in his journal that some had married into the families of the Native Americans: "This tract of country belongs to the tribe of Chickasaw Indians, a warlike race, and one that preserves a good understanding with America, which the latter is obligated to keep up by presents sent annually to them." He added, "They were very much dissatisfied with the Americans they said, for not sending them their accustomed presents."[5]

The description written by Baily provides a good indicator of what Winchester likely observed during his first visits to the bluff many years later. Baily called the Native Americans he encountered a "well-made, handsome race of men" and was particularly struck by how they dressed:

> The chief part of them were dressed in printed calico shirts, which (together with what they call a breech-clout) formed the whole of their dress, except a pair of mockasons, which served them for shoes. These mockasons are made of deer skins, which are smoked instead of tanned, and are thereby rendered very soft and pleasant to the feet; they are sowed together at the top with the sinews of the deer, and are finished oftentimes in a very curious manner with wampum and porcupine quills.[6]

As more settlers pushed into the Tennessee territory, Native Americans became increasingly reliant on gifts and payments from the United States. Chickasaw leaders realized they had to adapt to the changing environment in order to survive. They began to formally engage with the U.S. government, negotiating treaties that secured yearly payments to tribal leaders in return for maintaining peace among the settlers. These agreements also established government agents or factors, who served as liaisons between the Chickasaw and the federal government. These agents were responsible for managing Native American affairs, enforcing policies, and resolving disputes, with the ultimate goal of keeping White settlers safe and securing control of the land.

In 1802, President Thomas Jefferson initiated the establishment of a factory on the fourth Chickasaw bluff. Early trading posts were called factories because they were managed by a person called a factor. "Factor" comes from the Latin verb *facere*, meaning "to do" or "to make." Over time, the word evolved to mean someone who "does business" on behalf of someone else. In this case, factors traded goods with Native Americans, hunters, and trappers in exchange primarily for animal skins on behalf of the United States. The factory on the fourth Chickasaw bluff was part of a broader network of government-operated trading posts and was a crucial point of social gatherings, news, and business until it was moved in 1818.

If you visited the bluff in 1809, in addition to the government factory, you would have found a future president serving as commander of a fort located further south from the Wolf River. Although he had not yet earned the nickname "Old Rough and Ready," at just twenty-four, Zachary Taylor had parlayed his fame as an Indian fighter into a short stint commanding Fort Pickering. Built around 1800 and replacing two previous forts, Adams and Pike, it was named after George Washington's secretary of state, James Pickering. It was surely a difficult assignment for Taylor since his older brother, William Dabney Strother Taylor, had been killed by a group of Native Americans a year earlier at the same fort while serving in the U.S. Army's artillery regiment.

Fortescue Cuming, an Irishman who had purchased land in Ohio and was exploring the area, happened to visit the bluff during the short period Taylor was in charge. As he navigated down the river, Cuming first saw Benjamin Fooy's "handsome settlement and good frame house" across from the bluff. Cuming also noted "Mr. Fooy's negro quarter gives his pleasantly situated settlement the appearance of a village or a hamlet." Crossing the river, they landed their flatboat under Fort Pickering. Cuming and his party soon realized they were not alone:

> An Indian was at the landing observing us. He was painted in such a manner as to leave us in doubt as to his sex until we noticed a bow

and arrow in his hand. His natural color was entirely concealed under the bright vermillion, the white, and the blue grey, with which he was covered ... he was drest very fantastically in an old fashioned, large figured, high coloured calico shirt—deer skin leggings and mockesons, ornamented with beads, and a plume of beautiful heron's feathers nodding over his forehead from the back of his head.[7]

Cuming and his party began making their way up the side of the bluff using the one hundred twenty steps that had been made by cutting logs into squares. Already on alert, their concern turned to worry as they noticed a trail of fresh blood on the steps. Cuming's first thought was that the Chickasaw had murdered those in the fort, and he and his party were headed for the same fate. Upon reaching the top, he observed around fifty Chickasaw relaxing on the lawn in front of the fort but was relieved to see a "good-looking White soldier" guarding the entrance:

> We were ushered by a soldier to the officers' quarters where we were received by lieut. Taylor the commandant, with civility not unmixed with a small degree of the pompous stiffness of office. He however answered politely enough a few interroigatories we made respecting the Indians. He said they were friendly, and made frequent visits to the garrison, but except a few of the chiefs on business, none of them were ever admitted within the stoccado, and that this was a jubilee or gala day, on account of their having just received presents from the United States' government.[8]

Taylor's time at Fort Pickering was short, and he soon returned to his home in Louisville, Kentucky, to recover from what is thought to have been a case of yellow fever that nearly ended his life.

The fourth Chickasaw bluff was the last stop before the mysterious death of one of the most famous visitors to Fort Pickering. In early September 1809, explorer Meriwether Lewis, of Lewis and Clark fame, was the new governor of the Louisiana Territory. He was traveling from St. Louis to Washington City with a stop at Fort Pickering. His plan was to continue from the bluff down the Mississippi River to New Orleans and from there, travel by ship to the nation's capital. While at Fort Pickering, Captain Gilbert C. Russell noticed that Lewis was not doing well physically or mentally. He later testified:

> The Commanding officer of the Fort on discovering his situation,

and learning from the Crew that he had made two attempts to Kill himself, in one of which he had nearly succeeded, resolved at once to take possession of him and his papers, and detain them there until he recovered, or some friend might arrive in whose hands he could depart in safety.[9]

After a few days, Lewis's health seemed to have improved, so Russell allowed him to resume his travels. Lewis changed his plans and decided to travel to Washington by land. He departed Fort Pickering on September 29. Twelve days later, Lewis was found dead at Grinder's Stand on the Natchez Trace. Whether he was murdered or took his own life is one of history's great mysteries and is still debated today.

The motivations of the men in whose footsteps Marcus Winchester followed were varied. De Soto, Marquette, Joliet, Bienville, Gayoso, and others had their own reasons for their time at the fourth Chickasaw bluff. Winchester's purpose was clear, at least at first—Andrew Jackson sent him.

Chapter Six Endnotes

1. Alexander Koch, Chris Brierley, Mark M. Maslin, and Simon L. Lewis, "Earth System Impacts of the European Arrival and Great Dying in the Americas after 1492," *Quaternary Science Reviews* 207 (2019): 13–36.
2. James D. Davis, *History of Memphis* (Memphis: Hite, Crumpton & Kelly, 1973), 168.
3. Davis, *Memphis*, 46.
4. James Roper, *The Founding of Memphis, 1818–1820* (Memphis: The Memphis Sesquicentennial, Inc., 1970), 23.
5. Francis Bailey, *Journal of a Tour in Unsettled Parts of North America in 1796 and 1797* (London: Baily Bros., 1856), 272.
6. Bailey, *Journal*, 273.
7. Fortescue Cuming, *Sketches of a Tour to the Western Country, Through the States of Ohio and Kentucky* (Pittsburgh: Cramer, Spear & Eichbaum, 1810), 257.
8. Cuming, *Sketches*, 268.
9. James E. Starrs and Kira Gale, *The Death of Meriwether Lewis: A Historic Crime Scene Investigation* (Omaha: River Junction Press, 2009), 251.

A. HIEKE,
PORTRAIT PAINTER
Studio over Stoball & Mitchell's,
NO. 293, MAIN ST., CORNER MADISON,
MEMPHIS, TENN.

CHAS. POTTER,
Cash Dealer in
GROCERIES
AND PROVISIONS,
NO. 88, FRONT ROW,

Opposite the Steamboat Landing,

MEMPHIS, TENN.

GRANGER & Co.,
Manufacturers of
MINERAL WATER,
AND DEALERS IN
ALES, PORTER & CIDER,
No. 9, EXCHANGE BUILDING,
MEMPHIS.

From Rainey's Memphis City Directory, 1855/56

Chapter Seven: Hello Memphis

John Overton purchases the John Rice tract

On April 12, 1942, *The Commercial Appeal* included a story written by real estate editor Lillard M'Gee with the headline "Old Weakley County Book Shows John Rice Transfer of City of Memphis Land." A clerk in the Weakley County registrar's office in Dresden, Tennessee, had stumbled across a dusty, leather-bound deed book. As she blew decades of dust from the book and carefully began inspecting it, the clerk discovered grants and deeds of transfer for land in West Tennessee. Included among the old documents was a deed of transfer for a piece of property by John Rice to Elisha Rice. The clerk read that on June 14, 1784, John Rice:

> ... conveyed 5,000 acres of land lying on the Chickasaw Bluff, one mile below the mouth of Wolf River, at a white oak marked J.R., running north 27 degrees west 310 pole to a cottonwood tree, then due east 1377.1 poles to a mulberry tree, then south 625 poles to a stake, then west 1204 poles to the beginning.

The survey was dated December 1, 1786, and handwritten in the lower right-hand corner, obviously much later, was "Memphis is on this tract."

John Rice had begun promoting the fourth Chickasaw bluff for settlement nearly twenty years before Tennessee was granted statehood. He placed an ad in a Maryland publication with the intent of enticing adventurous Marylanders to migrate westward. He wrote, "A settlement is intended to be made at the Chickasaw-Bluff, on the Mississippi-river, and Western District of North-Carolina, in the spring of 1792." Rice described the land as having "timber of all kind of the largest growth, constantly running springs, and fertile soil." Settlers would not have to worry who their neighbors would be. Rice had agreed to "furnish a respectable number of families from Cumberland to join in the settlement . . . along with several families in Frederick, Ann-Arundel, Montgomery, and Charles-Counties." Among the list of names of those who had committed to invest in the enterprise were Marcus Winchester's uncles, William and Stephen. This is the first known connection of Marcus Winchester to the bluff that would become Memphis.[1]

Regarding the fear many living in the north had of Native Americans, Rice concluded, "Add to this, its happy situation with respect to Indian tribes—the largest being the Chickasaw nation; whose towns lay down in Georgia, about 120 miles distant; and are a peaceable, friendly, and humane people."[2]

Ironically, Rice's life—and his plans for the bluff—came to an end in 1791 when he was killed by Native Americans as he transported goods down the Cumberland River near Nashville. He left no heirs, so a will he had written in 1784 was executed, transferring the five-thousand-acre tract to his brother, Elisha Rice. Elisha cashed in and sold the tract to John Overton in 1794 for five hundred dollars, much less than what Rice originally paid. Two years later, Overton transferred half his interest to Andrew Jackson. Records reflect the cost to Jackson was one hundred dollars, but it is likely he paid nothing, and the land was a gift from Overton to his oldest friend. On July 3, 1797, Jackson sold one eighth portions of his half to James Winchester's brothers, Stephen and Richard, for $312.50 each.

Thirteen years later, Stephen Winchester, living in Sumner County, Tennessee at the time, sold his one-eighth interest to their brother in Baltimore, William, for five hundred dollars. Richard, living then in Jefferson County, Kentucky, sold his one-eighth interest to James Winchester for $500.

Of course, all these transactions were made with the understanding that it was only a matter of time before a treaty was made with the Chickasaw Nation, and the grants could be activated. But that did not become a reality until Andrew Jackson made it happen on October 19, 1818, with a treaty often referred to as The Jackson Purchase. Two months later, on December 12, 1818, he sold another one-eighth of his small portion to James Winchester. His price was no longer $500, as it had been for the others. Now that he had made the land officially open to settlement, he sold it to James Winchester for $5,000—making a significant profit.

Although he is often mentioned as one of the founders of Memphis—and he certainly profited from Overton's gift—it is questionable if Andrew Jackson ever even paid the fourth Chickasaw bluff a visit beyond one very frustrating afternoon. He claimed to have spent a considerable amount of time trying to dislodge his flatboat from a sandbar just above Fort Pickering in 1813 while on his way to Natchez.[3]

By 1823, as Jackson was preparing to run for president, it became clear that profiting off land he made available by a treaty he negotiated would provide his enemies with ammunition to question his ethics. He sold his remaining piece of the Rice tract to John Christmas McLemore, Tennessee's surveyor general and the husband of Jackson's niece, Elizabeth Donelson.

Like John Overton and James Winchester, McLemore was always looking for a good land investment. He was, at the time, the largest landowner in Tennessee.[4] Overton wrote to Winchester that he saw McLemore's involvement as a good thing for their partnership, as he would be much more invested in the outcome than Jackson had been.

While McLemore was indeed more invested and actually put down roots in Memphis for many years, the idea of Andrew Jackson as a founder of Memphis remains firmly established as part of the city's origin story.

Chapter Seven Endnotes

1. Lawrence Kinnaird, *Spain in the Mississippi Valley, 1765-1794*, in *Annual Report of the American Historical Association for the Year 1945*, vol. 2, pt. 1 (Washington, D.C.: U.S. Government Printing Office, 1949), 317.
2. Kinnaird, *Spain in the Mississippi Valley*, 317.
3. John Spencer Bassett, ed., *Correspondence of Andrew Jackson*, 7 vols. (Washington, D.C.: Carnegie Institution of Washington, 1926), 1:264–65.
4. Cleo A. Hughes, "Speculation and Settlement in West Tennessee" (M.A. thesis, George Peabody College for Teachers, 1968), 35.

ECLIPSE
COTTON GIN STANDS!

BEADLE, PAYNE & CO.,

Continue to Manufacture these superior Gin Stands at **THEIR OLD STAND**, on *POPLAR STREET*, opposite the Union Foundry, MEMPHIS, TENNESSEE.

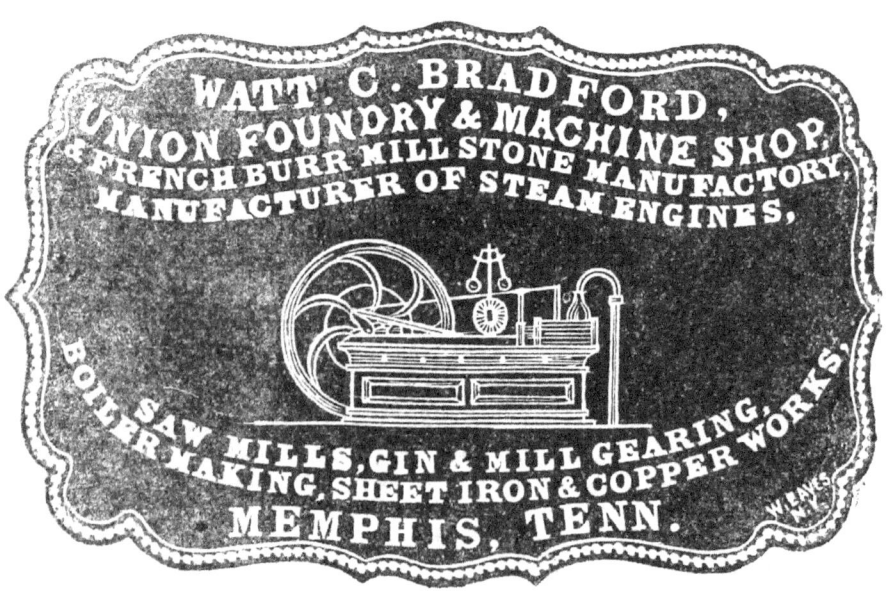

From Rainey's Memphis City Directory, 1855/56

Part Two

Chapter Eight: Chickasaw Special

*Marcus Winchester with Andrew Jackson
at The Jackson Purchase*

For Andrew Jackson, expansionism took precedence over civil liberties of any kind. Historians agree securing the nation against hostility from both Native Americans and foreign adversaries bordered on obsession for the Tennessee soldier and politician. In 1816, he negotiated a treaty with the Creek Nation, acquiring millions of acres of land in present-day Alabama and Georgia earmarked for White settlement. Then Jackson turned his attention westward. In October 1817, he opened a letter from Secretary of War George Graham that read:

> I am directed by the President to request that you would take such measures as you may deem proper, to ascertain whether a negotiation can now be entered into with the Chickasaws, with a prospect of a favorable termination, for the extinguishment of their claim to the lands held by them within the limits of the States of Kentucky and Tennessee, and advise the department of the result.[1]

For Jackson, the slow pace of land acquisition that had been taking place with the Native Americans for decades had gone on long enough. Early in his presidency, George Washington wrote, "The Government of the United States are determined that their Administration of Indian Affairs shall be directed entirely by the great principles of Justice and humanity."[2] Washington initially sought to establish treaties and set boundaries with Native American tribes, but most White settlers paid no attention to the boundaries. In the end, he wrote, "I believe scarcely anything short of a Chinese wall, or a line of troops, will restrain

Land jobbers, and the encroachment of settlers upon the Indian territory."[3]

Thomas Jefferson took a different approach. He wrote a letter to William Henry Harrison on February 27, 1803, that was marked "unofficial and private." He explained the need for confidentiality, writing, "I may with safety give you a more extensive view of our policy respecting the Indians, that you may the better comprehend the parts dealt out to you in detail through the official channel…"[4]

In the letter, he suggested getting the Native Americans into debt through trade would result in their being forced to give up their land in order to settle that debt. He explained this would allow the United States to expand its settlements and Native Americans could either assimilate into White society or be pushed far west of the Mississippi River to land that was deemed less valuable. Jefferson also stressed the need to appear friendly to Native Americans while showing strength.

Lastly, the letter underscored that these plans should be kept secret, especially from leaders of the Native American tribes.

Unlike Jefferson, Andrew Jackson made his plans clear in both word and deed. In 1830, he wrote, "My original convictions upon this subject have been confirmed by the course of events for several years, and experience is every day adding to their strength … those tribes cannot exist surrounded by our settlements and in continual contact with our citizens is certain,"[5] He wanted them gone:

> They have neither the intelligence, the industry, the moral habits, nor the desire of improvement which are essential to any favorable change in their condition. Established in the midst of another and a superior race, and without appreciating the causes of their inferiority or seeking to control them, they must necessarily yield to the force of circumstances and ere long disappear."[6]

Andrew Jackson was not alone. At the time, most settlers and political leaders believed that those of Anglo-Saxon or northern European descent were inherently superior to other races. This shaped policies and social structures and was the justification for the forced displacement of Native Americans and the justification of slavery as an economic necessity.

Members of the Cherokee tribe had played a crucial role in the Battle of Horseshoe Bend, aligning with Jackson and providing vital support by attacking the Creeks from the rear. Their efforts did nothing to garner Jackson's favor. As author Peter Cozzens points out in his book, *A Brutal Reckoning*, Jackson nor his second in command, John Coffee, ever publicly acknowledged the role the Cherokee played in the victory. Cherokee Indian agent Return J. Meigs wrote in his report of the battle: "The daring, intrepid, and persevering bravery of the Cherokee warriors probably saved the lives of 1,000 white men."[7]

Marcus Winchester was well aware of the complicated and often deadly relationship between Native Americans and White individuals in the early nineteenth century. He witnessed some Native Americans seeking to align themselves with White settlers through acts of loyalty and assimilation, while others resisted the loss of their lands and independence. These relationships were unpredictable and ever-changing, with deep divisions not only between tribes but also within them.

Winchester knew his uncle had been murdered by Native Americans, and growing up at Cragfont, he surely heard stories from his father about "fighting Indians" during the early years of settling Sumner County. However, he had also witnessed courage and bravery among some of the Native Americans he encountered while serving as his father's aide during the War of 1812.

One example was mixed-race Shawnee Spemica Lawba who had been captured as a young teenager by Kentucky militia leader Benjamin Logan during a raid by Kentucky mounted militiamen across the Ohio River on the Machachac Tribe towns of the Shawnee Nation. He quickly learned English and adopted the name Johnny Logan. While serving as a spy for William Henry Harrison and providing critical intelligence for James Winchester, Logan was killed by men loyal to Tecumseh, and his body was taken back to Fort Defiance where he was buried with full military honors. It was likely Marcus Winchester who took down his father's report to Harrison, writing, "More firmness and consummate bravery has seldom appeared in the military theatre."[8]

The treatment Logan received was the exception. Most White men and women that Marcus Winchester knew would never admit Native Americans were anything other than inferior. One early Memphis settler later shared a story that reflected the prevailing feelings of most at the time:

> Colonel Thomas H. Person, one of the first settlers of this country who lived a few miles south on Nonconnah, took an Indian boy, some ten or twelve years old, as an experiment, to see if he could be civilized and raised up with white principles. As the boy progressed in years, his wild nature began to develop itself—he greatly preferred the woods to the field and the gun to his books. He became ungovernable and the Colonel had to send him back to his parents. You may make a white man an Indian, but you can never make an Indian a white man—example, Sam Houston.[9]

Following years of treaty negotiations, triumph in the War of 1812, the defeat of the Red Sticks during the Creek War, and an increasing demand for land, the settlers of the southern United States turned their full attention to expansion. The desired outcome was, by then, crystal clear. The United States would send any remaining Native Americans to land far to the west where they would be out of sight and out of mind. An especially important strategy was to wrestle ownership of the rest of West Tennessee and Kentucky away from the approximately 3,500 Chickasaw that remained in the region.

Kentucky historian Thomas D. Clark points out, there were several reasons this became a priority. First, there was the need to create space between the southern and northwestern tribes to prevent another leader like Tecumseh from once again uniting the tribes against the White settlers. Second, the Chickasaw lands included numerous smaller rivers and tributaries that led to the Mississippi River and provided the best route to New Orleans. Finally, Tennessee and Kentucky politicians were growing increasingly bold in Washington with their claims to what they saw as land that belonged to their constituents.[10]

On March 16, 1818, the time had come. The Tennessee legislature formally asked Congress to take action to acquire the western Chickasaw lands. On April 3, Congress set up a commission to negotiate with the Chickasaw and appropriated $53,000 for the treaty negotiations. Superintendent of Indian Trade Colonel Thomas L. McKenney was instructed to purchase $6,500 in gifts to be delivered to the fourth Chickasaw bluff to begin the talks.

The new secretary of war, John C. Calhoun, sent letters to Andrew Jackson and Isaac Shelby dated May 2, 1818, essentially firing the starting pistol. He wrote:

> I have the honor to enclose to you a commission to treat with the Chickasaw Indians, for that portion of their country which lies in the States of Kentucky and Tennessee. The object and importance of extinguishing their title to that tract of the country, are so obvious as to require no comment; and the President anticipates, from your weight of character, and knowledge of the Indians, that the object in view will be very effected. . . . the President is very anxious to remove the Indians on this side, to the west of the Mississippi.[11]

The letter also included compensation: Jackson and Shelby would each receive eight dollars per day, and a secretary of their choosing would be paid five dollars per day. Colonel Robert Butler was hired for that role by Jackson. Butler and his siblings had become the wards of Andrew Jackson and his wife in 1805 after their father died of yellow fever. Robert Butler attended West Point and was

Jackson's assistant at the Battle of New Orleans and when Jackson served for a short time as governor of Florida. Butler officially joined the Jackson family in August 1808 when he married Rachel Jackson's niece.

The negotiations that would take place east of the Chickasaw Old Town in Northwest Mississippi, near present-day Tupelo, would come with a multitude of challenges. Shelby was sixty-seven and was so infirm, he had recently declined President James Monroe's request to serve the country as secretary of war. Shelby was overweight and suffering from numerous ailments, although a massive stroke that would result in the loss of the use of the right side of his body was still two years away.

The bulk of the planning would be left up to Jackson, but he was not in much better shape. Although he was only fifty-one, the long-term effects of frontier diseases along with his many days and nights on the battlefield, rendered him nearly incapacitated at times. His tendency to want to settle personal scores by dueling also impacted his long-term health. Years after his death, hair samples indicated that the lead bullet fragments still in his body had slowly poisoned Jackson for years, resulting in numerous ailments.

Another challenge in the negotiation could have been avoided if the United States government had paid its bills on time. In the Treaty of Council House, signed in 1816, the Chickasaw ceded close to six million acres in what is now southwestern Tennessee and northern and western Alabama. The United States agreed to provide the Chickasaw with presents and an annual payment of $12,000 additional dollars in cash for the next ten years. They also agreed to settle any debts the Chickasaw owed to American citizens.

Jackson discovered the country was behind on those cash payments. The previous Indian agent was no longer in place, and a new one had to be appointed before making any further payments. To make matters worse, a shipment of presents that had been sent to the fourth Chickasaw bluff on a steamboat, ironically named the *Good Hope*, had wrecked. Jackson was told by the Chickasaw that many of the items on the boat had arrived damaged. Someone on whom he could depend needed to get there quickly to check out the shipment and report back. Jackson chose Marcus Winchester, just twenty-two years old, for the important task. The future president must have seen something in the young man he thought he could trust. Little did either of them know that short visit would change the course of the rest of Winchester's life.

Chapter Eight Endnotes

1. The Jackson Purchase Historical Society, *Jackson Purchase 150 Years, A Sesquicentennial*, (Mayfield, Ky: *The Mayfield Messenger*, 1969), 8.
2. George Washington to the Commissioners to the Southern Indians, August 29, 1789, *Founders Online*, National Archives, originally published in *The Papers of George Washington, Presidential Series*, vol. 3, 15 June 1789–5 September 1789, ed. Dorothy Twohig (Charlottesville: University Press of Virginia, 1989), 551.
3. George Washington to Timothy Pickering, July 1, 1796, *Founders Online*, National Archives, originally published in *The Papers of George Washington, Presidential Series*, vol. 20, 1 April–21 September 1796, ed. David R. Hoth and William M. Ferraro (Charlottesville: University of Virginia Press, 2019), 349–50.
4. President Thomas Jefferson to Governor William Henry Harrison, February 27, 1803, in Clarence E. Carter, ed., *The Territorial Papers of the United States*, vol. 7, *The Territory of Indiana, 1800–1810* (Washington, D.C.: Government Printing Office, 1939), 90–92.
5. Andrew Jackson, "Second Annual Message to Congress," December 6, 1830, in *A Compilation of the Messages and Papers of the Presidents, 1789–1897*, ed. James D. Richardson, vol. 2 (Washington, D.C.: Government Printing Office, 1896), 519–20.
6. Jackson, *Second Annual Mesage*, 520.
7. Peter Cozzens, *A Brutal Reckoning: The Creek War and the Epic Story of Red Stick Defeat* (New York: Vintage Books, 2023), 298.
8. Charles Poinsatte, *Outpost in the Wilderness: Fort Wayne, 1706-1828* (Allen County, Ind.: Fort Wayne Historical Society, 1976), 77.
9. "The Aborigines of West Tennessee," *Old Folks Record*, no. 4 (January 1875): 180.
10. Thomas D. Clark, "The Jackson Purchase: A Dramatic Chapter in Southern Indian Policy and Relations," *Jackson Purchase Historical Society Journal* 45, no. 1 (1988): 307.
11. Henry Dearborn to James Wilkinson, September 6, 1806, *Records of the Bureau of Indian Affairs*, Record Group 75, vol. D, 151, National Archives, Washington, D.C..

J. & M. JONES,
PLASTERERS
AND
SLATERS!

CAUSEY STREET,
BET. LINDEN AND BROWN'S AVENUE,

Are prepared to execute all kinds of

PLAIN AND ORNAMENTAL
PLASTERING
AND
CEMENTING.

We are constantly receiving every variety of

NEW CENTER-PIECES.
SLATING

DONE IN THE VERY BEST STYLE.
Orders from the country solicited.

From Rainey's Memphis City Directory, 1855/56

Chapter Nine: Memphis Blues

*Andrew Jackson sends
Marcus Winchester to the bluff*

John Overton, Andrew Jackson, and the Winchester brothers had invested in the promise of the great financial reward they believed would come from developing and then selling lots on the fourth Chickasaw bluff. At the time, it was not clear to any of them how long it would take or how difficult it would be. Marcus Winchester was likely the first to realize the magnitude of the challenge. It would have been difficult for anyone to see the bluff as a diamond in the rough in those early years. A writer for *The Navigator* described the few residents that lived there: "The settlement is thin and composed of what is called the half breed; that is a mixture of the whites and the Indians, a race of men too indolent to do any permanent good for themselves or society."[1] That writer also saw access as a problem noting, "a landing may be had a little above Fort Pickering, but it is not a very good one."[2]

The governor of the Mississippi Territory, William C. C. Claiborne, provided another first-hand observation in an 1801 letter to James Madison, then secretary of state under Thomas Jefferson. He noted the large number of boats that were stranded or sunk in the river because the crew had either died or was too sick to work: "A few posts to render aid in such cases, with hospital stores for the sick would greatly promote commerce and the peopling of this remote territory." He added, "The humanizing effecting on the Indians of such stations would soon be felt."[3]

An early visitor arriving by river wrote, "Towards sundown we came in sight of Memphis at the end of a long reach in the river. It is situated on a bluff of naked clay soil, marked here and there with iron and having a barren and unpromising appearance."[4]

The names of some of those earliest settlers who were making their home on the bluff were included in another visitor's journal:

> In 1797, I find at this place four white families who came here two and three years ago. The man of most consequence is Kenneth Ferguson, a Scotchman and agent of Panton, Leslie & Company, of Pensacola—very active in the Spanish interests. He is extensively engaged in the Indian trade and sells at the most exorbitant rates. Another of these people is William Mizell, a native of North Carolina, who was at Pensacola under British protection, when it surrendered to the Spaniards. He is no friend to them, and I find him very useful as an interpreter as he resided fifteen years among the Chickasaws and speaks their language well.[5]

William Mizell seemed to make a noteworthy impression on those he encountered and was frequently written about by early visitors to the bluff. He was a soldier who fought for the British against the Spanish and married a woman from the Chickasaw tribe. He worked as a hunter, trader, and interpreter for thirty years. In 1795, Chickasaw war chief and diplomat, Piomingo, wrote to General James Robertson, one of the founders of Nashville:

> Dear Sir as you know that the Interpreter that was aloted to me lives there I Request that you will have William Mizell put in as he can talk or write and do our business and there is no other hear that can, so be pleased have him put in so he can do our business.[6]

Missionary Joseph Bullard visited the bluff, and in his journal entry on May 28, 1799, he wrote, "This day became acquainted with William Mizle, long resident in this nation and sometime interpreter at the Bluffs. From him I learnt something of the customs and language of the Chickasaws; he says the method of healing in this nation is to take water, soak roots in it, and blow in it with a pipe, and say over it a number of words by way of charm, and wash the body of the sick with this preparation."[7]

In a journal entry made on February 8, 1803, by Thomas Peterkin, the first factor appointed to the bluff, one finds an account of Mizell selling furs to the agency: "He sold 46 pounds of deerskins at 50 cents a pound, 3 foxskins at the same price, 2 small bearskins at 50 cents a pound and ½ pound of beaverskins for which he was paid $1.50."[8] A later entry stated that Mizell was a hunter, trader, and interpreter working for the factory, and he was paid $200 for a year's work. Mizell later purchased land across the river in Arkansas where he died in 1825.

Another factor assigned to work on the bluff was Isaac Rawlings Jr., referred to in later years as "Old Ike." In time, he rose to prominence, eventually becoming Memphis's second mayor and one of the city's most influential business and community leaders.

Like Marcus Winchester, Rawlings's wealthy family hailed from Maryland, were among the earliest American settlers, and fought for independence from the British in the revolution. Rawlings was the namesake son of a physician who was also a major landowner, possessing numerous plantations, including Rawlings Choice.

In the spring of 1809, when he was twenty-one, young Rawlings began working as a clerk at the new factory built at Fort Osage, sitting high on a bluff overlooking the Missouri River. The construction of the three-and-one-half story fort had been overseen by William Clark, who selected the location on his first expedition with Meriwether Lewis.

At twenty-six, Rawlings was promoted from clerk to Indian agent and factor and was assigned to the factory at Fort Pickering on the fourth Chickasaw bluff. The job of factor was a challenging one, since part of their job description was "to secure the friendship of the Indians in our country in a way the most beneficial and the most effectual and economical to the United States, and to inspire confidence in the honor and integrity of the government."[9] Inspiring Native Americans to have confidence in the honor and integrity of the government would have been a truly arduous task, all things considered.

Rawlings's role evolved to that of leader for the early community of "rogues and rascals" living on the bluff. He had experience in both business and government and earned the respect—and fear when needed—of those living and working around the factory. According to the earliest records that have survived, Rawlings presided as an unofficial judge before the fourth Chickasaw bluff was even a town. His legal decisions are the first for which there is any record. The cases were mostly petty thefts and assault and battery, while the punishment was typically public whipping or banishment.[10]

By late 1817, it was clear the need for a factory on the bluff was coming to an end. Rawlings was instructed to approve only maintenance and repairs around Fort Pickering that were absolutely necessary. The factory was not the only thing that began falling apart. Years of living and working on the river had affected his health, so when Rawlings's assignment at the factory on the bluff ended, he returned to his family home in Maryland.

Once his health improved, and Rawlings was ready to return to work, he was assigned the role of managing the new factory that was being built on the Arkansas River at Illinois Bayou, about two hundred miles west of the fourth Chickasaw bluff near the present-day town of Russellville, Arkansas. His primary focus was setting up a post to do business with the Cherokee who were being forced to settle in that area. Rawlings served there until spring 1820. Soon after celebrating his thirty-second birthday, he resigned—again because of his health—and returned home to Maryland. Superintendent of Indian affairs, Thomas L. McKenney, praised the job he had done:

> Since you must leave the service of the Govt as factor, I must consent to part from you. Your reasons are well-founded, as without health there is no enjoyment of life. I part from you with reluctance and shall always be happy to bear my testimony to the able and honourable manner in which you have discharged your duties.[11]

Meanwhile, Marcus Winchester was experiencing his first visit to the bluff. When he arrived, he learned Paul Ballio was functioning as the government factor. However, Ballio was no Isaac Rawlings. He had been ordered to Prairie du Chien, in the Territory of Michigan, but had ignored the order and remained at the bluff. He confided in Winchester that he feared he would not be paid by the United States government for the work he was then doing. Winchester quickly located the damaged presents and confirmed the Chickasaw had been correct. As they claimed, the goods sent as presents had been damaged when the *Good Hope* wrecked. There had been two shipments, the first of which was not damaged. The soaked barrels and crates in the second shipment had been opened to allow them to dry, but Ballio had not bothered to keep the two shipments separated, and any records had been misplaced. It was therefore impossible for Winchester to tell what was missing.

His report on the damaged goods for Andrew Jackson was thorough, not only showcasing his attention to detail but also providing a fascinating historical account of what was valued by Native Americans at the time. Among the gifts were saddles of "very inferior quality." They were so badly damaged that Winchester noted they were worth only half their original value. The shipment also included nine pieces of high-quality strouds, described as being "in tolerable order." Strouds, decorated with stripes in various colors, were brushed and pressed during finishing, unlike other broadcloths that were raised and trimmed to create a nap. This textile was a staple in fur trade inventories and was considered the most valuable fabric to Native Americans.

Winchester's inventory also included other textiles like flannel, scarlet cloth for making blankets, and swanskin. Swanskin was a white woolen fabric that was valued by Native Americans because it was waterproof. Winchester noted fish hooks and scissors included in the shipment that were "rusted very much," and needles that were ruined. An assortment of looking glasses—an early word for mirrors—was also damaged. Finally, the presents included weapons and ammunition. Most were "a good deal rusted," and one box of rifles was damaged beyond use. About half the gun powder was unusable.[12]

Winchester finished his work and returned to the Chickasaw Council House, where he found the negotiations were not going well. From the moment Shelby, Jackson, and their party arrived, it was apparent that the discussions would be challenging. Jackson, usually a figure of robust energy, was noticeably unwell and extremely weak. Several key members of the Chickasaw tribe, whose participation was crucial for meaningful dialogue, failed to even show up. Even Jackson and Shelby, who should have presented a united front, found themselves at odds over a particular point in the negotiation, nearly coming to blows.

In spite of all the challenges, Jackson's message to the Chickasaw remained consistent and left no room for interpretation:

> Brothers, this piece of land is claimed by your Nation, but our whites paid for it many years ago—and our father the President has kept them away from it that his red children might hunt on it, but the game is now gone, and his white children claim it now from him. . . . Next year, your white Brethren will have nearly one hundred steam ships running up and down the Mississippi River, and they will want much wood for their fires that make them go on the water, and when a ship gets broke, your white brethren wants to be on the shore with their own people until it is mended.[13]

Jackson's relentless determination—and a few strategically placed bribes—began working. The Chickasaw leaders in charge of the treaty negotiation on behalf of the tribe, Levi Colbert, George Colbert, Chinubby, and Tishomingo, recognized their dwindling options in the face of encroaching settlers and a changing political landscape and attempted to at least depart with as much as they could. They agreed to Jackson's terms. The Treaty of 1818—eventually better known as the Jackson Purchase—was signed on October 19, 1818. For the vast expanse of 6,848,000 acres, the Chickasaw were to receive $20,000, paid out over a period of fifteen years—a mere four-and-a-half cents per acre. While certainly a terrible deal for the Native Americans—Jackson sold James Winchester just a few acres of the Rice Tract for $5,000—they ultimately knew they had little choice.

The treaty witnesses, including notable Tennesseans like General John Coffee, signed the agreement, ensuring the legal ratification of the treaty and the formal transfer of the land. Among the witnesses to sign their names on that historic document was Marcus B. Winchester.

During that short visit to the fourth Chickasaw bluff, he must have found something that appealed to him. He immediately headed back and agreed to serve as one of the representatives for "the proprietors," James Winchester, John Overton, and Andrew Jackson. Marcus Winchester was now at the helm of the project that would eventually transform the bluff from a hard-scrabble little community to the second largest city on the Mississippi River.

Chapter Nine Endnotes

1. Zadok Cramer, *The Navigator* (Pittsburgh: Cramer, Spear & Eichbaum, 1814), 187.
2. Cramer, *The Navigator, 187,*
3. Cramer, *The Navigator, 150.*
4. John E. Semmes, *John H. B. Latrobe and His Times, 1803-1891* (Baltimore: Norman Remington & Co., 1917), 616.
5. Semmes, *John H. B. Latrobe*, 50.
6. Piomingo to General James Robertson, September 29, 1795, *James Robertson Papers*, Vanderbilt University Special Collections, Nashville, Tenn.
7. "William Mizell - Chickasaw Indian Interpreter, Trader and Trapper," *Ancestry.com*, uploaded by Pearcy, August 11, 2009, accessed December 2, 2024.
8. William Mizell," Ancestry.com.
9. James E. Roper, "Isaac Rawlings, Frontier Merchant," *Tennessee Historical Quarterly* 20, no. 3 (1961): 266-269.
10. *Proceedings of the Seventh Annual Meeting of the Bar Association of Tennessee* (Nashville: Marshall & Bruce C., 1899), 88.
11. Roper, *Rawlings*, 271.
12. Jackson Purchase Historical Society, *Jackson Purchase 150 Years: A Sesquicentennial* (Mayfield, KY: The Mayfield Messenger, 1969), 6.
13. Jackson Purchase Historical Society, *Jackson Purchase 150 Years*, 6.

J. & A. WOODRUFF,

CARRIAGE
MANUFACTURERS AND
DEALERS,
NOS. 3 & 4,
EXCHANGE BUILDINGS,
MEMPHIS, TENN.,

Have always on hand a large assortment of
CARRIAGES
from the
BEST MANUFACTURERS
in the United States.
Every description of **CARRIAGES BUILT** to order, and
REPAIRING DONE IN THE BEST MANNER
and at the shortest notice.
ALL WORK SOLD BY US FULLY GURANTEED.

From Rainey's Memphis City Directory, 1855/56

Chapter Ten: Walking in Memphis

*Marcus Winchester and William Lawrence
arrive and begin surveying the bluff*

He was barely out of his teens when he arrived in Memphis in 1818, but fortunately, young Marcus Winchester had a strong mentor in fifty-year-old John Overton, even if the two occasionally did not agree. It was Overton that young Winchester would communicate with most frequently about the development of Memphis. Overton would also push the hardest to keep the investment from becoming "nothing more than a mere harbor for a few drunken boatmen," as he put it in a letter to James Winchester. In a touch of humor or arrogance—or perhaps a combination of both—he added to the sentence in parenthesis, "(besides those now there)."

It was also Overton who pulled strings and used his influence in back rooms with Tennessee's politicians to benefit the growth and development of the community forming on the bluff. Normally measured and unemotional in his approach, he was impatient when it came to the development of Memphis. Only days after the treaty with the Chickasaw was complete, he wrote to James Winchester:

> You will see an official account from Genl. Jackson that he has made a treaty with the Chickasaws of Tennessee and Kentucky. So that the claim to our tract at the Bluff is also extinguished and Marcus Winchester is there long before this. He has fine weather to explore our land there and will bring us an accurate description of the Bluff tract.... We must proceed to lay off a town by this time in 12 months. I suspect if the country settles as fast as I think it will.[1]

Historian James Roper believed that at some point before January 7, 1818, John Overton, James Winchester, and Andrew Jackson met, likely at the Hermitage, to begin planning how they could get the best return on their investment. In August 1819, Overton wrote Winchester a letter letting him know Jackson would be at the Hermitage early September so the three men could meet to continue their discussions. The name of the new town on the fourth Chickasaw bluff was likely a topic of conversation. Although Andrew Jackson often gets the credit, it was James Winchester who came up with the name Memphis.

In 1844, Charles Cassedy—who had helped Winchester defend himself against his critics following the War of 1812—wrote a letter to the editor of *Memphis Weekly American Eagle* to set the record straight on the origin of the name:

> The name of your city, formerly known by the military cognomen of Fort Pickering, was given to it by Gen. James Winchester as he informed me himself, [because of] the fancied or real resemblance of the great river Mississippi, and the unrivalled richness and fertility of its banks, to the far-famed Nile of ancient Egypt, and the exhaustless fertility of its great valley, once granary of eastern Europe, western Asia and northern Africa.[2]

Winchester's choice of name for the fourth Chickasaw bluff was likely influenced by his fascination with the classical civilizations of ancient Greece and Rome. After all, the names Winchester chose for his sons included Marcus Brutus, Lucilius J. (possibly Junious), Napoleon, and Valerius Publicola—who understandably decided to go by "Val."

Winchester had christened his first river town Cairo, Tennessee, but only after he first tried using the name Ça ira—French for "things will work out." It was a phrase in a song popular during the French Revolution but was introduced to American popular culture by Benjamin Franklin, who liked to work it in when telling stories about the revolution in later years. Since early settlers in present-day Middle Tennessee had little interest in practicing their French pronunciations, the name of Winchester's little town on the Cumberland became Cairo by default.

The antebellum South's fascination with the classical civilizations of ancient Greece and Rome was deeply rooted in the social, political, and intellectual culture that was developing among the Southern planter aristocracy at the time. Providing a classical education for their sons was important for southerners who expected those sons would one day take over the family businesses. One reason an emphasis on the study of the classics was central to the upbringing of Southern elites is clear today—justification of slavery.

Like Marcus Winchester, the boys who came from families with money and growing land holdings were often educated in the classics before settling down in the South. They were encouraged to view themselves as modern-day Roman citizens, occupying the pinnacle of the social hierarchy. As historian Kenneth M. Stampp pointed out in his book *The Peculiar Institution*, "The Athenians, as Americans of the ante-bellum South were fond of recalling, attained unprecedented heights of intellectual and artistic achievement in a society built upon a foundation of servitude."[3]

Drawing parallels between the American South and ancient Athens was effortless for those who metaphorically squinted just right and were sufficiently motivated. Some even persuaded themselves that their growing reliance on enslaved labor was not shameful and that its obvious negative aspects could easily be justified.

"After all," they told themselves, "We're just like the ancient Greeks." As historian Eugene D. Genovese notes, "the Southern planter class fashioned itself as the modern equivalent of the Roman patrician class, seeing themselves as defenders of a republicanism that they believed to be in keeping with ancient traditions."[4]

The original Egyptian Memphis on the Nile River had been a center of commerce, trade, and a home to kings. The investors of Memphis River on the Mississippi—or the proprietors as they came to be called—were only focused on commerce and trade, and it was never a place any of them planned to call home, as their castles were in Middle Tennessee. Memphis journalist and historian Perre Magness observed, "the founders of Memphis were men who lived in gracious houses along the Cumberland and conceived of Memphis as a profitable real estate investment rather than a place to live."[5]

When surveyor William Lawrence was hired to join Marcus Winchester in preparing the bluff, the proprietors had found two young men who would not only embrace the vision for commerce and profit but would also make Memphis home for the rest of their lives. Both Lawrence and Winchester would meet their wives, build homes, have children, and start their own businesses on the bluff.

By the spring of 1819, the two young men were eager to begin surveying the bluff and dividing it into lots. However, they had to wait for the Cumberland River to rise high enough to allow them to travel by flatboat, loaded with supplies, from Cairo to Memphis.

There were several ways to reach Memphis over land, but all were challenging, slow, and often required crossing streams and rivers that, depending on the season, meant building a raft. One of the earliest settlers of Memphis, James Brown, described the Native American trails that led into and away from the bluff. The Cherokee Trace, an east–west route, began at Tuscumbia Landing in Alabama, passed through present-day Raleigh, and entered Memphis at Bayou Gayoso near today's St. Jude Children's Research Hospital. The Chickasaw Trail, by contrast, was a shorter north–south path from Mississippi into Memphis. Settlers later widened it, calling it Pigeon Roost Road. It was eventually named Lamar Avenue. One settler, who as a boy lived about ten miles northeast of Memphis, recalled the hardships his family faced when traveling these rough trails to the city for supplies.

> We saw but little signs of civilization—very few settlers. The whole country was heavily timbered. There were no hostile Indians, but every other object that the settlers of a new country ever had to contend, was met with in the Western District of Tennessee ... and to reach Memphis, only ten miles distant was no small job. Think for a moment. Surrounded by no unbroken forest, no roads, no bridges, no mills, no schoolhouses, no church."[6]

Frenchman Gustave de Beaumont wrote of his trip from Nashville to Memphis via stagecoach in 1831:

> Frightful roads. Precipitous descents. No regular highway. The road is only an opening cut in the forest. The stumps of the trees not completely cut away, so that they form so many impediments over which we jolt incessantly. . . . After Nashville, not one town on the road; only a few villages scattered here and there till we reach Memphis.[7]

The stagecoach was only able to travel around thirty miles each day. De Beaumont received no sympathy from the stagecoach driver after complaining when the axel broke, delaying his arrival even more. He was told a recent traveler broke his arm while traveling through the same area, while another broke his leg.

The routes by waterway were equally challenging and provided a different set of obstacles. Noah Ludlow was an actor who decided to travel from Nashville to New Orleans in 1817 to launch the first company of English-speaking actors in that city. A number of his fellow thespians, along with the husbands of the female actors, were willing to join him for the adventure. In writing about the trip in his memoir, Ludlow provided a glimpse at the route Marcus Winchester and others used to travel on water from Nashville to Memphis, Natchez, and New Orleans by boat.

Ludlow wrote with great flourish, "We took leave of many kind friends, and on a beautiful afternoon about the 20th of October, 1817, we bid farewell to the good people of Nashville and committed our lives and fortunes to the waters of the Cumberland, Ohio, and Mississippi Rivers."[8]

Ludlow purchased an old keelboat for the journey for two hundred dollars. The long, narrow boats typically ranged from forty to eighty feet in length and eight to twelve feet in width, coming to a point at both the bow and stern. They were built with a large center cabin for shelter or storage and were often equipped with sails and rigging for use when the wind was favorable. They could be rowed, poled, or hand-winched upstream when it was not—which was most of the time. The cabin of the keelboat Ludlow purchased had already been divided into small rooms, making it perfect for his needs.

Ludlow and his fellow actors descended the Cumberland River to the Ohio River, then stopped at Smithland, a village of half a dozen houses. Not finding the supplies they needed, they moved on. They next landed in America, Illinois. When writing about the trip years later, he expressed doubt that the town was still in existence, writing, "I am of the opinion that it has passed away into the great receptacle of small things and small ideas called oblivion."[9] Today, America is an unincorporated community that is home to a little more than one hundred residents who might take issue with Ludlow's opinion.

When passing the "barren pile of mud" Ludlow observed accumulated at the confluence of the Ohio and the Mississippi Rivers, he predicted, "Some day there will be a great commercial city here." That prediction came true, at least for a while. Thanks to its location, a major hub for the steamboat and railroad industries sprang up there, and the Illinois town was named Cairo, like James Winchester's town in Tennessee. Cairo, Illinois became a major link for commerce between the Deep South and the Great Lakes. By the late 1800s, Cairo was booming with grand hotels and elegant homes lining its streets and bustling docks along its riverfront.

As railroads and highways gradually replaced riverboats in the twentieth century, the city's importance as a port diminished, and Cairo found itself bypassed by modern transportation. Flooding also played a major role. The catastrophic flood of 1937 led to the construction of massive levee systems designed to protect the town, but the levees also cut Cairo off from the rivers that had once fueled its growth and prosperity. Economic stagnation followed.

Many businesses left entirely, leading to a loss of jobs and deepening poverty. The city's struggles worsened when Cairo became a national flashpoint during the civil rights movement as Black residents faced systemic segregation, discrimination, and racially motivated violence. Home to over fifteen thousand in its heyday, Cairo has sadly declined to a population of fewer than fifteen hundred today. The town that once bragged it was "the Gateway to the South" is now filled with crumbling buildings, boarded up storefronts, and neighborhoods that have been all but abandoned.

Further down the Mississippi River, Noah Ludlow and his troupe of actors docked at a riverbank and found what Ludlow described as "a shack where corn was stored." They purchased eggs and milk from the one family living there at the time. The town where that shack was located eventually became Hickman, Kentucky.

Stopping next in New Madrid, Missouri, they heard first-hand stories of the New Madrid earthquakes of 1811 and 1812. Ranked among the largest in U.S. history since its settlement, the earthquakes are believed to have been ten times more powerful than the one that struck San Francisco in 1906. Northwest Tennessee's paradise for waterfowl hunting, fishing, and birdwatching—Reelfoot Lake—was formed nearby when, during the most powerful of the quakes, a chasm opened, allowing water from the Mississippi River to rush in and fill it. Locals in New Madrid told Ludlow they were still afraid to go to sleep, fearing they would wake up underwater.

The group traveled onward. They approached Plum Point, Island Thirty-Seven, and the Devil's Elbow on high alert. It was a section of the river known for robberies by, as Ludlow called them, "river-thieves." Especially concerning for the group were rumors that a gang headed by John Murrell operated there. The outlaw, later nicknamed the "Great Western Land Pirate," was just beginning his road to notoriety. Whether a gang was active that day is unknown, but Ludlow felt they had a close call as they approached a flatboat tied to the riverbank. Those on the boat called out, claiming they had been robbed and needed provisions. After discussing, the actors decided not to risk it and continued their journey without stopping. About fifty miles further downriver, they came to the fourth Chickasaw bluff. Ludlow wrote:

> When I first beheld this beautiful site for a city there was not a building, hut or habitation of any kind on it, at least where the city is now built; but two miles below the mouth of the Wolf River, near the southern end of the bluff, stood the remains of a block-house. This blockhouse was once a portion of the fortification of Fort Pickering, and had been turned into a kind of trading-store, furnishing powder, shot, whiskey, and other destructives to the Indians, who came there to trade.[10]

The group purchased some venison from a Native American looking to sell a deer he had draped across his horse. Ludlow's final observation about the fourth Chickasaw bluff was about that Native American and was written, it seems, to make the point that Native Americans were not inferior to Whites. "We found him as sharp at a bargain as any of his white brethren."[11] And with that, the group continued their journey to New Orleans.

Chapter Ten Endnotes

1. John Overton to James Winchester, October 25, 1818, *James Winchester Papers, 1787-1953*, Tennessee State Library and Archives.
2. "The Name of Memphis," *Commercial Appeal*, December 09, 1926, 136.
3. Kenneth M. Stampp, *The Peculiar Institution, Slavery in the American South* (New York: Alfred E. Knopf, 1956), 15.
4. Eugene D. Genovese, *The Mind of the Master Class: History and Faith in the Southern Slaveholders' Worldview* (Cambridge: Cambridge University Press, 2005), 66.
5. Perre Magness, "Founders Had Eye on Quick Profits," *Commercial Appeal*, July 21, 1988, 25.
6. William B. Waldran, "Anniversary Address of W. B. Waldran," *Old Folks Record* 1 (December 1874): 100.
7. Alexis de Tocqueville, *Memoir, Letters, and Remains of Alexis de Tocqueville, vol. 1* (Cambridge: Macmillan and Co., 1861), 27.
8. N. M. Ludlow, *Dramatic Life, As I Found it* (St. Louis: G. I. Jones and Company, 1880), 123.
9. Ludlow, *Dramatic Life*, 124.
10. Ludlow, *Dramatic Life*, 127.
11. Ludlow, *Dramatic Life*, 128.

J. J. PRESCOTT & CO.,
LARD OIL,
SOAP & CANDLE
MANUFACTURERS,
NEAR THE LANDING,
Front of Commercial Hotel.
MEMPHIS, TENN.

☞ Having increased our facilities for making Soap, by constructing new Works and Fixtures, and having engaged the services of an Experienced Boston Soap Maker, we are enabled to furnish

THE BEST ARTICLE

manufactured in the Mississippi Valley, and on as good terms.

MERCHANTS

will find it

To Their Interest

TO CALL AND EXAMINE OUR SOAP

before buying, either in the city or elsewhere.

☞ TALLOW AND SOAP GREASE WANTED.

From Rainey's Memphis City Directory, 1855/56

Chapter Eleven: Changes Comin' On

Marcus Winchester takes care of business in Memphis

On May 16, 1977, James E. Roper spoke to the West Tennessee Historical Society on the topic of Paddy Meagher, Tom Huling, and the Bell Tavern. Roper, a respected author, historian, and professor in Memphis at Southwestern—today's Rhodes College—was considered the foremost living authority on the history of Memphis. A fifth-generation Memphian, the city's civic and political leaders called on Roper anytime an important visitor needed a tour of the city.

However, by the late 1970s, Roper was mad. Regarding the tours, he told a reporter for *The Commercial Appeal*, "I don't like to do it anymore. I got tired of pointing to an empty lot or parking lot and saying that's where such-and-such was."[1] Much of his frustration came from the lack of cooperation he found among the city's leaders for preserving its history:

> A gleaming example of the lack of cooperation in this city was our effort to save the old railroad depot for a museum. We were told by the city we had 18 months to save the money and buy it. We needed $120,000. But three months after they said that, they got out the bulldozers and knocked it down without even telling us. Once it was down, the city told us we could have gotten half the amount through a government historical revision plan.[2]

The Memphis politicos of the 1970s may not have been interested in the city's history, but Roper would not have a problem finding a passionate audience when speaking to the West Tennessee Historical Society. This particular night, he had something especially exciting to share. During a project to organize a massive number of files at the Tennessee State Library and Archives, a letter had been discovered filed away under the heading "anonymous." The last page with the signature was missing, and the handwriting was so poor, it was difficult to read. At some point, someone had filed it away. The letter, begun on April 15, 1819, was written by Marcus Winchester to John Overton, and it shed light on the very first days after Winchester and William Lawrence arrived in Memphis. Roper was thrilled. Like the old deed of transfer for the Rice Grant found in the Weakley County registrar's office nearly three decades earlier, this discovery was like receiving a message from the past. The letter not only included details and dates that had previously been unknown, it provided a first-hand look at the problems the two young men had to solve during their first days on the bluff:

> I do myself the pleasure to inform you that Mr. Lawrence and myself landed in the mouth of Wolf on the morning of the 9th instant. By sunrise on the succeeding morning, we had extended our line one mile and 39 poles—beginning at the mouth; though not without escaping the observation of Mr. Irvine, who seems sensibly alive to all our operations. So much so, that our arrival seems to have induced him to decline a trip to New Orleans, when upon the very eve of sailing. The influence of this man upon the Bluffs if he is devoid of principle (which I am unwilling to believe) as to exercise it, may either dam up every source which could lead us to knowledge of the spot where the beginning corner stood, or so foul them as to induce those who could testify to the fact to depose, even that it stood above the measured distance given by the plat . . . Old Patrick Meghar, who is a kind of equivocating menial devoted to Irvine, Mr. Lawrence and myself have flattered on to the extent of our abilities. . . . We have paid Judge Fooy a visit, and had a long conversation with him. I spoke with freedom and I believe with candor. He has no recollection of any tree known certainly as Rice's corner. He well recollects that when the Spanish garrison stood near the Wolf, the commandant had several marked trees cut down—the marks upon which was carefully transcribed and shown to Judge Fooy, but so great is the length of time that he has no remembrance, either of what the marks were, or of the situation of the trees—neither does he know the manner the commandant disposed of the book, in which they were noted.[3]

After the area had been acquired with the Louisiana Purchase in 1803, Judge

Fooy's Camp de la Esperanza, across the river from the bluff, had been renamed Hopefield. Fooy was allowed to stay and was given the position of magistrate. He became a much-trusted resource in the early days of settlement on the bluff and a good neighbor to Winchester, Lawrence, and other settlers until his death in 1823.

After twenty days on the Mississippi River surrounded by brown muddy water and mile after mile of riverbank, it must have been a relief for the two young men to see the Wolf River. The water was so clear, steamboat captains would use it to clean their boilers. It was spring when they arrived. Wild grasses had already begun growing, and the trees were filled with new leaves. Right from the start, Winchester and Lawrence saw the power of the Mississippi River and the challenges the instability of its bank could cause. A large section of the path along the bluff had caved in, causing them to have to detour through the thick woods and tangled undergrowth just behind the path. The two men wasted no time and began working immediately.

According to tradition, it was at Patrick "Paddy" Meagher's makeshift tavern where they spent the first few nights. Meagher is a colorful character in the history of Memphis, memorialized by Paddy's Hen and Chickens—a collection of mud and silt islands that once lay in the Mississippi River about six miles upstream from the fourth Chickasaw bluff. For several years, Meagher operated a small business selling wood and supplies to boats from one of those islands. These islands are considered historically significant today because they are associated with the deadliest maritime disaster in U.S. history. On April 27, 1865, the steamboat *Sultana*, loaded beyond capacity with more than two thousand passengers, experienced a catastrophic boiler explosion near Paddy's Hen and Chickens. The disaster resulted in the deaths of an estimated eighteen hundred passengers, many of them Union soldiers recently released from Confederate prisons. While the shifting course of the Mississippi, along with channel realignment, ultimately caused these islands to vanish, the Sultana Disaster Museum in Marion, Arkansas, tells the story and memorializes those lost in the tragedy.

Paddy Meagher most likely arrived in the United States as a soldier in the British army and was among the soldiers captured by George Rogers Clark in what is now Indiana. Along the way, Meagher switched sides and enrolled in the company of Robert George in Louisville, Kentucky. For his service, Meagher received a land grant in Ohio, which he immediately sold.

One theory is that Meagher made the acquaintance of Scottish trader James Logan Colbert and they began a business relationship which led to Meagher settling on the bluff. He was an important resource for Winchester and Lawrence, especially in their first weeks on the bluff. It was at Meagher's tavern where depositions with other early settlers were taken to help determine the starting point of the original Rice grant. The river had moved, and most of the markers in the grant were long gone. Before the men could start laying out lots, they had to prove what part of the bluff the proprietors actually owned.

Among those who testified was James Stewart, who came forward and shared "the dying words" of Mr. Matthews which Marcus Winchester recorded:

> Matthews declared that in his opinion the mouth of the Wolf River now was greatly higher up than when he first knew it. That when he first knew it, it was nearly opposite to Meagher's house. That he thought it was now 300 yards above where it was then when Matthew's first knew.[4]

Winchester also discovered the strip of land that had previously been noted as a place to easily land a flatboat at the bluff, had been swallowed up, and boats had begun docking further south at the base of the old blockhouse near where Fort Pickering had once stood.

When not assisting Lawrence in the survey and laying out lots, Winchester was busy with the construction of a shelter that he used to store the first shipment of inventory that had arrived from Cairo. Marcus had written to his father, "bring whatever quantity of whiskey you can procure at 50 cents . . . indeed almost anything you have to sell, we can vend to considerable advantage here."[5]

Before the end of the year, Marcus Winchester traveled to Baltimore, where he visited family members and ordered more merchandise to sell in the new Memphis mercantile, Winchester & Carr. Winchester had too much to accomplish alone, so he had gone into business with Anderson B. Carr. Carr and his two brothers, Thomas and Overton, had been on their way to "Indian country" when they stopped at the bluff for supplies. They were told about the treaty Jackson had negotiated and that land would soon be for sale, so they decided to stay. While in Baltimore, Winchester also had an engraving of a map of Memphis made and sent to his father at Cragfont. On January 11, 1820, Marcus wrote a letter to John Overton in which he shares more detail about the map he had produced:

> In pursuance of your directions that if an engraving of a plan of the town of Memphis did not exceed $100 I might contract for the execution of the same, I have engaged a gentleman of the city of Baltimore . . . I have caused a typographical chart of Major Long to be embodied in the plate, a steam boat to be moored at the old Spanish landing, and a barge to be represented under full

sail entering the harbor of Wolf River.[6]

Supervising the building of the store and then stocking it with the supplies took more of Winchester's time than Lawrence would have liked. In a letter to Overton dated June 4, 1819, he wrote that he was finished laying off the lots but they were not yet numbered, then added that the arrival of the merchandise had "operated some against me as Winchester could not give me as much assistance afterwards as before."[7] Lawrence was acting as the agent on behalf of Overton and Jackson—and later John C. McLemore—while Winchester was agent on behalf of his father, uncle, and cousins. Overton was not happy reading about Winchester's focus on the store rather than preparing lots to sell. He wrote to James Winchester, "Marcus and Carr are securely selling their goods with them whether it is a town in their day or not is not so material. Lawrence is in the woods surveying. It is not from them I learn things."[8]

Another time, Overton received word from William Cage that "as they came up, there was no wood for the steam boats at the mouth of Wolf river." This left Overton, using his word, "grieved." Overton's vision of hospitality as a key to the growth of Memphis was evident in his response:

> I was grieved at this as I had particularly urged Marcus to be attentive to keeping a constant supply of wood for steamboats—If you travel a high road will you not call at a Tavern where the tavern keeper receives you at the door before you get down, makes you easy in his house and furnishes you everything you want? ... Let me beg of you to write to your son, seriously, on this subject, and everything connected, with (accommodation the most polite) to the passengers of the river ... write to Marcus & Carr I beg of you.[9]

James Winchester sometimes kept the peace between his son and Overton, but he too had his hands full. He had just been appointed by President James Madison to manage an important survey. The recent treaty had transferred ownership of West Tennessee to the United States, but North Mississippi still belonged to the Chickasaw. When Congress established Tennessee as a state on June 1, 1796, the southern boarder was determined to run along the thirty-fifth parallel. It would be up to Winchester to figure out exactly where that dividing line was. Andrew Jackson was certainly invested in anything relating to the Chickasaw and was eager to suggest next steps:

> Colberts Ferry will be a proper point for you to assemble and

meet the chiefs, if you cannot get transportation for all you may obtain a canoe for some of your party to pass down the river to the line the balance can pass down on the west side of the river, as it may be difficult without a boat to cross the Tennessee at the line—The distance by land I suppose from Colberts Ferry to the line is about thirty-five mile—and mostly through a barren or poor country which skirts a valuable one.[10]

Winchester and the survey team he put together arrived on June 7, 1819, and prepared to run the survey lines. They first needed to connect with the representatives of the Chickasaw, but by June 10, they still had not arrived, so Winchester proceeded without them. Several days later, after they had surveyed around six miles of the line, James Colbert Jr. arrived and shared that he would be serving as one representative, but the other, Samuel Seely, was ill. Seely's health improved enough for him to rejoin the group by June 14, by which time they had already surveyed sixteen miles. Winchester later noted, the pair questioned the validity of the results that came from the tools he used instead of the rising and setting sun. "It was in vain that I told them the sun did not set in the West at midsummer."[11]

Surveying in the early 19th-century involved a variety of methods, tools, and somewhat standardized legal guidelines to follow. Those charged with finding the boundaries of a piece of property—large or small—had to mark the lines and create detailed maps and certificates.

Surveys were often based on natural landmarks such as waterways, trees—called witness trees—or rocks, all of which could be moved or altered over time. The tools of the trade included instruments such as a tripod, Jacob's staff, and compass. A Jacob's staff could be used in place of a tripod, which was sometimes cumbersome to transport across uncleared land filled with old-growth forests and tangled brush, like what James Winchester encountered. It resembled a large walking stick with a knob the size of a tennis ball on top that was used to mount a compass called a circumferentor.

The land was measured with a tool called a Gunter's chain, invented by Englishman Edmund Gunter in the early 1600s. The chain consisted of one hundred links and measured sixty-six feet in length, with ten chains equaling one acre. Surveyors typically carried a small notebook to record measurements and various details about the land they surveyed.

It was important to note man-made landmarks, such as paths, mills, and bridges, as well as natural features like minerals, salt springs, or mountains. The survey of Tennessee's southern border, for example, took James Winchester west across portions of the White Oak, Hatchie, and Wolf Rivers. Upon completion, Winchester's survey recorded the line ending at the Mississippi River, approximately three-fourths of a mile below Presidents Island.

As the survey party neared the Mississippi River, Colbert and Seely departed, stating they would return later for a final meeting with James Winchester on the bluff. When the two arrived for that final meeting, however, they infuriated Winchester by claiming that the line had not been run correctly. They argued that Winchester's survey had allotted too much land to the United States and too little to the Chickasaw Nation.

Winchester defended his survey in an August 2, 1819, letter to Secretary of War John C. Calhoun, asserting his belief that the line was correct and should never need to be remeasured. The validity of Winchester's line remained in question for several decades, especially with so much valuable cotton land—and the city of Memphis—at stake. Eventually, a new survey was conducted, which determined that Winchester's line was incorrect. However, rather than reducing Tennessee's land, the new survey placed the state line four miles farther south. As a result, those living in Memphis remained Tennesseans.

While James Winchester was busy running the survey line between Chickasaw country and Tennessee, John Overton had distractions of his own. On July 28, 1820, the fifty-four-year-old bachelor married thirty-seven-year-old widow Mary McConnell White May. She was the daughter of Knoxville founder James White and the widow of the late Dr. Francis May, who had been Andrew Jackson's doctor. According to family stories, Overton, always practical, proposed by telling May that, while he did not love her, he would promise to always provide for her and her children. He then gave her twenty minutes to think the offer over.

As a woman in the early nineteenth century, her options were limited, so she accepted. John Overton became a husband and step-father to his new wife's five children. At the time, she had two adult sons and three children under twelve. Three more children soon followed: John Jr. was born in 1821, Anne Coleman in 1823, and Elizabeth Belle in 1826. Overton was an enthusiastic and engaged father and step-father to his suddenly large family, seeing to their education and preparing them for their future. Of course, that included instructing them on how to manage a large plantation and the enslaved population that worked on it. An inventory from 1835 registered fifty-three enslaved people belonging to the Overton family at Travellers Rest.[12]

Meanwhile, in Memphis, the official land office opened on December 6, 1820, at the home of Anderson B. Carr's brother, Thomas. The first public sale of lots took place the following day. James Winchester and John and Mary Overton traveled to Memphis on horseback for the occasion. Marcus met them at Reynoldsburgh where the Natchez Trace crossed the Tennessee River and rode with them to Memphis.[13] Overton was not one to leave anything to chance. In

October, he had written Jackson, "Do you know of anyone we can probably get who will make a good Cryer, at the public sale of our lots? Much depends on a lively, witty and agreeable Cryer."[14]

Although sales were disappointing at first, a few buyers began showing up as word spread. Land speculator Joseph B. Porter arrived with his son and nephew, James Brown. In later years, Brown noted, "At this time there were but three white men residing in this part of the purchase, Thos. D. Carr, A. B. Carr and a hired man named Overton . . . The Messrs. Carr had arrived at this place but two or three weeks prior to our arrival. They had been traveling down the Mississippi River from Virginia, but when they arrived to the bluff, they decided to stay."[15] Brown also remembered the first sales of lots in Memphis and the first lots that were given by the proprietors for improvements. "They gave T. D. Carr two lots to build a tavern to serve visitors to the land office. The tavern consisted of six or eight small, round-pole cabins with boat plank floors and clay-filled cracks, much like Indian huts. They also gave A. B. Carr a lot for a horse mill and another by Bayou Gayoso for a tannery."[16]

Samuel Brown, the first sheriff in Memphis, would soon open a hotel on the north side of Auction Street across from Auction Square. Until then, the cabins Brown remembered were primarily for prospective buyers. Overton also began running ads in newspapers around the country describing Memphis as being located on "the handsomest site on the Mississippi below St. Louis."[17]

The layout of the town created by Marcus Winchester and William Lawrence had a similar look and feel to other cities springing up in the South. That was not an accident. All who worked on the plan for Memphis had spent time in the east, were well read, and had a financial interest in a city design that residential and commercial buyers would find appealing.

They were also likely all well aware of the success of Philadelphia's city plan that was designed by Quaker William Penn and surveyor Thomas Holme in 1682. It was the first plan for a city in the United States to use a grid pattern for streets and to include open public squares or parks that were intended to be used by those living in or visiting the city. Penn's plan included a central square at the intersection of the two main streets and four additional squares in each quarter of the original grid pattern.

He also varied street widths according to their purpose—broad main avenues carried major traffic, while narrower streets served lighter use. Historian Richard C. Wade found that many American towns adopted Philadelphia as their model, and travelers often noticed and recorded the resemblance: William Faux thought Lexington's "outline is large and resembling Philadelphia," Henry B. Featon wrote that Cincinnati was "built on the model of Philadelphia," John Cotton observed that Pittsburgh's streets were "mostly laid out like those of Philadelphia," and

John Palmer remarked that Zanesville, Ohio, was platted "after the manner of Philadelphia."[18]

Eventually, the same could be said for Memphis. It initially covered an area roughly two by four miles, bordered on the south by Union Avenue, on the east by East Parkway North, on the north by Vollintine Avenue, and on the west by the Mississippi River. The streets north of Poplar Avenue were named after James Winchester, Andrew Jackson, and John Overton, while those south of Poplar were named after the first five presidents: George Washington, John Adams, Thomas Jefferson, James Monroe, and James Madison. Today's Front Street was originally named Mississippi Row and overlooked the river. North of Jackson, the street was called Chickasaw Street, and south of Union Avenue, it was called Shelby Street. Main Street served as the primary commercial thoroughfare.

The design included four major north-south streets and a public promenade along the riverbank south of Jackson Street called Mississippi Row. No buildings were allowed along the promenade, as it was intended to serve as a scenic, uninterrupted walkway from one end of town to the other—an aspect of the plan that was frequently challenged and would eventually have to be resolved by the Tennessee Supreme Court. The plan for Memphis also included four large public squares—Auction, Exchange, Market, and Court—strategically placed and named based on how they were to be used.

Marcus Winchester later testified, "Squares were intended for different and specific purposes from each other, and were located in different parts of the town because it was designated that the public easements or advantages should be scattered as to benefit the greatest number of people ... for the proprietors at that early day considered Memphis was destined to become a large city."[19]

Winchester also pointed out that Auction Square, placed close to the public landing and the center of the town at that time, was designed to support large amounts of commerce. He wrote:

> It was believed a large amount of auction sales and other transactions of a similar nature would be transacted, and where it was believed more room than a simple street would be required for the temporary resting and accommodation of cotton bales, tobacco hogsheads, sugar hogsheads, loaded wagons, burthen cars and other cumbrous articles of merchandise, and the arrangements of transporting merchandise would be required.[20]

There was no mention of enslaved individuals when referencing commerce on Auction Square. Today, there is a large granite slab at Auction Square, now called Auction Park, that many incorrectly identify as a place enslaved people stood as they were auctioned. It was not placed there until 1924 by the Colonial Dames, long after slavery ended.

While questions about the original purpose of the Memphis waterfront and the public areas designated by the proprietors still comes up from time to time, Winchester knew first-hand what was originally intended. He was there:

> In relation to the piece of public ground called the public promenade, in the growth of a city as large as it was believed Memphis would come to be, with a dense population, it was believed to be indispensably necessary that a large public walk should be laid out and dedicated in such a way that it could never be interfered with by individual or corporate authorities over which citizens or strangers might freely pass, without let or hindrance.[21]

When the sale of lots on the bluff proved disappointing at first, John Overton wasted no time unleashing his public relations skills. He paid for what now would be considered an advertorial in the *Port Folio*, a literary and political journal that was published in Philadelphia from 1801 to 1827. Included in the 1820 issue of the journal, alongside articles with titles like "The Book of Psalms; Translated from the Hebrew," "On the Principles of Historical Composition," and "The History of Ismayl and Maryam, an Arabian Tale," was a spotlight on a new town on the Mississippi River that seemed to have come right from Overton's pen—because it did.

Chapter Eleven Endnotes

1. Audrey West, "Historian Says Memphis Neglects Its Past," *Memphis Press-Scimitar*, May 25, 1977, 17.
2. West, "Historian Says Memphis Neglects Its Past."
3. James E. Roper, "Paddy Meagher, Tom Huling, and the Bell Tavern," *West Tennessee Historical Society Papers*, no. 31 (1977): 13–15.
4. Roper, "Paddy Meahgher," 14.
5. Walter Durham, *James Winchester: Tennessee Pioneer* (Gallatin: Sumner County Library Board, 1979), 219.
6. Roper, *The Founding of Memphis*, 71.
7. William Lawrence to John Overton, June 4, 1819, William Lawrence Correspondence, Archives Division, Tennessee State Library and Archives.
8. John Overton to James Winchester, April 4, 1823, James Winchester Correspondence, Archives Division, Tennessee State Library and Archives.
9. Durham, *James Winchester*, 225.
10. Jackson to Winchester, April 13, 1819, James Winchester Correspondence, Archives Division, Tennessee State Library and Archives.
11. Durham, *James Winchester*, 217.
12 *A Past Uncovered: The Story of the Enslaved People of Travellers Rest*, Travellers Rest Historic House Museum, Nashville, Tenn., exhibit.
13. John Overton to James Winchester, October 15, 1820, Winchester Papers, Tennessee State Library and Museum.
14. Fletch Coke, *Dear Judge: Selected Letters of John Overton of Travellers' Rest* (Nashville: Travellers' Rest Historic Museum House, 1978), 61.
15. J. P. Young, *Standard History of Memphis, Tennessee* (Knoxville, Tenn: H. W. Crew & Co., 1912), 61.
16. Young, Standard History of Memphis, 62.
17. Young, Standard History of Memphis, 63.
18. Richard C. Wade, *The Urban Frontier: The Rise of Western Cities, 1790–1830* (Cambridge, Mass.: Harvard University Press, 1959), 314.
19. James H. Malone, "History of Early Land Grants for Public Purposes in Memphis," *The Commercial Appeal*, March 21, 1915, 12.
20. Malone, "History of Early Land Grants."
21. Malone, "History of Early Land Grants."

S. A. MOORE. W. W. WAIR

S. A. MOORE & Co.,

WHOLESALE AND RETAIL

GROCERS,

Forwarding and Commission

MERCHANTS,

and Agents for the sale of

VIRGINIA, KENTUCKY AND MISSOURI

TOBACCO,

NO. 2, SHELBY STREET,

MEMPHIS, TENN.

Particular attention paid to

SELLING AND STORING COTTON.

LIBERAL

CASH ADVANCES MADE

on Produce assigned to them.

From Rainey's Memphis City Directory, 1855/56

Chapter Twelve: Considering a Move to Memphis

John Overton advertises the new town on the east bank of the Mississippi River

Writing under the pseudonym "Oliver Oldschool," Joseph Dennie was credited as author, but he certainly had a lot of help from John Overton. Many of the talking points the Tennessee judge used in ads and letters can be seen in the article reprinted here in its entirety.

Memphis, A New Town on the Mississippi

A town of the above name has been laid off on the east bank of the Mississippi river, at the lower Chickasaw Bluffs, in the county of Shelby, State of Tennessee. It is also within the Western District, lately acquired by treaty from the Chickasaw Indians.

The plan and local situation of Memphis is such as to authorize the expectation that it is destined to become a populous city. It is laid off parallel with the Mississippi, the course of which at this place is nearly due south, with Wolf river emptying into it at the northern extremity of the town. Three hundred and sixty-two lots are designated upon its present plat; and there is any quantity of elevated level land adjoining, suited to the purpose of enlarging it at pleasure. The streets run to the cardinal points. They are wide and spacious, and, together with a number of alleys, afford a free and abundant circulation of air.

There is, besides, four public squares, in different parts of the town, and between the front lots and the river an ample vacant place reserved as a promenade; all of which must contribute very much to the health and comfort of the place, as well as to its security and ornament.

The bluff on which Memphis is situated is remarkably high and level, as it is a large tract of country which extends for many miles at right angles from the Mississippi. Being from twenty to thirty feet above the highest flood, it is always dry and commands a complete view of the river, which, at this place, is rather more than three-quarters of a mile wide.

The scenery from the town is quite picturesque and delightful, presenting a rich and extensive plain in the rear, with improvements skirting the opposite shore, as well as a vast expanse of water, chequered by islands which are covered by the heaviest and tallest timber. In casting the eye up the river, a water view is obtained for several miles, interrupted and varied by a cluster of islands about three quarters of a mile distant, commonly known by the name of Paddy's Hen and Chickens, through which the Mississippi is seen discharging its immense column of water in two or three different channels.

Upon directing the attention down the river the eye enjoys an equally extensive range, where is presented, within the space of three miles. President's Island, which contains several thousand acres of land, a considerable portion of which is very fertile, and entirely free from inundation. In addition to this, the frequent passage of steamboats and crafts of every description, up and down the Mississippi, give a grandeur even to the prospect, and an active and commercial appearance to the place, which is only one remove from a position on the sea-board.

This is the only site for a town of any magnitude on the Mississippi, between the mouth of the Ohio and Natchez. The western bank is uniformly too low and subject to inundation, and the eastern affords no other situation sufficiently high, dry, level and extensive, together with a rich surrounding county, competent to support it. Neither can an eligible position be selected, for this purpose, on any of the rivers which empty themselves into the Mississippi, between the Tennessee river and the Bluff, in consequence of their being greatly incommoded by swamps as high as they are navigable. It is consequently the only desirable site, and is considered by many superior to any upon the Mississippi river. Natchez cannot vie with it, and it even excels Baton Rouge, inasmuch as the banks are higher and more uniformly level and commanding, the surrounding prospects more beautiful and interesting, and, from its situation, necessarily more healthy. Thus, by nature, it is so situated that much competition cannot arise by the erection of other towns between the mouth of the Ohio and Natchez.

The general advantages of Memphis are owing to its being founded on the Mississippi, one of the largest and most important rivers on the globe, and the high road for all the commerce of the vast and fertile valley through which it flows. This noble river, which may with propriety be denominated the American Nile, is about two thousand five hundred and eighty miles from its head to its mouth, and, with its branches, waters two-thirds of the territory of the United

States.

Memphis lies thirty-five degrees six minutes of north latitude, and thirteen degrees west longitude from Washington. The adjacent and surrounding country, which is to be relied on to support it, is one of the most extensive and beautiful bodies of land, contiguous to the Mississippi river, between the mouth of the Ohio and New Orleans. It is elevated, dry and level, possessing a fertile and productive soil, and extending east northeast, south and southeast, for nearly one hundred miles.

No tract of country can be better accommodated to the principal staples of the western world. Corn, cotton, wheat and tobacco may be cultivated to great advantage. It is also well adapted to the growth of blue and herd grass, clover, etc., and must consequently be happily suited to the rearing of stock.

The climate is certainly a desirable one, in consequence of its uniformity and being free from those extremes of heat and cold to which the country, either father north or south, is generally subjected. Such a climate must be very congenial to the constitution, and to the vigorous maturity of most of the vegetable productions of the temperate regions. From the locality of Memphis, the largest portion of the produce hereafter to be raised for market, in the extreme tract of country lying between the Tennessee river and Bluff, must necessarily be concentrated at that point for exportation, as the rivers by which it is watered are not uniformly navigable.

The superiority of the Bluff on which Memphis stands over the few situations of high ground on the Mississippi river, is evinced by its having been first selected by the French, as early as the year 1736, as a suitable position for a garrison. Whilst Louisiana was in the possession of Spain, this Bluff was again chosen as a healthy and commanding site for a similar establishment. A fort and garrison had been built and occupied, and the adjacent land cleared and cultivated for many years anterior to their being surrendered to the United States, agreeably to the Treaty of St. Ildefonso.[1]

Chapter Twelve Endnotes

1. Oliver Oldschool, "Memphis, A New Town on the Mississippi," *The Port Folio* 9, no. 1 (1820): 489–94.

J. Henry A. Lownes, Memphis.   Edmond Orgill, Memphis.   Wm. Orgill, New York.

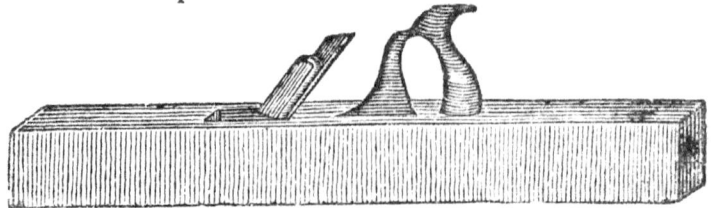

LOWNES, ORGILL & CO.,

Importers of

HARDWARE, CUTLERY

Guns, French Window Glass,

AND DEALERS IN

AGRICULTURAL IMPLEMENTS,

Iron, Nails, Castings, Plows, &c.,

NO. 18, FRONT ROW,

Corner of Monroe Street,

MEMPHIS, TENN.

Every variety of

TOOLS

fo

Blacksmiths, House & Ship

CARPENTERS,

COOPERS AND TINNERS.

Also, Agents for the sale of

CUMBERLAND, TENNESSEE IRON,

AND RICHE'S CELEBRATED

FIRE PROOF SAFES.

From Rainey's Memphis City Directory, 1855/56

Chapter Thirteen: That's how I got to Memphis

The new town of Memphis begins to grow under Marcus Winchester's leadership

Benjamin Fooy made Memphis history on May 22, 1819, when he was recorded as the recipient of lot number fifty-three facing the river. It was the first entered in the deed book and was one of several lots given by the proprietors to some of those first settlers who had been living on the bluff since before Marcus Winchester arrived. This served the dual purpose of kick-starting economic development while proactively making nice with those whose lives were about to change.

Knickerbocker and Wright soon bought a lot to build a warehouse, the first brick building in Memphis. Early Memphis writer James Davis claimed that as they were building that warehouse, they came across buried sections of Spain's Fort San Fernando de las Barrancas that had been abandoned by Gayoso twenty-five years earlier.

Paddy Meagher officially registered lot forty-four in the name of his daughter, Sally. This lot also faced the Mississippi River with Water Street—later changed to Overton Street—running alongside. Beneath it was the best location for arrivals to and departures from the bluff. Locals quickly dubbed it "Meagher's Landing."

Catherine Grace purchased a lot at the mouth of the Bayou Gayoso, then shortly afterwards, married Joab Bean. He was a skilled gunsmith, having learned the craft from his father, who taught him how to build, repair, and maintain firearms. Bean came from one of Tennessee's first families. His grandfather, William Bean Jr., his father, Jesse Bean, and his four uncles served as part of Colonel John Sevier's Riflemen in the Battle of King's Mountain during the Revolutionary War. Joab's grandparents, William and Lydia Bean, were the first White settlers in Tennessee, and Joab's Uncle Russell Bean was considered "the first White child" born in Tennessee. His parents, Jesse and Elizabeth, were the first settlers of Franklin County, Tennessee, settling on "Bean's Creek" and naming the settlement "Bean Station." Joab Bean would make history in Memphis for a different reason. His purchase of a young Black man for one hundred dollars was Memphis's first recorded sale of an enslaved person.[1]

Marcus Winchester claimed the lot at present-day Jackson and Front Streets on which he quickly began building a store that would also function as the Memphis post office and an informal bank for decades to come. Today, the Front Street substation stands on that lot, across from the Memphis Pyramid. Across the frequently muddy road was a grove of locust trees, a popular campsite for travelers coming to Memphis to buy, sell, or trade supplies. That site is now the on-ramp to Interstate 40, leading to the Hernando de Soto Bridge into Arkansas.

It seems clear that, by this time, Marcus Winchester was in Memphis to stay. After the proprietors divided up the portion of the tract that had not yet been laid off, James Winchester gave Marcus 420 additional acres on the southeast corner of the tract, bounded by today's Manassas and McNeil Streets and Poplar, and Union Avenues.[2]

Marcus Winchester operated a one-man chamber of commerce, general store, welcome center, real estate firm, and economic development office all rolled into one. His salesmanship even drew notice in a clipping from the Arkansas World, preserved in the Crittenden County courthouse. The writer observed that Memphis then contained only small wooden houses and a handful of stores, one of them Winchester & Carr. Of Winchester himself, the visitor wrote that he was "agreeable, pleasant, hospitable, and generous." He also noted:

> He imparted to us much valuable information regarding the country and expressed high hopes of the future of Memphis as a point of extensive commerce, assuring us of his confidence that it would become a large city in no distant day, and advising us to make large investments in lands adjacent to the town, telling us it could then be bought it very low figures.[3]

Twenty-year-old Victor Moreau Murphey paid the bluff a visit in the summer of 1825 and included a few details in a letter to his father, Archibald D. Murphey. He wrote, "We went from this down to Memphis where I had the pleasure of washing my hands in the Mississippi River. This is not to be compared with any stream I ever saw before. Memphis is situated on a high bluff, and affords of most delightful prospect of the River."[4] While the river impressed young Murphey, Memphis itself disappointed. "The whole Town does not contain a decent looking house and but one or two respectable looking men."[5] One of those men was Marcus Winchester. Murphey wrote:

> Mr. Winchester was particularly kind to me, invited me to his house and shewed every disposition to render me agreeable while there, and told me anything in the world he had, if I stood in need to Call on him for it, and even went so far, as to tell me if I should be unfortunate while in this country and get out of money, to apply to him. To meet with such a friend at that distance from home, and in the midst of Strangers, is a circumstance which seldom happens and one which I shall long remember.[6]

Murphey also mentioned seeing William Lawrence whom he evidently already knew: "I then saw Mr. Lawrence. I intended going to his house. He lives 4 or 5 miles in the Country. But my horse was much fatigued and began to decline."[7]

Qunicy K. Underwood arrived in Memphis from North Alabama as a 4-year-old boy with his family on April 1, 1826. He later wrote about Winchester and remembered he and his friends would pass the time at Winchester & Carr. However, he noted, "we would vanish with marked rapidity from our loitering around said store when half a dozen of the red men of the forest, after frequent potations, gave the Indian yell, which we construed as the war-whoop!"[8]

Underwood also wrote that his father, Washington Underwood, was the first teacher on the bluff, and Underwood and his brother, Washington L. Underwood, apprenticed at the *Memphis Advocate* newspaper as boys. When working as a newspaper delivery boy, he wrote he could always count on Marcus Winchester for fifty cents in silver at Christmas. The Underwood brothers later moved to Arkansas where they established the Helena, Arkansas, *Southern Shield* newspaper, and Quincy served as a county judge.

The first Memphis wedding took place that May when Overton Carr married Mary Hill. William Lawrence then wed Eliza Brown, a daughter of Daniel R. Brown and sister of early settler Samuel R. Brown, on November 22, 1821.

Marcus Winchester hired William Irvin to run a ferry from Memphis to Arkansas. It is likely this was the same Mr. Irvin that canceled his trip to New Orleans when Winchester and Lawrence first arrived at the bluff. The price for each man and horse to ferry across the river was one dollar. A four-wheeled wagon drawn by four horses was three dollars if empty and five dollars if loaded.

Another good description of Memphis in the late 1820s came from Frances Trollope in her book *Domestic Manners of the Americans*:

> The river here is so wide as to give it the appearance of a noble lake; an island covered with lofty forest trees divides it, and relieves

by its broad mass of shadow the uniformity of the waters. The town stretches in a rambling irregular manner along the cliff, from the Wolf River, one of the innumerable tributaries to the Mississippi, to about a mile below it. Half a mile more of the cliff beyond the town is cleared of trees and produces good pasture for horses, cows, and pigs; sheep they had none. At either end of this space the forest again rears its dark wall and seems to say to man, 'so far shalt thy come, and no farther!'[9]

As one early resident remembered in 1898, it was still less of a town and still more of a trading post in 1824:

Main Street was simply a public road and a bad one at that. Exchange Street was another public road crossing Main Street. Front Street was the whole town. Where the Cotton Exchange building is now was the north edge of a pond or a low place that became a pond after big rains. About the corner of Union and Second streets was the pond proper. The river front was lined with trading boats at that time, and they made business good for the three stores.[10]

Food and shelter were the primary concerns for Memphis's first settlers, leaving little time for establishing a place of worship. When Christian missionary Jeremiah Evarts, known by his pen name, William Penn, visited in May 1826, he wrote sarcastically that the town "was not yet so rich or so populous as the ancient capital of Egypt." He added, "There are four or five stores, and perhaps ten log houses, with two or three poor framed houses. A large framed house is to be erected here this season for a tavern."[11] That was likely a reference to Paddy's Bell Tavern. He wrote, "In regard to Memphis and the neighborhood, I could not learn that there is any moral culture of the inhabitants. A Methodist preacher has sometimes conducted public worship; but the people were not desirous of hearing him, as he is intemperate."[12]

Early pioneer evangelists came down the river and preached when and where they could. One of the first on the bluff was Elijah Coffee. A cobbler by trade, he arrived from St. Louis one Sunday in March 1824 to save Memphis souls—and soles—preaching from a flatboat tied up on the Wolf River. He was such a success, his makeshift congregation moved from the riverbank to Barney Flynn's nearby cabin. The good Reverend Coffee had found a home. He was a tough character, some said on the run from the law or a wife in St. Louis, and some said both. True or not, in one story passed down, a man who heard one of Coffee's sermons said, "Brother, that was the damndest meanest sermon I ever heard," To which Coffee replied, "Well, I generally tries to match my preaching to the congregation."[13]

Coffee joined forces with 24-year-old circuit rider Thomas P. Davidson, or Uncle Tommy as he came to be called, and formed the First Methodist Society of Memphis in February 1826. Joining Davidson was Henry, an enslaved man he owned. Henry was mute but created his own version of sign language he used to communicate.[14] In addition to Coffee, there were only two other members: a young widow, Paulina Perkins, and Mr. Dickins, who was "of Portuguese descent."

The little group held their meetings in various locations, including a log cabin near the mouth of the Wolf River where Coffee's flatboat had originally been tied, the schoolhouse on Court Square, and even in the dining room of the Blue Ruin tavern. By 1832, the congregation had grown to eleven. Marcus Winchester sold them a lot at the corner of Poplar and Second Streets where they constructed Memphis's first church building. Today, it is the location of Memphis First United Methodist Church.

A receipt for a newspaper subscription given to Coffee by Winchester is one of the first items of Memphis ephemera recorded. Written on the receipt is: "Rec'd (by the hands of Maj. M. B. Winchester, three dollars,) from E. Coffee for the Memphis Advocate for one year, commencing on the 10th of January, 1827."[15]

It is unknown if Coffee was still a subscriber in January 1859 when an article appeared in the Memphis newspaper about his arrest: "Elijah Coffee, who was the first preacher on the bluffs, was arrested yesterday for being drunk, and was locked up. He swore terribly, and wanted to fight the officers."[16]

It wasn't long before a Catholic church was established in Memphis. Irish immigrant Eugene Magevney arrived in the city in 1833 by way of Philadelphia and took a teaching position at the school on Court Square. As early Memphis journalist John Hutchison wrote nearly a century ago:

> In a gumlog cabin that stood for many years in what is now Court Square, the stern son of the Ould Sod held forth from his great chair. . . . In a drawer under the hard seat of that chair he kept his foolscap and quills. On the broad desk arm he rested his book as he taught those early Memphis moppets their letters.[17]

To one of his former students, the school seemed like it was "a mile out of town." The student also recalled, "He was an excellent teacher but a terror, as he should have been, to us rude boys."[18] While educating the rude boys of Memphis was important, Magevney soon realized land speculation was more lucrative, and he eventually became quite wealthy.

In 1838, Magevney purchased the home at 198 Adams, where he had been boarding with the Manning family. The home had been built around 1836 by John M. Manning. While it originally consisted of four rooms and a downstairs hall, Magevney expanded the house and used it as both his home and a private school. It was the site of the city's first Catholic Mass in 1839. Magevney also played a crucial role in the establishment of the city's first Catholic church, St. Peter's, and was instrumental in the establishment of Memphis's first public schools. Today, Eugene Magevney's home still stands and is recognized as the oldest surviving house in Memphis. And safely archived in the collection of Memphis's Pink Palace Museum and Mansion is that old chair Magevney used in the "gumlog cabin" on Court Square.

As the town grew, it was obvious to Marcus Winchester a newspaper was an important next step. He included his plans in a letter to Overton dated January 15, 1826. He wrote, "Mr. Lawrence has informed you of the plan we have in contemplation for the establishment of a Press here." In addition to himself, Winchester proposed that John Overton, James Winchester, John C. Mclemore, William Winchester, George Winchester, Anderson B. Carr, and William Lawrence each invest $100 to purchase a press suitable to produce a small newspaper.[19] Marcus Winchester achieved his goal, and by the end of that year, *The Memphis Advocate and Western District Intelligencer*, published by Thomas Phoebus, began rolling off the press.

In the October 1832 issue of the paper, a notice was published that W. B. McClellan and H. G. Kearney would be publishing "another newspaper in the town of Memphis," named the *Memphis Advocate* because, "it is one which is associated with the early history and prosperity of the now flourishing town in which we are located." They also noted, "we cannot but hope that former friends of that paper will extend a moiety of their patronage to us, so long as we endeavor sedulously to avoid any of the errors into which its former editor may have inadvertently fallen."[20] Most of the earliest issues of Memphis newspapers are lost, so exactly what those errors were and which editor fell into them is unknown.

Other newspapers would soon follow. Early in 1832, T. Woods & Co. began printing a weekly publication, *The Western Times and Memphis Commercial Advertiser*, and *The Memphis Gazette* was begun in 1834 by P. G. Gaines. In January 1839, Dr. Solon Borlon began printing the first issues of the *Western World and Memphis Banner of the Constitution* that was later purchased by Van Pelt.

In the early years of American journalism, newspapers were unapologetically partisan, serving as the mouthpieces for political factions rather than striving for impartiality. Editors openly aligned themselves with political parties, and filled their pages with articles, essays, and even "news" stories crafted to advance their side's policies and attack the opposition.

For example, John Overton wrote and asked Marcus Winchester to encourage Memphis residents to subscribe to a new newspaper that supported Andrew Jackson titled the *Nashville Globe* and to have Phoebus reprint articles from it in the *Memphis Advocate*. Overton had heard rumors that, as the town grew, some residents were beginning to oppose Jackson. Letters between the two show Overton had also begun to suspect Winchester was not as loyal to the Jacksonian cause as he claimed to be. He asked Winchester if it was true that a newspaper supporting Henry Clay was being started in Memphis and stressed such a move would be seen as a serious betrayal. In response, Winchester assured his mentor he knew of no such plans.

In addition to politics, the *Memphis Advocate* also covered some social topics and business news of the day:

> A reasonable portion of our paper shall be devoted to the cause of Religion, Education Literature, and the Fine Arts. The various improvements in the various branches of Agriculture and Manufacturers will be particularly observed and published; and it should be our particular care, that our readers are kept well appraised of every change in the New Orleans and other Markets.[21]

As people and presses moved west, so did politics and propaganda. In the article announcing the *Memphis Advocate*, McClellan or Kearney wrote:

> We are decidedly in favor of the re-election of Andrew Jackson as president of the United States, and we are as decidedly opposed to the system of protecting Manufacturing at the expense of Agricultural interests of our country; We are opposed to the assumption of a right, in the general government to carry on a system of Internal Improvements by means of protecting taxation; we are in favor of a general and early sale of the public lands; we are opposed to "Nullification" in its every grade and every hue ...[22]

In the early nineteenth century, as pioneers were settling the frontier, nullification—the idea that a state had the right to declare a federal law null and void if they considered it unconstitutional—became a major issue. The Tariff of 1828, known by those who opposed it as "The Tariff of Abominations," was bad for the Southern agricultural economy while benefiting those states with manufacturing and industrial interests.

In response, Vice President John C. Calhoun of South Carolina anonymously authored a document called *The South Carolina Exposition and Protest*, arguing that states had the right to nullify federal laws they deemed unconstitutional. This debate over state sovereignty culminated in the Nullification Crisis, which reached its peak during Andrew Jackson's presidency. By 1830, this states' rights position was increasingly used to resist abolitionist efforts and potential federal restrictions on slavery.

On April 13, 1830, Jackson stood to make a toast at the annual Democratic Jefferson Day dinner. Little did those in the audience know that he was about to make news and create an often-repeated quote in the days leading up to the Civil War thirty years later. Jackson raised his glass and included in his toast the words, "Our Federal Union, it must be preserved!" It was a rebuke of Calhoun and was later inscribed at the base of Clark Mills' equestrian statue of the Jackson in the center of Lafayette Square in Washington, D.C.

Increasingly, farmers and their families arrived to take advantage of the farmland east of the bluff. William and Sarah Patterson Bettis, along with several of their extended family members, were among the first. Included in the group was their son, Tillman "Till," and his wife, Sally, as well as their sons, John and James. Sarah's brother, Drury Patterson, and his son also joined the group. They were headed to Texas from South Carolina and stopped in Memphis for supplies. They learned about the opportunity to acquire large amounts of inexpensive farmland, so some members of the family stayed while others continued their journey to Texas. According to tradition, Till and Sally's fifth child, Mary Jane, was the first White child born in Memphis. Till Bettis was active in county government for many years.

As James Davis, who was a close, personal friend of Bettis, remembered, "Till was rather on the free and easy order, fond of his glass, his friends and a good joke; took the world easy and seemed to care but little about the opinions of others."[23] The Bettis family farmed a large tract of land in today's Midtown Memphis, framed by Poplar to Union Avenues and McNeil to Cooper Streets. Their small family cemetery—one of the oldest in Shelby County today—can be found next door to the chain grocery store in Memphis between Avalon and Angelus Streets.

Members of the Bettis family, along with other early Memphians, can be found on an important historical document discovered in the early 1980s. While cataloging old papers at the Tennessee State Library and Archives, Memphis historian Annice Boulton made a significant discovery.

Tucked away in a long-overlooked file of legal documents was a petition signed by many of Memphis's earliest residents. The petition, addressed to the state legislature, called for the formation of a new county—an appeal that would shape the region's future. Not surprisingly, this was not an idea they came up with on their own.

John Overton and James Winchester knew the lots they had for sale in Memphis would be made more valuable if they could get the legislature to approve the formation of a county, and Memphis could be designated as the county seat. In July 1819, Overton drafted a petition and sent it to James Winchester for his approval. Winchester made a few changes and mailed it to Anderson B. Carr to circulate among the inhabitants of the bluff to sign.

Glancing down the list of more than seventy signatures on the petition, in addition to the Bettis family, one sees the signatures of Marcus Winchester, William Lawrence, Anderson B. Carr, George Winchester, Joab Bean, and Paddy Meagher, along with many others.

Thanks to the petition—and Overton's powers of persuasion at the state capital—the Tennessee state legislature voted in November 1819 to establish Shelby County and name it after Isaac Shelby, to honor him for his contribution to the Treaty of 1818. The Tennesseans surely lamented they could not honor Andrew Jackson instead of a Kentuckian, but there had already been a Jackson County in Tennessee for nearly twenty years.

The new county needed someone from the state to work out of Memphis, so Jacob Tipton was sent in May 1820. Tipton had served as an ensign in the War of 1812, was surveyor general of the eleventh district of Tennessee, and had been a clerk for the House of Representatives in the Tennessee General Assembly. One of his first actions was the swearing in of Marcus Winchester, William Irwin, Thomas D. Carter, and Benjamin Willis as justices of the peace. The next day, they appointed William Lawrence as county clerk, Samuel Brown as sheriff, Thomas Taylor as registrar, William A. Davis as trustee, William Bettis and William Dean as constables, and John Perkins as solicitor.

Many of the settlers who arrived in Memphis in the early years were single, but Tipton arrived with his wife, Lorina Taylor Tipton, and young son, Landon. Lorina was a daughter of Nathaniel Taylor, an early Tennessee settler and land owner who served as a brigadier general under Andrew Jackson in the War of 1812. After her father's unexpected death in 1816, Lorina's mother, Mary Patton Taylor, completed the large home that had been under construction in Elizabethtown, Tennessee when her husband died. She named the plantation Sabine Hill and led the family in growing their businesses that included a grist mill, saw mill, iron works, and several large farms. Some of Lorina's siblings migrated with her and Jacob to West Tennessee, where they settled on land granted to them for their father's military service.

In 1821, a meeting was held at the home of William Lawrence, where Thomas Carr was authorized, and $175 was appropriated to construct the first county courthouse, jury room, and jail at the northeast corner of Main and Winchester Streets. However, the following May, it was Marcus Winchester who presented the invoice for fifty dollars for costs on the courthouse project. In that meeting, "William A. Davis & M. B. Winchester Esquires" were approved to spend 125 dollars to build a jail."[24]

It was a sign of things to come for Winchester when another of the first items of county business involved Paddy Meagher. Meagher had, for many years, sold wood, whiskey, tobacco, groceries, and sometimes room and board out of his tavern above Meagher's Landing. It was only natural that as business in the area grew, he would want to take full advantage of the settlers' taste for whiskey and the increasing number of visitors stopping in Memphis seeking a place to eat and drink. In compliance with the new law, Meagher applied for a license to run a tavern. While his application for the tavern was approved, he did not have the $1,250 needed to post a bond, so his request to serve alcohol was denied. One can imagine his great frustration at having been in business for a decade only to be denied by these new county restrictions. The amount, which seems excessive for that time, is especially suspicious when you learn Thomas Carr had been given lots forty-five and forty-six—directly across Water Street from Meagher's tavern—to build a new tavern on behalf of the proprietors.

Meagher ignored the new rules and continued selling whiskey as he had done for years. By the end of that summer, charges from the grand jury were brought against him. *The State of Tennessee v. Meagher* is a great example of what was to come as Winchester attempted to serve the state, the proprietors, and the residents of Memphis. Meagher pled guilty and was charged a one dollar fine. To solve the problem, Marcus Winchester and Thomas Carr chipped in and paid the bond themselves so Meagher could legally operate his tavern and sell as much whiskey as he liked. Less than two years later, Thomas Carr gave up the two lots on which he was supposed to build a tavern for the proprietors and purchased Meagher's lot from him. The Bell Tavern was constructed there in 1826, and Meagher was hired as proprietor. Tradition says the name came from a fifty-pound iron bell Meagher attached to a post at the entrance. It was just wood and nails, but it was a building that, in the years to come, would represent the heart of early Memphis. When it was finally torn down in 1915, a writer for *The Commercial Appeal* reported:

> It was a quaint old structure, built of odds and ends of lumber, nailed to cedar posts stuck in the ground. Hand-made nails were used in applying the weatherboarding, but the framing was put together with wooden pins . . . the material for the old tavern

was probably carried up the bluffs from the river, the timbers having had every appearance that they were at one time portions of flatboats. Bullet holes studded the posts. The stories they might have told were buried with those who knew them.[25]

Another of the county court's first actions was to commission William Lawrence to survey the county. After three years and a cost of $142.50, he declared Shelby County officially spanned 625 square miles. Those who owned a portion of it were going to have to pay. To fund county services, the court implemented a property tax in 1820, set at 6¼ cents per one hundred acres of land. These funds supported programs to help the poor by providing food, shelter, and burial services. During its first session, the court granted various licenses, including one for a ferry, and took measures to protect the population from wildlife such as wolves, which were still plentiful in both town and countryside. Their numbers declined after the court set a bounty of three dollars for each wolf pelt.

Early settlers also hunted to survive. In a public address in 1874, William B. Waldron, who arrived in Memphis in 1825 as young boy, shared that many of the families on the bluff were so poor, "they had to subdue the forest and bring it into cultivation before they had the promise of bread." He added, "The killing of bear, deer and turkeys saved many a family from suffering."[26]

Of course, West Tennessee's congressman and self-proclaimed King of the Wild Frontier, David Crockett, built a whole personal brand out of killing bear, but unlike the theme song, it was long after he was three. He noted in his autobiography that in 1825-26, he had an especially successful year hunting bear: "As soon as the time come for them to quit their houses and come out again in the spring, I took a notion to hunt a little more, and in about one month I killed forty-seven more, which made one hundred and five bears I had killed in less than one year from that time."[27]

Bear and other wild animals were seen less around Memphis as settlers moved in, bringing with them the hustle and bustle of a big city. However, they did make an appearance from time to time. When he was an old man and the lone survivor of the first generation of Memphians, Joseph Rawlings wrote about the Sunday morning in 1825 when a bear showed up in Memphis and created terror as it made its way up the center of town. He wrote, "I heard a fuss and jumped up and ran out and found every boy, black and white, and every fice and pug nose dog in town were at his heels hooping and hallowing."[28] Unfortunately, the story Rawlings told did not have a happy ending for Paddy Meagher's bulldogs or the bear.

By the end of the 1820s, Memphis was a very different place than it had been a decade earlier. A Memphis resident or visitor to town who picked up a copy of the February 23,1828, *Memphis Advocate and Western-District Intelligencer* would find a bit of local and national news, entertainment content, and ads for everything from medicine and land to enslaved men, women, and children, and farm equipment. That particular issue included a letter from David Crockett to his Shelby County constituency touting his vacant land bill, news of a treaty with the Creek nation for the purchase of the final strip of land they claimed ownership of in Georgia, and details of a dinner given in Bowling Green, Kentucky in honor of James Pitts. He was the first to navigate the Green and Barren Rivers in a steamboat.

Businesses opened and closed; some failed quickly while others would be around to serve the next generation of Memphians. Anderson B. Carr and D. W. Woods announced a new mercantile named Carr & Wood that had just opened on Winchester Street next door to Nathaniel Anderson's new hotel at Winchester and Main Streets. They had just received an assortment of staple and "fancy" goods that were for sale. Their ad noted, "The senior partner of the concern has been engaged in business in Memphis for the last eight years."

Nathaniel Anderson, hotel proprietor, ran his own ad that illustrates today what was important to the early nineteenth-century visitor to Memphis—a comfortable room, a stocked bar, and space set aside for horses to be fed:

> The Proprietor has the pleasure to apprize the public, that his establishment is at length in a situation to enable him to afford accommodations of the most comfortable kind. His chambers are fitted in superior style; his bar is well supplied with choice drink, and his stables, which are large and commodious, with provender and careful Hostlers.

On another page of the newspaper, Anderson let readers know he "likely had two or three negro men for sale, for cash." Alexander Pope was opening a dry goods store in the location previously occupied by F. A. & T. Young on Chickasaw Street, and J. Hatley advertised an auction with "Negroes for Sale." That auction would take place in Hardeman County, and one would be able to bid on "one negro man, one woman and two children" that were part of the estate of the late Major Lewis Dillahunty, who fought under Andrew Jackson in the War of 1812.

Had he been alive, Dillahunty, a substantial landowner, might have taken interest in the advertisement placed by William Lawrence. He was offering his services as a land agent and would handle taxes, attend to the division of land, record deeds, and for five percent of the price, handle land that was for sale. He included John Overton, John C. McLemore, Jacob Tipton, and Marcus Winchester as references.

In other ads, Memphians were offered Liverpool salt, superior old whiskey, Irish linens, and lots for sale in Memphis that were to be sold at auction. The proprietors' pitch may have raised eyebrows among a few of those who had already purchased Memphis lots that they learned were considered "inferior":

> So strong is the emigration to the Western District, of the State of Tennessee, and such the disposition to acquire property in this town, situated as it is, on a high and beautiful bank of the great river Mississippi, that the proprietors have thought proper for the encouragement of the settlement of the town and country, to offer for sale, the unsold lots in said town, which forms much the largest and handsomest part; with but few exceptions, it was only the inferior lots which have been sold at private sale.[29]

While many were glad to call it home, Memphis was certainly not for everyone. Whenever sales slowed and things got tough for those in the Memphis real estate market, the old timers were fond of telling the story of Hamp Angel, owner of a flatboat that frequently docked in Memphis. He was given the price of five dollars to purchase a piece of property on Front Row near Auction Street. He returned to his flatboat and remarked to the pilot, "I would not give $5 for the whole damned town."[30]

Reuben Davis knew the day he arrived, Memphis was not for him. After studying medicine with his brother-in-law in Hamilton, Mississippi, he was looking for a place to settle down. He thought perhaps the new town on the Mississippi River he had been hearing about might be a nice place for a young doctor to open a new practice:

> After several days' journey on horseback, I reached Memphis late one summer afternoon. It was a small town—ugly, dirty, and sickly. While supper was being prepared for me at the tavern, I walked through the miserable streets and out upon the banks of the river. I shall never forget the dreariness of that night, nor the despondency into which I fell when I tried to bring myself to consider this as my future home. I passed much of the night in reflection and became convinced that I could not maintain myself there. Everything pointed to the certainty that, in a short time, this squalid village must grow to be a great and wealthy city, but I had no confidence in my destiny as one of the builders of it. For

many years, the population would be rough and lawless, and the locality and sanitary conditions of the town promised that disease and death would hold carnival there.[31]

Davis eventually found success becoming a prominent lawyer, politician, and military figure—in Mississippi.

Through all the activity of new men and women arriving to town, log cabins being torn down and wood frame and brick buildings going up, Marcus Winchester stood watch. After the unofficial postmaster, Thomas Stewart, died in 1823, Winchester began running an official mail service out of his store. He accepted the position of "the first official postmaster of Memphis" and served in that role for the next twenty-six years. One writer captured what Winchester's days may have been like around that time:

> What was it like to be postmaster in a town the size of Memphis in the early days? For a moment, if you will, picture Marcus Winchester in his general store, swapping hats among his various jobs from justice of the peace to postmaster. Supplies from New Orleans are arriving today on the river. The stage from Jackson is expected and the mail must be sorted and placed into pouches. A trader arrives and wants to cash in two Kentucky paper banknotes. Marcus has to make the proper discounts on the money. Children are playing in the street in front of the store. New settlers, hearing about the newly created town of Memphis, arrive almost daily and seek provisions at Winchester's store. News is brought by these settlers from Nashville, Louisville, and points east. The land across the Mississippi River is still a territory. Reelfoot Lake is but 25 years old. History is being made here.[32]

As seriously as Winchester took his work, any researcher reading his correspondence can attest that his handwriting was nearly illegible, and it got worse as he aged. At one point, the postmaster general of the United States wrote to Winchester that his letters gave him more trouble to read than all the others he received combined. He concluded, "writing is designed to communicate our ideas and should be readable."[33] That was a concept Marcus Winchester never seemed to have grasped.

One would never know from his handwriting the importance Winchester seemed to place on how he presented himself publicly. One writer described him as a "singularly handsome man, of winning manners, polished address and rather foppish in dress."³⁴ At that time, the word foppish was used to describe someone who was "excessively refined and fastidious in taste and manner." That certainly caused Winchester to stand out from the rest of the men on the bluff in those early years. He also stood out from the others because he was a representative of the proprietors—not always a good thing for "they were not in good odor with the townsfolk."³⁵ The same writer who described Winchester's style as foppish also noted Winchester's difficult position:

> He was a man of undoubted ability and proved himself equal to the demands of his office in such a way that, though handicapped by his connection with the proprietors, he in time came to be so trusted by the rank and file of the people that they would not receive paper money until he had passed judgment on it and pronounced it good.³⁶

The exchange of money for goods and services was a challenge in the early years. Joseph Rawlings noted the exchange of goods for payment was a combination of trade and "cut money." He wrote, "We cut a dollar into four pieces for quarters, a half into four pieces for bits, as they were called, and a quarter into four pieces for picayunes."³⁷

One settler who worked in an early Memphis mercantile remembered that credit was easy to get, and most Memphians usually paid their bills on time. Although, once Texas opened up for settlement, he noted it became safer to only offer credit to married men because, "their wheels were locked down."³⁸ Single men were more likely to run their credit up and leave for Texas without paying.

Marcus Winchester's wheels were very much locked down, and his work had unique challenges that only he experienced when trying to keep the peace between the proprietors and the residents of Memphis. An example of the frustration the rest of the town had with the proprietors came from the very thing everyone most counted on for success—the river. After one of John Overton's visits to Memphis, he was angered when he discovered a street had been cut across the promenade to give the residents easier access to the river. In January 1828, he wrote to Lawrence and Winchester, "A certain quantity of ground, well-defined and laid down in the plan of said town, was set apart for a promenade. . . . It was with no small degree of regret that on my landing on the bank at Memphis . . . it was perceived that a public street had been deeply cut through this same promenade without the consent of the owners of the soil, who set apart this same piece of ground for a special purpose and for none other."³⁹

The proprietors' frustrations with the residents of the town had begun almost immediately. James Winchester, not one to acquiesce to the demands of anyone, quickly tired of their requests, as he shared in August 1820 with John Overton. "The people of Memphis have taken it into their heads that they're settling there is to make the proprietors immensely rich and that enough cannot be done for them." He added sarcastically, "If we were to give them all lots, they would then want us to build for them houses, and next to boil for them their coffee."[40]

Marcus Winchester was different from his father when it came to dealing with the working-class residents of Memphis. He was, by then, one of them. While the Kentucky soldiers who had served under James Winchester viewed him as arrogant and "having the appearance of a supercilious officer," Marcus possessed a natural charisma and was well-liked by the early settlers, even as he served as a mediator between them and the proprietors. As one of Memphis's first settlers later recalled, Marcus had a heated exchange over "a matter long forgotten now":

> Maj. Anderson became irritated to an unusual degree, and in his frank manly, impetuous way, blurted out his indignation at what he supposed at the moment was Maj. Winchester's indisposition to deal fairly: 'Maj. Winchester, if you insist on that you are a rascal sir.' Winchester rose to his feet, with that courtly dignity for which he was so distinguished, and with perfectly unruffled temper, bowing as only a Chesterfield could have bowed, and responded, 'I am very sorry, Anderson, that you could possibly think so.' Troubled at once by a sense of injustice, Anderson replied, 'Stop Winchester, damned if I do think so—I was wrong.'[41]

Meanwhile, John Overton was busy in Murfreesboro—the capitol of Tennessee from 1818 to 1826—fighting hard to keep the seat of Shelby County in Memphis. In his estimation, this would determine the future of the county—and the value of his investment. An opposing group was working equally hard to have that designation moved to the nearby town of Sanderlin's Bluff, eleven miles northeast of Memphis on the Wolf River. Overton wrote to James Winchester:

> Those wishing to take the courthouse away (which will be its ruin) are numerous and active . . . without immediate prompt attention and action we are to be put down. . . . Should Memphis be put back in that way it may never survive so fatal a blow. . . . This business is the most arduous I was ever engaged in.[42]

His intense lobbying was to no avail. Despite six visits to the state legislature to campaign in favor of leaving the business of the county in Memphis, in December 1824, Sanderlin's Bluff was selected as the seat of Shelby County. The town's name was changed to Raleigh by Joseph Graham, the first Circuit Court Clerk, in honor of his hometown of Raleigh, North Carolina.

It is impossible to know the impact moving the county seat had on Memphis. It certainly drew some business away but was ultimately not the fatal blow Overton feared. Isaac Rawlings loaned his nephew, Joseph, three thousand dollars' worth of merchandise and sent him to Raleigh to set up a mercantile there. Rawlings later wrote, "Raleigh at that time was a good place for a new-beginner, good society and honest people, pretty girls and accomplished young men. I had some happy times there."[43] Happy times aside, Rawlings was grateful to return to Memphis in 1847. He later worked for a number of early Memphis businesses including the Desoto Insurance Company, Union and Planters Bank, the New Orleans Steam Packet Company, and the Cotton Exchange.

Not until 1868 did the seat of Shelby County move back to Memphis from Raleigh. Had he been alive then, John Overton would have no doubt smiled as he read an article about Raleigh in the August 5, 1894, issue of *The Commercial Appeal*, more than sixty years after his death. The headline alone would have caught his eye: "Memphis had a Rival Then." He then would have read:

> People who visit the springs, if only for a few hours through the day, could not spend a portion of the time to better advantage than by walking through this ancient village. They will find many ruins to interest them. They will see the crumbling remains of the old brick jail, built half a century ago. The 'oldest inhabitant' will point out where the courthouse used to stand, but that historic building has been so long removed that trees as large around as a man's body have grown up on the spot.[44]

Chapter Thirteen Endnotes

1. G. Wayne Dowdy, *Enslavement in Memphis* (United States: History Press, 2021), 15.
2. Walter Durham, *James Winchester: Tennessee Pioneer* (Gallatin: Sumner County Library Board, 1979), 224.
3. James E. Roper, "Marcus B. Winchester, First Mayor of Memphis," *Tennessee Historical Quarterly* 18, no. 1 (1959): 7.
4. William Henry Hoyt, *The Papers of Archibald D. Murphey* (Raleigh: E. M. Uzzell & Co., State Printers, 1914), 313.
5. Hoyt, *Papers of Archibald D. Murphey*, 313.
6. Hoyt, *Papers of Archibald D. Murphey*, 314.
7. Hoyt, *Papers of Archibald D. Murphey*, 315.
8. Quincy K. Underwood, "Address of Judge Q. K. Underwood," *Old Folks Record*, no. 12 (September 1875): 531–32.
9. Frances Trollope, *Domestic Manners of the Americans* (New York: Alfred A. Knopf, 1949), 25.
10. "Indians Got Drunk," *Commercial Appeal*, December 25, 1898, 10.
11. Ebenezer Carter Tracy, *Memoir of the Life of Jeremiah Evarts* (Boston: Crocker and Brewster, 1845), 238.
12. Tracy, *Memoir of the Life of Jeremiah Evarts*, 238.
13. Perre Magness, "Methodists Helped Tame Rivertown," *Commercial Appeal*, November 22, 1992, E2.
14. Dowdy, *Enslavement*, 9.
15. "A Relic of the Olden Time," *The Memphis Daily Avalanche*, April 29, 1859, 3.
16. "Minister Has Troubles," *The Commercial Appeal*, December 9, 1926, 172.
17. John Hutchison, "Building Was There When Megeveny Came," *The Commercial Appeal*, January 8, 1939, 41.
18. "Address of Judge Q. K. Underwood," *Old Folks Record*, no. 12 (September 1875): 532.
19. *Old Folks Record, no. 12 (September 1875): 533–534.*
20. "Proposals for Publishing in Memphis, Tennessee," *Memphis Advocate and Western District Intelligencer*, October 30, 1832, 4.
21. "Proposals," *Memphis Advocate*, 4.
22. "Proposals," *Memphis Advocate*, 4.
23. Davis, *History of Memphis*, 304.
24. Roper, "Winchester and the Earliest Years," 338.
25. George L. Fossick, "The Old Bell Tavern," *Commercial Appeal*, November 28, 1915, 64.
26. William B. Waldran, "Anniversary Address," *Old Folks Record* 1 (December 1874): 102.
27. David Crockett, *A Narrative of the Life of David Crockett, of the State of Tennessee* (Philadelphia: E.L. Carey and A. Hart, 1834), 195.
28. Rawlings, "Miscellaneous Writings," 26.
29. "Lots in Memphis," *Memphis Advocate and Western-District Intelligencer*, February 23, 1828, 4.
30. Joe Curtis, "Memphis Wharfage Fee Fight Was Long and Hard Battle, Finally Won by Tobias Wolfe," *Commercial Appeal*, October 19, 1941, 17.
31. Reuben Davis, *Recollections of Mississippi and Mississippians* (Boston and New York: Houghton, Mifflin and Company, 1889), 24.
32. Captain Henry A. Hudson Jr., USNR, "Marcus Winchester and Early Memphis Postal History," *Ansearchin' News* (Winter 1997): 22.
33. Post Office Department, *Letters Sent*, Book 0-2 (August 13, 1845), 458.
34. "Great City Now Stands on Chickasaw Bluffs," *Tennessean*, July 26, 1910, 156.
35. John M. Keating, *History of Memphis, Tennessee* (Syracuse, NY: D. Mason & Co., 1888), 121.
36. Great City Now Stands on Chickasaw Bluffs," *Tennessean*, July 26, 1910, 156.
37. J. J. Rawlings, Miscellaneous Writings and Reminiscences of J. J. Rawlings (Memphis: United Charities, 1896), 3.
38. W. Waldran, "Anniversary Address," 102.

39. Overton to Winchester, January 21, 1828, *James Winchester Correspondence*, Archives Division, Tennessee State Library and Archives.
40. Durham, *James Winchester*, 222.
41. "Old Folks at Home," *Memphis Daily Appeal* (Memphis, TN), July 26, 1867, 3.
42. John Hibbert De Witt, "General James Winchester," *Tennessee Historical Magazine* (Nashville: The Society, 1915), 200–202.
43. Joseph J. Rawlings, *Miscellaneous Writings and Reminiscences of J. J. Rawlings* (Memphis: Self-published), 11.
44. "Memphis Had a Rival Then," *Commercial Appeal*, August 5, 1894, 16,

J. C. DOUGHERTY,

EAST SIDE OF MAIN STREET, BET. MADISON AND MONROE
MEMPHIS, TENN., Dealer in

Fancy and Staple Dry-Goods,

AND MERCHANDISE GENERALLY;

Keeps constantly on hand a supply of

Ready-made Clothing, Boots, Shoes, Hats, Caps

Will offer extraordinary inducements to Cash buyers.

☞ CALL AND SEE! ☜

F. LANE.   NEWTON FORD.   A. C. TREADWELL.

F. LANE & CO.,

COTTON FACTORS

—AND—

Commission Merchants,

NO. 2, SOUTH SIDE OF UNION STREET,

MEMPHIS, TENN.

SCHNEIDER & GLASSICK,

GUNSMITHS

AND GENERAL REPAIRER,

No. 20, Jefferson Street, opposite Commercial Hotel,
MEMPHIS, TENN.

We ask the patronage of citizens and those visiting Memphis. We warrant all of our work, and our long experience in the business, will enable us to make or repair guns and other fire arms in a superior and workman-like manner.

NEW DRY-GOODS HOUSE.

Wm. WASH.   J. C. BAKER.

WASH & BAKER,

DEALERS IN

STAPLE AND FANCY DRY GOODS,

Fowlkes' old stand, opposite U. S. Hotel,

182 Main Street, Memphis.

From Rainey's Memphis City Directory, 1855/56

Chapter Fourteen: Memphis Bound Blues

*Marcus Winchester befriends Isaac Rawlings,
David Crockett, and Frances Wright*

In the 1820s, three individuals entered the lives of Marcus and Amarante Loiselle Winchester who would go on to play major roles in shaping their world: Isaac Rawlings, David Crockett, and Frances Wright. Each represented a distinct facet of Marcus Winchester's evolving relationship with Memphis—Rawlings symbolized business, Crockett embodied politics, and Wright reflected Winchester's growing engagement with social reform.

Isaac "Old Ike" Rawlings Jr. returned to Memphis in February 1821 at age thirty-two—already middle-aged at that time. As a government factor, he had been an employee of the United States. He had bought, sold, and traded merchandise with the Native Americans but, as a salaried employee, was forbidden from participating in any type of commercial enterprise from which he would personally benefit. With years of frontier retail experience and seeing potential in Memphis, he opened his own mercantile, and this time, he was able to keep any profit for himself. For his customer base, Rawlings first targeted those he knew best, the Native Americans who still came to Memphis to trade at that time. They frequently camped by a stream that was located near the present-day campus of St. Jude Children's Research Hospital.

Rawlings hired Jack Meazels, a "half-breed Cherokee" who spoke English, Choctaw, and Chickasaw, to work in the store. One early Memphian remembered, "the Indians came in caravans, with their ponies well packed with cow-hides, deer skins, beaver, bear and otter, and an innumerable quantity of coon-skins, which were exchanged for blankets, striped domestics, tobacco, whiskey, &c."[1]

By 1824, Rawlings's store had become so successful that he sent for his sixteen-year-old nephew, Joseph J. Rawlings, who was living in Maryland. Joseph, the young son of Rawlings's brother, Thomas, quickly adapted to frontier life on the bluff and, with the help of Meazels, even learned to conduct business with the Chickasaw in their own language. Unfortunately, after teaching Rawlings enough of the language to be able take care of business behind the counter, Meazels found himself out of a job.

The first meeting of Isaac Rawlings and Marcus Winchester was not documented, but we know at least a bit about their friendship because James Davis shared his memories of the two men in *The Memphis Daily* in 1871:

> When I first became acquainted with Winchester, I thought him the handsomest man I ever saw. In addition to his fine appearances, his manners were those of a Chesterfield. He was prepossessing and popular. In politics he was a strong Democrat; in religion he was skeptical, and might be called a non-believer. He never attended church. Isaac Rawlings was low in stature. Nothing pre-possessing about him. He had an impediment in his speech but a fine head and a very intellectual countenance. He was as strong, an old line Whig as Winchester was a Democrat. They were good friends; had frequent political controversies, but it never interrupted their kind personal relations. Unlike Winchester the old man was very piously inclined—a thorough Episcopalian in sentiment . . . and attended divine service at his church whenever his rheumatics would admit.[2]

The term "Chesterfield" Davis used when writing of Winchester originated with Philip Stanhope, the 4th Earl of Chesterfield. He was an English statesman who wrote letters to his son emphasizing politeness, tact, and good manners. In Davis's time, the word "Chesterfield" had become synonymous with a true gentleman who displayed polish, formal etiquette, and charm.

Both Rawlings and Winchester came from similar backgrounds, had relatives in Maryland, and were both running mercantile businesses while simultaneously investing in as much land as they could grab. Winchester would be the first county mayor, but Rawlings was right behind him, serving as the second. There would be many occasions when they relied on each other to ensure the success of the city they shared and from which they both stood to benefit. For thirty-five years, the two men served side-by-side on committees, in city and county leadership, and working together to make Memphis a town thousands of others would choose to make home. They may have been united in objective, but they were not always in agreement regarding strategy.

Nineteenth-century lawyer and Tennessee politician James Phelan argued

Rawlings and Winchester represented "two opposing tendencies." He remembered Rawlings being blunt, suspicious of innovation, and well satisfied with the order of things—unless they were working to his disadvantage. Phelan believed Winchester, on the other hand, had a quick mind, clear judgement, and a spirit of restless inquiry. Of their politics, he wrote, "Rawlings was conservative; Winchester was liberal, Rawlings was a Whig and Winchester a Democrat."[3]

One early disagreement between the two was on the topic of the incorporation of Memphis, something Winchester and the proprietors had been pushing for at the state capital, apparently without keeping others in Memphis informed. Incorporation was a significant milestone for small towns, and Overton believed it was crucial for growth. Incorporation offered a number of benefits including the ability to self-govern, manage resources, and plan for future expansion.

After a local government was put into place, the city leaders could pass laws, levy taxes, and make decisions at the city level rather than relying on state authorities for day-to-day governance. For the proprietors, it also meant the small community that was developing on the bluff would grow more quickly, generating more sales. People were more likely to settle down and live in a town that had a local government, enforcement of established laws, and public services. They were also more likely to open and run a business in a community where there was an infrastructure and a stable customer base on which they could count.

The Tennessee state legislature approved the incorporation of Memphis on December 9, 1826. The news caught many in Memphis, including Isaac Rawlings, by surprise and generated frustration that was directed at Marcus Winchester and the proprietors. Historian John Preston Young recounted the town meeting that was subsequently called by Rawlings:

> Isaac Rawlings was made chairman of this meeting and he made a speech against the new act announcing it as "a trick of the proprietors." He held that the small community could not support a city government; that it must grow in population and wealth before such an act could be considered. He said that it would be an advantage only to the proprietors and well-to-do class, while the poor on the outskirts of the proposed town would suffer hardships thereby. Speakers on the other side put forward the advantages of a corporation and offered to leave out the poor 'on the outskirts' to satisfy Mr. Rawlings and his partisans.[4]

The incorporation moved forward. Election of aldermen in Memphis took place, and those elected were Marcus Winchester, Joseph L. Davis, John Hook, N. B. Atwood, George F. Graham, John R. Dougherty, and William D. Neely.

The aldermen elected Marcus Winchester as the city's first mayor. Memphis didn't have a mayor elected by the citizens until the city was rechartered in 1895 after the yellow fever epidemic.

Before Winchester's second term as mayor, the city charter added a provision that the city mayor could not also hold a federal position—like postmaster. Winchester chose to withdraw his name from consideration for mayor so he could continue serving as postmaster, a paying job he had come to enjoy—and that provided an annual salary and more prestige than that of mayor. The position of mayor would remain an unpaid role until Mayor William Spickernagle received an annual salary of five hundred dollars in 1841. After Winchester, Rawlings was elected mayor, serving five one-year terms with a break after he lost the election of 1831.

That election was won by twenty-three-year-old lawyer Seth Wheatley, who—according to local lore—managed to turn a group of voters living in shacks along Catfish Bay against Rawlings, thereby influencing the aldermen's vote that year. Catfish Bay was a poor community at the mouth of Bayou Gayoso, on the outskirts of town, that later became known as the Pinch. Supposedly, in retaliation for their campaign against Rawlings, a local tannery dumped rotting animal carcasses into the bayou.

Rawlings won the election the following year, but Wheatley went down in history as Memphis's youngest mayor. He later became the president of Farmers' and Merchants' Bank and built a home on Adams Street where he hosted many parties and events. According to the writer of an 1874 biographical sketch, Wheatley "was not brilliant, but of sound, practical, good sense, and by steady, patient toil, and rigid economy, gathered wealth."[5]

James Phelan had much good to say about Rawlings's years as a public servant, noting he was long known as the model mayor.

> Rawlings was vain, stubborn, self-willed, and imperious, impatient of contradiction and conservative to a fault. But he was also honest, clear-minded, law abiding, determined to be obeyed, and economical. He took the duties of his position in earnest rigorously enforced the law, preserved order, looked after the disbursement of the public funds with scrupulous care, and was remarkably energetic.[6]

David Crockett also showed up in Memphis around this time. After three sessions in the Tennessee state legislature, his career in state politics ended in October 1824. He declined to run again and set his sights on a seat in the U.S.

House of Representatives. Crockett returned home to Northwest Tennessee to determine his next steps.

He was content to be back in the woods around his home in Northwest Tennessee hunting for bear once again, but the woods also gave him an idea of how he could raise some much-needed campaign funds for the next election.

Throughout the region were thick forests of old-growth trees that could be cut down and used in a variety of ways including being trimmed into the beveled staves used in the production of barrels. All types of goods around the country were stored and shipped in barrels, as they could be rolled down gangplanks of steamboats, keelboats, and flatboats, easily loaded onto wagons or pack animals, and then stored as long as needed to keep the contents protected. Used barrels could also be found throughout the country, sliced in half and used for all sorts of purposes from feeding animals to rocking babies to sleep.

Crockett hired a few men to cut cypress trees down on his property and trim them into staves, likely using a water-powered sawmill he had built there on the Obion River specifically for that purpose. The crew also got busy building two large keelboats on the edge of the river. The plan was simple: load the strips of cypress wood onto the boats and then sail down the Obion River, into the Mississippi River, and on down to New Orleans, where he would sell the staves and the boats for a nice profit. It was a good idea—on paper.

By the time the two boats were finished and ready for the trip, Crockett wrote the crew had produced thirty-thousand staves. Making their way down the smaller tributary was no problem, and the men Crockett had hired seemed to know what they were doing. But when they entered the much larger and more powerful Mississippi River, Crockett quickly discovered he had underestimated the current of the river and overestimated the abilities of his crew. Although they had planned to stop at one of the ports along the way, Crockett nor the others could regain control of the boats, so they had no other choice but to tie the two boats together, head down river, and hope for the best.

Shortly before they reached Memphis, the boats hit Paddy's Hen and Chickens at full speed and were destroyed. The only way out of the cabin of the keelboat for Crockett was through a small hole in the side of the sinking boat. With a bit of maneuvering, he was able to get his head and arms through the hole, but the rest of his body was stuck inside the shell that was quickly headed to the bottom of the river. Finally, at the last minute, some of the crew were able to pull him through. He was, as he described, "skinned like a rabbit," and what little clothes he had been wearing were torn off along with some of his skin. Naked and freezing, he waited there with the rest of the crew on a small section of their boat, now lodged in the mud. The following morning, they waved down a steamboat that took them to Memphis, where Crockett would meet Marcus

Winchester for the first time. James Davis wrote of the occasion:

> Winchester being among the first to witness his condition, taking an ocular measurement of his person, procured the necessary raiment, hastened down and soon afterward returned, supporting the unfortunate adventurer, whom he conducted to his resident. An hour or two later, he appeared at the store door in the finest suit of clothes, it was supposed he had ever worn. . . . Other persons were also liberal to the unfortunates in this affair, for those were liberal days and Crockett and his friends were toasted around to considerable extent; when, warmed up by the few imbibings, he became eloquent, told jokes and laughable stories…and it may be that the misfortune at the head of the Old hen was the starting point for his future importance and notoriety.[7]

Winchester was impressed after meeting Crockett, and the feeling was mutual. Memphis's first mayor even began contributing financially to Crockett's campaigns, but did so secretly because of the growing animosity between the future congressman and Andrew Jackson. Of his unplanned visit to Memphis, Crockett wrote, "Here I met with a friend, that I never can forget as long as I am able to go ahead at any thing; it was a Major Winchester, a merchant of that place: he let us all have hats, and shoes, and some little money to go upon, and so we all parted."[8]

Crockett biographer James Shackford believed it was Winchester to whom Crockett refers many times as a "good friend" who gave him money to fund at least one of his congressional campaigns. There are also other historical references to a close friendship between the two men, including a letter to Winchester from John Overton chastising him for "continued support" of Congressman Crockett.

The inability to control the Tennessee congressman had been a frustration to Overton and other supporters of Andrew Jackson for years. Crockett finally broke with Jackson once and for all when he voted against Jackson's Indian Removal Act of 1830, opposing it on moral grounds.

The act authorized the U.S. government to force the remaining Native American tribes to move west of the Mississippi River. Anticipating the suffering it would cause, Crockett condemned the law as "inhumane" and wrote that act would "bring shame and reproach on the American name."[9]

Its passage set in motion the removal of more than 60,000 Native Americans from Georgia, Tennessee, Alabama, North Carolina and Florida. Beginning in 1831, members of the Five Civilized Tribes—Cherokee, Chickasaw, Choctaw,

Creek and Seminole—were driven from their homelands in the southern interior of the United States, a region stretching from the Cumberland River in the north to the Mississippi Valley in the west.

Marcus Winchester personally witnessed Crockett's prediction come true as thousands of Choctaws arrived in Memphis via the road passing through Raleigh. One Memphian, who clearly did not grasp the gravity of the situation, wrote of seeing thousands of Native Americans camped along the river in Memphis during their journey west. He wrote, "'Twas the fall of the year, and every evening, when the Indian camp-fires were burning, hundreds of citizens would stroll down to see the Indians." He added, "[They] left thousands of dollars here in trade, as they were here for some weeks, and had just received cash for their lands. Red blankets, butcher knives, and frying pans were all sold out."[10]

Frenchmen Alexis de Tocqueville did comprehend the suffering of the Native Americans he saw in Memphis. He and Gustave de Beaumont traveled across the country in 1831 and 1832, studying American prisons on behalf of their home country. During that particularly harsh winter, they arrived in Memphis after a grueling stagecoach journey from Louisville with a short stop in Nashville. It was nearly Christmas, December 17, 1831, when the two finally arrived. Beaumont was especially disappointed with the town they found on the bluff and recorded in his journal, "What a letdown ... Nothing to see, neither people nor things."[11] The two had time to kill, so they hired a group of Cherokee to take them hunting in the old growth forest on the edge of town.

Later that week, Tocqueville wrote of seeing a large group of the first Native Americans forced to migrate west. Some, like this band of Choctaws, traveled through Memphis. Tocqueville's memory of the site and sound of the migrants stayed with him for the rest of his life:

> At the end of the year 1831, whilst I was on the left bank of the Mississippi at a place named by Europeans, Memphis, there arrived a numerous band of Choctaws (or Chactas, as they are called by the French in Louisiana). These savages had left their country, and were endeavoring to gain the right bank of the Mississippi, where they hoped to find an asylum which had been promised them by the American government. It was then the middle of winter, and the cold was unusually severe; the snow had frozen hard upon the ground, and the river was drifting huge masses of ice. The Indians had their families with them; and they brought in their train the wounded and sick, with children newly born, and old men upon the verge of death. They possessed neither

tents nor wagons, but only their arms and some provisions. I saw them embark to pass the mighty river, and never will that solemn spectacle fade from my remembrance. No cry, no sob was heard amongst the assembled crowd; all were silent. Their calamities were of ancient date, and they knew them to be irremediable. The Indians had all stepped into the bark which was to carry them across, but their dogs remained upon the bank. As soon as these animals perceived that their masters were finally leaving the shore, they set up a dismal howl, and, plunging all together into the icy waters of the Mississippi, they swam after the boat.[12]

Tocqueville also described the hopelessness of their situation:

It is impossible to conceive the extent of the sufferings which attend these forced emigrations. They are undertaken by a people already exhausted and reduced; and the countries to which the newcomers betake themselves are inhabited by other tribes which receive them with jealous hostility. Hunger is in the rear; war awaits them, and misery besets them on all sides.[13]

Around fourteen hundred Choctaws were ferried across the Mississippi River from Memphis in 1831 and 1832. During a removal in 1832, cholera was being spread from riverport to riverport by those traveling on steamboats. Many of the Native American emigrants died from the disease before ever making it to Memphis. Over the next decade, around sixty thousand Native Americans would make the dangerous journey from their homes in the southern states to resettle in Indian Territory. After the Choctaw, the Seminoles—based in present-day Florida—were forced to leave in 1832. The Creek removal occurred in 1834, followed by the Chickasaw in 1837 and the Cherokee in 1838.

The Chickasaw tribe, who had regarded West Tennessee as their hunting grounds prior to the 1818 treaty negotiated by Andrew Jackson, was among the last to migrate westward. Although their journey of hundreds of miles exposed them to severe hardships and the extremes of both heat and cold, they endured relatively less suffering compared to other tribes. This was partly due to their familiarity with the weather patterns along the first part of the route and the foresight of their leaders, who negotiated for departures during the most favorable travel months.

Unlike the Chickasaw, the leaders of the Cherokee Nation resisted resettlement. Afterall, they had played a crucial role in the Battle of Horseshoe Bend, aligning with Jackson and providing vital support. As a tribe, they had proven their loyalty to the United States. Through the years, many adapted well and lived lives similar to those of their White neighbors. They built homes, operated mills, grew and harvested corn, cotton, and other crops, and raised sheep and cattle.

The Cherokee had developed a written language and established schools for their children, with some even attending the nation's most prestigious colleges. They published their own weekly newspaper, *The Cherokee Phoenix*—the first Native American newspaper in the United States—and even adopted their own constitution. Some of the Cherokee were also enslavers. By 1809, there were six hundred enslaved men, women, and children living in the Cherokee Nation, and by 1835, that number had increased to sixteen hundred.

The Cherokee had long held treaties with the United States affirming their right to tribal lands in Georgia, where they lived in peace. When that right was threatened by White settlers seeking their land and by Georgia's evolving laws aimed against them, the Cherokee chose not to resist through violence but instead turned to the American legal system.

In *Cherokee Nation v. Georgia*, the Supreme Court declined to rule on the merits of the case, declaring the Cherokee were a "domestic dependent nation" and, therefore, lacked standing. But one year later, in *Worcester v. Georgia*, the Court ruled decisively that the Cherokee Nation was sovereign and immune from Georgia's jurisdiction.

President Andrew Jackson, however, was not one to be restrained by the judiciary. In a letter to his close friend John Coffee, he dismissed the Court's authority: "The decision of the Supreme Court has fell still born, and they find that it cannot coerce Georgia to yield to its mandate."[14] Many historians interpret this as one of the most profound early tests of the balance of power between the executive branch, the judiciary, and state governments in U.S. history.

Jackson refused to enforce the ruling. Instead, he secured the Treaty of New Echota in 1835, signed not by the elected leaders of the Cherokee Nation but by a minority faction led by Major Ridge. The vast majority of Cherokee people, under Principal Chief John Ross, vehemently opposed the treaty and fought it for years. Their efforts ultimately failed. In 1838, federal troops and Georgia militia forcibly removed the Cherokee from their homes with little warning. Thousands perished along the brutal journey west—known today as the Trail of Tears.

On the harsh journey, an estimated four thousand of the sixteen thousand Cherokee driven from their homeland died of disease, starvation, and harsh weather conditions. In nearly every instance of forced removals, Native Americans were not given the supplies or help they had been promised, leading to widespread suffering and death. Overall, tens of thousands of Native Americans—some estimates nearing one hundred thousand—lost their lives and their homelands during the series of forced removals. Because so many of those who did not survive the journey were the youngest and the oldest, the Cherokee who reached Indian Territory had, in a symbolic sense, lost both their past and their future.

While there were no immediate consequences for Andrew Jackson disregarding the directive of the Supreme Court, Jackson's decision to ignore constitutional limits are widely viewed as a stain on American democracy. David Crockett's prediction that Jackson's policies toward the Native Americans would bring shame and reproach on the American name did ultimately come true. Celebrated historian of Native American history Angie Debo wrote, "But among the skeletons on our national conscience, surely none is more difficult for us to closet than our treatment of the American Indians. And one chapter in that story, the account of their dispossession and removal, remains most difficult for us to countenance, even today."[15]

For many southern tribes, crossing the Mississippi River represented the point of no return, leaving behind the lives they had known and the spirits of the ancestors who had come before them. For young White settlers eager to take their land, their departure was a necessity. For those old enough to remember the Indian wars of earlier years and the deaths of friends and family, it was the ultimate victory. After one group of Choctaw departed the harbor in Vicksburg, Mississippi, aboard the steamboat the *Huran*, a local reporter wrote:

> They are going away! With a visible reluctance which nothing has overcome but the stern necessity they feel impelling them, they have looked their last on the graves of their sires—the scenes of their youth, and have taken up their slow toilsome march with their household goods among them to their new homes in a strange land. They leave names to many of our rivers, towns, and counties, and so long as our State remains the Choctaws who once owned most of her soil will be remembered.[16]

Marcus Winchester's friend, David Crockett, would also cross the Mississippi River as he left the United States for the last time. On October 31, 1835, he wrote to his brother, "I am on the eve of Starting to the Texes—on to morrow morning myself Abner Burgin and Lindsy K Tinkle & our Newphew William Patton from the Lowar Country this will make our Company and we will go through Arkinsaw and I want to explore the Texes well before our return."[17]

The next day, Crockett and his entourage set out on their journey. As they arrived in Memphis, the politician, who had become one of the first internationally recognized American celebrities, must have thought back to 1826 and that chance meeting with Marcus Winchester. At that time, his idea of harvesting wood and taking it downriver to New Orleans had failed miserably. Perhaps he smiled when that crossed his mind as he and his crew rode down the muddy street along the bluff overlooking the river. Happy to see his friend, Winchester gathered a few Memphis men for an impromptu farewell party for Crockett and his entourage.

They began their evening at the Union Inn at Adams and Third Streets. As the party grew, they moved first to Hart's Saloon on Market Street, then next door to Neil McCool's Saloon. The room was now packed with revelers excited they were getting to experience a celebrity in person. Crockett was encouraged to hop up on the bar and give a speech, which of course, he was more than happy to do. He included the "and they can go to hell" talking point that never failed to elicit a response from an audience. As if on cue, the crowd erupted in cheers as he finished. He soaked in the response and jumped down.

The alcohol began to take effect, and some in the crowd—by then numbering more then one hundred—began to get rowdy. Crockett suggested they call it a night. Rather than head back to the hotel, he and a small group of friends parted ways to make it appear as though the evening had come to an end, then Winchester, Crockett, Robert Lawrence, James Davis, and a few others met up at the door of Cooper's mercantile.

Although his establishment was not a tavern, Cooper sold liquor by the barrel and was known to have the best quality alcohol in Memphis. They just needed to get into the store, above which Cooper also lived. The men knew that Cooper had to wake up and go down to the docks anytime, day or night, when a steamboat arrived with his merchandise. Lawrence banged on the door and shouted, "Freight, Freight!" Cooper made his way downstairs and opened the door, and the group shoved their way in to begin the last part of their evening.

Davis, who claimed to have been among the small group of friends that evening, remembered, "We all got tight—I might say, yes, very tight … men who never were tight before, and never have been tight since, were certainly VERY TIGHT then."[18] As Winchester, Crockett, and the others drank, laughed, and swapped stories, no one knew that the their friend would never return to Tennessee. As Davis wrote of the evening, "The best of feeling prevailed to a late hour."[19]

The next morning, a small group made their way down to the Wolf River, where Crockett and his party would board the ferry managed by Winchester and operated by one of his enslaved men, Limus. Davis wrote of Crockett's last minutes east of the Mississippi River:

> In the days of which I speak there were no steam ferry-boats, there was simply a ferry-flat, propelled by 'snatch oars,' with a

> noted old negro, named Limus, as Captain. The ferry landing was then in the mouth of the Wolf river. My recollection of how he looked is as vivid as if it were yesterday.... The day I saw him he had been the guest of a few personal friends, Edwin Hickman, C. D. McLean, M. B. Winchester, Robert Lawrence, Gus Young, and others, at the City Hotel. He had left the hotel, accompanied by these gentlemen on foot, for the landing. I followed in silent admiration for the river. He wore that same veritable coonskin cap and hunting shirt, bearing upon his shoulder his ever faithful rifle. No other equipments save his shot-pouch and powder-horn, do I remember seeing.[20]

According to Davis's account, Marcus Winchester and the others then said their goodbyes. Crockett and those who remained with him, including nephew William Patton and friends Abner Burgin and Lindsey Tinkle, stepped onto Winchester's flatboat. Davis wrote, "The chain was untied from the stob, and thrown with a rattle by old Limus into the bow of the boat, it pushed away from the shore, and floating lazily down the little Wolf, out into the big river, and rowed across to the other side, bearing that remarkable man away from his State and his kindred forever."[21]

Because he was killed just a few months later at the Alamo, David Crockett was not around to witness the final waves of Native American removal. In December 1838, Jackson's successor to the White House, Martin Van Buren, bragged about the "success" of the relocation in his second annual message to Congress:

> It affords me sincere pleasure to be able to apprise you of the entire removal of the Cherokee Nation of Indians to their new homes west of the Mississippi. The measures authorized by Congress at its last session, with a view to the long-standing controversy with them, have had the happiest effects ... they have emigrated without any apparent reluctance.[22]

Van Buren failed to mention that the forced relocation was still underway and that thousands of Cherokee men, women, and children were already dead.

The Winchesters' strong ties to the King of the Wild Frontier pales in comparison to their connection with the woman who came to be known by many as the Red Harlot of Infidelity, Frances Wright. Wright, called Fanny by her friends, was a bold figure championing a variety of progressive and—

increasingly controversial—causes. Thirty years old, she arrived in Memphis on horseback, traveling with George Flower, a married friend and business partner with whom she was also romantically involved. Wright wasted no time letting Marcus Winchester and William Lawrence know that she was in the market for land and that Andrew Jackson himself had sent her.

It was October 1825 when Winchester showed her a piece of real estate on the Wolf River near present-day Germantown, Tennessee. October is one of the prettiest times of the year in West Tennessee, and the leaves that were not crunching under their feet had turned the old-growth trees brilliant shades of red, yellow, and orange. The cool nip in the air and the gentle breeze hid the fact that, in just a few months, anyone standing in the same spot would be experiencing oppressive humidity, scorching heat, and the relentless swarms of mosquitoes experienced during a West Tennessee summer. As Wright surveyed the landscape, she decided this was the place. Here, she would implement her bold and ambitious plans to end slavery.

Wright was born in Dundee, Scotland, on February 6, 1795, to a couple of radicals who supported the cause of the "common folk," in spite of coming from money themselves. Wright's father, James Wright, was a wealthy Scottish landowner who was a supporter of the revolutions in America and France and distributed pamphlets like *The Rights of Man* by Thomas Paine in his home country. After James and his wife died when Frances was only three, she and her younger sister, Camilla, were sent to live with their aunt in England.

Wright's great-uncle was James Mylne, a professor of moral philosophy at Glasgow College. At the age of eighteen, Wright was browsing through his library when she stumbled upon Carlo Botta's *History of the War of the Independence of the United States of America*. That moment altered the trajectory of the rest of her life. She became, in her word, "riveted" by the United States. The tales of courage, the principles of democracy, and the promise of a society built on equality and individual freedom resonated with young Wright. For her, the book was more than a history lesson—it was a window into a bold social experiment that seemed to offer hope for humanity.

Inspired by the stories she read, young Wright began to view America as a land of possibility and a beacon of progress. The ideals and bravery of American revolutionaries nurtured her emerging belief in human potential and social reform. She wrote, "I immediately collected every work which promised to throw any light on the institutions, character and condition of the American people, and as, at that period, little satisfactory information on these subjects could be gleaned in Europe, I visited this country in person."[23]

In 1818, Wright and Camilla, who had inherited a large amount of money from their late father, embarked on a two-year tour of the United States. While in New York, with the assistance of a banker's son who likely had romantic intentions, a theater company staged a play she had written, *A Tale of Freedom*. Although she was the writer of the play, when it received a standing ovation, no one knew they were applauding her work. It had been credited to "anonymous" so as not to offend the male critics.

Six months after the sisters returned home from what was an eye-opening experience for Frances Wright, she published *Views of Society and Manners in America*, a detailed account of their time in the United States. For many, it became an introduction to what was going on across the ocean in that strange country called America that had fought for independence and won.

Wright remained amazed by this new and unique version of democracy and heartily embraced the freedoms she saw lived out in its people. In one example of her infatuation with America, she wrote, "It is singular to look round upon a country where the dreams of sages, smiled at as utopian, seem distinctly realized, a people voluntarily submitting to laws of their own imposing, with arms in their hands respecting the voice of a government which their breath created and which their breath could in a moment destroy!"[24] In the land of the free Wright wrote of, every home was comfortable, no one experienced poverty or disease, there was no crime, and the entire population was made up of enlightened philosophers.

Because of their mutual love for America, Wright began a friendship with the Marquis de Lafayette, then an international celebrity. The French aristocrat and military officer played a role in both the American and French revolutions. At the age of nineteen—and despite orders to the contrary from the French government—Lafayette secretly arranged and financed his voyage to America on a ship named *La Victoire*. Driven by his commitment to the ideals of liberty and independence, Lafayette set sail from Spain in 1777 and traveled to the United States. He volunteered his services to the Continental Army and became an aide-de-camp and close confidant of George Washington. Lafayette's contributions included securing French military aid, leading troops in critical battles such as the Battle of Brandywine, and aiding in the eventual victory at Yorktown.

After returning to France, he served as a leader in the French Revolution and continued to use his influence to advocate for America. He also played a significant role in bolstering the idea of democracy, freedom, and independence around the world.

A symbol of Lafayette's passion for freedom and the deep mutual respect between him and George Washington can be found in a key hanging on the wall of Washington's historic estate at Mount Vernon, Virginia. Bastille Prison was stormed, and the seven political prisoners it held were set free on July 14, 1789.

It was a pivotal moment in the French Revolution.

Revolutionaries presented a key to the prison to Lafayette, who was the head of the Paris National Guard at the time. The simple wrought-iron key came to represent freedom, liberty, and equality. Lafayette sent it and a drawing of the prison to George Washington along with a note that read:

> Give me leave, My dear General, to present you with a picture of the Bastille just as it looked a few days after I Had ordered its demolition, with the Main Key of that fortress of despotism—it is a tribute Which I owe as A Son to My Adoptive father, as an aid de Camp to My General, as a Missionary of liberty to its patriarch.[25]

Just before finishing his second term as president in early 1797, Washington took the encased key and drawing to Mount Vernon, where it first hung in the "Lafayette bedchamber" and then in the first-floor entry hall. It can still be seen on the tour of Washington's home today.

In spite of their nearly forty-year age difference, Lafayette, a widower, and Frances Wright quickly became friends—and some say lovers—in a relationship that would last until his death in 1834. Friends and foes from Paris to London to Washington, D.C. gossiped about this young woman with whom Lafayette was spending, in the opinion of some, too much time. The two had a perfectly reasonable explanation—she was working on his biography, they explained. Though Lafayette described the relationship as paternal, his family remained unconvinced and strongly disapproved of Wright, especially when they discovered Lafayette was considering adopting Wright. They had no intention of welcoming Wright into their family in any capacity.

In 1824, the United States was celebrating the fiftieth anniversary of the Revolution, and Lafayette, as the last surviving major general of the Continental Army, was invited to return for an early public relations stunt—a grand tour of the country he helped liberate. While his children put an end to the idea of Wright joining Lafayette as part of his official delegation, she and her sister followed him to America on the next ship out. Once they arrived in the United States, they accompanied Lafayette to parties and events around the country. For Wright, this provided an introduction to many of the notable politicians of the day including Thomas Jefferson, James Madison, James Monroe, and Tennesseans Sam Houston and Andrew Jackson. These men were as infatuated with this tall, outgoing woman as Lafayette was.

Southern historian and journalist John Egerton noted, "She never hesitated to do whatever she wanted to do, regardless of convention. The men she met seemed utterly charmed by her intelligence, her beauty, and her confidence, while the ladies were dismayed by her daring."[26]

As she spent time touring America on the arm of Layfette, she was forced to come to terms with the dichotomy of a country celebrated for freedom and liberty also embracing the idea of enslaving other human beings. One wonders if George or Martha Washington ever thought it ironic that the key representing freedom that was hanging in a case on the wall in their home was no doubt kept free of dust by enslaved housekeepers. While acknowledging that some seemed to treat their enslaved workers decently, Wright pointed out "to break the chains would be more generous than to gild them."[27]

However, like many others at that time, the idea of broken chains came with stipulations. The prevailing thought in the early nineteenth century was that immediate freedom would actually be harmful for the enslaved. Many of America's brightest thinkers of the day advocated for a gradual approach to abolishing the institution of slavery. They believed that freeing the enslaved immediately would create such social instability that it would jeopardize the future of the entire country. James Madison, Henry Clay, and leaders of some abolitionist groups promoted the idea that formerly enslaved individuals should be "prepared" for freedom through education, a viewpoint that reflected a mixture of authentic humanitarian concerns and blatant racism.

Propaganda that today seems preposterous was used to justify keeping Black individuals enslaved by portraying them as perpetual children incapable of achieving mental or social adulthood. An 1850 issue of the most widely circulated magazine in the South, *De Bow's Review*, included an article by the editor that captures the sentiments of many during that time:

> Children are fond of the company of negroes, not only because the deference shown them makes them feel full at ease, but the subjects of conversation are on a level with their capacity; while the simple tales, and the witch and ghost stories so common among negroes, excite the young imagination, and enlist the feelings.[28]

By all accounts, Wright accepted this assessment but believed that enslaved individuals could become self-sufficient with substantial training and education. After attending British industrialist Robert Owen's lecture, "Discourse on a New System of Society," in Washington City, Wright began exploring his utopian philosophy as a possible solution to the problem of slavery that so troubled her.

Owen was, at the time, a leader of New Harmony, one of the utopian socialist communities that were springing up in America in the early nineteenth century. America's version of democracy and capitalism was still new, so some were open to exploring socialism and other alternatives as potential paths forward for the new country. Utopian socialist like Owen envisioned a society based on cooperation instead of competition as a way to eliminate poverty and unemployment. They believed a system driven by collaboration rather than profit would transfer resources to the people who needed them. They also embraced "Noblesse oblige," the idea that the privileged have a responsibility to help those less fortunate. They wanted to avoid an economy in which a majority of Americans had little and a few had much.

Owen had seen poor orphans forced to work grueling jobs in filthy mills, women making only a small percentage of what men made for the same job, and workers forced to endure inhumane conditions and a lifestyle that too frequently led to an early grave. He attempted to apply utopian principals on thirty thousand acres of land in New Harmony, Indiana. His plan was for eight hundred or so residents to grow their own crops and produce goods which would be sold. The proceeds would be shared by all based on their need, not their contribution. Raising children was to be a group effort, and because he believed education had the power to shape human nature, it would be provided for free, and all would be encouraged to learn new skills and share ideas.

After spending time with Owen at New Harmony, Wright became deeply committed to creating a version of his utopian community that would end slavery. In Wright's utopia, the enslaved would work together and earn enough to purchase their freedom. Simultaneously, they would receive a free education and gain skills necessary to serve as a productive member of society—though far away in different countries and in communities set up just for them.

While at New Harmony, Wright was drawn to George Flower, an Englishman who had been part of an antislavery collective in Albion, Illinois. She decided to take him on as a partner in turning her plan into a reality. Together, they coauthored a tract titled *A Plan for the Gradual Abolition of Slavery in the United States without Danger of Loss to the Citizens of the South* that shared their views with the world. The tract acknowledged that any plan to abolish slavery must take into consideration the economic impact on enslavers:

> It is conceived that any plan of emancipation, to be effectual, must consult at once the pecuniary interests and prevailing opinions of the southern planters, and bend itself into the existing laws of the southern states ... it appears indispensable, that emancipation be connected with colonization, and that it demand no pecuniary

sacrifice from existing slave-holders, and entail no loss of property on their children.[29]

The first step was to find a location. Through Lafayette, Wright met Andrew Jackson who, of course, sent her to his friends in Memphis. Those who made their home on the bluff were used to big personalities living life on the fringes. But even there, Wright stood out from the moment she arrived in town. She was taller than the average women of the day and dressed in clothing that was considered more masculine than what was worn by other women. Occasionally, she even completed her outfit with a man's top hat.

One Tennessee reporter described her as "a tall and willowy figure, handsome and magnificently proportioned." He wrote: "As she walked down the street she looked neither to the right nor to the left. She simply went about her own business in her own way."[30] Another young Memphian, Ellen Douglas Jarnagin McCallie, who was just a girl at the time she encountered Wright, wrote that Wright rode her horse side-saddle into Memphis dressed "in a semimanish fashion," in an ensemble that included dark pantaloons; a short, black skirt and coat; leggings; and boots, topped off with a black, silk top hat. McCallie's father was Spencer Jarnagin, an East Tennessee lawyer, notable Whig, and United States Senator who settled with his family in Memphis. He worked with Wright, handling some of her contracts and agreements. The bold abolitionist made a big impression on young McCallie as the little girl eavesdropped on her father and Wright working in his office together. She wrote, "Her voice was rather deep, but sweet and mellow, for I remember how I would love to hear her talk, though not understanding the conversation."[31]

Once Wright had selected land along the bank of the Wolf River for her community, she quickly purchased 320 acres from the proprietors. The name James Richardson shows up as a witness on the deed, a fact that would prove ironic since that same Richardson, a Scottish physician Wright met in Memphis, would one day contribute in a significant way to the failure of her plan.

Wright and George Flower rolled up their sleeves and got to work. She wrote to a friend, Madame Charles de Lasteyrie, about the pride she felt in the success of her first weeks in West Tennessee:

> After having passed through an immense extent of country, consulted by letter and personal interview all the most important persons in the vicinity and observed the character of the people living in the towns and villages, here I am at last, property owner in the forests of this new territory, bought from the Indians by

the United States about five years ago and still inhabited by bears, wolves, and panthers. But do not be alarmed, I have traveled the length and breadth of this territory two times, doing forty miles a day on horseback, through unbroken country spending the night in cabins open to the air on all sides, or in the woods themselves, a bear skin for my bed, my saddle for a pillow, and I am perfectly well. My health is better—I am stronger than I have ever been in my life. I have braved all weathers, heat and cold, and I have caught neither cold nor fever.[32]

Also in the letter, she described Memphis to her friend as "a little town with nothing but dozens of log cabins that had been baptized with the imposing name of Memphis." Describing it as "nothing but a station for furs traded by Native Americans," she added Memphis was perhaps "as wretched as the Memphis of ancient Egypt."[33]

In Nashville, Wright purchased eleven enslaved people for around $500 each and returned to Memphis where she selected the name Nashoba—the word the Chickasaw's used for the Wolf River—for her little community. One day, a South Carolinian named Robert Wilson showed up at Nashoba with a pregnant enslaved woman named Lukey and six little enslaved girls he had inherited. Wilson was opposed to slavery, but if he freed them, he would have to pay to send them to another country, something he could not afford to do. He was there to "donate" them to Wright's cause in hopes they would eventually earn their freedom according to her plan. Marcus Winchester was a witness on the agreement Wilson made with Wright in which she promised to treat the girls humanely, feed and care for them, and free them within fifteen years. The agreement also included a clause that the girls would be resettled in Liberia, Haiti, or Mexico.[34]

Marcus and Amarante Winchester became friends with Wright and her sister, and Marcus's name shows up as a witness on many legal documents and receipts relating to Nashoba. Some early historians have even suggested than Marcus Winchester was a partner in Nashoba, but his name was never included as a deed holder. One writer observed that as long as the Wright sisters lived in West Tennessee, Amarante Winchester was "one of their most loved and honored women friends."[35] When Camilla Wright gave birth to a little boy on February 21, 1829, some believe it was at the Winchester's home in Memphis, and for a while, Camilla lived next door.

Another interesting connection can be found in the name the Winchesters chose for their first-born son, Robert Owen, born in 1827 and named in honor of the founder of New Harmony. When their next child was born in 1829, they named the little girl Frances Wright.

It is clear that Marcus Winchester, while representing the trinity of early Tennessee capitalism—James Winchester, John Overton, and Andrew Jackson—made his own decisions when it came to social issues like race, religion, and politics.

Chapter Fourteen Endnotes

1. "The Aborigines of West Tennessee," *Old Folks Record*, no. 4 (January 1874): 179.
2. "Old Times," *Memphis Daily Appeal*, June 18, 1871, 2.
3. James Phelan, *History of Tennessee: The Making of a State* (Boston: Houghton, Mifflin and Company, 1888), 324.
4. J. P. Young, *Standard History of Memphis* (Knoxville: H. W. Crew & Co., 1912), 71.
5. *Elmwood Cemetery Biographical Sketches*, "Seth Wheatley" (Memphis: Elmwood Cemetery, 1874).
6. Phelan, *History of Tennessee*, 326.
7. James D. Davis, History of Memphis (Memphis: Hite, Crumpton & Kelly, 1873), 149-150.
8. David Crockett, *A Narrative of the Life of David Crockett of the State of Tennessee*. Originally published 1834. Reprint, *Autobiography of David Crockett* (New York: Charles Scribner's Sons, 1923), 128.
9. David Crockett, "David Crockett's Circular," February 28, 1831, Rare Books Division, Library of Congress.
10. "The Memphis of Forty-two Years Ago," *The Daily Memphis Avalanche*, April 3, 1881, 2.
11. Alexis de Tocqueville, *Memoir, Letters, and Remains of Alexis de Tocqueville*, vol. 1 (Cambridge: Macmillan and Co., 1861), 29.
12. Alexis De Tocqueville, *Democracy in America* (London: Saunders and Otley, 1835), 372-73.
13. Tocqueville, *Democracy in America*, 373.
14. Andrew Jackson to John Coffee, April 1832, in *Correspondence of Andrew Jackson*, ed. John Spencer Bassett, vol. 4 (Washington, DC: Carnegie Institution, 1929), 430.
15. Grant Foreman, *Indian Removal, the Emigration of the Five Civilized Tribes of Indians* (Norman: The University of Oklahoma Press, 1974), 5.
16. Arthur H. DeRosier, *The Removal of the Choctaw Indians* (Knoxville: The University of Tennessee Press, 1999), 4.
17. James Atkins Shackford, *David Crockett: The Man and the Legend* (Chapel Hill: University of North Carolina Press, 1956), 210.
18. Davis, *History of Memphis*, 147-148.
19. Davis, *History of Memphis*, 148.
20. Davis, *History of Memphis*, 139-140.
21. Davis, *History of Memphis*, 141.
22. Martin Van Buren, "Second Annual Message," December 3, 1838, in *The American Presidency Project*, ed. John T. Woolley and Gerhard Peters, accessed December 3, 2024.
23. *Frances Wright, Course of Popular Lectures as Delivered by Frances Wright* (New York: Office of the *Free Enquirer*, 1829), 7.
24. Frances Wright, *Views of Society and Manners in America: In a Series of Letters from That Country to a Friend in England, During the Years 1818, 1819, and 1820* (London: Longman, Hurst, Rees, Orme, and Brown, 1821), 362.
25. Marquis de Lafayette to George Washington, March 17, 1790, in *The Papers of George Washington, Presidential Series*, vol. 5, ed. Dorothy Twohig (Charlottesville: University Press of Virginia, 1996).
26. John Egerton, *Visions of Utopia* (The University of Tennessee Press: Knoxville, Tennessee, 1977), 17.
27. Wright, *Views of Society*, 290.
28. "Southern Review of De Bow's Review," vol. 19 (September 1855): 363.
29. Frances Wright, *A Plan for the Gradual Abolition of Slavery in the United States, Without Danger or Loss to the Citizens of the South* (Baltimore: Benjamin Lundy, 1825), 3.
30. "Career of Fannie Wright in West Tennessee," *Tennessean*, Dec 25, 1901, 8.
31. Ellen Douglas Jarnagin McCallie, "Early Advocate of Women's Rights," *Chattanooga News*, November 10, 1914, 20.
32. A. J. G. Perkins and Theresa Wolfson, *Frances Wright: Free Enquirer, The Study of a Temperament* (Philadelphia: Porcupine Press, 1972), 144.
33. Perkins and Wolfson, Frances Wright, 144.
34. Perkins and Wolfson, Frances Wright, 145-146.
35. Perkins and Wolfson, Frances Wright, 144.

NEGROES WANTED!
WE WISH TO BUY
ONE HUNDRED
GOOD
NEGROES
FOR THE
SOUTHERN MARKET,
BY
THE FIRST OF OCTOBER.

We will pay the highest cash price for all sound, likely young negroes offered for sale. Bring them to our office, as this is the place to trade. We will have for sale in our yard, by the first of October, a full supply of all sorts of negroes, from Virginia and Kentucky, selected by the best of buyers, where all can be supplied with the best of servants.

BOLTON, DICKENS & CO.
MEMPHIS, TENN.

From Rainey's Memphis City Directory, 1855/56

Chapter Fifteen: Anywhere but Memphis

Death and disease come to the city on the bluff

Joseph J. Rawlings, Marcus Winchester, and Walter D. Dabney traveled together on horseback to the Indian agency in Mississippi. They intended to collect on unpaid debts owed to them by Native Americans for merchandise purchased in their stores on credit. After waiting a week with no sign of the agent, the trio of friends began their journey back to Memphis empty-handed. Their plan had been to spend the night in an empty cabin they knew of along the way. After getting lost, they found themselves with no choice but to wait out the night in a swampy area called Cold Water Bottom. Years later, Rawlings shared his memories of that night:

> We commenced to stay in that horrible place all night. Our first effort was to get a light—no matches in them days. We had spunk and steel, and with all our efforts we could never get a fire. We gave it up for a bad job and spread our saddles on the ground. Sleep was not expected. Foxes and wolves were barking all around us, owls hooting—plenty of music—that was not the worst of it. There were millions of mosquitos to the square inch, and it was as much as we could do to save our lives from the infernal pests. Next day we reached home after a sleepless night. On looking in the glass, we did not know ourselves. You could not put the point of a pin on our faces and hands where there was not a mosquito bite.[1]

The stagnant floodwaters, combined with Memphis's heat and humidity, created ideal breeding grounds for mosquitos. Memphians, like those in other river cities and low-lying areas, found them annoying, but they were unaware at the time that the pests were also spreading diseases such as malaria and yellow fever. Early visitors to the bluff observed the Chickasaw sleeping on raised beds on stilts. Beneath these beds were placed smudge pots in which they burned materials like green wood or plants. The smoke acted as a natural repellent, driving mosquitoes—and disease—away from the raised bed.

At the time, it was believed by White settlers that diseases could be attributed to "miasmas" or foul air, so they focused on keeping bad smells away, rather than adopting practices like smudge pots. The true culprits—mosquitos—remained unidentified as hundreds of thousands died of disease.

A Memphis resident wrote in 1836, "Memphis is pronounced by all strangers visiting it to be the filthiest and most deadly appearing town in the Union."[2] William Walden, who settled in Memphis in 1825, remembered, "almost everyone had the chills and fever."[3] In September 1872, Walden addressed members of the Old Folks Society and spoke about the impact of yellow fever. He shared memories of managing a mercantile in Memphis's early years before railroads and when river traffic consisted primarily of flatboats. Farmers had to market their goods when the water was high enough. At times, that would lead to a surplus that would drive prices down. He claimed sometimes he saw more than two thousand flatboats waiting to unload their supplies at the landing in Memphis or to get supplies that would allow them to make it further down the river to New Orleans. "If rumors of an outbreak of yellow fever in New Orleans began to spread, the owners of the flatboats would sell everything in Memphis—including the boats—as quickly as they could," he remembered. "They then booked passage on the first steamboat that would take them back up the river, or head home as quickly as possible over land."[4]

A writer for *The Railroad Record* visited Memphis in 1851 and saw nothing threatening in the city's future. As if tempting fate, he wrote:

> Its high position has secured its health so far, that neither cholera nor yellow fever have visited it, in the several forms in which they have prevailed in almost all the southern cities. This immunity is likely to continue, for it lies in both high and dry ground, and has purer and better air than any place in the region.[5]

Known as the "Yellow Jack," yellow fever caused high fever, jaundice, and internal bleeding. Outbreaks of the disease struck Memphis periodically during Marcus Winchester's lifetime, but more than twenty years after Winchester's death, *The Railroad Record* writer's prediction of immunity was proven very wrong. During the summer of 1878, Memphis experienced one of the most devastating yellow fever epidemics in American history. It swept through the city and the surrounding area, killing more than five thousand—half the population at the time. The epidemic overwhelmed the city, leading to mass graves, the collapse of the local economy, and the loss of the city's charter for several years. It would be John Overton's namesake grandson who would contribute to the survival of the city by holding the title of "President of the Taxing District" after Memphis lost its charter. His 1903 obituary noted that Overton was "the originator of the taxing form of government under which Memphis recuperated from the devastation caused by yellow fever."[6]

It was not the only disease early Memphians had to worry about. As the number of boats docking on the bluff increased, so did the risk of outbreaks of smallpox. It was spread through respiratory droplets released when an infected person coughed, sneezed, or even spoke. In a letter to John Overton dated January 15, 1826, Marcus Winchester informed the proprietor that all was not well in Memphis. Smallpox had come to the home of the Irvins where six members of the family were infected. Winchester feared smallpox would soon spread across the city.

Those who contracted smallpox first came down with flu-like symptoms including a severe headache, high fever, and body aches. Within a few days, a rash would start to form on their face, arms, and legs, eventually spreading to the rest of their body. The rash would turn into raised bumps that filled with clear fluid which would then turn into hard, pus-filled blisters. As the disease progressed, those pustules covered nearly every inch of their skin, making every movement excruciatingly painful. About one in three people infected died. Those who survived were left with deep, disfiguring scars. Native Americans had a very descriptive name for the disease—rotting face.

A smallpox vaccine, the first successful attempt at preventing a contagious disease through inoculation, was developed by Edward Jenner in 1796. He noticed those who worked around cows and contracted cowpox, a disease with only mild symptoms, developed an immunity to smallpox. After much trial and error, he proved that by giving people a mild dose of cowpox, you could prevent smallpox. In the early 1800s, the virus used to make the vaccine changed from cowpox to the vaccinia virus. By the time Winchester was writing to Overton about his fear of an outbreak in 1826, the vaccine was available but difficult to get. "We have no vaccine matter, and most of our people are without the security which vaccination imparts to them," he wrote. "If the matter can be procured in Nashville, a little might be forwarded by mail, and yet received in time to arrest the progress of the destroyer."[7]

Winchester was right to be worried. A smallpox epidemic in 1837, spread by the *SS St. Peter*, a steamboat of the American Fur Company, killed more than 17,000 living along the Missouri River and completely wiped out several Native American tribes. The steamboat had traveled up the Mississippi and Missouri Rivers from St. Louis to Fort Union, in present-day North Dakota, carrying infected passengers who spread the disease to others. That nightmare scenario could very easily have happened in Memphis.

For Marcus Winchester and others living in the early nineteenth century, the death of a loved one was always around the corner. Of the babies born in 1800, only around half lived to see their fifth birthday. Men and women born in 1800 who lived to experience the Civil War had beaten the odds, and they were the oldest residents in their communities.

In a letter dated October 26, 1815, Marcus's father, James, shared his philosophy of living life to the fullest with his brother, David, in Baltimore. Then sixty-three years old, Winchester was writing after learning of the death of their sister, Katherine Winchester Hotchkiss. She and her husband had made their home in Kaskaskia, Illinois, a city on the Mississippi River between Memphis and St. Louis:

> Your sorrowful letter of the 9th instant has burned; our family once smug and content for many years was unmarked by the great destroyer of the human race but now scattered over a vast extent of country; His unwelcome visits are very frequent; of ten brothers and sisters of us, only half that number left. Their frequent memorials of our mortality are a great drawback to the pleasure of accumulating property in this world; as one knows not how soon one may be summoned to leave it <u>never never</u> to return; and then the uncertainty of the use which will be made after by those who are to come after us; they may be wise or foolish; If the latter they cannot keep it; if the former they can amass it. Therefore I hold it wisdom to take a full share of the good things of this world as we go along never denying ourselves one rational enjoyment within our reach for the sake of leaving our heirs rich; and above all sacrifice nothing on the shrine of popularity and pursue an independent and correct course of conduct; self-approbation is a treasure of inestimable solace.[8]

In addition to David, James Winchester's surviving siblings in 1815 included his sisters, Elizabeth and Lydia, and his brother, Richard. A poignant reminder of both the permanence of death and the ever-changing power of the Mississippi

River, a descendant who searched for Katherine Winchester Hotchkiss's grave wrote, "Due to changes in the river's course, the cemetery where she was buried has disappeared. No further trace of this branch has been discovered."[9]

In the hot Tennessee summer of 1826, the "great destroyer of the human race" paid an unwelcome visit to Cragfont—this time it was there for seventy-four-year-old James Winchester. He had been sick for weeks with a painful illness that left him bedridden and growing weaker each day. He knew the time of his death was likely drawing near. Not surprising for those who knew him, he took control and organized his own departure. He even had the undertaker take his measurements for the coffin while he lay in bed, and he chose the style, demanding something "plain and neat."

James Winchester died on July 27, 1826, with members of his family at his side. He and his wife, Susan, still had three young children at home. James Martin was ten, Helen Marr was seven, and George was only four. A hyperbole-filled obituary in the *National Banner and Nashville Whig* paid tribute: "The patriot, the philanthropist is gone! From a long acquaintance, I am persuaded I can say with a truth that excludes all false panegyric, that he was the personification of the social virtues. As a parent, a husband, a friend, a citizen, surely, he had few equals."[10]

Winchester was buried in the family cemetery at Cragfont near his brother, George, who had been killed by Native Americans more than thirty years earlier. Also in the family cemetery were his infant daughters, Cynthia and Malvina, and his son, Napoleon, who had died at just eighteen in the fall of 1824 after an illness that lasted nineteen days.

Old friend Charles Cassedy was hired to write Winchester's epitaph which was also included on his grave marker:

> How oft, alas! we see the worthless name
> Bedecked by fraud with trophies of the brave;
> While lost forgotten or unknown to fame,
> Oblivion's wing obscures the Patriots grave.
> But when false claims to Glory meet their Doom,
> And Truth with clarion note, once more shall rise,
> The historic Muse will point to this lone tomb,
> Where native worth and spotless honor lies.

Cassedy was pointing out that sometimes people who do not deserve recognition manage to be celebrated, while real heroes like Winchester are often forgotten or ignored. He acknowledged the damage done to Winchester's reputation—he believed falsely—during the War of 1812, but assured the reader the "truth" will eventually come out, and history will give proper credit. When that happens, history will point to the grave where James Winchester lies, "a person of real worth and unblemished honor." Cassedy wrote to Winchester's daughter, Maria Winchester Breedlove, years later:

> The epitaph I wrote on your deceased and honored father and which appears on his tomb recognizes prophetically, a period on which ample justice would be done to his memory and his virtues—as well as to the base defamations and their authors, by which his character was assailed during life. I knew it would be impossible to stem the torrent of malignity and popular prejudice against him while living, such are the wrong headedness and injustice of mankind.[11]

Winchester's death also hastened the demise of the town he built, Cairo, Tennessee. As new roads and transportation routes were established elsewhere, Cairo was gradually bypassed, its commercial importance eclipsed by new centers of trade in Nashville. Over time, the town faded into obscurity.

While his material success quickly evaporated, Winchester's real legacy, his family, thrived. In 1989, a descendant of James and Susan Winchester was looking through a random assortment of old files and papers belonging to her late mother, when she discovered an unfinished manuscript written by her late grandmother, Susan Winchester Powell Scales.

Scales, who lived to the age of 101, was the daughter of George Winchester, Marcus Winchester's youngest brother, and his wife, Malvina Gaines. George, having just finished college, married Malvina in March 1851, and together they began their married life at Cragfont. George's widowed mother, Susan Winchester, was the matriarch of the plantation and, along with many enslaved people, ran the daily operations that included farming cotton, tobacco, and other crops. It required constant attention—hoeing, weeding, and harvesting by hand. Beyond the fields, livestock needed tending, fences required mending, and roads had to be kept passable for transporting goods to market. Inside Cragfont, Susan Winchester oversaw preparation of meals, procurement of supplies, and management of the enslaved who worked inside and outside the house.

Scales wrote that her mother, who was shy and timid, was fascinated with her new mother-in-law, Susan Winchester, who had been a widow for a quarter century when they arrived. She quietly observed from an upstairs balcony each morning as Susan, who the family called Mammy, departed the house riding her horse, Zephyr. Of her grandmother, Scales wrote:

> Grandmother was a pioneer … she was the widow of a soldier of the Revolution. She may have lived in a cabin or tent while this beautiful house was being built, stone on stone, of rock quarried on the place, the beams and rafters held by wooden pegs and the nails made in the shop on the grounds. Her husband (much older than she) and their eldest son were in the War of 1812, and a younger son in the Mexican War. Their 14 children were married or dead, and she was left a widow.[12]

Susan Winchester died at Cragfont on December 7, 1864, at eighty-seven years old. In an article published in the *Nashville Banner*, she was remembered as having rare personal beauty, strong intellect, and an incredible thirst for knowledge. The writer noted that when the demands of pioneer life passed, "she graced the manor as beautifully as she had blossomed in the wilderness."[13] She had been a widow for thirty-eight years, and at the time of her death, she had outlived seven of her twelve children, including Marcus Winchester.

Back in Memphis, after his father's death, Marcus Winchester facilitated the selection of four acres of land adjacent to what was then known as the Second Bayou to be used as a cemetery. It was named the Winchester Burying Ground. In 1847, around seven more acres were purchased as a for-profit endeavor by William R. Smith, and that came to be known as The New Winchester Burying Ground. The original portion of the cemetery donated by Marcus Winchester was later referred to as The Old Winchester Cemetery. Eventually, the entire area was called The Winchester Cemetery.[14] It became the final resting place for hundreds of Memphians for the next quarter century until other cemeteries, like Elmwood, opened.

The proprietors of Memphis were then John Overton who owned half, John McLemore who owned one fourth, William Winchester's heirs who owned one eighth, and Marcus Winchester and nine other family members who owned a final eighth. In addition to the small percentage of the bluff he inherited, Marcus owned several lots in Memphis and the land just outside the town his father had gifted him years earlier. By the early 1830s, he began acquiring land across the river in Arkansas, and by 1842, he owned nearly 2,600 acres. Included was much of the land that had belonged to Benjamin Fooy when Winchester first arrived to the bluff.[15]

With James Winchester gone, John Overton began leaning even more heavily on Marcus. Overton was busy with many business and political endeavors. He worked on Andrew Jackson's presidential campaigns in both 1824 and 1828, serving as chairman of the Nashville Committee for Jackson's election. There were similar committees around the country, but Nashville's was the only one to have Jackson's oldest friend at the helm.

Overton was also a key figure in the loosely organized group known as the Nashville Junto—an inner circle of Andrew Jackson's closest allies, including influential politicians, businessmen, and newspaper editors. In the contentious 1824 presidential election, an act often called the "Corrupt Bargain" resulted in Jackson losing the presidency to John Quincy Adams despite winning the most popular and electoral votes. Determined to overturn this defeat in the next election, the Nashville Junto sought to harness the growing enthusiasm for Jackson, propel him to the White House in 1828, and secure positions of power for themselves and their allies.

In addition to Overton, the members of the group included Felix Grundy, a Tennessee congressman, senator, and U.S. attorney general; John Eaton, a Tennessee military commander, lawyer, and the youngest senator in American history; and James K. Polk, a Tennessee lawyer and politician, chairman of the Ways and Means Committee, Speaker of the House, and, from 1845 to 1849, the nation's eleventh president.

The campaign of 1828 between Andrew Jackson and incumbent John Q. Adams marked a turning point in American politics. For the first time, political parties actively courted the support of ordinary voters through large rallies, parades, and direct appeals in party-affiliated newspapers that openly backed their chosen candidates. Jackson's ultimate victory marked the decline of the old system of elite-controlled politics and the rise of a more populist, democratic political culture. It also cemented the Democratic Party as a dominant force, reshaping the landscape of American politics forever.

Jackson's support was strongest in the southern and western regions where he was seen as a champion of the common man against aristocratic elites. Small farmers, frontiersmen, settlers, and working-class voters admired his bravery, military heroism, and his image as a self-made man. Jackson's aggressive stance on Native American removal and territorial expansion resonated with White settlers eager for land. Among pro-slavery advocates, particularly in the South, support for Jackson was also strong. As a plantation owner and enslaver, he was viewed as a staunch defender of slavery at a time when abolitionist sentiment was growing in the North. His unwavering opposition to federal interference in state affairs reassured wealthy planters that he would not allow the government to threaten their way of life.

This contrasted sharply with his opponent, John Q. Adams, who was portrayed by Jackson's supporters as an out-of-touch aristocrat who was corrupt and elitist. The election was one of the most vicious in American history, filled with personal attacks and scandalous accusations. Adams's supporters depicted Jackson as an uneducated, violent frontiersman. Both sides engaged in relentless mudslinging, personal attacks, and accusations—many of them false.

Nothing was off limits. Jackson's opponents even revived the scandal surrounding his marriage to Rachel, accusing her of bigamy and claiming she was not sophisticated enough to represent the nation in the White House. William B. Lewis wrote John Coffee, "The floodgates of falsehood slander and abuse have been hoisted and the most nauseating filth is poured in torrents on the head of not on Jackson but all his prominent supporters."[16]

John Overton organized the effort to defend the couple publicly in the nation's first political sex scandal. In a long, editorial-style defense, Overton wrote the story of his friends' meeting, the innocence of their courtship, and the belief of both that she was legally divorced at the time of their marriage. Overton also defended the couple's honor, essentially attempting to prove publicly they did not have sex before they were married:

> Continuously together during our attendance on wilderness courts, whilst other young men were indulging in familiarities with females of relaxed morals, no suspicion of this kind of the world's censure ever fell to Jackson's share. In this—his singularly-delicate sense of honor, and doing what I thought his chivalrous conceptions of the female sex, it occurred to me that he was distinguishable from every other person with whom I was acquainted. . . . Since the year 1791, General Jackson and myself have never been much apart, except when he was in the army. I have been intimate in his family, and from the mutual and uninterrupted happiness of the General and Mrs. Jackson, which I have at times witnessed with pleasure, as well as those delicate and polite attentions which have ever been reciprocated between them, I have long been confirmed in the opinion, that there never existed any other than what was believed to be the most honorable and virtuous intercourse between them. Before their going to Natchez, I had daily opportunities of being convinced that there was none other; before being married in the Natchez country after was understood the divorce had been granted by the legislature of Virginia, it is believed there was none.[17]

Overton also addressed Rachel's personal character. "A more exemplary woman in all relations of life, as a wife, friend, neighbor, relative or mistress of slaves, never lived," he wrote. "She has a warm heart, gracious manners and a hospitable temper and made her home very attractive to visitors."[18]

Rachel Jackson, a deeply religious Christian, was mortified by the national attention focused on her first marriage, questionable divorce, sex life, and the implications that she was a "fallen woman." She confided to friends that she dreaded the spotlight she would have to endure if her husband were elected president. In the election held from October 31 to December 2, 1828, Jackson won 55.5 percent of the popular vote and 178 electoral votes, compared with John Quincy Adams's 83. Andrew Jackson became the seventh president of the United States.

Rachel Jackson grew increasingly ill toward the end of the campaign. She complained of severe chest pains and difficulty breathing. In mid-December, she suffered what was described as a "violent attack" of pain in her chest, shoulder, and arm—most likely a heart attack. On the evening of December 22, she collapsed, and despite efforts to revive her, she died just two months before her husband's inauguration. Andrew Jackson buried his wife on Christmas Eve in the white gown she had intended to wear at his inaugural ball. Jackson built a permanent, Greek-styled gazebo over her grave and wrote the words for the epitaph himself:

> Here lie the remains of Mrs. Rachel Jackson, wife of President Jackson, who died December 22nd 1828, aged 61. Her face was fair, her person pleasing, her temper amiable, and her heart kind. She delighted in relieving the wants of her fellow-creatures, and cultivated that divine pleasure by the most liberal and unpretending methods. To the poor she was a benefactress; to the rich she was an example; to the wretched a comforter; to the prosperous an ornament. Her piety went hand in hand with her benevolence; and she thanked her Creator for being able to do good. A being so gentle and so virtuous, slander might wound but could not dishonor. Even death, when he tore her from the arms of her husband, could but transplant her to the bosom of her God.

The efforts of John Overton and the Nashville Junto were not the last time the Jacksons would be defended by a group of passionate Nashvillians. A 1936 Metro Goldwin Mayer film, *The Gorgeous Hussy,* told the story of Andrew Jackson, portrayed by Lionel Barrymore, defending Peggy Eaton, portrayed by Joan Crawford. In real life, Peggy was the attractive and charismatic daughter of a popular boarding house owner. Her marriage to Tennessee senator and member of the Nashville Junto, John Eaton, created a national controversy. After Jackson was elected president, he selected Eaton as his secretary of war. The Eatons had married months earlier, after her first husband committed suicide. As the society women of Washington City were quick to point out, the relationship had begun before her first husband's death. Other wives of Jackson's cabinet members refused to speak to her, but the president came to her defense. As one writer put it, "She had a few marriages, a host of suitors and Jackson's ear."[19] The political fallout of the public snubbing of Peggy Eaton, Jackson's unwavering support, and the months that followed became a national controversy known as the Petticoat Affair.

The Gorgeous Hussy was not written as an accurate retelling of historical facts, and it seems character actress Beulah Bondi—who later played the role of Jimmy Stewart's mother in *It's a Wonderful Life*—was no Rachel Jackson. When the movie came out, a group in Nashville was outraged, and they had no intention of seeing the reputations of their hometown hero and his beloved wife besmirched without a fight. After seeing the movie posters and photos from the film, the group, including the officers of the Ladies Hermitage Association, demanded and received a preview of the film by the Nashville Board of Censors.

To put it mildly, they were horrified and declared the film "outrageous and preposterous." Tensions rose in the Lowes Vendome Theater the moment Beulah Bondi's Rachel first appeared on the screen with "her coarse face and stringy hair," smoking a pipe.[20] After the screening, comments from the group ranged from "Lionel Barrymore as General Jackson looks like an old woman" to "I feel like I have been to a funeral."[21]

Judge John H. DeWitt, president of the Tennessee Historical Society—and a man with a passion for accuracy—noted indignantly, "their dates are all twisted." Graeme McGregor Smith, state regent of the Daughters of the American Revolution and a great-great-niece of Rachel Jackson, wrote, "I felt as one who had seen a loved one butchered. I saw this greatest combination of statesman and warrior, the indomitable Andrew Jackson, portrayed as an illiterate, uncouth, irresponsible, senile, old man—a travesty on all that I have been taught."[22] The Nashville Board of Censors simply shrugged and let the group know they saw nothing immoral on the screen and that anything beyond that was not their problem.

After Rachel Jackson's death and funeral, Andrew Jackson departed for Washington City. John Overton supported his friend through the early months of his grief. He attended the inauguration, vacationed with the president, and visited him at The White House at least once a year. In 1831, Artist Ralph E. W. Earl wrote to Overton, "The President often speaks of you, nothing seems to give him more satisfaction than to receive a letter from his old and well tried friend of Travellers Rest."[23] Overton wrote about his friendship with Jackson in a letter to Overton's nephew in 1824:

> We commenced our career together, we slept, ate, and suffered together, and I always entertained the same view of his talents and character, and I have the consolation to think that I have never been mistaken in him. What opinion he entertains of me, I know not. I have my part to play, marked out, I believe, by Providence, and he has had his part, and it may seem strange, but it is true.[24]

As Marcus Winchester matured into his role as a leader in Memphis, he became less likely to do exactly as the old judge demanded, and their relationship became strained. Overton valued blind obedience and, like Jackson, demanded one hundred percent allegiance to the person and the party. When he even suspected that was not the case, he acted swiftly. Overton had accused Winchester of supporting the publishing of a new anti-Jackson newspaper and of helping fund David Crockett's campaign for congressman—an accusation that was very likely true. At one point, Overton even reminded Winchester he had influence over who served as the postmaster of Memphis.

On his part, Winchester grew increasingly frustrated by Overton's lack of compassion for the poor residents of Memphis. To Winchester, they were his friends and neighbors. To Overton, they were a nuisance. The winter of 1831 was the coldest in at least fifty years. There was so much snow and ice, travel by wagon was impossible. Pilots on the Mississippi River found their boats damaged or even destroyed by large sheets of ice with edges as sharp as razor blades.

Reverend John Bergen, in middle Illinois, experienced similar weather in December 1830 and carried the memory of that winter with him the rest of his life. In his journal, he wrote, "The snow became so deep, the cold so intense, the crust at times so hard, and the people were so unprepared for such an extreme season, that it became almost impossible in many parts of the country to obtain bread for family use, though amid stocks of wheat and fields of corn."[25]

Many of the families in Memphis ran out of firewood and could not get wagons out of the city, so they turned to Winchester for permission to cut trees on the edge of town. The land on which those trees grew belonged to the proprietors. Overton forbid access, even when they offered to purchase it. Winchester was infuriated, especially since Overton was among the wealthiest planters in Tennessee by that time. Memphians would speak of that winter for years to come and tell stories of how some of the older buildings, including the

Bell Tavern, were stripped of wood to use for fires.

By his mid-sixties, John Overton appeared even older than his years according to Harry A. Wise, who spent an evening with the judge at The Hermitage in 1828:

> He was a man who had made his mark in law and politics, but was not pious and was a queer-looking little old man. Small in stature, and cut into sharpe angles at every salient point, a round, prominent, gourd-like, bald cranium, a peaked, Roman nose, a prominent, sharp, but manly chin, and he had lost his teeth and swallowed his lips.[26]

In April 1832, sicty-seven-year-old Overton had been ill, but he insisted on continuing with his plan to travel for three weeks to and from Baltimore and Philadelphia. When he finally returned home, he was very weak, and once he got into bed, he never got out. Dr. Samuel Hogg was called to Travellers Rest to treat the old judge. Fearing death was imminent, Overton had John M. Lea, his future son-in-law, burn many of the letters he had received from Andrew Jackson through the years. Early historian W. W. Clayton wrote about the event:

> A few days before Judge Overton's death he caused all the correspondence of Gen. Jackson, embracing a life-time (for Judge Overton never lost or mislaid a paper or letter), to be brought to his bedside. Political excitement was then at the highest pitch, and the war between Jackson and the Bank was raging. He reflected that, after his death, many of those letters, intended for his own eye, might fall into the hands of his friend's enemies, and garbled extracts find their way to the public,—such a thing had happened and might happen again—few would be living who could explain the circumstances under which they were written, time and the events of life might have induced a change of opinion concerning men and things, and with a singular prudence he committed the correspondence to the flames, remarking that, living or dead, he would not betray the confidence of a friend.[27]

John Overton was thinking of his friend, Andrew Jackson, to the very end. Marcus Winchester received a letter dated April 14, 1833, from Richard H. Berry, the husband of Overton's stepdaughter, that included details of the old judge's death. He wrote, "I heard him request Dr. Hogg to say to General Jackson that he saw him die and that he died a man and a soldier, so you see he clung to the general to his last moments."[28]

Overton was buried at Travellers Rest, but he and others buried there, including Samuel Overton, Ann Overton Brinkley, Richard Barry, Mary Barry, H. L. Barry, and Andrew Jackson May, were reinterred at the Mt. Olivet Cemetery in Nashville on November 20, 1868, where Mary, John Overton's wife, had been buried when she died in 1862. Mary requested the graves be moved before her death, out of fear the house and cemetery would be destroyed during the Civil War.

At the time of his death, Overton's estate was valued at around three-hundred thousand dollars, approximately ten million today. His will directed his considerable land holdings, businesses, and investments be divided among his wife, children, step-children, and friends. Travellers Rest and his interest in Memphis was left to his wife, and upon her death, it went to his son, John Overton Jr., who was twelve at the time of his father's death.

The inventory of the estate submitted to the Davidson County, Tennessee, court on April 9, 1835, included household furniture, paintings of Andrew Jackson and George Washington, spinning wheels, a loom, a carriage and harness, three copper stills, and a variety of plows and farm tools. Also included was a list of the fifty-three enslaved people owned by John Overton: twenty-two men, eleven women, and twenty children.

As executor of his will, John Overton selected John Samuel Claybrooke, the son of Overton's youngest sister, Sarah. She had married well, choosing John Claybrooke for a husband and had remained in Louisa County, Virginia. He was a well-established descendant of English settlers who had arrived on the James River around 1600. The Claybrookes were prominent landowners with substantial holdings.

Claybrooke received the best classical education available at the time, studying the culture, history, literature, and languages of ancient Greece and Rome. His education included the study of Latin and Greek.

In 1828, at the age of twenty-one, Claybrooke moved to Travellers Rest, where he lived and worked with his uncle. Overton was clearly impressed by his ambitious young nephew, who shared his enthusiasm for books and education. Claybrooke later settled in Hardeman's Cross Roads, a community along the Harpeth River, halfway between present-day Franklin and Murfreesboro. The area would later become the community of Triune. He worked as a teacher at the Harpeth Union Male Academy, which became Hardeman Academy after its first year. An 1834 advertisement promoting Hardeman Academy described Claybrooke as "a gentleman highly qualified by his ability, assiduity, and experience in teaching."

Despite the great amount of promise Claybrooke displayed, he was an unusual choice for Overton to have selected as executor. Overton knew every businessman in Middle Tennessee and had a long list of friends who were lawyers and bankers who managed large, complicated estates, yet he trusted a twenty-five-year-old teacher to manage his family's wealth after his death. Although he was an excellent teacher, Claybrooke was untried in business and law at that point. However, by all accounts, Overton's last business decision was as solid as those that came before, and Claybrooke managed the judge's estate well.

After his uncle's death, Claybrooke married Mary Ann Perkins and began a family of his own. The Claybrookes eventually had ten children together. In addition to helping manage the Overton estate on behalf of John Overton Jr., who had not yet reached adulthood, Claybrooke began working with Marcus Winchester on the development of Memphis. Over the years, Claybrooke would become one of Winchester's closest friends—a steadfast ally Winchester would soon find invaluable.

Chapter Fifteen Endnotes

1. J. J. Rawlings, *Miscellaneous Writings and Reminiscences of J. J. Rawlings* (Memphis: United Charities, 1896), 23.
2. *Memphis Enquirer*, August 25, 1836, 1.
3. W. B. Waldran, "Anniversary Address," *Old Folks Record* 1 (December 1874): 100.
4. Waldran, "Anniversary Address," 101.
5. W. H. Rainey, *Rainey's Memphis: Memphis City Directory, 1855–56* (Memphis: H. B. Wolfkill, 1855), 34.
6. "Last Rites Today," *Tennessean*, December 13, 1903, 3.
7. Marcus Winchester to John Overton, January 15, 1826, *John Overton Papers, 1769–1866*, Tennessee State Library and Archives, Nashville, Tenn.
8. James Winchester, Letter of Condolence to David Winchester, 1752–1826, Gilder Lehrman Institute of American History, GLC06997.55, accessed via Adam Matthew, *American History*, 1493–1945.
9. Louis Farrell, *Descendants of William Winchester*, 3
10. "Obituary," *National Banner and Nashville Whig*, August 5, 1826, 3.
11. Charles Cassedy to Maria Breedlove, regarding biography of James Winchester, Gilder Lehrman Institute of American History, GLC06997.77, accessed via Adam Matthew, *American History*, 1493–1945.
12. Susan Winchester Powel Scales, *My Mother, A Biography* (unpublished manuscript, 1950), 6–7.
13. Douglas Anderson, "G. W. Winchester of Bledsoe's 'Lick'," *Nashville Banner*, August 16, 1925, 35.
14. Midge H. Gurley, "Abandoned, Abused, and a Municipal Pariah: The Life and Death of Winchester Burying Ground," *The West Tennessee Historical Society Papers*, 2018, 1.
15. James E. Roper, "Marcus B. Winchester," *Tennessee Historical Quarterly* 18, no. 1 (1959): 16–17.
16. Clifton, Frances. "John Overton as Andrew Jackson's Friend." *Tennessee Historical Quarterly* 11, no. 1 (1952): 30.
17. James Parton, *Life of Andrew Jackson, Volume I* (New York: Mason Brothers, 1861), 152-153.
18. E. P. Blair, "The Real Rachel Jackson, *Nashville Tennessean*, September 6, 1936, 1.
19. Frank Nugent, "The Screen," *New York Times*, September 5, 1936, 7.
20. "Movie Built Around Jackson OK'd by Censors," *Nashville Banner*, September 4, 1936, 18.
21. "Movie Built Around Jackson OK'd by Censors," *Nashville Banner*.
22. "Movie Built Around Jackson OK'd by Censors," *Nashville Banner*.
23. Fletch Coke, "Profiles of John Overton," *Tennessee Historical Quarterly* 37, no. 4 (1978): 401.
24. Samuel Gordon Heiskell, *Andrew Jackson and Early Tennessee History* (Nashville: Ambrose Printing Co., 1918), 436.
25. History of Sangamon County, Illinois: Together with Sketches of Its Cities, Villages and Townships (Chicago, Interstate Publishing Company, 1881**)**, 431.
26. Heiskell, *Andrew Jackson and Early Tennessee History*, 324.
27. William W. Clayton, *History of Davidson County, Tennessee, with Illustrations and Biographical Sketches of Its Prominent Men and Pioneers* (Philadelphia: J. W. Lewis & Co., 1880), 99.
28. Richard H. Barry to Marcus B. Winchester, April 14, 1833, Tennessee State Library and Archives, Nashville, Tenn.

BYRD HILL & SON,
ADAMS STREET,
MEMPHIS, TENN.,

Being permanently located, for the

PURCHASE OF NEGROES,

will pay the highest market value. They will also

BUY AND SELL ON COMMISSION,

having a suitable yard for their safe keeping.

☞ Particular attention paid to the selection of homes for favorite servants.

☞ **NEGROES FOR SALE AT ALL TIMES.**

BATH HOUSE
On the Mississippi,
at the
FOOT OF EXCHANGE STREET

With the National Flag, which can be seen from any part of Front Row, where

BATHS OF THE BEST KIND

can always be had.

GEORGE FRITZ.

From Rainey's Memphis City Directory, 1855/56

Part Three

Chapter Sixteen: Tired of Being Alone

*Marcus Winchester marries Amarante Loiselle,
a free woman of color from St. Louis*

Things about Memphis noted by visitors in those early years included the large number of people sick with fevers, the rainbow of colors visible when the sun struck the mud on the side of the bluff just right, and the mixed races of the people who lived there. One visitor described Memphis as "composed of people of mixed blood, some a cross of whites and Indians, some of whites and negroes, others again of negroes and Indians."[1]

Newspaper editor and historian John M. Keating published a history of Memphis in 1888 in which he expressed his opinion on why White men had married "Indian women" rather than "respectable" White women in Memphis:

> There were Indian women and black girls in abundance; not a respectable white woman was to be seen once a month ... two or three respectable men married Indian women; excuse no white women about. They lived together apparently well satisfied, and raised half-breed families. *One white man married a quadroon but his was a solitary instance.*[2]

That "one White man" was Marcus Winchester. And the "quadroon?" That was Amarante Loiselle. Today, barely a trace remains of Loiselle, despite her being Winchester's wife for sixteen years and the mother of his eight children.

In the Tennessee State Library and Archives, one can find hundreds of letters written by and to the Winchester, Breedlove, Overton, and Claybrooke families, sharing news, updates, and gossip about Marcus Winchester's extended family. Yet, there is no mention of his first wife. It is certainly possible, though unproven, that mentions of Amarante were intentionally destroyed after her death to protect the Winchester children from the social stigma of being mixed race—much like John Overton destroyed his letters exchanged with Andrew Jackson.

Amarante was so thoroughly erased from the historical record that some early chroniclers of Memphis assigned the marital status of bachelor to Marcus Winchester. "While he never married, his gracious manners had a peculiar charm for woman,"[3] one journalist wrote in 1909—overlooking the existence of Amarante, Winchester's eight children, and his second wife, Lucy.

In the void created by the absence of facts, writers who did acknowledge Amarante have spun the tale of Marcus and Amarante Loiselle Winchester into whatever narrative they chose, often with a flair for the dramatic. The marriage of Marcus Winchester also became a powerful cautionary tale, passed down by those warning of the dangers that awaited White men who dared to defy the social norms and laws of the day by marrying outside their race.

One Memphis journalist, Linton Weeks, writing more than 125 years after Winchester's death, proclaimed, "Of all the dramatic personae to grace the stage of Memphis history, perhaps the most illustrious, imaginative character was Marcus Brutus Winchester, the town's first fallen hero." Weeks continued his version of Winchester's life, casting him as a "dashing, dapperly dressed young man" who was "outwardly genteel and affable, inwardly a searching and brooding fellow," that is, until he met "the beautiful quadroon abandoned in Memphis by Thomas Hart Benton." Weeks described Amarante Loiselle as "bewitching, gentle, hearty, and gracious." Was the word *bewitching* used to imply that Winchester was not to blame for his "indiscretion?" Weeks also noted that Winchester and his *bewitching* bride, the forbidden lovers, "would have been run out of town if not for the friendship of Isaac Rawlings."[4]

To some, being the victim of a bewitching was certainly preferable to a man choosing to marry someone with even one drop of Black blood and attempting to sneak her across the color line as his wife. After all, the "one-drop rule" classified anyone with even a single ancestor of African descent as Black, regardless of their appearance or the percentage of African ancestry. While not formally written into law during Winchester's time, the concept was increasingly used socially to enforce racial segregation and maintain a system of White supremacy as the fight over slavery intensified. Of course, the irony was Marcus Winchester himself would have been considered Black under this obviously misguided system.

The word "quadroon" played an especially significant role in the complex racial language of the early nineteenth century, particularly in places like New Orleans, where racial identity carried heavy social and legal implications. A person identified as quadroon was one-quarter Black and three-quarters White. In the antebellum South, terms like "quadroon" were not only used to define legal status but also influenced social mobility and even where one was allowed to go. In other cases, it resulted in sex trafficking and prostitution.

In one example, "Quadroon balls" occasionally occurred in some of the hotels of New Orleans. Gatherings of mixed-race women—identified as quadroons—were introduced to wealthy White men in the hopes of forming "social or financial connections." These individuals, despite being considered free or enslaved Black women, were sometimes seen as more desirable due to their lighter complexion.

While traveling through the South, Edward King, author of *The Great South, a Record of Journeys*, wrote in his journal, "The quadroons of New Orleans are celebrated for their beauty, and many of them are not distinguishable from white persons in personal appearance. They are the offspring of white fathers and mulatto mothers, and partake generally of the characteristics of the two races, though the fairness of complexion predominates."[5] This system of raising lighter-skinned women to a higher level also reinforced the evolving racial boundaries that governed Southern society.

In some legal contexts, a person labeled as a quadroon might be treated differently than someone categorized as "mulatto" or "octoroon." Mulatto referred to those of mixed Black and White heritage. It was derived from the Spanish word Mulatto, meaning mule—which is a hybrid of a horse and donkey. Of course, it was racist and intentionally derogatory, reflecting the view of racial mixing as unnatural. It can also be found in legal and census documents to classify individuals of a variety of mixed races.

"Octoroon" was used to describe someone who was one-eighth Black and seven-eighths White, while "Creole" was a term that could have a range of meanings, depending on the location and context. It generally referred to people of mixed European and African descent who were born in North America. The racial meaning of Creole, especially in cities like New Orleans and St. Louis, was often complex and frequently used when it might not be an accurate description of an individual's actual origin or racial heritage.

A "Melungeon" was a term historically used to describe a mixed-ethnic group of people primarily found in the Appalachian region of the United States in parts of eastern Tennessee, southwestern Virginia, and eastern Kentucky. The origins of the Melungeons were the subject of much debate and speculation for many years, with many descendants claiming to be of Portuguese heritage rather than African. Today, DNA testing has proven the families historically called Melungeons are the offspring of sub-Saharan Africans and Whites of northern or central European origin.[6] In other words, their ancestors were intermarried Back and White men and women.

In cities like Memphis, New Orleans, and St. Louis, racial identity became more relevant as the community and social structure grew and became more complex. The race of your neighbor's parents did not matter when you were just trying to survive from one day to the next. As opportunity, income, and a social hierarchy developed, so did displays of overt racism and laws passed to establish and retain White supremacy.

Marcus and Amarante became a living example of the idea of interracial marriage. Leaning into the romantic aspect of the story, one writer proclaimed, "Winchester fell in love with a bewitching, honey-skinned woman, lived proudly in the face of social scorn, and died in poverty, a broken man. All for love."[7] Once again, the word "bewitching" was used in reference to Amarante, and this writer pointed out she was "honey-skinned," indicating she was more akin to the women of the New Orleans quadroon balls than the Black enslaved women in the cotton fields of the Delta.

"Women were scarce, and consequently it was commonplace for men to openly have mistresses of mixed blood and to father children of the relationships," wrote another. "But it was unheard of for a man to marry his mistress."[8]

Describing the Winchesters in her biography of Frances Wright, Alice Perkins wrote of Marcus, "He was tall, black-haired, and very handsome, with a manner that impressed everyone with its mixture of bonhomie and dignity. He seemed assured of a brilliant future in the history of his state *if it had not been for one tragic limitation*."[9] That limitation was his choice of a wife.

Most of what has been written about Marcus Winchester and Amarante Loiselle in the last century and a half can be traced back to a narrative created by one man, James Dick Davis. Historians later proved much of what Davis wrote was adapted from secondhand accounts, faulty recollections, and a flair for the dramatic and never intended to be an accurate historical record. Davis was, above all, a storyteller—not a historian.

His version of the story of Marcus and Amarante Winchester was shared in newspaper articles and in a compilation of those articles turned into a book published in 1873, *The History of the City of Memphis*. Picking up on what Davis wrote, Linton Weeks's account focused on Thomas Hart Benton's role as the villain of the story—by introducing a transactional element. He wrote that Benton passed Amarante off to Winchester then, "to assuage his guilt, Benton plopped a bag of gold on the counter and assured Winchester that money did not matter."[10]

Most versions of the story of Marcus and Amarante include Benton, something first found in the account written by Davis. In his version, Thomas Benton, Andrew Jackson's aide-de-camp and future Missouri Senator, took a "beautiful French Quadroon woman" home with him from New Orleans. When he tired of her, he "turned her adrift" but provided a little financial support, which he gave to Marcus Winchester to manage. Marcus fell in love with the beautiful Amarante Loiselle, and she with him. Together, the two traveled to Louisiana, where there was no law permitting interracial marriage. Throwing caution to the wind, the wealthy, good-looking, White Winchester made the beautiful and charming Quadroon his lawfully wedded wife.

Davis's account was a tragic love story. Although Amarante, who went by the name Mary in later years, tried to prove her worthiness to the locals in Memphis "by acts of charity and liberal donations to religious purposes," she was ostracized by the White community. He claimed eventually some in Memphis turned against the Winchester family to such a degree, it became dangerous for them to go out in public. Eventually, Marcus and Amarante Winchester had to flee the city and move with their children to their farm, Muscogee Camp, about three miles outside the city limits. The city's first mayor had been banished from the town he built. In Davis's story, because of a broken heart, Marcus turned to drink and died in poverty, a broken shell of the man he once was.

James Davis, the writer who shared that story, was born on September 2, 1810, in Pennsylvania. He arrived in Memphis at age seventeen in 1827 by way of Tuscumbia, Alabama. Davis married Mary Jane Smythe on December 15, 1834, and together they raised at least seven children in Memphis. He fancied himself an author and poet but fed his large family by working as a municipal harbormaster and house painter.

Along the way, Davis developed a deep appreciation for Memphis history. As a young man, he heard stories of the past directly from those who had lived through the birth of the city, and he felt an obligation to preserve those memories. Through his storytelling, Davis provided vivid—and frequently embellished—versions of the events that shaped Memphis's early years, blending history with his personal observations and gossip he heard along the way.

It had not taken Memphians long to embrace their heritage. The Old Folks of Shelby County, an organization for original settlers and their families who had been in Memphis for twenty years or more, was founded in 1857. Only around forty years had passed since Marcus Winchester and William Lawrence first navigated their flatboat to a spot on the bank of the river, made their way up the fourth Chickasaw bluff, and introduced themselves to Paddy Meagher.

The group's official publication, *The Old Folks Record*, published volume one, number one, in October 1874. In that issue, they requested "biographical sketches of old neighbors, anecdotes of old citizens, and traditions of the neighborhoods of Memphis."[11] The publication featured short stories, poems, news of the members, and historical anecdotes. Davis was one of the earliest members, officers, and editors.

Family tradition suggests that Davis's principles took precedence over his popularity when he publicly declared himself as one of the five men in Shelby County who voted against Tennessee's secession from the Union.

After the war, it appears all was forgiven. His articles about the history of Memphis appeared in *The Old Folks Record*, in local newspapers, and in his book, *The History of the City of Memphis*, turning Davis into a local celebrity. The forward for his book included some high praise for his writing:

> He appears as a chronicler of events forgotten by nearly all the living, and unrecorded by those who have died. Interesting beyond measure is the simple recital of facts and let us say that even Sterne the divinest master of pure English never wrote a more admirable and touching recital in more faultless language ... it is a masterpiece of simple elegance. Read and improve it who can. It is matchless because it rises superior to all art.[12]

The Memphis writer whose work "rose superior to all art" died at age seventy on October 3, 1880. His dedication to recording Memphis history was acknowledged in his obituary, but the writer also downgraded Davis's book from "superior to all art" to "readable." He wrote:

> The venerable James D. Davis one of the oldest of the old folks society and familiar with scenes and events on the bluff since long before the Indians left, died last night. Mr. Davis was held in high esteem by the older settlers of this vicinity, and he was well worthy of all the respect he commanded. Some years ago he wrote a readable book containing many facts concerning the early history of this section, interspersed with anecdotes, incidents and personal mention of notable people.[13]

In advance of his first article about Marcus and Amarante Winchester in the January 16, 1871, issue of the *Memphis Daily Appeal*, Davis was described as one of the oldest citizens of Memphis and a writer whose narrative "is distinguished by its naive simplicity and truthfulness."[14] But was his story about the Winchesters *really* truthful?

Journalist Gary Moore tried to find out for an article in the May 1993 issue of *Memphis Magazine* titled "Memphis Belle." As Moore discovered, "only small scraps of evidence exist by which to conjure up the ghost of Amarante Loiselle."[15] Moore first examined historical and census records to determine whether there was any truth to the story that Thomas Hart Benton, the villain in Davis's account, really met Loiselle in New Orleans, took her as a companion, only to later enlisted Winchester's help in "dealing with her." As it turns out, Moore did find a connection between Winchester, Benton, and Loiselle, but it was a complicated story to research. Moore wrote, "Digging into this mystery is like mining the river bottom. The mire keeps shifting and nothing is certain except that down there somewhere is the ship-wrecked foundation of race relations."[16]

Thomas Hart Benton was born in 1782 near Hillsborough, North Carolina. His father died before he was three, and his mother moved the family to Tennessee. They settled on three thousand acres twenty-five miles south of Nashville. Benton received his license to practice law from John Overton and two other Tennessee Superior Court judges. At the outbreak of the War of 1812, Andrew Jackson made Benton his aide-de-camp, with a commission as a lieutenant colonel. Benton was assigned to represent Jackson's interests to military officials in Washington City. He quickly grew frustrated with this administrative role, as it denied him direct combat experience. Despite his lack of heroism on the battlefield, he played a crucial role in organizing logistics for Jackson's forces and developed important relationships with those working in Washington City.

Benton's fiery temper greatly impacted his early years and political career in Tennessee. He was smart and ambitious but quickly developed political aspirations that were often derailed by his confrontational nature. This led to numerous conflicts—including one with his former mentor that nearly changed the course of American history. Thomas Benton's brother, Jesse, had a minor disagreement with William Carroll, a future governor of Tennessee, that escalated to Jesse Benton challenging Carroll to a duel. Andrew Jackson, friends with both, reluctantly acted as Carroll's second. Both Carroll and Benton survived the duel, but both were slightly injured. Jesse Benton received an injury that was as embarrassing as it was painful—a shot in his buttocks. Thomas Benton publically blamed Jackson for not stopping the duel before it escalated to that point. The two exchanged letters that grew increasingly hostile.

On September 4, 1813, Jackson and a few of his friends had a near-deadly encounter with the Benton brothers near the Nashville Inn. Jackson was the initial aggressor, allegedly rushing at Benton yelling, "Now defend yourself, you damned rascal!" Pistols were drawn, and the fight escalated from verbal altercation to street brawl. Ultimately, Jackson was shot in the arm and shoulder by Thomas Benton, while both Benton brothers were slightly wounded by members of Jackson's entourage. In *The Life of Andrew Jackson*, Marquis James paints a vivid picture of the aftermath:

> General Jackson's wounds soaked two mattresses with blood at the Nashville Inn. He was nearly dead… while every physician in Nashville tried to staunch the flow of blood, Colonel Benton and his partisans gathered before the Inn shouting defiance. Benton broke a small-sword of Jackson's that he had found at the scene of conflict. All the doctors save one declared for the amputation of the arm. Jackson barely understood. "I'll keep my arm," he said.[17]

The confrontation was widely reported throughout Tennessee, where Jackson was revered as a hero. Benton's political future in the state came to an abrupt end. He wrote to a friend, "The meanest wretches under heaven to contend with: liars, affidavit-makers, and shameless cowards…all the puppies of Jackson are at work on me."[18]

Benton chose nearby Missouri to start over, setting up a law practice and founding a newspaper, the *Missouri Enquirer*. Perhaps a little wiser after the fallout from his battle with Jackson, he quickly became a dominant political figure, serving as Missouri's first senator, a position he held for thirty years. Despite their very public confrontation in Nashville, Benton later became one of Jackson's strongest allies in the Senate. When asked about their fight in later years, he replied, "Didn't everyone fight with Andrew Jackson when we were all young?"

Benton was also a major supporter of those in the fur trade. Thanks to his efforts, on May 6, 1822, Congress passed a law abolishing the government-managed trading posts that did business with the Native Americans. This absence of the factories created an opportunity for fur traders to fill in the gap and accumulate wealth.

Benton married Elizabeth McDowell, the daughter of Colonel James McDowell, on March 27, 1821, and the first of their six children was born in 1822. Their daughter Jessie, born in 1824, would one day marry John C. Frémont, the celebrated explorer of the American West and the first presidential candidate of the Republican Party.

Elizabeth's family was well-established in Rockbridge County, Virginia, and held a prominent position in society. Benton's marriage into the McDowell family strengthened his political and social standing among the wealthy elite in Washington—ironically, the very group he frequently denounced during his campaigns. Despite his populist rhetoric, the union provided him with valuable connections that bolstered his influence in national politics. Together, he and Elizabeth had six children. Theodore Roosevelt, who wrote a biography of Benton, displayed his admiration when he noted:

> He was a faithful friend and a bitter foe; he was vain, proud,

utterly fearless.... Without being a great orator or writer, or even an original thinker, he yet possessed marked ability; and his abounding vitality and marvelous memory, his indomitable energy and industry, and his tenacious persistency and personal courage, all combined to give him a position and influence such as few American statesmen have ever held.[19]

Gary Moore did discover a connection between Benton and Amarante Loiselle, but it was not a romantic one. In 1815, Benton was recorded as living on F Street in St. Louis. The 1821 St. Louis directory lists fur trader Pierre Baribeau, Loiselle's father or stepfather, living at 126 North Church, on the southwest corner of F Street. Amarante Loiselle was born around 1809, so she was only around six years old when her family could have first met their new neighbor, Benton.

Baribeau had owned property in St. Louis since before the territory became the state of Missouri. In an 1805 document, Baribeau is listed among the names of other property owners. His name also appears on a letter, dated December 27, 1805, addressed to President Thomas Jefferson from citizens of the territory, expressing their support and confidence in Governor James Wilkinson. It was support that was misguided at best. Wilkinson schemed to have Kentucky and Tennessee secede from the United States, and while serving as a turncoat on behalf of the Spanish government, he was suspected of attempting to sabotage the Lewis and Clark expedition in 1804.

Jefferson's first vice president, Aaron Burr—most remembered today for the duel with Alexander Hamilton that inspired a Broadway musical—persuaded Jefferson to appoint James Wilkinson as the first territorial governor. Burr and Wilkinson then collaborated on a plan to separate the land west of the Appalachian Mountains from the United States and establish a new country. They worked hard to persuade prominent St. Louis's property-owning male residents, such as Baribeau, to join their scheme. Wilkinson later turned against Burr and confessed everything to Jefferson. While neither man was ultimately indicted for their misdeeds, both were removed from their respective offices. Although Wilkinson continued to serve in the U.S. Army and held various commands during the War of 1812, he went down in history as a symbol of incompetence, corruption, and treachery.

Burr and Wilkinson were not alone in their greed, inspired by the potential riches the region promised. The Louisiana Purchase of 1804 had opened the exciting new territory to the United States, setting the stage for a booming fur trade. Reports of abundant beaver populations in the upper Missouri from the Lewis and Clark expedition triggered a frenzy among fur trading companies.

French Canadian fur traders like Baribeau, long familiar with the waterways and wilderness of the northern territories, saw in these new lands an opportunity to make their own fortunes. While inland frontiersmen and pioneers traveled along Indian trails or carved out new paths traveling on horseback or in wagons, the trails of the fur traders were rivers like the Missouri, Ohio, and Mississippi. Their modes of transportation were the various styles of barges, birchbark canoes, keelboats, and flatboats that evolved based on the types of waters they navigated.

One group of boatsmen that stood out from the others were the Creoles from Canada that typically piloted large barges. Often, they had Native American, Black, or mixed-race heritage. According to historian Leland Baldwin, they traditionally wore a unique style of clothing: "When on the boats, they often worked stripped to the waist, but at other times they wore fringed buckskin trousers, bright red shirts, and blue surtouts reaching almost to the knees. Rough caps, moccasins, and red woolen sashes completed the costumes."[20]

It was in this environment of discovery and exploration that Amarante was born and raised by her mother—and Pierre Baribeau's common-law wife—Victoire Loiselle. Whether Baribeau was Amarante Loiselle's father is unproven. In a real estate transaction, Baribeau referred to her as "daughter of my wife, Victoire Loiselle," suggesting that Baribeau may have been Amarante's stepfather, rather than her biological father. It could also have been a formal legal phrase used to specify the familial connection in a way that avoided ambiguity considering he was not yet legally married to Victoire.

It appears Victoire Loiselle and Pierre Baribeau had at least three other children together: Therese, Perry, and Adrien. Therese later settled in Memphis, Perry remained in St. Louis, and Adrien made New Orleans his home.

What race was Amarante's mother? The name Victoire was common in France, and Loiselle is a French surname. St. Louis, founded by the French in 1764, remained under French and Spanish control until the United States acquired it in the Louisiana Purchase of 1804. By the time Amarante Loiselle was born, St. Louis had a significant French-speaking Creole population, which also included white settlers as well as mixed-race individuals of French and Native American or African ancestry.

Victoire Loiselle had a child who died in infancy. When "Child Loisel" was buried in St. Louis King of France Cemetery on July 31, 1806, the baby's race was recorded as "free colored." This suggests that Victoire Loiselle may have been Creole, mixed-race, or a free Black woman.

Many French-Canadian fur traders intermarried with Native American women, particularly from the Osage, Kaskaskia, or Dakota tribes. Since Pierre Baribeau was involved in the fur trade, he may have been Métis (of mixed French and Indigenous ancestry), a common identity among traders in the Upper Mississippi and Missouri River regions.

In early nineteenth-century St. Louis, White American settlers often viewed French Canadians as "other" because of their French language, Catholic faith, and close ties to Native Americans—ties that were strengthened through both intermarriage and relationships made through the fur trade. Regardless of their racial background, both Victoire Loiselle and Pierre Baribeau likely faced a degree of discrimination and racism. While French Canadians initially held some power in cities like St. Louis and New Orleans, especially in trade, Catholic institutions, and politics, White settlers eventually became the dominant force. French Canadians were gradually marginalized.

Because Amarante's father remains unidentified and her mother's exact heritage is unknown, her racial identity cannot be determined with certainty. What is certain, however, is that she was not considered White—a fact that carried consequences for both her and Marcus Winchester in antebellum Memphis. She was, however, a landowner.

As part of the research for his article, Moore found records indicating that Baribeau deeded Amarante part of the property he owned on F Street on April 21, 1819. In the antebellum South, the ability of women to own land—while legally restricted—shaped pockets of society in profound ways, particularly in growing urban centers like St. Louis and, eventually, Memphis.

Most women were excluded from owning property due to social and legal restrictions, but widows and unmarried women sometimes inherited, purchased, or managed property in their own names. In St. Louis, where French and Spanish colonial laws had once granted women limited rights to property, free women of color and White widows continued this legacy.

Records show that Baribeau eventually married Amarante's mother but not until December 27, 1827, about a month before her death on January 24, 1828, at age fifty-three. This was likely to avoid complications in settling her estate. By the time her mother died, Amarante was twenty-two, already living in Memphis, and the mother of two young children fathered by her husband, Marcus Winchester.

Stories passed down through the years claim that Winchester and Loiselle met on a steamboat. Although unproven, it seems more plausible that Benton, a neighbor and family friend, was part of a group that included Loiselle traveling from St. Louis to either Memphis, Natchez, or New Orleans. Winchester frequently traveled to New Orleans for business and to visit family living there. Either on the boat or during a stop in Memphis, it is possible that Amarante Loiselle became acquainted with the city's handsome founder.

It is likely that those who later disapproved of interracial marriage seized on her connection to Benton—unpopular in Tennessee—and spread rumors and gossip, which eventually became accepted as fact. Benton biographer William N. Chambers also agrees any romantic relationship between Amarante and Benton seems very unlikely:

> The fact that Benton was not at New Orleans with Jackson, but in Washington, and the fact that he moved to St. Louis in the late summer or fall of 1815, makes it hard to understand when or how he acquired the girl, or how he could have kept her in Tennessee two or three years. Finally, the whole thing seems out of character for Benton.[21]

Regardless of how Marcus and Amarante met, it is thought they married soon afterward. According to the late Arthur Webb, the couple married in New Orleans in 1823 when Winchester was twenty-seven and Amarante was still a young teenager. Webb was a well-respected genealogist, historian, and journalist who dedicated his life to exploring and reporting on the history of African Americans in Memphis. He joined the *Tri-State Defender* newspaper staff in 1978, where he worked for twenty-eight years, rising to the rank of associate editor before his death on October 25, 2006.

After Webb's death, portions of his research were donated to the Memphis and Shelby County Room at the Benjamin L. Hooks Central Library. Unfortunately, the evidence he claimed to have found of a legal marriage between Marcus and Amarante is not included in that collection. If such proof exists, it would be significant, as it would suggest Winchester's intention for Loiselle to be his legal wife despite a Tennessee law passed in 1822 that made interracial marriages illegal in the state.

Both before and after that law was passed, some White men lived with free and enslaved Black women as though they were husband and wife but never formally married. Some White men were even legally the masters of the enslaved women they referred to as their wives. Of course, many of those relationships existed because the enslaved woman had no other options. She had to survive with an absence of any agency over her life or that of her enslaved children. There are many known cases of enslavers selling the children they fathered with enslaved women.

Isaac Rawlings, for example, was in a public relationship with an enslaved woman, who was both his sole domestic partner and the mother of his son. After moving his mercantile into town, Rawlings continued to expand his wealth and political influence in Shelby County, serving as mayor from 1829 to 1831 and again from 1833 to 1836. One young man who knew Rawlings for many years described him as "a dude, or dandy, as we then called, and wore ruffled shirts and long waving hair."[22]

In 1828, Rawlings relocated his store to a small building with tiny windows and a deep cellar on the south side of Commerce Street, near Toncray's Alley between Front and Main Streets, positioning it closer to Winchester & Carr and another mercantile, Henderson & Fern. Rawlings also acquired 342 acres north of the Loosahatchie River at the Shelby-Tipton County line, 500 acres along the Wolf River, and part of an entire block on Market Square in Memphis. Additionally, he maintained investments in several Memphis businesses, including the Memphis Wharf Company. He also served as president of the Memphis Marine and Fire Insurance Company.

One early settler recalled that living with the bachelor Rawlings were his clerks, who helped with his business, and "two negro women who did the cooking and the washing." One of those women was named Hannah and was described as "a good-looking Indian woman of which Rawlings was very fond."[23]

Isaac Rawlings's nephew, Joseph J. Rawlings, remained close to his uncle, and other members of their extended family migrated from Maryland to Memphis. Included in that group was Isaac's unmarried sister, Juliet, and another nephew, Thomas. According to James Davis, Isaac Rawlings was instrumental in the founding and much of the funding of Memphis's Calvary Episcopal Church. At one point, he and his family were its only members.

Eventually, another family member joined the household—a son, William Isaac Rawlings. He was born to the enslaved woman Isaac treated as his wife. Since Isaac Rawlings was the church's most important member—and its primary funder—no one appears to have protested when Rawlings had his son, technically his enslaved boy, baptized at Calvary Episcopal Church. William Isaac Rawlings was raised as though he were free and White, despite the fact that by law, he and his mother were counted among those Rawlings enslaved.

Down the street, the Winchester family was growing as well. Because no written details remain, most of the facts about their early years can only be inferred from the few legal documents and census records available. Winchester sold his wife lot 710 on September 24, 1824. The transaction was witnessed by Robert Lawrence. In 1827, Winchester deeded more property to her at the corner of Jackson and Main Streets and transferred ownership of two enslaved people to her for one dollar.

Winchester left no written opinions on slavery, but his actions provide insight into his views. On one hand, he came from a family of enslavers and owned enslaved people himself. On the other, he married a free woman of color and provided help in freeing enslaved individuals when he could. During his life, many turned to Winchester when they wanted to ensure that, after their death, their slaves would be freed. Two enslaved women, Sarah and Barbara, along with five enslaved children, were willed to Winchester by William Bell. The two men had agreed that Winchester would take care of the legalities of freeing them, then help them settle in a free state, which he did. In another case, Ruthie Ann Boyd asked Winchester to purchase her and then free her once she had paid him back what he paid for her. Winchester later sold her to Jacob N. Moon with the same understanding. She became a free woman in January 1850.

John M. Keating observed:

> The kindliest feeling existed between the Negroes and the white people of the town and vicinity, and the strong tendency toward manumission and deportation that then outcropped in many places at the South was nowhere stronger than in Memphis and Shelby County. Leading Men like Winchester helped in schemes for the education of the Negro and he particularly had an understanding with his Negroes that they could work out their freedom.[24]

Until freedom for the enslaved became a near impossibility, Winchester's store was known as one of the few places where enslaved men and women could deposit money they earned. It was kept safe by Winchester until they had saved enough to purchase their freedom or that of their loved ones. James Davis wrote:

> I have heard that Winchester opened a regular account with all his slaves, charging them with their purchase [of] food, clothing, etc., and crediting them with all their services, with a view to their ultimate emancipation. Another class that had the greatest confidence in the Major, was the women, who never doubted his honor. I allude to the widows and such as had estates to manage and I will venture to say that not one of them had ever cause to regret it.[25]

Obviously, Winchester's philosophy regarding race had to be influenced by the fact that he was the father of mixed-race children. He and Amarante eventually had eight. The couple's first child, Laura, was born around 1826, quickly followed by their first son, Robert Owen, who was born around 1827. Baptism records at the St. Louis Cathedral show a child named Regis Pierre Winchester was born to a couple named "Marcus Winchester and Amaranthe Loisel" on August 25, 1827, and baptized on September 28, 1828. Some believe that Regis Pierre was their eldest son and that his name was later changed to Robert Owen.

Owen was followed by Frances in 1829. The 1830 census shows a female

"A. Loiselle" living in Memphis in a home that included five free "colored" and four enslaved people. Three of the "free colored persons" were likely Winchester and Loiselle's three youngest children. Marcus was recorded as living a few doors down. Why, if they were legally married, they were recorded living separately and why she was listed as Loiselle and not Winchester remains a mystery.

More children continued to arrive. Louise was born in 1832, Loiselle in 1835, Valeria in 1837, Selima in 1838, and Mary Lisida, the youngest, in 1839. The children of Marcus and Amarante Winchester were considered free Black, mixed-race, or Mulatto. This meant that no matter the significance of the roles played by their father and grandfather in founding the town in which they lived, they would never truly be free.

Chapter Sixteen Endnotes

1. James E. Roper, "Marcus B. Winchester," *Tennessee Historical Quarterly* 18, no. 1 (1959): 6.
2. John M. Keating, *History of the City of Memphis* (Syracuse, NY: D. Mason & Co., 1888), 151–52.
3. "Half Forgotten Pages in the History of Memphis." *Commercial Appeal*, December 12, 1909, 67.
4. "Half Forgotten Pages in the History of Memphis," *Commercial Appeal*.
5. Edward King, *The Great South* (Hartford: American Publishing Company, 1875), 517.
6. Travis Loller, "'A Whole Lot of People Upset by This Study': DNA & the Truth About Appalachia's Melungeons," *News Leader* (Staunton, VA), March 8, 2021, 12.
7. Linton Weeks, *Memphis: A Folk History* (Little Rock: Parkhurst Publishers, 1982), 34–35.
8. Weeks, Memphis: *A Folk History*, 36.
9. A. J. G. Perkins and Theresa Wolfson, *Frances Wright: Free Enquirer, The Study of a Temperament* (Philadelphia: Porcupine Press, 1972), 144.
10. Weeks, *Memphis: A Folk History*, 27.
11. *Old Folks Record*, vol. 1, no. 1 (October 1874): 1.
12. James Davis, *The History of the City of Memphis* (Memphis: Lippincott & Co., 1873), 78.
13. *Public Ledger*, October 4, 1880, 4.
14. *Memphis Daily Appeal*, January 16, 1871, 3.
15. Gary Moore, "Memphis Belle," *Memphis Magazine*, May 1943, 79.
16. Moore, "Memphis Belle," 77.
17. Marquis James, *The Life of Andrew Jackson* (Indianapolis: Bobbs-Merrill, 1938), 154.
18. H. W. Brands, *Andrew Jackson, His Life and Times* (Doubleday: New York, 2005), 191.
19. Theodore Roosevelt, *American Statesman, Thomas Hart Benton* (Boston: The Riverside Press, 1886), 364-365.
20. Leeland D. Baldwin, *The Keelboat Age on Western Waters*, Pittsburg: The University of Pittsburg Press, 1941), 86.
21. William Nisbet Chambers, *Old Bullion Benton* (Boston: Little, Brown and Company, 1956), 56.
22. "Old Landmarks in Memphis," *Memphis Avalanche*, May 27, 1888, 2.
23. "The Old Folks," *Memphis Daily Appeal*, June 18, 1871, 2.
24. Keating, *History of Memphis*, 190-192
25. James Davis, "Winchester's Peculiarities," *Memphis Daily Appeal*, January 6, 1871, 3.

LEWIS PUTNEY,
COMMISSION MERCHANT
AND DEALER IN
SALT,
No. 11 Exchange Buildings,
MEMPHIS, TENNESSEE.

L. GITTER & Co.,
PIANO MAKER AND TUNER.

SECOND DOOR FROM CORNER OF GAYOSO & SECOND STS.
Particular attention paid to Tuning and Repairing Pianos and other Musical Instruments.

H. HOEFER,
GILDER AND MANUFACTURER
of all descriptions of
FRAMES FOR LOOKING GLASSES, PICTURES, &C.
☞ ALSO, Orders taken for Steamboat Work, &c. &c.

From Rainey's Memphis City Directory, 1855/56

Chapter Seventeen: I am Somebody

The battle over slavery

It is striking today when one realizes many of those advocating for liberty and freedom in America were themselves owners of enslaved men, women, and children. Some enslaved children were even fathered by those same men. Twelve of the first eighteen presidents and around half of the fifty-five men who signed the Constitution were enslavers. The Declaration of Independence asserted that all people were endowed with unalienable rights, including life, liberty, and the pursuit of happiness. Yet, according to one study, forty-one of the fifty-six men who signed the Declaration on August 2, 1776, enslaved other human beings. Freedom certainly did not extend to the approximately 500,000 people held in bondage at the time—about 20 percent of the young nation's population.[1]

Slavery was an issue that grew more contentious through the years, ultimately leading to laws at the federal, state, and even county levels that were designed to uphold and protect White male authority. With the passage of each law, the chain around the neck of every non-White man and woman tightened, whether they were enslaved or not. The Northwest Ordinance, passed in 1787, prohibited slavery in territories east of the Mississippi River and north of the Ohio River, while the Fugitive Slave Act of 1793 enforced the capture and return of escaped slaves across state lines. This act introduced the element of slave hunters, who often did not care whether the non-White individuals they captured were legally free or enslaved.

The Missouri Compromise, passed in 1820, admitted Missouri as a slave state and Maine as a free state, and prohibited slavery in the Louisiana Purchase territories north of the 36°30´ line (except in Missouri itself). Looking back, the path that led to the Confederate attack on Fort Sumter in Charleston Harbor,

South Carolina, on April 12, 1861, can be seen falling into place. In the decades before the Civil War, politicians on both sides grappled with the issue of slavery, striving to avert a conflict that, in hindsight, seems inevitable. Their dread of a war between the North and the South was well-founded. By the time the Civil War ended at the Appomattox Court House in Virginia, on April 9, 1865, more than 700,000 Americans would be dead.[2]

Many Tennesseans can be counted among those trying to address the question of how to end slavery in the early decades of the nineteenth century. Because Tennessee was part of North Carolina until 1790, many of the state's initial laws regarding slavery and the rights of free Black individuals originated from there. In 1741, North Carolina legislators passed a number of laws intended to eliminate any chance enslaved individuals might be able to gain their freedom, even if they had the money to purchase it.

Some who were enslaved had developed skills essential to building the new country. Enslavers occasionally allowed those enslaved craftspeople to keep a portion of the money they earned when they were "loaned out" to others. Some enslavers kept the money for themselves. In 1821, John Overton drafted a written contract detailing an arrangement with Joseph Wright regarding one of Overton's enslaved women, Matilda.

Under this agreement, Matilda worked as a weaver for Wright, who provided her with food, shelter, and clothing while she was learning the trade. In return, Overton received twenty-two dollars' worth of woven goods. Once her work with Wright was completed, she returned to Overton's plantation. He purchased a loom for Matilda, and required her to use her newly acquired skills at Travellers Rest.[3]

Overton worked out similar arrangements to train other enslaved individuals as blacksmiths, coopers, mule spinners, and seamstresses, ensuring they developed specialized skills that benefited his plantation. As the skills and contributions of some enslaved individuals became indispensable to the young economy, their yearning for freedom grew and was met with harsher restrictions designed to suppress any aspirations for independence. Laws were enacted to stifle even small acts of autonomy. Enslaved individuals may have provided crucial labor on Southern plantations, but they were usually prohibited from opportunities such as raising their own livestock or poultry, denying them a chance at even limited self-reliance. They were also forbidden from carrying guns or hunting unless explicitly authorized by their enslavers, ensuring they remained defenseless.

Plantations were not the only places where enslaved individuals were forced to live and work. As business grew in Memphis, so did the number of enslaved individuals working on boats and on the river, loading and unloading goods of all kinds, especially cotton. They also worked in the hotels and taverns as housekeepers, bartenders, and porters.

In the early years, trade and commerce on the Memphis bluff primarily took place with Native Americans trading fur for goods of all kinds. By the 1830s, the region experienced growth in agricultural products, particularly in timber, tobacco, and cotton, along with significant advancements in river transportation. This opened new markets for the products West Tennessee farmers were able to produce. Flatboats, keelboats, and small rafts were gradually replaced by steamboats and larger barges, revolutionizing the way those products were transported.

The introduction of steamboats on the Mississippi River not only improved transportation but also reshaped the economies of river cities like Memphis. In 1811, the *New Orleans*, funded by Robert Fulton and Robert Livingston, became the first steamboat to navigate the Mississippi. While demonstrating the viability of steam-powered travel, those aboard also witnessed the devastating New Madrid earthquakes. Entire sections of land collapsed into the river, islands vanished, and massive waves surged upstream, briefly creating the illusion of waterfalls.

When the *New Orleans* finally reached its destination in January 1812, it had survived not only floating debris, sandbars, and a powerful earthquake but also the skepticism of those who doubted steam power could ever replace traditional boats.

Henry Miller Shreve had no doubts. He had honed his navigational skills as captain of the *Enterprise* during the War of 1812. He transported supplies for Andrew Jackson's army and participated in the Battle of New Orleans. Shreve recognized the need for vessels designed specifically for the Mississippi's frequently shallow waters and strong currents. His entry into the steamboat field, the *Washington*, launched in 1816. It was the first steamboat to feature a shallow-draft hull and twin decks, setting the standard for future river steamboats. The *Washington* made history in 1817 when it completed a round-trip voyage from Louisville to New Orleans in just 41 days, proving to naysayers that steam power was commercially viable. With Shreve's innovations, steamboats could now traverse the river more efficiently, carrying both passengers and goods with unprecedented speed and consistency.

While Shreve did not have to fight an earthquake, he did have to battle two formidable challengers: Robert Fulton and Robert Livingston, funders of the *New Orleans*. New York State had granted Fulton and Livingston exclusive rights to operate steamboats on its waterways, which they used to restrict competition from other steamboat operators. After a series of court battles against rivals, including Shreve, Fulton's company eventually lost its legal grip, clearing the way for entrepreneurs to invest in steamboat experimentation and production.

By the 1830s, hundreds of steamboats traveled up and down the rivers, revolutionizing trade and travel. Many of the towns along the Mississippi increasingly had a direct connection to national and international markets through St. Louis and New Orleans. Memphis was well on the way to joining them in becoming a bustling commercial hub thanks to the bluff and an infrastructure that supported merchants, traders, and settlers eager to capitalize on the developments made in transportation. As business along the riverfront grew, men like Marcus Winchester and Isaac Rawlings became increasingly prosperous as they sold land and supplies to new settlers drawn to Memphis thanks to the many jobs created by the booming waterfront industry.

Agriculture in Tennessee was prosperous most years as well. The federal census of 1830 recorded that around 70,000 new residents had flooded into West Tennessee to take advantage of the land, a portion of which was ideal for growing cotton. Even better, the tributaries that fed into the Mississippi River addressed one of the greatest challenges with cotton as well as other products—transporting it to market. As one historian wrote about West Tennessee:

> The rapid settlement and development of this section of the state has no parallel in the history of the Southwest. In the early days many settlers were unruly—many pirates and outlaws raged along the Mississippi especially—but soon the population became predominantly substantial and prosperous. It was due chiefly to the new division—West Tennessee—that in 1825 the cotton culture became so important in Tennessee that about 40,000 bales were produced, an increase of 38,500 bales over the crop produced in 1816.[4]

Some who grew and picked cotton on small farms in West Tennessee did so with family members or hired hands. However, a large workforce was required to grow, harvest, and transport cotton from the fields on large plantations to market. Most of that labor came from enslaved workers. Tennesseans like James Winchester, John Overton, Andrew Jackson, and most of their contemporaries were successful, respected businessmen—and unapologetic enslavers.

In 1820, James Winchester sent a shipment of merchandise to Marcus from Cairo. It included 712 gallons of whiskey, 3,250 pounds of bacon, and Prince, an enslaved craftsman whom he offered to sell to Anderson B. Carr for $800. In a letter to Marcus, James wrote, "Prince is sober, honest, and faithful; a tolerably good carpenter and shoemaker, and soon might make a good tanner."[5]

In an 1817 letter to his son-in-law, James Breedlove, Winchester remarked on the increasing value of enslaved individuals, stating, "the price of negroes has risen astonishingly." He added, "Frank Youree has lately arrived from Maryland with a drove of females. If from amongst them I can select one which I think will suit you on tolerable terms, will purchase and send to you."[6]

Andrew Jackson purchased his first slave, Nancy, shortly after arriving in Tennessee in 1788. Historian Mark R. Cheathem, who has done much contemporary research about Jackson and those enslaved by him, points out that the buying and selling of slaves was something Jackson did frequently throughout his adult life. He wrote, "A preliminary assessment of his slave transactions indicates that he bought and sold 125 slaves in sixty-five separate transactions over the course of his lifetime, with the transactions involving slaves in Tennessee, Alabama, Florida, Mississippi, South Carolina, Virginia, and the District of Columbia."[7]

In the list of John Overton's taxable property in 1820 are the names of fourteen enslaved males and eight enslaved females. In 1829, Overton's estate inventory listed more than fifty enslaved people, but this was only a snapshot at the time of his death. Given his long career as a land speculator and plantation owner, it is highly likely that he, like Andrew Jackson, bought and sold more than one hundred enslaved people over his lifetime. His financial records and transactions indicate that he used enslaved labor both for plantation work and to clear and develop land. In his 1957 book *Slavery in Tennessee,* historian Chase C. Mooney wrote, "John Overton might be classed as a slave trader—but not of the coffle-driving type—for he both purchased and sold quite a number of Negroes."[8] A coffle was a group of enslaved people chained or bound together and marched long distances, often from the Upper South to the Deep South, as part of the large-scale domestic slave trade. Slave traders who engaged in this practice were often considered the most notorious figures in the trade, dealing in high volumes of enslaved individuals and often transporting them in the most brutal conditions.

Although they bought, sold, and traded enslaved people, men like James Winchester, Andrew Jackson, and John Overton would not have been considered slave traders in the nineteenth century. Many today understandably blur the distinction between enslavers and slave traders. Those in the antebellum period recognized—and at times debated—the differences between the two.

An enslaver, or slaveholder as they were then called, was someone who owned enslaved people for the purposes of forced labor. Many considered themselves benevolent caretakers, a self-serving delusion that is difficult to comprehend today. By contrast, slave traders were viewed, even in the South, as occupying a lower moral and social rung. Traders made slavery look exactly as it was—the buying and selling of human beings for profit. It was challenging to position oneself as a benevolent Christian while separating families, marching people through city streets in chains, and auctioning them like livestock with financial profit the only objective.

As Mooney discovered in his research, like other goods, the price of enslaved individuals rose with demand and inflation. In 1790, the average price of an enslaved man or woman was between $150 to $200. Sixty years later, that price had risen dramatically: "In Memphis, in 1846 and 1847, carpenters sold for $2,500; a hammerer, or a helper, for a blacksmith for $1,114; painters $1,005; fieldhands from $750 to $1,000; boys about 12 years of age for $700; and girls between 12 and 18 from $600 to $800."[9] In 1850, $1,000 had a purchasing power equivalent to approximately $40,000 today.

By comparison, the price of good farmland—especially in West Tennessee, where cotton and tobacco thrived—could range from five to twenty dollars per acre, depending on improvements like fencing, buildings, and soil fertility. A story in 1836 in *The Anti-Slavery Record* noted that in Tennessee, "the price of slaves was never known to be higher nor people ever more madly bent on continuing the practice of slavery."[10]

Not everyone was willing to remain silent in the face of what John Wesley, the founder of the Methodist Church, called "the sum of all villainies." Opposition to slavery, while present from the birth of the country, intensified during this period through increasingly active, vocal, and organized efforts. During the first three decades of the nineteenth century, anti-slavery sentiment continued to gain momentum, frequently led by Quakers. Known for their commitment to equality and pacifism, Quakers denounced slavery as a moral failing and advocated for immediate manumission—the complete emancipation of all enslaved individuals.

Opinions on the abolition of slavery and the treatment of free Black individuals varied across Tennessee, depending largely on geography and economic factors. Those who openly opposed slavery were concentrated in East Tennessee, a region with mountainous terrain, a climate unsuitable for large-scale cotton farming, and a significant population of Quaker settlers. These settlers, guided by their religious beliefs, often advocated for abolition. Prominent abolitionist Joshua Leavitt of Boston acknowledged these regional differences during an anti-slavery convention held in London in 1843:

> The people of East Tennessee, a race of hardy mountaineers, find their interests so little regarded by the dominant slave-holders of

other parts of the state that they are taking measures to become a separate state. They are holding anti-slavery meetings, and meetings of political associations with great freedom, discussing their questions, rousing up the people and showing how slavery curses them, in order to bring them to the point of action.[11]

At that time, immediate manumission by an enslaver was possible but very difficult. It was not simply a matter of "setting one's slaves free." In most states, enslavers could only free individuals who performed "meritorious services." The term was so vaguely defined that it was often manipulated to deny freedom. Even if an enslaver wished to grant manumission, the final decision often belonged within the county court, which rarely ruled in favor of the enslaved. The vague definition of "meritorious services" ensured that freedom remained out of reach for most, reinforcing a system of lifelong servitude. These legal barriers underscored the pervasive fear among enslavers that even the smallest hope could unravel the institution—a fear that fueled their relentless efforts to tighten control and prevent even the tiniest possibility of freedom. That does not mean those who believed America should be the land of the free gave up.

The first anti-slavery society in Tennessee, the Tennessee Society for Promoting the Manumission of Slaves, was formed in 1815 at the Lost Creek Meeting House in Jefferson County, Tennessee. The abolitionist movement quickly spread from East Tennessee throughout the region. In 1820, Quaker Elihu Embree began publication of a newspaper in Jonesboro, Tennessee, called *The Manumission Intelligencer*. It was the first newspaper ever published in the United States dedicated exclusively to ending slavery. In the first issue, Embree wrote:

> This paper is especially designed by the editor to advocate the abolition of slavery, and to be a repository of tracts on that interesting and important subject. It will contain all the necessary information that the editor can obtain of the progress of the abolition of slavery of the descendants of Africa, together with a concise history of their introduction into slavery, collected from the best authorities.[12]

What impact Elihu Embree and his publication might have made will never be known. After producing seven issues and gaining more than 2,000 subscribers, he died unexpectedly at the age of thirty-eight—likely from malaria—just eight months after the first issue rolled off the press.

Embree was not alone in searching for ways to abolish slavery. Frances Wright returned to her experimental Tennessee commune, Nashoba, in June 1826 after spending time at Robert Owen's colony in New Harmony, Indiana. She arrived exhausted and ill-prepared for the challenges ahead. To make matters worse, 1826 was the summer of a dengue fever outbreak.

Wright seemed to consider herself as impervious to disease as she was to criticism. Without understanding that the fever was spread by mosquitos, she took no measures to protect herself or her sister, and both became ill with the fever. Symptoms included excruciating headaches, pain behind the eyes, nausea, vomiting, and a severe rash. However, it was the intense muscle and joint pain, particularly in the legs and back, that earned dengue its nickname: Breakbone Fever.

Wright also faced emotional pain as she struggled physically. George Flower, her partner who had been managing operations at Nashoba, brought his wife and children to live with him. When Wright returned, he and his family quickly departed. Wright's biographer, Celia Morris Eckhardt, believes that Flower and Wright had an intense romantic relationship during their first months together but that it ended due to his family obligations. Afterward, they could no longer work together. Flower did not include Frances Wright or Nashoba in his autobiography, written thirty years later. He merely referred to that time as the only exception to an otherwise happy life. Eckhardt suggested that it was "one of Fannie's great misfortunes that George Flower was long since married when they met."[13]

Wright's health continued to deteriorate until she finally decided to return to Europe, accompanied by Robert Dale Owen, son of Robert Owen, to recuperate. On May 14, 1827, they attended a farewell dinner at the home of Marcus and Amarante Winchester and departed the next morning for New Orleans aboard the *Helen McGregor*. Only thirty-two months later, that same steamboat's boilers exploded while departing the dock at the Memphis wharf, killing approximately fifty of its passengers. Many of the victims were buried in the newly established Winchester Burying Ground.

While in New Orleans and before departing for Europe, Owen wrote to Camilla that Wright had taken the opportunity to speak with many free Black and mixed-race men and women about her plans to end slavery through her experiment at Nashoba. He also commented on the "wonderful relationships" he observed between White men and Mulatto women but added a dose of reality: "The world, as you probably recollect, is a tedious, uninteresting world."[14]

Wright entrusted Camilla, Richeson Whitby, and James Richardson, the Scottish physician she met in Memphis, with managing Nashoba in her absence.

During an earlier visit to New Harmony, the Wright sisters had both been captivated by Whitby, a reserved young Quaker who ardently embraced the community's socialist ideals. Frances Wright saw in Whitby the potential to be an excellent foreman, while Camilla apparently saw him as a potential husband.

Despite Camilla's public denunciation of marriage, the two became husband and wife while Frances Wright was in Europe. Although Wright was no doubt shocked by the development, an unexpected brother-in-law would soon prove to be the least of her worries.

Without the vision and direction of Frances Wright and George Flower, the new Mr. and Mrs. Whitby and James Richardson led Nashoba down a path that strayed far from Wright's original intentions and descended into a nightmare of mistreatment and abuse for the enslaved living there. James Richardson, with the knowledge of both Camilla and Whitby, submitted what amounted to a status report to *The Genius of Universal Emancipation*, a new version of Elihu Embree's *The Emancipator*. It had been purchased by Benjamin Lundy, who renamed it and moved its production to Baltimore, Maryland.

It is difficult to comprehend what Camilla, Whitby, or Richardson were thinking during these appalling incidents, let alone why they chose to publicize their actions. One can only deduce they saw nothing wrong with their behavior or their treatment of the enslaved. The once "utopian" community had become a place of horrific abuse that included separating children from their parents, flogging, and sexual exploitation. One account was especially chilling: "Two women slaves tied up and flogged by James Richardson in presence of Camilla and all the slaves. Two dozen and one dozen on the back with a cowskin."[15]

Even more damning among the pro-slavery crowd was an entry about Richardson himself: "James Richardson informed that last night Mamselle Josephine and he began to live together and he took this occasion of repeating to them our views on color, and on the sexual relation."[16] Josephine was the mixed-race daughter of a teacher hired to teach Nashoba's children. Of course, their views on "color and the sexual relation" was that all races should be free to have consenting sexual relations with individuals from any other race—and without marriage.

When Wright discovered what was happening in Tennessee, she quickly made plans to return to Nashoba to do damage control and restore her vision for the commune. This time, she was in the company of a friend—forty-eight-year-old Frances Trollope.

By all accounts, Trollope was the life of every party she hosted or attended. When she married Thomas Anthony Trollope, a London barrister, their future appeared secure. Thomas Trollope was the sole heir to the fortune of his very wealthy uncle. The only obstacle to the Trollopes enjoying that windfall was the fact that his uncle refused to die.

The Trollopes built a luxurious mansion on leased land and led a life filled with lavish parties, international travel, and the finest in fashionable clothes for husband, wife, and five children. Their expenses far exceeded their income, but they believed it was only a matter of time before Thomas's uncle passed away and they could pay their debts. Unfortunately for the Trollopes, the uncle had many years of life left and even married a much younger woman, with whom he began having children—heirs who took Thomas Trollope's place.

Matters were further complicated by Thomas Trollope's chronic headaches, which were treated with large doses of calomel. The resulting mercury poisoning left him with debilitating symptoms, making work increasingly difficult and eventually impossible.

During a fundraising excursion, Wright visited the Trollopes's home and spoke passionately about her utopian community, Nashoba, emphasizing the exceptional opportunities it could offer young men like their son, Henry Trollope.

Wright clearly knew which buttons to push. Frances Trollope was deeply worried about Henry, who appeared to be following too closely in his father's footsteps. Wright convinced Trollope to accompany her to Tennessee, bringing her youngest son, Henry, and two daughters, Cecilia and Emily. Her husband and two older sons, Thomas and Anthony, remained in England, moving into a smaller rented home after being forced out of their mansion.

In January 1828, Frances Trollope, her children, and their servants arrived in New Orleans aboard the *Edward*. They were accompanied by Wright and a French artist, Auguste Hervieu, who was to tutor Trollope's children and others at the Nashoba school. From New Orleans, the group traveled up the Mississippi River toward Memphis. Their journey, already arduous, was further delayed when their steamboat became stuck in the mud near Natchez. After many days, the group finally reached Memphis at midnight, only to be met by torrential rain. The weather made it nearly impossible to ascend from the boat to Nathaniel Anderson's new hotel on the bluff. Undeterred, Wright led the group upward through the storm. Trollope wrote:

> The heavy rain which had been falling for many hours would have made any steep assent difficult, but unfortunately a new road had recently been marked out, which beguiled us into its almost bottomless mud, from the firmer footing of the unbroken cliff. Shoes and gloves were lost in the mire, for we were glad to avail

ourselves of all limbs as we reached the grand hotel in a most deplorable state.[17]

The next morning, Marcus Winchester was one of the first Memphians Trollope met. She described him as "a pleasing gentlemanlike man" who seemed "strangely misplaced on a little town on the Mississippi."[18] During dinner, which she and Wright had in the main dining room of the hotel, Trollope noted all the shopkeepers in town joined them. She was told that since the hotel had been completed, all the men of the town had their meals there served by Nathaniel Anderson's wife. Trollope wrote, "The good women of Memphis being well content to let their lords partake of Mrs. Anderson's turkeys and venison, (without their having the trouble of cooking for them), whilst they regale themselves on mush and milk at home."[19]

While a humorous scene—and more than a little condescending—Trollope was no doubt taking a few liberties with the truth. It is unlikely that Nathaniel Anderson's wife cooked turkeys for the men of Memphis every evening. Nathaniel and Mildred Moon Anderson had come to Memphis in 1823 from Virginia and were among the wealthiest and most prominent citizens of the city. Anderson later became a cotton broker and banker with offices in Memphis and New Orleans. He was a partner with Marcus Winchester in various projects. While Winchester served early on as an unofficial, one-man chamber of commerce, Anderson served as the head of the first official one. He organized and served as the first president of the Memphis Businessmen's Club.

When the ground dried enough for them to finally make it to Nashoba, it only took one look for Trollope's hopes to come crashing down. This was neither a solution to her money problems nor a way to provide a brighter future for her struggling son, Henry:

> One glance sufficed to convince me that every idea I had formed of the place was as far as possible from the truth. Desolation was the only feeling—the only word that presented itself; but it was not spoken. I think, however, that Miss Wright was aware of the painful impression the sight of her forest home produced on me, and I doubt not that the conviction reached us both at the same moment, that we had erred in thinking that in a few months passed together at this spot could be productive of pleasure to either.[20]

When Auguste Hervieu, the artist who came along as tutor, saw the commune and discovered they had not even begun building a school, he was angry and immediately demanded to be taken back to Memphis. They convinced him to stay—at least for a few weeks.

Only ten days after arriving, Trollope borrowed $300 from Wright and departed Nashoba. The January 27, 1828, records from the commune include the notation "Frances Trollope and family with their manservant William Abbot and Esther Rust, her maid, and Auguste Hervieu, left us for Memphis."[21] Trollope sent Henry to New Harmony with Robert Owen while she and the rest of her entourage headed for Cincinnati on the first steamboat out of Memphis five days later.

In Ohio, Trollope opened a precursor to today's shopping malls she named the Cincinnati Bazaar. Her idea was inspired by European markets and intended to introduce a more refined shopping experience to the frontier town. She was clearly ahead of her time. The business struggled due to local resistance to her lofty concept and financial mismanagement. Disillusioned by her experience and looking for anything that would help her make money to support her family, Trollope turned to writing. Her book, *Domestic Manners of the Americans*, published in 1832, was a satirical critique of American culture and social norms. It was initially funded by Auguste Hervieu, who had found financial success as a portrait painter in London. A pencil sketch the artist made of Nashoba was included in Trollope's book, providing the only visual record of Wright's commune.

Trollope's son, Anthony, followed in her footsteps many years later and became one of the most respected English novelists of the Victorian era. Of his mother's decision to travel to Memphis with Wright he wrote:

> In 1827 she went to America, having been partly instigated by the social and communistic ideas of a lady whom I well remember,—a certain Miss Wright. . . . Her chief desire, however, was to establish my brother Henry; and perhaps joined with that was the additional object of breaking up her English home without pleading broken fortunes to all the world.[22]

Trollope's book became an instant best seller, and she went on to write other novels and travelogues that finally mended her "broken fortunes" and secured her family's financial stability for the remainder of her life.

The hard work required of him at New Harmony was something Henry Trollope had neither anticipated nor intended to endure for long. Within weeks, he rejoined his family in Cincinnati where he worked for his mother on her various enterprises. Young Trollope's health declined due to numerous illnesses including fevers, likely brought on by malaria possibly contracted at Nashoba. He returned to Europe where he died of consumption on December 23, 1834, in his mid-twenties.

As Frances Trollope predicted, Frances Wright's experimental utopian community ultimately failed. The reasons for its failure vary, but Wright's unconventional ideas and James Richardson's decision to share them with the media did not help her cause. As her fame and notoriety grew, Wright became increasingly bold in sharing her own controversial opinions. Her ideas about ending slavery, advocating for the rights of the working class, and championing free education for all children were concepts that initially garnered some support. However, her other beliefs were far more provocative. She argued not only that all races should be free but also that there was no reason they should not mix socially or sexually. She dismissed the institution of marriage as unnecessary and rejected all forms of organized religion.

Few Americans at that time were as progressive as Wright had supposed, and the backlash against her was both swift and severe. While her promotion of socialist ideals was controversial enough, her advocacy for free love and sexual freedom pushed public tolerance beyond its limits, earning her the nickname "The Red Harlot of Infidelity."

However, historian Allison M. Parker argues that Wright's radical ideas had less impact on Nashoba's failure than has been previously suggested by historians. She writes:

> In fact, Wright embodied the spirit of boundlessness and the volatility that characterized antebellum America. She embraced, exploited, and sometimes personified the Jacksonian era's weak federal government, its stronger state and local governments, its political conflicts and social turmoil, as well as its democratization and visionary plans. Her emphasis on state rather than national legislation found a sympathetic audience with Jacksonian democrats who wanted to limit the power of the federal government.... Although she supported miscegenation, Wright's language and actions betrayed her commonality with most white Americans who believed in a racial hierarchy in which whites were, in her words, "the master race."[23]

During the 1820s and 1830s, many Americans were open to exploring new ideas, and society was less rigid for many of the settlers, making some of Frances Wright's ideas worth considering. Parker points out, "it was not until the tenor of the age became more ordered and conservative that she was marginalized."[24]

While Frances Wright's nonconformity and liberal social ideas drew significant negative attention and undermined her vision for educating and colonizing enslaved individuals, Nashoba faced additional challenges. Chief among them was the inability to farm the poor-quality land they had selected. Frances, Camilla, and their hired workers were also inexperienced in essential survival practices of the time and unprepared for the long-term commitment required to transform the Tennessee wilderness into a productive farm.

The Nashoba experiment came to an end only five years after Wright first arrived in Memphis. She decided that she could make a greater impact through lecturing, writing, and publishing a newspaper than by focusing her efforts on the freedom of "a few slaves." Wright left Camilla's husband, Richeson Whitby, in charge of Nashoba and settled pregnant Camilla in her Memphis home next to the Winchesters. With scheduled public appearances along the way, Wright departed for New York to begin her next chapter.

Prominent early nineteenth-century activist Catherine Beecher, a champion of equal access to education for women, was not a supporter of Wright. This is surprising, given that activism was deeply ingrained in Beecher's family. Her siblings included Harriet Beecher Stowe, the celebrated author of the best-selling antislavery novel *Uncle Tom's Cabin*; Isabella Beecher Hooker, a prominent leader in the women's suffrage movement; and Henry Ward Beecher, a renowned Brooklyn pastor whose powerful lectures against slavery and in support of temperance and women's rights drew thousands of eager listeners. About Wright, Catherine Beecher wrote:

> Who can look without disgust and abhorrence upon such a one as Fanny Wright, with her great masculine person, her loud voice, her untasteful attire, going about unprotected, and feeling no need of protection, mingling with men in stormy debate, and standing up with bare-faced impudence, to lecture to a public assembly . . . I cannot conceive of any thing in the shape of woman, more intolerably offensive and disgusting.[25]

Camilla's baby, Frances, named after his aunt, was born in late January after a difficult birth in the Winchester's home. Already weakened by the fevers she had survived at Nashoba, the new mother struggled to regain her health. Meanwhile, Frances Wright had shifted her focus entirely away from West Tennessee. In addition to writing, publishing, and lecturing, she purchased an old church and named it *The Hall of Science*. Essentially, it was a new type of church but designed for antebellum, free-thinking liberals. The hall hosted lectures by like-minded speakers on social issues of the day and produced pamphlets and books, which were sold in an adjoining bookstore.

Seven months after the two sisters had last been together, Camilla was ready to rejoin Wright in New York. Marcus Winchester accompanied Camilla to Cincinnati, where he entrusted her to Frances Trollope. Trollope later wrote to a friend that Camilla's baby was "one of very uncommon beauty, and appears in all respects just what a mother could wish."[26] Camilla and baby Frances continued their journey alone after departing Cincinnati. Once Frances Wright had settled Camilla in New York, she departed for a series of lectures in Boston and Philadelphia. For a brief time, it seemed Camilla had finally found some happiness. However, shortly after Wright was reunited with Camilla, her namesake nephew tragically died of a fever at just seven months old, leaving Camilla devastated. To make matters worse, while mourning her great loss, Camilla continued to suffer from the lingering effects of the illnesses she had contracted at Nashoba. She was broken both mentally and physically.

Around this time, Wright decided to fulfill her promise to free the enslaved inhabitants of her short-lived utopian community. The individuals were still living and working at Nashoba under the supervision of Camilla's estranged husband. Marcus Winchester and his brother-in-law, James Breedlove, who was living in New Orleans, helped plan Wright's journey to Haiti. They also saw her trip as an opportunity to her to fund her voyage and them to turn a profit. They arranged for her ship to be loaded with lard and pork, with instructions to trade them in Haiti for a shipment of coffee. She would then return to New Orleans, where Breedlove would secure buyers for the coffee.

Wright found only one person willing to accompany her to Haiti—Frenchman Guillaume Phiquepal D'Arusmont. The two met at New Harmony, and while they shared many of the same values, they made an unlikely pair. She was thirty-five, wealthy, tall, and still striking, while he was fifty-two, underemployed, and described as "short, muscular, and wiry."[27]

They departed in October 1829 aboard the *John Quincy Adams* for the 30-day voyage. The group included Frances Wright, her entourage, and thirty-one enslaved individuals—thirteen adults and eighteen children. Upon arrival in Haiti, Wright presented a letter from the Marquis de Lafayette, which quickly secured an introduction to Jean-Pierre Boyer, the president of the country.

President Boyer was the biracial son of a French father who worked as a tailor and a mother who was a former enslaved woman from the Congo. He played a significant role before, during, and after the Haitian Revolution, emerging as a key political figure following Haiti's independence. The Haitian Revolution began in 1791, when a group of enslaved men, inspired by the ideals of freedom and equality from the French and American Revolutions, launched an attack on a port city in Saint-Domingue. After a decade of brutal conflict, the revolutionaries triumphed, resulting in emancipation and the creation of the Black Republic of Haiti in 1804. This made Haiti the only nation in history to abolish slavery through rebellion and establish independence led by formerly enslaved individuals.

As slave masters and those they enslaved in the United States closely watched the Haitian conflict and eventual victory, one pressing question emerged: If it could happen there, could it happen here? During the first half of the nineteenth century, as the issue of slavery became a central debate and moral dilemma, Haiti remained a potent symbol. For enslavers, it served as a cautionary tale; for the enslaved, it stood as a beacon of hope.

For the formerly enslaved children and adults who had traveled from a small experimental community outside of Memphis to a country of free Black revolutionaries, it was not just a hope—it was, at least for that moment in time, freedom. They were given food and clothing and provided with homes and farms on Boyer's property. No evidence has been found to indicate what happened next to the newly freed Nashoba residents Wright left behind in Haiti.

While she accomplished her primary goal, the trip was a financial failure. After accounting for expenses, Marcus Winchester, James Breedlove, and Frances Wright each lost $431.48. However, this loss was minor compared to the $16,000—equivalent to approximately $640,000 today—that Nashoba ultimately cost Wright.

In her analysis of Frances Wright and Nashoba for an issue on race, ethnicity, and civic identity in *American Literary Magazine*, historian Gail Bederman suggests the failure of Nashoba was a turning point for Wright:

> From the moment Wright first glimpsed the U.S. until her original plan for Nashoba failed, she viewed America as the enlightened opposite of British corruption. She conceived Nashoba to further the cause of the republican utopia she had described in *Views of Manners and Morals*. Because slavery was a relic of British corruption, Wright had faith that Americans would gladly cast it off if they could afford to do so. Because she saw the US through the rosy lenses of British radicalism, she truly believed liberty-loving Americans, North and South, would recognize the efficacy of her plan, abolish slavery, and colonize all of the US's negroes within 85 years, painlessly and with no economic loss to the slaveholders.

Nashoba's collapse in 1826 turned Wright from a British to an American radical.[28]

Upon returning to New York from Haiti, Wright discovered Camilla was in worse shape than ever and decided it was time for a break for both of them. They headed to France where it seems Camilla's health and mental state improved. She even got an apartment of her own rather than staying with Wright. Sadly, on February 8, 1831, she died with Frances at her side "after a sudden attack of hemorrhage" at age thirty.[29]

Wright and D'Arusmont grew close during their time in Haiti, and the bond between them soon deepened into a romance. When she reached Paris, Wright discovered she was pregnant. The activist who had so often and confidently spoken out against marriage did not practice what she preached. She and D'Arusmont married and soon welcomed daughter, Frances Sylva, to the new family.

The next decades of Wright's life were marked by sadness and misfortune. Her public appearances were met with protests and threats against her life, making them too risky to continue. She endured numerous lawsuits, a contentious divorce, and estrangement from her daughter, who, by all accounts, she deeply loved. Wright visited the formerly enslaved individuals she had freed in Haiti and her former commune at Nashoba to observe their progress. She wrote that she was pleased with what she saw.[30]

In 1851, Frances Wright slipped on ice in front of her home in Cincinnati and fell, breaking her hip. The injury resulted in a year of excruciating pain that left her frequently delirious and unable to function. She died on December 13, 1852, at age fifty-seven.

Frances Wright gradually faded into obscurity after her death. She did not live to witness the Civil War, the abolishment of slavery through the Thirteenth Amendment, the establishment of public education for all American children, the rise of the National Labor Union, the ratification of the Nineteenth Amendment granting women the right to vote, the Civil Rights Act of 1964, or other pivotal milestones in American history that reflected the basic human rights and freedoms she had passionately championed decades earlier. In many ways, she was a woman far ahead of her time.

Perhaps the best way to remember Frances Wright is through the recollections of a carpenter who worked on one of her homes. She moved in before his work was completed, and he assumed it was to push him to work faster and finish the job more quickly. He discovered the opposite was true, and later wrote:

> She didn't seem to have any idea to hurry us, in fact, it was the

other way. She actually hindered us by talking to us, advancing her theories for the advancement of working men. We carried our own dinners with us, but she insisted we should eat our dinners at her table. In this way I learned a great deal about her private thoughts on different subjects.... She could entertain you by the hour on ancient or modern history, on the sciences, geology, chemistry, astronomy, or natural history. She was a walking encyclopedia, an orator inferior to none, and superior to any I ever heard.[31]

Chapter Seventeen Endnotes

1. Paul Finkelman, *Slavery and the Founders: Race and Liberty in the Age of Jefferson* (Armonk, NY: M.E. Sharpe, 2001), 3–5.
2. J. David Hacker, "A Census-Based Count of the Civil War Dead," *Civil War History* 57, no. 4 (December 2011): 307–48.
3. Travellers Rest, *A Past Uncovered: The Story of the Enslaved People of Travellers Rest* (Nashville: Travellers Rest, 2025).
4. Mary S. Carroll, "Tennessee Sectionalism" (PhD diss., Duke University, 1931), 164–65.
5. Walter Durham, *James Winchester: Tennessee Pioneer* (Gallatin: Sumner County Library Board, 1979), 34.
6. Durham, *James Winchester*, 35.
7. Mark Cheathem, "The Evolution of the Enslaved Community at Andrew Jackson's Plantations, 1790s–1840s" (paper presented at the BrANCH Conference, Newcastle-upon-Tyne, Fall 2012), 1.
8. Chase C. Mooney, *Slavery in Tennessee* (Westport, Conn.: Negro Universities Press, 1971 [orig. 1957]), 34.
9. Mooney, *Slavery in Tennessee*, 37.
10. Mooney, Slavery in Tennessee, 38.
11. Joshua Leavitt, remarks at an anti-slavery convention, London, 1843, quoted in David S. Heidler and Jeanne T. Heidler, *David Farragut: Union Admiral* (Santa Barbara, CA: ABC-CLIO, 2010), 23.
12. E. E. Hoss, "Elihu Embree, Abolitionist," *The American Historical Magazine* 2, no. 2 (1897): 117.
13. Celia Morris Eckhardt, *Fanny Wright, Rebel in America* (Cambridge, Mass.: Harvard University Press, 1984), 133.
14. Eckhardt, *Fanny Wright*, 140.
15. Eckhardt, *Fanny Wright*, 144.
16. Eckhardt, *Fanny Wright*, 143.
17. Frances Trollope, *Domestic Manners of the Americans* (New York: Alfred A. Knopf, 1949), 23-24.
18. Trollope, *Domestic Manners*, 24-25.
19. Trollope, *Domestic Manners*, 25.
20. Trollope, *Domestic Manners*, 27.
21. Alice J. G. Perkins and Theresa Wolfson, Frances Wright, Free Enquirer: The Study of a Temperament (New York: Harper & Brothers, 1939), 190.
22. Anthony Trollope, Autobiography of Anthony Trollope (New York: Dodd, Mead & Company, 1905), 30.
23. Alison M. Parker, "'What We Do Expect the People Legislatively to Effect': Frances Wright, Moral Reform, and State Legislation," in *Women and the Unstable State in Nineteenth-Century America*, ed. Alison M. Parker and Stephanie Cole (College Station: Texas A&M University Press, 2000), 62–63.
24. Parker, "'What We Do Expect the People Legislatively to Effect,'" 64.
25. Quoted in Michael Warner, "Publics and Counterpublics (abbreviated version)," *Quarterly Journal of Speech* 88, no. 4 (2002): 413-425.
26. Eckhardt, *Fanny Wright*, 196.
27. Margaret Lane, *Frances Wright and the Great Experiment* (Manchester : Manchester University Press, 1972), 36.
28. Gail Bederman, "Revisiting Nashoba: Slavery, Utopia, and Frances Wright in America, 1818-1826," *American Literary History* 17, no. 3 (2005): 454.
29. Eckhardt, *Fanny Wright*, 229.
30. Lane, *Frances Wright*, 44.
31. Lane, *Frances Wright*, 44-45.

JOS. SPECHT,

Manufacturer of

CONFECTIONS

IN ALL BRANCHES.

American, French and German styles.

MADISON, BETW'N MAIN AND SECOND, St's,

MEMPHIS, TENN.

FANCY AND PLAIN

CANDIER,

IN GREAT VARIETY

WHOLESALE AND RETAIL

ICE CREAM SALOON,

FOR LADIES AND GENTLEMEN.

CREAMS OF ALL FLAVORS,

FROZEN LEMONADE,

SHERBERTS AND ROMAN PUNCH,

Small or Large Quantity.

WEDDINGS, BALLS & PARTIES,

Furnished with Ornaments; Pyramids; Cakes; Candies; Jellies, Charlotte Russ and Parisian; Blanc Mange; Bavarois; Nougat, &c., &c — In style, variety, BON GOUTI and workmanship he can't be surpassed. Keeps constantly for sale, syrups of all flavors, fine wines, champagne, fruit in juice, cordials, and all sorts of nuts, prunes, chocolates, raisins, and figs, pickles, oranges, lemons, &c.

Orders from the country promptly attended to.

From Rainey's Memphis City Directory, 1855/56

Chapter Eighteen: Soul Man

Racism impacts the Marcus Winchester family

There was a brief moment in history when the world inhabited by Marcus and Amarante Winchester—and the future of the country—might have taken a different turn. What many do not realize today is that in America's early years, there was widespread agreement that slavery was wrong, unsustainable, and an institution destined to end. Daniel Webster reflected on this earlier attitude in his famous Seventh of March speech: "The most eminent men, and nearly all the conspicuous politicians of the South, held the same sentiments—that slavery was an evil, a blight, a scourge, and a curse. There was no diversity of opinion upon this point."[1]

In emerging cities like Memphis, racial identity gained increasing significance as communities and social structures evolved and became more complex. As opportunities expanded, income levels increased, and social hierarchies began to develop, overt displays of racism and laws designed to establish and uphold White supremacy began to emerge.

These developments affected both free Black individuals and the enslaved. Amarante Loiselle owned her own property, and all the members of her family were free. She was likely far more educated than many others in Memphis and, due to her assumed heritage, was probably bilingual. However, she was of mixed race. As abolitionist voices grew louder and fears of slave insurrections intensified, life became increasingly intolerable and dangerous for even free mixed-race individuals like Marcus Winchester's wife and children.

In 1800, Tennessee was home to a little over 300 free Black men and women, a figure that rose to 7,300 by 1860, making up less than one percent of the population.[2] Early in Tennessee's history, free Black men could own property, conduct business, and testify in court. Similar to White men, free Black men were even able to vote if they owned property. However, their social standing remained precarious, as they were still regarded as second-class citizens, if that. Throughout the early nineteenth century, any rights or security they may have once held was gradually stripped away by White men to minimize perceived threats to the institution of slavery or to minimize the risk of violent rebellions.

Then in 1806, Tennessee enacted a law that made it nearly impossible for formerly enslaved residents to remain in the state after gaining their freedom. The law required them to leave Tennessee within twelve months of being freed. If they failed to do so, they could be re-enslaved and sold to the highest bidder. The Winchester children and other offspring of interracial marriages faced similar threats to their legal and political rights as free Black individuals. During the 1830s, Tennessee implemented additional laws that restricted where free Black residents could travel and the circumstances under which they could gather in groups. Free Black men and women were required to obtain special permission from the courts before traveling across county or state lines. Furthermore, laws prohibited gatherings of free and enslaved Black men and women to reduce the risk of organized resistance.

There was little hope for change. Elijah E. Hoss, Bishop of the Methodist Episcopal Church, summarized the state of slavery by 1840 as "a fixed thing." He wrote, "free debate concerning it was no longer tolerated though many persons continued to cherish in silence the conviction that it was a great evil."[3] He attributed the sudden silence to southerners' growing resentment of interference by abolitionists in the North, fear generated by numerous slave uprisings, anxiety over what would happen economically and socially if all slaves were suddenly freed, and greed.

One writer described the need for slavery in the South: "Here you will ask, what do they want with so many negroes, the answer is, to make more Money—again, you will ask what do they want with so much Money, the answer is to buy more Negroes. . . a Man's merit in this country, is estimated, according to the number of Negroes he works in the field."[4]

In 1993, Kenneth Stampp received the prestigious Lincoln Prize for lifetime achievement from the Civil War Institute at Gettysburg College, recognizing his distinguished career as a historian specializing in slavery, the Civil War, and reconstruction. His first major book, *The Peculiar Institution: Slavery in the Ante-Bellum South*, was published in 1956. He was among the first historians to argue that the moral debate over slavery was the true cause of the Civil War, challenging the view presented by many that it stemmed primarily from a conflict over states' rights. Of the evolution of the permanence of slavery, Stampp wrote:

By the 1830's the fateful decision had been made. Slavery, now an integral part of the southern way of life, was to be preserved, not as a transitory evil, an unfortunate legacy of the past, but as a permanent institution—a positive good. To think of abolition was an idol dream. Now even native Southerners criticized the peculiar institution at their peril.[5]

James Davis experienced firsthand the change in treatment of enslaved residents of Memphis:

A large portion of the money here then belonged to negroes, generally in small savings, but almost all boasted of having money in 'massa's hands,' and was not unfrequently enough to buy themselves. Slavery was then very different from what it was ten or twenty years afterward, after abolitionism rose up.[6]

John C. Calhoun, South Carolina senator, vice president of the United States under both John Q. Adams and Andrew Jackson, and the Senate's most prominent states' rights advocate, said of slavery in 1838, "Many in the South once believed that it was a moral and political evil; that folly and delusion are gone; we see it now in its true light, and regard it as the most safe and stable basis for free institutions in the world."[7]

In 1834, the Tennessee General Assembly organized a convention to amend the state constitution, just nine years after the original constitution had been adopted. All three candidates running to represent Shelby County at the convention—Charles Stuart, Isaac Rawlings, and Adam Alexander—supported ending slavery, but their views on how differed slightly. Stuart advocated for the immediate emancipation of all enslaved individuals. In contrast, Rawlings and Alexander aligned with those in the nation, like Frances Wright, who supported the colonization of formerly enslaved individuals rather than granting them outright freedom within the United States. Adam Alexander won the election and attended the convention in May 1834 to represent the people of Memphis.

Historian J. P. Young suggested that Alexander's victory reflected the prevailing sentiment in the Memphis community at the time. He wrote, "Another proof of the feeling in favor of emancipation in that period is that many petitions were sent to the convention from a number of counties, praying that some system of gradual emancipation be agreed upon."[8]

Sixty delegates gathered for the Tennessee State Constitutional Convention to address issues like taxation, the state court system, and how to govern a state that had grown rapidly and was becoming more urban. Beneath the surface of Tennessee's political and social climate in the early 1830s lay the contentious and divisive question: what should be done about slavery? This issue became particularly urgent in the aftermath of the Nat Turner insurrection in August 1831, the deadliest slave revolt in American history. Turner, an enslaved minister, led more than fifty followers in a violent rebellion in Southampton, Virginia, killing nearly sixty White people, most of whom were women and children. Although the uprising was suppressed by dawn the following day, with most of the rebels captured or killed, it left an indelible mark on the minds of enslavers across the South. Many, previously lulled into complacency by the belief that their enslaved workers were content, began to scrutinize their plantations—and those of their neighbors—for any signs of brewing rebellion.

As news of the revolt spread, so did fear. In Virginia, the General Assembly enacted sweeping measures aimed at preventing future insurrections. These laws targeted both enslaved and free Black individuals, prohibiting the teaching of reading and writing to the enslaved, strictly regulating gatherings, and requiring written authorization from enslavers for travel. For Marcus Winchester, these developments were deeply troubling. He recognized that restrictions imposed on free Black individuals in Virginia—like his own children—would inevitably spread to Tennessee and beyond.

The limitations on mobility were a minor inconvenience compared to the far greater dangers confronting free Black and mixed-race men, women, and children. Today, many are aware of the Underground Railroad through which some enslaved escaped to the North to some measure of freedom. What is less known is that just as many free individuals were captured and spent the rest of their lives enslaved in a system known by some historians today as the Reverse Underground Railroad. Stories like those of Solomon Northup, Cornelius Sinclair, and Jude Hall's sons highlight the pervasive fear and vulnerability experienced by free and mixed-race men, women, and children who, despite their legal status, were forced to live in constant vigilance.

Solomon Northup was a married father of three who was a mixed-race violinist and farmer. He was lured to Washington City in 1841 with the promise of work in a circus, only to be drugged, kidnapped, and sold into slavery. He spent twelve years enslaved in Louisiana, being forced to work on sugar and cotton plantations before regaining his freedom. Once freed, he wrote a book, *Twelve Years a Slave,* that became a bestseller and an important piece of anti-slavery literature. Northup's account of his ordeal sold thirty thousand copies in three years and provided a firsthand account of the horrors that many enslaved people had to endure. Northup's writing about Patsey, one enslaved woman he befriended during his time enslaved, was particularly poignant. She was frequently abused by enslavers Edwin Epps and his cruel wife, but one beating Northup witnesses destroyed both Patsey's body and spirit:

> Indeed, from that time forward she was not what she had been. The burden of a deep melancholy weighed heavily on her spirits. She no longer moved with that buoyant and elastic step—there was not that mirthful sparkle in her eyes that formerly distinguished her. The bounding vigor—the sprightly, laughter-loving spirit of her youth, were gone. She fell into a mournful and desponding mood, and oftentimes would start up in her sleep, and with raised hands, plead for mercy. She became more silent than she was, toiling all day in our midst, not uttering a word. A care-worn, pitiful expression settled on her face, and it was her humor now to weep, rather than rejoice. If ever there was a broken heart—one crushed and blighted by the rude grasp of suffering and misfortune—it was Patsey's.[9]

In a situation similar to Northup's, Cornelius Sinclair, a ten-year-old free Black boy, was grabbed, gagged, and thrown into a wagon while walking through a market in Philadelphia. Sinclair was kidnapped that day, along with five other boys, by a slave-trading ring led by the notorious Patty Cannon. She and her gang abducted hundreds of free Black individuals and sold them into slavery in the South.

When they realized their son was missing, Sinclair's parents quickly placed a missing-person notice in the newspaper. It directed anyone with information to contact him at a merchant house near the Philadelphia dock where he worked as a porter.[10] No one did.

After being held aboard the ship, Sinclair and other young boys were transported along Delaware and Maryland's Eastern Shore. They then endured a grueling march over land through Georgia and into Alabama. In October 1825, Sinclair was sold for $300 to James Paul in Tuscaloosa, Alabama.

Unlike many stories of free Black men, women, and children, forced into slavery via the Reverse Underground Railroad, Sinclair's story has a happy ending. Methodist ministers Robert L. Kennon and Joshua Boucher learned of Cornelius's kidnapping and filed a lawsuit on his behalf, challenging his illegal enslavement. In March 1827, a jury of slaveholders in Tuscaloosa recognized Cornelius's free status and granted his release. Cornelius returned home to Philadelphia. He testified against one of the kidnappers, John Purnell, who was convicted and sentenced to forty-two years in prison. Purnell died five years later while incarcerated.

The story of Jude Hall underscores the fragility of freedom even for Black patriots. A free, land-owning veteran of the American Revolution, Hall was a celebrated figure in his home state of New Hampshire. He had fought in significant battles such as Bunker Hill, Ticonderoga, Trenton, Saratoga, and Monmouth, earning the nickname "Old Rock" for his strength and bravery. Yet, he suffered devastating personal losses when three of his sons—James, Aaron, and William—were kidnapped and sold into slavery at different times. Hall never saw his sons again. For free individuals like Marcus and Amarante Winchester, these stories represented their worst fear for their family.

An eighty-seven-page pamphlet published in 1829 by David Walker, a free Black man, expressed the sentiments of many others—like the Winchesters—who were free but whose lives were still shaped by discrimination against people of color:

> Our difference of color, the servitude of many and most of our brethren, and the prejudices which those circumstances have naturally occasioned will not allow us to hope, even if we could desire, to mingle with you one day, in the benefits of citizenship. As long as we remain among you, we must (and shall) be content to be a distinct cast, exposed to the indignities and dangers, physical and moral, to which our situation makes us liable.[11]

In this charged environment, the Tennessee Constitutional Convention convened on Monday, May 19, 1834, and appointed a three-member committee to explore the issue of slavery in the state and make a reccomendation. As expected, the report issued a month later opposed emancipation. The committee framed slavery as an unfortunate but "necessary" institution, arguing that the condition of enslaved people was preferable to the perceived poverty and mistreatment of free Black individuals. The report also warned that emancipation would destabilize society, leading to widespread poverty among freed individuals and violent uprisings that could spill across state lines and result in retaliation against White Tennesseans.

By a narrow majority, the convention also revoked the voting rights of Black land-owning men, a right they had held since 1796. Furthermore, free Black individuals were barred from voting on the passage of the new state constitution. Most damning was Article II, Section 31, which declared: "The General Assembly shall have no power to pass laws for the emancipation of slaves, without the consent of their owners."

When White, male Tennesseans cast their votes in March 1835, 71.4 percent approved the new constitution, effectively closing the door on any state-driven efforts to abolish slavery. Tennessee was not unique. After grappling with the question of slavery for decades, the answer across southern states became clear. They would fight to keep it intact.

For enslavers who wished to free those they enslaved, what was already difficult became nearly impossible, so some attempted to circumvent the system.

Duke William Sumner, a much-respected thoroughbred racehorse breeder in Davidson County, Tennessee, died at age 67 in 1844 without being able to free "his old servant" Pompey. However, Sumner attempted to provide a measure of freedom for Pompey in his will:

> My old servant Pompey, who has traveled faithfully from childhood thro the various scenes of life with me, If he survives me, he is to serve as a slave to no other man or person, he is to be at liberty to live with whomsoever he may think proper, and in case his own labour should be insufficient for his comfortable support, it is distinctly to be understood, that my estate shall support him and if it is thought most advisable by my executors, I authorize them to reserve a certain Sum out of my estate as they may think reasonable in case it may be needed for the use of this fine honest old man Pompey which they can judge by his situation. My great aim in this proviso is that this faithful servant may have a certain independence to keep him from suffering while he may live.[12]

If there was any doubt about the importance Sumner placed on this provision, he emphasized it by stating, "If this is neglected, I will rise in Judgment against you." If Sumner's wishes were carried out, Pompey would have been able to live out the remainder of his life with some measure of freedom, albeit within the constraints of enslavement.

In July 1844, an estate sale was held on Sumner's property on White's Creek. Items available for purchase included land, farming equipment, one-third ownership of a thoroughbred horse named *The Great Pacific*, two thoroughbred stallions, mares, colts, cattle, hogs, and sheep. Also up for bid that day were eight enslaved individuals, described in the promotional materials as "consisting of men, women, and children." The sale announcement noted, "There will be two of the negro men sold for cash; the balance of the negroes and chattel property on nine month's credit."[13] It is unknown if Pompey was one of those enslaved men or if Sumner was forced to "rise up in judgement."

Another attempt to provide an enslaved person with a measure of freedom in spirit if not in law is evident in the final wishes of Winifred Spicer of Vallabush, Mississippi. In her 1839 will, probated in Shelby County, she essentially left her slave a slave. Spicer bequeathed fourteen enslaved men and women to her grandson, Robert M. Spicer, naming them individually: Grace Delphia, George, Peter, John, Minerva, Maria, Lewis, Washington, Jackson, Matilda, Fanny, Henry, and Jim. One name was set apart from the others: "and my old woman Dolly . . . who has served me long and faithfully."

Winifred specified in her will, "I have not given her to my grandson for any service she may render him, but for the purpose that he may protect and provide for her." She went even further by instructing that another enslaved woman, Fanny—also listed among those left to Robert Spicer—should be tasked exclusively with caring for Dolly. In addition, Winifred bequeathed to Dolly several items for her use, including furniture, two cows, and a calf.[14]

Like Marcus Winchester, Isaac Rawlings closely observed the changes taking place across the South from his home in Memphis. At forty-nine, he was in poor health, suffering from advanced stages of what was diagnosed as arthritis but may have been bone cancer. He understood that if he died without securing his son's freedom, the boy could be condemned to a life of enslavement. As Rawlings wrote, from the moment of William's birth, Rawlings had treated his son as "a free person, never intending for him to be enslaved." This would be a key provision in proving his son had an agreement with his father that he would one day be freed. This would also prove to be a loophole that would allow William Isaac to remain in Tennessee rather than being forced to move up north.

In February 1837, when William Rawlings was not yet a teenager, his father petitioned the Shelby County Court to legally emancipate him. Under the law, the court first needed to approve the request, determining that freeing the enslaved individual aligned with "the interests of the state." Additionally, William Rawlings would be required to leave Tennessee unless Isaac could prove a prior "contract for freedom." Rawlings' petition, endorsed by John Pope, the court's chairman, argued that emancipating young Rawlings was in the state's best interest. The court issued a judgment in Rawlings's favor, declaring William "forever free" and entitled to all the rights of a free person, including permission to remain in Tennessee. This favorable ruling was unusual and reflected Rawlings' status and connections in Memphis rather than any compassion on the court's part.

Little is known about William's mother, who may have been Mary, an enslaved woman in Rawlings's household. In the summer of 1818, Mary worked as a cook on a crew with Rawlings transporting goods and supplies up the Mississippi to a new factory in Arkansas. Records show that Mary was paid sixteen dollars for two months of service, though it is likely Rawlings kept the payment. Alternatively, William's mother could have been Hannah, another enslaved woman mentioned in Rawlings's will. Rawlings purchased Hannah many years earlier from Thomas William Love, a trader from Virginia who settled near present-day Holly Springs, Mississippi. Love married Chickasaw Sally Colbert, the oldest daughter of James Logan Colbert. Chickasaw tradition allowed a husband to become a member of the wife's family, so Love became a member of Colbert's tribe. Seven of his sons became Chickasaw leaders, during and after the removal to Indian territory.

Isaac Rawlings died of spinal cancer on September 19, 1839, at age fifty-one, two years after emancipating his son. As he directed in his will, Rawlings was buried in the Raleigh Cemetery rather than the Winchester Burying Ground in Memphis. True to his meticulous nature, Rawlings' swill, witnessed on June 7, 1839, was detailed and left no room for misinterpretation. Rawlings left his sister Juliet three thousand dollars, to be distributed in annual installments of three hundred dollars for ten years or until her death. Juliet, who was forty-seven at the time, lived another five years and was buried near her brother in the Raleigh Cemetery following her death in November 1844.

Rawlings's will also addressed the fate of John, described as "the son of Clarisa, given to me by my sister Susanna Rawlings." John was to be given to Rawlings's son, William, and set free upon reaching the age of thirty. In reference to the law that required those who were enslaved to leave the state if freed, Rawlings added, "When free, if he cannot enjoy freedom in Tennessee, he can go elsewhere."

Aware of the evolving nature of Tennessee law and the mistreatment of free Black individuals, Rawlings put significant thought into his instructions. Regarding William, he wrote, "my natural son, whom I have always considered free and whom I have raised and educated in my house." Rawlings left nothing to chance:

> To William Isaac Rawlings ... who has now the care of my store and well-known to the witness to this will & whose freedom was acknowledged and established by the County Court for Shelby County, Tennessee on my position to set Court in February 1837 and Baptized 22nd July 1838, by Dr George Weller of the Protestant Episcopal Church I give & bequeath at my death all my property and Estate not disposed of as above mentioned. . . . I require and enjoying upon him to take care of Hanah, whom I purchased of Wm. Love of the Chickasaw Nation upwards of Twenty years ago also of her children and to provide for them reasonably out of the property I leave him and to give them their

freedom as he can. I further require him to treat & use well the colored Persons I leave him.[15]

Rawlings left to William his business; shares of stock in The Farmers' and Merchants' Bank of Georgetown in Washington City and Memphis; his plantation, Rousby Hall, and the land and personal property that was there; land in North Carolina; Rawlings's shares in his plantation, Rawlings Choice; 342 acres of land in Shelby and Tipton Counties; 500 acres on the Wolf River; numerous pieces of land and property in Memphis; and shares of stock in The Memphis Wharf Company. William Isaac Rawlings had been born enslaved, but although he was not yet of legal age, he was suddenly one of the richest individuals in West Tennessee. Rawlings also included in his will instructions intended to encourage his son to become "a man of character." He wrote:

> I require him to progress in his studies, as he advances to lawful age to apply himself early and constantly thereafter to business, that his habits may be regularly & correctly fixed & with the means he will have at his disposal without touching his real estate & the servants therewith, which he had better keep. I suggest to him the property of endeavoring to make himself a useful & respectful man of business, a high-minded Honorable man; but to be such he must also be virtuous & moral in his habits & practice, honest & prompt in his engagements, frugal in his expenses so as to keep always within his income, and benevolent in his dispositions, these will protect him against self-reapproach and sustain him through life.[16]

After Rawlings's death, William faced at least one legal challenge to his freedom. When he attempted to transfer a debt of two hundred dollars owed to his father by his uncle, Thomas J. Rawlings, his uncle contested the validity of the transaction, claiming that William was not free because he was still in Memphis. Thomas Rawlings's lawyer argued that William's emancipation was invalid because it did not fully comply with the 1831 state law requiring freed enslaved individuals to leave Tennessee unless they had a specific prior contract for freedom.

The case was brought before the Circuit Court of Shelby County in 1842, where William Rawlings had to defend his freedom without the support of his influential father. Ultimately, in *Greenlow v. Rawlings,* the court ruled in his favor, confirming his status as a free man and resolving any doubts regarding his emancipation. This ruling allowed William to assume legal tasks, such as endorsing promissory notes and managing his late father's businesses, as though he were White.

In the 1840 census, two years before the court's final ruling, William Rawlings was recorded as living in Shelby County. His household included two free White men aged fifteen to nineteen who were listed as "engaged in commerce."

In 1841, his cousin, Joseph J. Rawlings, posted a $15,000 bond to become administrator of his uncle's estate, although he was not mentioned in the original will. February 7, 1842, he wrote to the court, "I hereby report that as administrator of the estate of Isaac Rawlings dec'd that I have not been able to get any effects what ever of sd. estate in my hands, the personal property all having been removed out of the state."

From that entry and the fact Juliet's 1844 will did not mention her nephew, it appears someone helped William liquidate as much of his father's estate as possible. William Rawlings, along with Hannah and her children, seem to have left the state with what inheritance they could get. After that, the trail of William Isaac Rawlings goes cold.

Chapter Eighteen Endnotes

1. Daniel Webster, "Seventh of March Speech," March 7, 1850, in *The Works of Daniel Webster*, vol. 5 (Boston: Little, Brown and Company, 1853), 344
2. Edward Michael McCormack, *Slavery on the Tennessee Frontier* (Nashville: Tennessee American Revolution Bicentennial Commission, 1977), 22.
3. E. E. Hoss, "Elihu Embree, Abolitionist," in *Publications of the Vanderbilt Southern History Society*, vol. 2 (Nashville: University Press Company, 1897), 137.
4. John Mills to cousin Gilbert, May 19, 1807, John Mills Letters (Department of Archives and History, Louisiana State University); U.S.
5. Kenneth M. Stampp, *The Peculiar Institution* (New York: Knopf, 1956), 28.
6. James Davis, "Old Times," *Commercial Appeal*, January 16, 1871, 3.
7. John C. Calhoun, "Speech on the Reception of Abolition Petitions," February 6, 1837, in *The Works of John C. Calhoun*, ed. Richard K. Crallé, vol. 2 (New York: D. Appleton and Company, 1853), 630.
8. J. P. Young, *Standard History of Memphis, Tennessee* (Knoxville, TN: H. W. Crew & Co., 1912), 76.
9. Solomon Northup, *Twelve Years a Slave*, (Auburn: Derby and Miller, 1853), 258-259.
10. Richard Bell, *Stolen* (Simon & Schuster: New York, 2019), 8.
11. David Brion Davis, Antebellum American Culture (Lexington, Massachusetts: D.C. Heath and Company, 1979), 286.
12. "Will of Duke W. Sumner," *Tennessee, U.S., Wills and Probate Records, 1779-2008*, Davidson County, accessed November 7, 2024, Ancestry.com.
13. "Executor's Sale," *Republican Banner*, June 19, 1844, 3.
14. Winifred Spicer, *Will Books*, 1830–1862, Shelby County, Tennessee, in *Tennessee, U.S., Wills and Probate Records, 1779–2008*, Historical Records Project (Tennessee), Shelby County Probate Place, Ancestry.com (Lehi, UT: Ancestry.com Operations, Inc., 2015). Original data: Tennessee County, District, and Probate Courts.
15. Isaac Rawlings, will, *Shelby County Will Books, 1830–1862, Tennessee, U.S., Wills and Probate Records, 1779–2008*, accessed November 20, 2024, Ancestry.com.
16. Isaac Rawlings, will, *Shelby County Will Books, 1830–1862*.

FORREST & MAPLES,
SLAVE DEALERS,

87 Adams Street,
Between Second and Third,

MEMPHIS, TENNESSEE,

Have constantly on hand the best selected assortment of

FIELD HANDS, HOUSE SERVANTS & MECHANICS,

at their Negro Mart, to be found in the city. They are daily receiving from Virginia, Kentucky and Missouri, fresh supplies of likely Young Negroes.

Negroes Sold on Commission, and the highest market price always paid for good stock. Their Jail is capable of containing Three Hundred, and for comfort, neatness and safety, is the best arranged of any in the Union. Persons wishing to purchase, are invited to examine their stock before purchasing elsewhere.

They have on hand at present, Fifty likely young Negroes, comprising Field hands, Mechanics, House and Body Servants, &c.

From Rainey's Memphis City Directory, 1855/56

Chapter Nineteen: Memphis in the Meantime

Culture, hospitality, and community development come to Memphis

Henry Lewis was a landscape painter and set builder whose panorama of the Mississippi River premiered at the Odd Fellows' Hall in Washington City in 1850. The reporter for the *National Intelligencer and Washington Express* gave the experience a rave review: "To those of us who are familiar with the Mississippi river the illusion was so perfect that we could hardly divest ourselves of the idea that we were actually passing along its waters."[1] Few in the nation's capital—or, for that matter, anywhere else in the United States—had actually passed along the waters of the Mississippi. For them, he added, "To those who have never seen 'The Father of Waters' it was indeed a treat, being assured as we were ... that the semblance was perfect."[2]

In the early nineteenth century, panoramas offered a blend of art, education, and entertainment that captivated audiences across America and Europe. These immersive presentations, a precursor to the experience of watching a film in a theater as a group, allowed audiences to sit together or walk around and view massive circular or scrolling paintings. Panoramas provided a rare glimpse at rarely seen parts of the world, revisited historical events, and explored contemporary social issues by combining live narration, art, and storytelling. Moving panoramas, such as those created by Henry Lewis, heightened the illusion of motion by slowly unwinding long, continuous painted canvases by hand, enabling virtual travelers to watch scenes pass before them.

Henry Lewis's virtual journey down "The Father of Waters" titled *Panorama of the Mississippi River* was one of five panoramas that took audiences on a trip down the Mississippi in the 1840s.[3] It took around two hours for the entire canvas, illuminated by gaslight, to unroll. Theater staff made the experience more like a real journey down the river by adjusting the lighting to create the illusion of fire and the rising and setting of the sun. It was a financial endeavor, so if you enjoyed the piano music that accompanied the show, sheet music was for sale in the lobby along with other souvenirs.

The cost of admission for Lewis's panorama was fifty cents for adults and twenty-five cents for children with "liberal arrangements" made for schools. A reporter from the *St. Louis Weekly Reveille* observed, "Lewis can impart a more extensive and more accurate knowledge of the country in one hour than books will teach in a month."[4] For a nation focused on expansion, the idea of the Mississippi River was thrilling, and Lewis's panorama more than delivered on his promise of a unique experience, completely accurate or not. As author Adam Hofbauer observed, Harris left a few things out:

> He omitted the teeming details of life, the children in the streets and the crowds along the banks, the people fishing and waiting for the ferries. He included forts and omitted prisons, depicted the plantation of then president Zachary Taylor but left absent the hundreds of slaves who worked there. The river was rife with drama, and Lewis could have painted lynchings and floods. But he was an artist seeking to affirm, not to titillate, and so his scenes were impersonal, almost pious, more intending to advertise a lifestyle than to lure with scandal.[5]

The Memphis in Lewis's panorama and a subsequent book of color lithograph prints was based on first-hand observation gathered while living in St. Louis and traveling the Mississippi River from 1846 to 1848. His description of Memphis provides a vivid picture of the city during that period:

> The view of Memphis from the waterside is very beautiful and impressive. A short distance from the top of the bluff a handsome array of structures extends into various sections, lending it such an appearance of activity as is presented by few places of its size. This point was chosen by the United States government for the erection of a new navy yard, and the construction necessary to it is now being carried out on a grand scale. The fine location of the city of Memphis, its close connection with a beautiful country-side, as well as its great distance from every other point on the river where a large city could be built, guarantees it overwhelming advantages in becoming a place of importance. An immense quantity of cotton is raised in the interior, and this is the principal market and shipping

point for it. A hundred and twenty thousand bales of cotton are shipped from here annually. At present the city has six churches, one academy, two medical colleges, a number of private schools, a large number of stores, some of which do a considerable business, an electric telegraph office, and a population of 15,000.[6]

The reputation of Memphis was shifting from that of a rough river port to something more respectable. A writer for the *Saturday Evening Post* noticed and wrote of the city in 1833:

> It now has an intelligent class of merchants who find the position an important one for business, being the stopping point for travelers going to the vast regions on the Arkansas, Washita, and Red Rivers. It is one of the places on the Mississippi which passing steamboats generally honor with the discharge of their cannon as they ascend, and may stop for wood and water and to take in fresh provisions.[7]

Marcus Winchester's little town on the bluff had indeed come a long way. In Memphis's early years, most residents lived and worked in hastily constructed log cabins or repurposed huts originally built by Native Americans. By the 1850s, these rudimentary structures had disappeared, replaced by more permanent and refined buildings. Homes and commercial properties constructed with milled lumber frames, glass windowpanes, and sturdy brick chimneys lined the riverfront, reflecting the growing prosperity of those living and working in the city. As one historian put it, "the rifle and plow played their indispensable part in subduing the land, but Tennessee was civilized with architecture, with shipsaws, and adzes, remembered architectural traditions, and the house carpenter's handbooks, chisels, plans, and augers."[8]

The community of soldiers, fur traders, Native Americans, and factors of the first decade had paved the way for the other small business owners who arrived and made Marcus Winchester's vision for Memphis a reality. As Theodore Roosevelt observed, "The wood-choppers, game-hunters, and Indian-fighters who first came over the mountains, were the forerunners of the more regular settlers who followed them."[9] "Regular settlers" like Emanuel Young, with big plans to build something new, flooded into Memphis. Joseph J. Rawlings later remembered:

> In 1826 or 1827, an enterprising merchant, Emmanuel Young, came to Memphis, brought a half dozen good working boys with

him, built a brick house on the bank of the bluff convenient to steamboat trade. He stirred up things, got business on the boom, and taught our merchants that other business could be done besides trading with Indians.[10]

With the demand for new and improved architecture—and settlers with the means to pay for it—came skilled craftsmen and builders who helped shape the growing city. Dick Hinds established a brick manufacturing plant close to the wharf, enabling him to ship his bricks up and down the river. He arrived just in time for Joseph F. Andrews, who constructed the first house in Memphis made entirely of brick, setting a new standard for local architecture. John W. Fowler, regarded as one of the finest plasterers in the Southeast, also made Memphis his home. All these new residents had to work to "keep up with the Winchesters." Until they were banned from living within the city limits, some said they had the nicest house in town.

Among those "regular settlers" whom Theodore Roosevelt described were men and women whose trades relied on a town's population being large enough to sustain their businesses. Seth M. Nelson, for instance, opened one of Memphis's first bakeries. When residents required medicine, Dr. Frank Graham referred them to Nathaniel Rayland's newly opened apothecary. The Reverend Silas T. Toncray preached at the Baptist Church but became wealthy by pursuing multiple professions, including silversmithing, watchmaking, dentistry, and sign painting.

He even served as mayor for a short time. Although Toncray was White, James Davis wrote that he built a brick church with a prominent steeple at the corner of Main and Overton Streets for Black worshipers.[11] This was where he preferred to preach. Davis never forgot the last time he saw the minister:

> There are some, we doubt not, who will remember Silas Toncray—a man of universal genius and various callings. The last time we saw him he was alone in his little back room, giving the finishing touches to a mechanism of brass, by which (to use his own language) he was able to measure distances, irrespective of the inequalities of surface. He informed us he had applied for a patent, but as he died shortly after, and as our youthful comprehension failed to catch the idea he wished to convey, the world doubtless lost, in his death, a valuable invention. Near the northern extremity of Main street, he erected a brick church for the benefit of the colored population, which still remains as a monument of his benevolence and Christian charity.[12]

As Marcus Winchester and William Lawrence made their way through the city, they must have felt a sense of pride in the progress they could see had been made in the few years since their arrival. Like Winchester, Lawrence's close relationship with the proprietors, combined with his own ambition, had paid off handsomely. He, too, had become one of the wealthiest men in town. Lawrence and his wife, Eliza, began building an impressive home at 167 Court Street, located at the southwest corner of present-day Court Avenue and B.B. King Boulevard.

Dick Hinds had not yet opened his brick manufacturing plant, and Memphis lacked industrial kilns. However, one resource Memphis had in abundance was mud. Bricks were shaped from river mud using special tools, left to dry in the sun, and then baked in a circle around a fire. This slow and imprecise process often produced as many broken pieces as usable ones, especially if the builder lacked the necessary skill and expertise.

Craftspeople were essential to the city's development. When Isaac Rawlings returned to Memphis, one of his enslaved men he brought with him was a brick mason. In February 1821, John Overton wrote to Marcus Winchester underscoring just how vital this skill was to the fledgling town:

> McLemore mentions the wish of a Bricklayer who came with Mr. Rawlings. On this now there should be no hesitation. You are expressly authorized to permit him to make bricks at the same place without hindrance for three years, together, selecting the spot and making such other arrangements or contract respecting the same as you may think proper for the encouragement of the place and the benefit of the proprietors. You are not only authorized to do so in this but in any other instances that may occur where it may be advantageous. In doubtful cases it might be well to advise with us but in as plain cases as that of a Bricklayer never hesitate but act.[13]

The walls of William Lawrence's new house were constructed with three layers of brick, making the building remarkably strong. The structure stood for decades, a testament to the craftsmanship and materials used. Lawrence incorporated hand-hewn oak beams over the doors, and the glass-paned windows were complemented by painted shutters.[14] It was a beautiful home inside and out, but sadly, William Lawrence did not live to see it completed. He died on April 11, 1830, at just thirty-two years old. Likely one of the many victims of yellow fever or malaria, he was buried in the New Winchester Burying Ground.

In his will, Lawrence left his wife all his land, furniture, farming utensils, and other personal property, referred to as "chattel," with the exception of "his negroes." His will stipulated that "should any of the negroes become unruly then my executor with the consent of my wife may sell such negroe and appropriate the proceeds in educating my children or otherwise for their benefit." He left his oldest son, William, the gun that had belonged to his grandfather, William Lawrence, "whom he was named after." To his second son, Thomas, he bequeathed his large shotgun. The remainder of his estate was left to his wife for use during her lifetime, to be divided among his children after her death. Lawrence added, "I desire my children shall be well educated and for that purpose my executor is hereby authorized to sell land if necessary."

Reflecting the customs of the time, William Lawrence named his wife as the guardian of their daughter, Frances, while his brother, Robert Lawrence, was appointed executor of the estate and guardian to his sons.[15] Robert and William were two of five Lawrence brothers who all made Memphis home. Robert, who later became mayor and president of the Farmers' and Merchants' Bank, was, according to early Memphis newspaper editor John M. Keating, "a general favorite because of his democratic habits and obliging disposition."[16]

Although William and Eliza Lawrence had been married for only nine years, she never truly recovered from his death. She wore black mourning clothes for the rest of her long life. Of their children, only Frances and William Lawrence Jr. lived to adulthood, and Eliza outlived them both. She passed away at her son-in-law's home on February 14, 1875, at the age of seventy-three—still wearing black.[17]

Men were not the only ones at work building the city. Agnes Price Hawthorne first stepped onto the soil of the fourth Chickasaw bluff with Hugh—a very sick husband—and five hungry children in 1816. Because of his poor health, Hugh had been told by doctors he needed to live somewhere warmer and more humid than the Kentucky community they had helped settle. They outfitted a small flatboat and undertook the dangerous journey down the Ohio River to the Mississippi River, bound for Natchez. By the time they reached Memphis, Hugh Hawthorne was near death. Although she found no doctor in town, a group of Native Americans fed the family and helped nurse Hugh back to health so the family could continue the journey.

A few years later, Hugh Hawthorne died in Natchez, and Agnes began working as a housekeeper for a family there. She never forgot the kindness she had received on the bluff, that had since been named Memphis. In 1824, after saving enough money, she and her children returned, bought property from John C. McLemore, and built a log cabin near the Lawrence home.

In 1828, she was among the small group that helped establish the city's first Presbyterian congregation. They built a church on land donated by the city at the corner of Poplar Avenue and Third Street—present-day North B.B. King Boulevard—where Hawthorne taught Sunday School for many years.[18]

Rachel Tancray was a craftswoman who served Memphis's female population. A talented seamstress, she moved into town in 1827 and eventually opened the first women's hat shop in Memphis. In 1869, she had become so well known, she was hired to endorse Mansfield & Higbee's Magic Arnica Liniment. "I was struck down with paralysis, so I could not move my hand or foot," she was quoted in the newspaper advertisement. "I procured one bottle and it has relieved me entirely. I can now sew, and have the perfect use of my right arm and right side which were before lifeless."[19]

As the economic prosperity of Memphis residents increased, so did the demand for cultural enrichment and development. Richard C. Wade, in his book *The Urban Frontier*, points out that in the first years of developing communities, they were focused primarily on one thing—jobs. Culture, he wrote, came later:

> A city is many things: it is a cultural focus, a social resort, a political center, but before all—though not above all—it is a place where people earn a living. This priority is especially striking in young cities where a vigorous social and cultural life must await the establishment of a stable economic culture.[20]

The Memphis Thespian Society was organized in 1829. The first show occurred when organizers booked Solomon "Old Sol" Smith and his brother to perform at the home of Emmanuel Young, right next door to his warehouse. In his memoirs, Smith demoted the Wolf River when he called Memphis "a very small river town at the mouth of Wolf Creek." He wrote that Memphis only had about six hundred inhabitants and was considered a "thriving place." Sol and his brother performed eight nights, and receipts for the performances were $319.[21] This was early in Smith's career, and he returned to perform in Memphis many times. He later managed other acts and found success as a humorist. Smith spent the final years of his life working as a lawyer in St. Louis.

The Thespian Society also performed their own productions, sometimes at a tavern called the Blue Ruin at the corner of Jackson and Chickasaw Streets across from what was left of The Bell Tavern. Emanuel Young's son, Tom, played an active role in productions, and even Marcus Winchester showed off his acting skills, performing in at least one play, *She Stoops to Conquer*. J. M. Keating remembered the Blue Ruin had "tolerably good scenery and a drop curtain to use between scenes."

One of the first theatrical productions advertised in Memphis was an encore appearance of Chapman's Theatrical Steamboat on September 29, 1836.

> For Six Nights Only Chapman's Theatrical Steamboat
> The Messrs. Chapman take this opportunity of returning thanks for the liberal patronage they have heretofore received from the ladies and gentlemen of Memphis and beg to assure them that neither trouble nor expense has been spared to merit a continuance of their favors. This evening, Saturday, 1st October will be performed Kotzebue's play of STRANGER With a variety of Singing. To conclude with the farce of PERFECTION
> Great care has been taken to render the Wharf commodious for ladies.[22]

Memphis experienced live theater March through May of 1837, when actors Warrell and Grove opened to an overflow crowd on a riverboat with the plays *Timour the Tartar*, *Highland Reel*, and *The Robber's Wife*.

One early Memphis resident remembered attending a play given in a livery stable opposite Hart's Saloon. "It was fixed up as well as could be expected, and the play was Cooper's *Pilot*," he wrote. "Long Tom Coffin was very finely rendered by a fellow who was 6 feet 6, and looked every inch the sailor."[23] Long Tom Coffin is a character in James Fenimore Cooper's 1824 novel *The Pilot*.

With all that live entertainment also came music. Italian immigrant and organist Philip Flavio came to Memphis from his birthplace in France by way of New Orleans around 1840 and played the organ at Isaac Rawlings's Calvary Episcopal Church throughout the 1840s and 1850s. Flavio also organized and performed in concerts at the church and other places in Memphis and was the proprietor of the city's first music stores. They were located at 296 Main Street in the Calhoun Building, Jefferson Street under the Commercial Hotel, and on Madison Street. Flavio sold sheet music, pianos, and other instruments; gave lessons; and even published his own music.

An advertisement for one of his music stores in 1848 promoted sheet music for the latest hits, "The Memphis Quick Step," "The Memphis Gallop," and "The Covington Female Seminary Waltz."[24]

There is no doubt Memphis's musical roots run deep. Icons such as Alberta Hunter, Sam Phillips, W. C. Handy, Elvis Presley, Ruby Wilson, and B. B. King called the city home, while studios like Sun Studio, Stax Records, Royal Studios, American Sound Studio, and Ardent Studios established it as a hub of music production. With the tagline "Home of Blues, Soul and Rock 'n' Roll," Memphis Tourism has promoted the city as a music lover's mecca, and millions visit from around the world each year to "shake, rattle and roll." Yet, none realize that Philip Flavio was there first.

In addition to contributing to the arts in Memphis through his moment on the stage, Marcus Winchester also played an active role in decorating the homes and offices of early Memphians by selling engravings in his store. Engravings provided the general public access to affordable art that they would not have had otherwise. Portraits, landscapes, or scenes from historical events were transferred onto metal plates by engravers. They carved intricate designs, which were then coated with ink, wiped clean of excess, and pressed onto paper.

Some prints remained monochrome, while others were hand-colored to create an image that could be sold as a premium product. Winchester was an official distributor for the work of Ralph E. W. Earl, Andrew Jackson's official White House portrait painter and husband of the Jacksons' niece. In addition to Andrew and Rachel Jackson, Earl painted portraits of Marcus Winchester's parents—James and Susan Black Winchester—John Overton, Martin Van Buren, John Coffee, and many others in Jackson's circle. Earl had one of his portraits of Jackson engraved by James Barton Longacre of Philadelphia and sold prints through dealers like Marcus Winchester.

As the riverfront filled in and Memphis's business community grew, investors like Robertson Topp spotted an opportunity in the hotel sector. Topp, a twenty-three-year-old lawyer from Davidson County who had learned the ropes in his brother's office, was an early settler, arriving in 1831. It didn't take long for him to catch real-estate fever. Called "the picture of a true Southern gentleman," he began buying up land around South Memphis—where Marcus Winchester was also investing. Like Winchester, Topp was an advocate for combining South Memphis, Fort Pickering, and Memphis into one larger city. It would take a while. In 1849, Memphis formally annexed South Memphis, extending the city's corporate limits southward to Calhoun Street. By 1870, Memphis had absorbed Fort Pickering, consolidating control over the riverfront and uniting the three once-separate communities under one municipal government.[25]

Topp also served in the Tennessee state legislature and was a driving force in attracting new business to Memphis. Knowing all that new opportunities flowing into the city would also bring visitors looking for a place to sleep, Topp got to work raising money to build Memphis's first luxury hotel. For the location, he selected a spot a little below Poplar Avenue where, according to the 1849 city directory, there was "an old field, surrounded by open wood, where the youth of the city, who have yet but sparsely cultivated beards, were in the habit of shooting squirrels and other game."

Archibald Walker and Topp's brother-in-law, William L. Vance, joined forces with Topp in 1842. To design their hotel, they hired James Dakin, a founder of the American Institute of Architects and the designer of the St. Charles Hotel in New Orleans. They decided to name the hotel the Gayoso House, honoring Manuel Luis Gayoso de Lemos, who had secured the bluff for Spain in 1795. While the process by which they selected the name has been lost to history, one wonders whether their list of possibilities included other names such as DeSoto, Marquette, Joliet, Bienville, or other early visitors to the fourth Chickasaw bluff.

The cornerstone was laid on July 4, 1842, with a grand gala to celebrate the occasion. The Gayoso House officially opened its doors on March 11, 1844. The hotel was unlike anything most Memphians had ever seen. Its Greek Revival portico could be spotted from miles away by boats making their way along the Mississippi River or pulling up to the Gayoso House's private dock.

One reporter described the hotel as having been set in "landscape gardening and terraced to the river with wealth and social condition almost of Babylonian splendor."[26] Guests who arrived by steamboat walked up from the dock through landscaped gardens along a long red carpet. Those who arrived by horse and buggy entered through a large gate under an ornamental sign in which the name of the hotel was spelled out in giant wrought-iron letters. Standing before the entry's large arches and magnificent columns, it was evident to guests they were arriving at one of the South's most luxurious hotels.

Once inside, guests encountered the check-in counter and lobby bar. Over the registration desk was painted Gayoso's coat-of-arms.[27] According to one account, the lobby featured heavy iron railings down the middle to separate the women from the "dandies who like to lounge around the hotel." After checking in and paying $1.50 per day—which included horse boarding if needed—guests were escorted to rooms adorned with silver-plated doorknobs and hinges and hand-painted wallpaper.

Through the years, staying at the hotel, or the version built after a fire burned the original down, became a Memphis tradition. The hotel's guestbook had the signatures of several U.S. presidents including James K. Polk, Millard Fillmore, Zachary Taylor, Grover Cleveland, and Theodore Roosevelt, along with other notables including Sam Houston and Henry Clay. As an important part of the Memphis business community, Marcus Winchester would have attended many meetings, conferences, and events at the Gayoso House.

Winchester was also a participant in the Southwestern Convention on November 12, 1845. It was one of a series of conventions that took place in cities around the Southern United States from 1837 to 1859 with the objective of finding ways to increase the "fortunes of the South." That day, a number of influential men gathered at Memphis's Methodist Episcopal Church and focused on the development of a southern transcontinental railroad and improving transportation on the Mississippi River and its tributaries. The convention was presided over by John C. Calhoun, who gave a keynote address in which he noted the importance of the location of Memphis:

> The region occupied by the western and southern States is a vast extent it may be divided into three parts. The first and greatest is the magnificent valley in the midst of which we stand, and which is drained by the mighty stream whose current roles under the bluff on which your city is located. It extends north and south nearly through the entire breadth of the temperate zone, and east and west from the Rocky to the Allegheny mountains, and occupies in its northern extension a position midway between the Pacific and Atlantic oceans.[28]

As part of the convention, men were selected to serve on various committees relating to improvements. Winchester was appointed to a committee of three that focused on improving western mail delivery. By this time, the post office was one of the biggest providers of government jobs. In the 1840s, about three-fourths of all federal civilian employees worked for the post office—around fifteen thousand in 1841. The efficiency of each office depended on the individuals employed as postmaster. Local postmaster positions around the country were often filled as political rewards for those who supported the ruling party. The amount of mail being sent had also increased much faster than the population. By 1840, local post offices handled nearly three thousand letters and twenty-seven hundred newspapers per one thousand residents with varying levels of success.[29] Today, one of the taglines embraced by the Memphis business community is "America's Distribution Center." It could be said the path to that designation began at the Southwestern Convention of 1845.

Not only was Winchester focused on improvements in communication and transportation, he continued to invest in real estate. He eventually owned land in and around Memphis and had invested in South Memphis and Fort Pickering. He had been steadily buying land on the other side of the river as well. Winchester eventually owned twenty-six hundred acres, much of which would become West Memphis, Arkansas. Winchester owned all the land that had belonged to Benjamin Fooy except twenty acres around Fooy's homesite where his widow still lived.

The transportation of people and goods along the river was central to John Overton's vision for the potential of the fourth Chickasaw bluff when he acquired the Rice Tract in 1794. The men who navigated the river were as important as those who arrived to the bluff traveling on land. As historian Leland D. Baldwin pointed out, "In the gallery of American genre paintings, the boatmen deserve a place along with the pioneer, the steamboat pilot, the cowboy, and those other types that have enriched American life and lore."[30]

The men who made their living navigating the rivers were a tough lot. Baldwin separated them into three categories: regular bargemen, keelboatmen, and flatboatmen. Flatboatmen were the most industrious, as between trips down the river, they worked as farmers, trappers, and merchants or stayed on the river building boats.[31]

By the mid-1800s, the bustling river traffic and thriving commerce in Memphis would have undoubtedly surpassed even his most ambitious expectations, had Overton lived to see it. Steamboats had joined the thousands of flatboats, keelboats, and other vessels traveling up and down the river with goods and passengers.

By 1838, the original public landing at the Wolf River was made useless by a sandbar—called Mud Island today—that had begun developing years earlier. While the landing had been perfect for flatboats and keelboats, with its flat slope and shallow water, it was now impossible for steamboats to dock there. Wharf boats were used to take passengers and goods to and from the boat and the dock. It was time consuming and expensive. Eventually, four additional landings were established along the Memphis riverfront to accommodate boats of all types.

In his memoir about travels along the Mississippi River from 1815 to 1825, Timothy Flint wrote about the riverfront in nearby New Madrid, Missouri, about one hundred thirty miles upriver from Memphis. His observations provide a glimpse into what the Memphis riverfront must have been like when large numbers of steamboats were docked there:

> In one place there are boats loaded with pine plank, from the pine forests of the southwest of New York. In another quarter there are numerous boats with the Yankee notions of Ohio. From Kantucky pork, flour, whiskey, hemp, tobacco, bagging, and bale rope. From Tennessee there are the same articles together with great quantities of cotton. . . . There are boats fitted on purpose and loaded entirely with turkeys, that, having little else to do, gobble most furiously. . . . The hands travel about from boat to boat, make inquiries, and acquaintances, and form alliances to yield mutual assistance to each other, on their descent from this to New Orleans. Next morning at the first dawn, the bugles sound.

Every thing in and about the boats that has life, is in motion. The boats, in half an hour are all under way ... the fleet unites once more at Natchez, or New Orleans, and although they live on the same river, they may, perhaps, never meet each other again on the earth.[32]

While the advancement of river transportation brought cities and towns closer together, it also increased the ease of getting enslaved individuals more quickly from one location to another. Another Mississippi River traveler wrote of seeing a flatboat with human cargo on a river port: "You see peeping out of the holes the wooley heads of slaves transported from Virginia and Kentucky to the human flesh mart at New Orleans. They have come thousands of miles, and still have to proceed a thousand more before they arrive at their place of destination.[33]

All those boats docking in Memphis should have provided a revenue source for the city, but until the early 1840s, most flatboat and keelboat pilots resisted all efforts to impose docking fees. They simply refused to pay them. As steamboats began paying the fee, Mayor William Spickernagle hired a wharf master and gave him the job of collecting fees from all boats. Most of the flatboatmen still refused to pay, some even threatening violence.

One confrontation on the Memphis riverfront in 1842 came to be known as the Flatboatmen's War. It resulted in two companies of local militia being called and the death of one of the flatboat pilots. He had pulled out a knife with, it appeared, every intention of using it. Stories circulated after the pilot's death—no doubt by Mayor Spickernagle—that the dead flatboat pilot's last words were that he should have paid the tax but was being stubborn and did not want to give in.[34] While "war" was a bit of an exaggeration for the conflict, the point was made. Extracting a fee from the pilots on the river was going to be tough.

The next Memphis mayor, Edwin Hickman, found a solution in the form of Tobias Wolfe, a strong young man who was to become a Memphis institution on the riverfront for the next three decades. Wolfe and his wife, Narcissus, arrived in Memphis in 1841 from North Carolina and settled in nearby Raleigh. Something about Wolfe's brute strength and large presence impressed the new mayor who recruited him as wharf master and provided motivation by allowing Wolfe to keep twenty-five percent of anything he collected for the city's coffers. It is unclear whether young Wolfe knew the history of the job or the difficult role into which he was stepping. Regardless, he was successful.

Joe Curtis was a Mississippi riverboat pilot and journalist who covered the river trade for *The Commercial Appeal* in a daily column titled "In the Pilothouse." In a 1941 column, he explained how Tobias Wolfe became so effective at his job:

He went after those tough flatboat fellows with hammer and tongs, fought them with his fists, whaled the daylights out of their best fighters, and finally, forced every master and owner of a flatboat landed at Memphis to pay the city wharf tax. He made them like it and forced them to like him, for he was fair and just in all enforced demands.[35]

As Curtis remembered, the city later created an elected position of wharf master, and Tobias Wolfe ran unopposed. He filled the role for the next twenty years, only stopping when Union troops took over the city during the Civil War. After the war, Wolfe was called on again several times to serve as wharf master, but all those years seeing people arrive to the city looking for a place to stay inspired him to enter the hospitality business instead. In 1868, he purchased the Whitemore House located at 111 Adams Street, remodeled it, and changed the name to the Cumberland House. While his hotel was not as grand as the Gayoso House, it was advertised as being "centrally located, convenient to railroad, steamboat, theater, post office, all the churches, and in the most cleanly, quiet, and respectable portion of the city."[36] Wolfe's rates were $7 a week or $2.50 a day.

The same year Wolfe arrived in Memphis, Congress appointed a commission to locate a navy yard somewhere along the Mississippi River. Most southern politicians believed investment in the Navy was money that benefited a handful of eastern states primarily along the Atlantic Ocean. To address that, Congress began looking for a location for a shipyard for the Navy along either the Ohio or the Mississippi River.

Most Memphians were skeptical when they found out Memphis was being considered. James Davis wrote the general consensus was, "What! A navy-yard at Memphis, a thousand miles from the sea? Fudge."[37]

The Memphis business community eventually embraced the idea of a shipyard and depot in hopes it would bring new business into the city and would finally attract a railroad. After selecting Memphis, Congress paid the city $25,000 for eighty acres at the mouth of the Wolf River where the Memphis Pyramid sits today. The plans were extensive; a wall would be installed to hold back the mighty Mississippi, the banks around the yard would be reinforced, and homes and buildings of stone and lumber would be constructed. What could go wrong?

Everything. It began when buildings—even while under construction—sank into the muddy soil on which they were being built. Once the stone foundation of one building was complete, it sank nine feet before the next phase of construction could even begin.

In 1851, Army engineers, opposed to the project, evaluated Memphis to assess its suitability as a navy yard without regard to regional politics. Their report concluded that Memphis lacked the "essential requisites" for an effective navy yard, emphasizing the necessity of proximity to the ocean and strong fortifications. Memphis was too far inland; the bluff sat on sandy, unstable soil; and the whole site failed to meet basic criteria. The engineers did point out the obvious. The Mississippi River's low water levels and natural obstructions rendered Memphis impervious to enemy attacks from the sea.[38] James Davis was working on the riverfront at the time and experienced the early days of the navy yard's construction. He wrote, "The ignorant asked questions which were readily answered, and the whole thing was explained by the still more ignorant."[39]

After a history of political infighting, government waste, and foolish decision making, the navy yard in Memphis could point to one success: the outfitting and rigging of the *Alleghany*. It was the first all-iron ship and the first with paddlewheels on the underside of the hull.

In the end, the navy yard on the bluff was given back to the City of Memphis. Considered a failure, it cost the U.S. government $1,500,000 and left Memphis with a riverfront property that was home to a number of deserted buildings. The former navy yard eventually became home to a flour mill, the city's first cottonseed oil mill, and before it burned to the ground, an elegant building in the center of the yard became the offices of the Memphis & Ohio Railroad. Some of the out buildings were used to store cotton. By 1876, the City of Memphis wanted out of the property management business. On January 13, 1876, a crowd gathered around the former naval commander's house at the yard to bid on eighty lots carved from the riverfront property. Under the headline "Going, Going, Gone," a writer for the *Memphis Daily Appeal* covered the story:

> There was a time when Congress was good-natured to Memphis. On one occasion, it petted the town by starting a navy-yard here…. A whole navy-yard was a magnificent present, but there is a "but" to everything, and there was a "but" here. Offer a girl a necklace of glass beads and she will be in ecstasies; give her a horse-collar, useful and valuable as the horse-collar may be, she will turn up her nose on it. So the Memphis city council said a navy-yard was not a nice thing for a city to have at all, and they sent word to Congress that they felt very much obliged, and so on, but they wanted no navy-yard.[40]

Chapter Seventeen Endnotes

1. "Lewis' Panorama of the Mississippi," *National Intelligencer and Washington Express*, April 8, 1850, 4.
2. "Lewis' Panorama, *National Intelligencer and Washington Express*.
3. John Frances McDermott, *The Lost Panoramas of the Mississippi* (Chicago: The University of Chicago Press, 1958), 1-2.
4. *St. Louis Weekly Reveille*, September 6, 1849
5. Adam Hofbauer, "The Lost Films of the 1840s: The Mississippi River and the Tradition of Proto-Cinema," *Bright Lights Film Journal*, April 30, 2013.
6. Henry Lewis, *The Valley of the Mississippi Illustrated* (Düsseldorf: Arnz & Comp., 1857), 352.
7. George L. Sioussat, "Memphis as a Gateway to the West," *Tennessee Historical Magazine* 3, no. 1 (March 1917): 4.
8. James Patrick, *Architecture in Tennessee, 1768–1897* (Knoxville: The University of Tennessee Press, 1981), 9.
9. Theodore Roosevelt, *Thomas Hart Benton* (Boston: Houghton, Mifflin and Company, 1887), 5.
10. J. J. Rawlings, *Miscellaneous Writings* (Nashville: Cumberland Presbyterian Publishing House, 1888), 12.
11. James D. Davis, *History of Memphis* (Memphis: Hite, Crumpton & Kelly, 1873), 232.
12. Davis, *History of Memphis,* 120.
13. Fletch Coke, *Dear Judge: Selected Letters of John Overton of Travellers' Rest* (Nashville: Travellers' Rest Historic House Museum, 1978), 63.
14. "Memphis First Brick Home Goes to Make Way for Auto," *Commercial Appeal*, August 10, 1930, 57.
15. William Lawrence, will, January 17, 1830, *Shelby County, Tennessee, Will Books* 1830–1862, no. 1, Shelby County Archives.
16. John M. Keating, *History of Memphis, Tennessee* (Syracuse, NY: D. Mason & Co., 1888), 190.
17. *Old Folks Record*, "Eliza Lawrence," no. 7 (April 1875): 333.
18. Alice Redden James, "The Winchester Cemetery," *Commercial Appeal*, January 10, 1909, 52.
19. "Paralysis Cured," *Public Ledger*, October 27, 1870, 4.
20. Richard C. Wade, *The Urban Frontier: The Rise of Western Cities, 1790–1830* (Chicago: The University of Chicago Press, 1959), 39.
21. Sol Smith, *Theatrical Management in the West and the South for Thirty Years* (New York: Harper & Brothers, 1868), 57.
22. Raymond S. Hill, "Memphis Theatre, 1836–1846," *West Tennessee Historical Society Papers* 9 (1955): 48.
23. "The Memphis of Forty-two years ago," *Daily Memphis Avalanche*, April 3, 1881, 2.
24. "New Music," *The Memphis Daily Eagle*, April 20, 1848, 3.
25. H. A. Chapman, *Map of the City of Memphis: Including Fort Pickering and Hopefield, Ark.* (St. Louis: A. McLean Lithographer, 1858), Geography and Map Division, Library of Congress.
26. "Where Weary Travelers of Yesterday Found Rest in Memphis," *Commercial Appeal*, January 1, 1940, 16.
27. Eldon Roark, "A New Look into the Past," *Memphis Press-Scimitar*, March 30, 1953, 13.
28. *Journal of the Proceedings of the Southwestern Convention: Began and Held at the City of Memphis, on the 12th November, 1845* (Memphis: Southwestern Convention, November 15, 1845), 7.
29. Richard R John, *Spreading the News* (Cambridge: Harvard University Press, 1995), 3–4.
30. Leland D. Baldwin, *The Keelboat Age on Western Waters* (Pittsburg: University of Pittsburg Press, 1980), 5.
31. Baldwin, *The Keelpbat Age*, 85.
32. Timothy Flint, *Recollections of the Last Ten Years, Passed in Occasional Residences and Journeyings in the Valley of the Mississippi* (Boston: Cummings, Hilliard, and Co., 1826), 103–4.
33. Charles Sealsfield, *The Americans as They Are* (London: Hurst, Chance & Co., 1828), 108-109.
34. J. P. Young, *Standard History of Memphis, Tennessee* (Knoxville, TN: H. W. Crew & Co., 1912), 82.
35. Dan Curtis, "Memphis Wharfage Fee Fight," *West Tennessee Historical Society Papers* 12 (1958): 17.
36. "Cumberland House," *Memphis Daily Appeal*, December 2, 1868, 4.
37. Davis, *History of Memphis*, 206,

38. Stanley J. Adamiak, "A Naval Depot and Dockyard on the Western Waters: The Rise and Fall of the Memphis Naval Yard, 1844–1854," *International Journal of Naval History*, no. 1 (April 2002): 5.
39. Davis, *History of Memphis*, 210.
40. "Going, Going, Gone," *Memphis Daily Appeal*, January 13, 1876, 4.

D. LEVY & CO.,
FASHIONABLE
CLOTHIER,
No. 189 MAIN STREET.

We would respectfully call the attention of the public to our splendid stock of

READY MADE
CLOTHING,

which, for quality and style cannot be surpassed in the city, as we are in receipt, weekly, of all

THE LATEST STYLES,

Gentlemen would do well to call on us before purchasing elsewhere. We keep constantly on hand, a full assortment of

GENT'S WEARING APPAREL,

TRUNKS, CARPET BAGS, &C. &C.

GIVE US A CALL.

No trouble to show Goods!!

From Rainey's Memphis City Directory, 1855/56

Chapter Twenty: Memphis Money

*Marcus Winchester and the
fight for Memphis's first bank*

In the antebellum era, banks were begun by groups of investors and local merchants to create economic growth and support commercial expansion. They also knew they needed to provide a stable medium of exchange in a country that was developing more rapidly than the infrastructure that supported it. Settlers needed money to buy real estate, and often they did not have cash, so they borrowed it. Banking was less regulated and capital was scarce so interest rates could sometimes range from twelve to twenty-five percent or even more.

In Memphis, Marcus Winchester and Isaac Rawlings had been functioning as de facto bankers for many years and had earned the trust of Memphians who could take advantage of their knowledge and reputation for honesty—but their capabilities were limited.

In 1832, Memphis was at a crossroads. The economic growth of the city could not continue without capital, and for that, a city needed its own bank rather than having to depend on institutions in New Orleans, St. Louis, or Nashville. A committee of Memphis businessmen created a working group to address the problem and come up with a solution.

In addition to Winchester and Rawlings, the group included Robert Lawrence, brother of William Lawrence and among the earliest to arrive in Memphis with Winchester; Nathaniel Anderson, a close friend of Winchester who operated one of the city's first hotels, served as a leading cotton broker with offices in both Memphis and New Orleans, and was active in Democratic politics; and Seth Wheatley, Memphis's youngest mayor. Along with several other men of note at that time, they created a group eager to shape the economics of the city.

For Winchester, a bank was crucial to creating economic strength and power to rival that of Nashville, seen more as a competitor than as a neighbor. "Our wives and daughters wish to enjoy some of life's luxuries, yet we are unable to provide them," he pointed out at the first meeting of the working group. "That is why we have gathered here today—to find a solution to this problem. With a bank, we too can dress in fine clothes, live comfortably, and enjoy the prosperity that other communities take for granted."[1]

There was, however, great economic instability on the frontier at the time, and banks often created as many problems as they solved. As settlers moved into towns like Memphis or carved farms out of what was once wilderness, the need for a reliable medium of exchange and the ability to borrow money was crucial to growth. Most banks were chartered by states rather than the federal government and issued their own banknotes. To bring order to this system, Congress chartered the Second Bank of the United States in 1816, giving it broad power to regulate the nation's currency and restrain irresponsible state banks. President Andrew Jackson, however, viewed the Bank as an undemocratic concentration of wealth and power. After a bitter political struggle, he succeeded in withdrawing federal deposits and, in 1836, effectively killed the Bank. What followed was a fragmented financial system in which state banks, often poorly managed and inadequately backed, operated with little oversight. The "Bank War," as Jackson's campaign against the institution became known, destabilized credit markets and contributed to years of monetary turbulence, including the Panic of 1837, which struck only months after he left office.[2]

Specie—gold and silver coins—remained the most reliable form of money during the antebellum period. Unlike banknotes, which depended on the trustworthiness of the bank that issued them, specie had intrinsic value due to the precious metals it contained. The federal government minted coins that were widely accepted as payment, especially for large transactions or international trade. State banks were usually required to keep specie reserves to back their notes, but in practice, many overextended themselves, lending heavily for land purchases and issuing far more paper than they could redeem in gold or silver. When confidence faltered, depositors demanded their money in specie, and runs on banks often followed.

For frontier communities like Memphis, this cycle of easy credit, speculation, and collapse defined much of the early economic life of the city. Ultimately, the little group of businessmen working on solving the money problem in Memphis disagreed about some of the specifics, but they were unanimous in the solution. They agreed to send Marcus Winchester and William Lawrence to Nashville to petition the state for a bank to be located in Memphis. The men's trip prooved succesful, and they soon opened the Farmers' and Merchants' Bank at the corner of Main and Winchester Streets. For more than a century, little else was known about the origins of Memphis's first bank. That changed when a forgotten pamphlet, long gathering dust on a library shelf, was brought to light by Memphis historian James E. Roper.

For many years, Roper was on the hunt for primary sources and documents that provided insight into the history of his hometown. In the late 1950s, he made a fascinating discovery. Sitting on a shelf at Harvard at the Baker Library of the School of Business Administration was *The Chronicles of the Farmers' and Merchants' Bank*. The unusual pamphlet—the only copy known to exist—was donated to Harvard by Shakespearean scholar Horace Howard Furness of Philadelphia in 1873. Written anonymously by a writer who used the pseudonym Jesse, the "Scribe," it tells the story of the bank's beginnings and subsequent troubles. The style, however, was reminiscent of the writings of Shakespeare—a unique mashup of Hamlet, Macbeth, and King Lear with the early settlers of the Tennessee frontier on a Mississippi River bluff.

Of his discovery, Roper wrote, "Although *The Chronicles of the Farmers' and Merchants' Bank* does indeed turn a bright light on the devious ways of antibellum capitalism, it is perhaps even more to be treasured as the contemporary record of a very obscure period in Memphis's general history."[3] As Roper knew well, very little of the history of Memphis's first decades survived to tell the story of the birth of the city beyond a few newspapers, a small number of letters, and the writings of James Davis—whose mind Roper noted was "forgetful, distorting, and often purely concocting."[4] Roper wrote, "*The Chronicles* brings forth into the daylight men and events which have until now been only shadowy, or else completely unknown. It is comprehensive, informed, and above all, contemporaneous."[5]

The anonymous author of the pamphlet knew enough details to have either been present—or very close to someone who was—at the meetings where the issue was discussed and a solution found and implemented. Whomever recorded this important piece of Memphis history intended to be anonymous, and anonymous they have remained.

Jesse, the "Scribe" opened his tale of Memphis banking with "Now it so happened that previous to the year 1832, the western portion of the state of Tennessee enjoyed no banking facilities. Now this thing sorely grieved the Monied Men, and the men of commerce in the said portion of the tribe."[6] Not only was this an economic problem, it was a matter of pride. "They reasoned together thus: now we are not men of money and enterprise as well as our brethren of the central location, and have not we financial talents sufficient to carrying on a western bank?"

According to Jesse, it was Marcus Winchester who first initiated the idea of a bank. In speaking to the members of the tribe, Winchester pointed out that they were "behind some of the more favored tribes." But this version of Marcus Winchester, in flowing robes and a powdered wig, had a solution.

Following is a portion of *The Chronicles of the Farmers' and Merchants' Bank* slightly edited into contemporary language—but retaining the Shakespearean intent—to provide insight into elements of the antebellum frontier economy, and the personalities of Marcus Winchester and his contemporaries.

The Chronicles of the Farmers' and Merchants' Bank

By Jesse, the "Scribe"

Chapter 1

Before 1832, the western part of Tennessee had no banks and had to rely entirely on the central state banks for money circulation. This situation deeply troubled the wealthy and business-minded men of the region. They reasoned among themselves:

Are we not just as capable in business and finance as the people in the central part of the state? Do we not have the same financial skills to run a bank in the west? It wounds our pride and humiliates us to have to beg for favors from those who are no better than us, just to access banking services from the state's institutions.

Let us come together and petition the leaders of our government, when they meet in the General Assembly, to grant us a privileged monopoly—a bank of our own. We can deposit our surplus funds in its vaults and withdraw what we need in return. We believe that every successful institution is based on mutual benefit: if we contribute our surplus in good faith, we should receive support in return.

The people welcomed this idea enthusiastically. They declared:

Let it be done, just as the scribes have written! Let us call a public meeting of all good citizens in the region to discuss it. If they agree, we will raise our voices as one—'The voice of the people is the voice of God'—and send our request to the General Assembly. When our rulers hear the people's voice, they will grant us a bank that will serve our interests.

This plan greatly pleased the people, and they all agreed to gather. The scribes then proclaimed:

Let the trumpets sound and a mighty wind sweep through the land, louder than anything ever heard here before! Let the call go out until everyone hears it and gathers in the streets and highways. Let them declare that our people are strong and independent—not worshipers of idols like others who build great temples to commerce. While other cities call upon scribes, Pharisees, and even foreigners to worship at their financial altars, we shall proclaim our own greatness.

We are a thriving people, rich in trade and agriculture. Our hills are covered with wool-producing sheep, and our valleys overflow with grapes and honey. Our surplus is so abundant that we must find a way to trade it effectively. Other cities have their own shipping, gold, and silver, and the legislature is only waiting for a powerful outcry from the people before granting our request.

So, the trumpets sounded, the message spread far and wide, and the people were summoned from every corner. When the great convention gathered, the assembly was full. Then, one humble citizen, Marcus Winchester, who had lived an honest life, was chosen to lead the meeting. He stood and addressed the crowd:

Men of the Western District and Brothers of This Tribe, I would be disrespectful to both myself and to you if I did not express my deep gratitude for the unexpected honor you have bestowed upon me by asking an ordinary citizen, inexperienced in formal proceedings, to preside over this important gathering.

I trust, my brothers, that you will support me with both your wisdom and your patience, so that I may fulfill this duty honorably, ensuring that our discussions remain productive and unified. Looking around this gathering, seeing our community leaders all present, I know that we must be here to discuss a matter of great importance—one that will either benefit or harm us all. However, I must admit, I feel some uncertainty in having to explain to you the full purpose of this assembly. Still, I am strengthened by my conviction that the issue before us is vital, one that will impact our future and deserves serious discussion.

Brothers, our tribe has a long history. We read in the records of our ancestors that we existed even before the time of the great Andrew Jackson. Some ancient traditions say that long before his days, our forefathers lived as a distinct community in a land called 'Rip Van Winkle.' But, as generations passed, they left that place due to lack of land for farming and raising livestock. Eventually, they arrived here, in what we now see as our own promised land—our 'El Dorado'—where we have finally found the opportunity to fulfill our dreams.

This land is rich and fertile. Our vineyards, fig trees, and myrtles flourish naturally. Our hills are black with cattle, our valleys full of horses, sheep, and oxen. Mules and hogs are so common that we barely take notice of them. But, my brothers, despite our wealth in agriculture, we still lag behind other regions. Though our lands yield more than we could ever need, we lack a proper financial system. Our commerce is limited, reduced to simple bartering. We have no way to exchange goods fairly when values differ. Our wives and daughters wish to enjoy some of life's luxuries, yet we are unable to provide them. That is why we have gathered here today—to find a solution to this problem.

So, what is the answer? The solution seems clear to me, and I hope it will be met with enthusiasm from all of you. We must establish a bank in this city, along the great Mississippi River, with a capital of half a million dollars and the ability to issue three times that amount in currency. This institution will fill the void in our financial system, enabling us to trade on equal footing with others. With this bank, we too can dress in fine clothes, live comfortably, and enjoy the prosperity that other communities take for granted.

As soon as he finished speaking, a wave of applause swept through the assembly. The people cheered in agreement, and finally, in one united voice, they cried out: "Let us have a bank!"

Chapter 2

After the chiefs of the tribe gave a unified and enthusiastic approval to Marcus's suggestions, the assembly came to order. Marcus rose to address them once more and began by expressing his gratitude for the warm reception of his previous words. He admitted that, while he had always hoped for the success of the project that had brought them together, he had not expected such a wholehearted response from the people. He was therefore not prepared to adequately express his thanks for the honor bestowed upon him. As a return, he suggested that each person in the assembly should speak their thoughts on the matter at hand. He continued:

My brothers, we are only at the beginning of this important discussion. Our current actions are merely preparatory to the real decisions we will make later. Even though each of us may feel confident about our success, I believe it is best that all the strong arguments in favor of our plan be presented here. This will help us build a powerful case that will impress others and strengthen our position when we approach the other tribes. But, my brothers, since I have already taken up much of your time, I must thank you for your attention to my humble suggestions, and, since Nathaniel Anderson, Seth Wheatley, Isaac Rawlings, Jacob Moon, and Robert Lawrence are all here, I would now be happy to hear their thoughts.

Marcus then returned to his seat. At this point, Nathaniel Anderson rose and spoke, saying, "Since Isaac is one of the founding fathers of our tribe and has offered us much wisdom and good advice in the past, I would be very pleased to hear his thoughts. Rather than say anything myself, I ask Isaac to speak." Isaac stood among his brothers and, looking around at the group, began, "I am hesitant to share my thoughts immediately, because this issue is so important to the tribe.

I am not unwilling to speak, but I would prefer to listen to the views of others first, so I ask Nathaniel to speak first." He then sat down. Nathaniel stood once again and said:

My beloved brothers, I truly wanted Isaac to speak, not because I fear any harm from my own words, but because I value his wisdom. He has lived through many experiences that have sharpened his judgment. But I will now give you my thoughts, even though they may be humble, leaving it up to you to decide how to use or interpret them.

My brothers, I felt a great sense of pride and admiration as I listened to Marcus. I am proud to live in the land he described, among such enlightened people. Marcus is the first to remind us of our tribe's history, to call attention to our noble beginnings, and to inspire us with lofty goals. I believe Marcus should be honored as a High Priest in whatever temple we build, and that as time passes and current events fade from memory, his name will endure. Even when the names of other tribes are forgotten, his name will survive and be passed down through generations, linking us with our descendants. This way, we will know that we did not live in vain.

I am sure I am speaking for all of us when I say that we are grateful to Marcus for showing us the way forward. But I must not take up too much of your time, so I will turn directly to the matter at hand.

Marcus wisely suggested that our leaders present a strong case for our plan, backed by facts and arguments that will attract the attention and admiration of other tribes. We must make sure we have solid reasons for whatever we propose. I completely agree with Marcus about the greatness of our tribe, the fertility of our land, and the growth of our commerce. Our domestic goods flourish here, but we need a way to import and export goods that matches our growing needs. While we are overflowing with native products, we cannot access foreign goods because they are effectively shut out of our ports. I see no better solution than Marcus's proposal for a bank with a half-million-dollar capital, with the additional ability to issue an unlimited amount of currency. I would only suggest that the amount of money in circulation be controlled solely by the bank's financial council, adjusting it as needed to serve the best interests of our people. This will allow us to fully develop our resources and create a stable market for our surplus goods, ensuring our prosperity for generations to come. My brothers, I have finished for now, but before I sit down, I would like Seth to share his thoughts next.

Nathaniel then took his seat. In response to Nathaniel's request, Seth stood and said:

My brothers, you all know that I am young, and so I must be cautious in speaking. However, I must admit that I have been deeply impressed by Marcus's brilliant and eloquent speech. I now see the importance of the issues we are discussing, and I am in awe of the wisdom Marcus has shown in addressing them. I admire both his modesty and the elegance of his ideas.

The future has always seemed mysterious and unknowable to me, but through Marcus's clear vision, I am beginning to see the potential of our tribe in a way that I never could have imagined. It is almost as though he has the ability to see into the future and reveal the greatness that awaits us. I am filled with wonder at the magnitude of his thoughts, and I am amazed by the way he solves the challenges we face. He is truly a great man with a powerful mind.

We should be proud that our tribe has firmly secured a place in history today. As time passes and the affairs of humanity improve, we will move forward with those improvements, rising from one achievement to the next, until we reach the highest pinnacle of success. Future generations will look back on this day with admiration, amazed by the accomplishments we are making now.

This day will be forever remembered as the beginning of something monumental. Historians in the future will mark the year 1832 as a defining moment in our history. This day, with all of its significance, will stand as a testament to our greatness, withstanding the passage of time. As Marcus has rightly said, we are a great people.

The praises Nathaniel heaped on Marcus's description of our progress have not been lost on me. Generations before us could only have dreamed of what we are now achieving. But to reach our full potential, I agree with both Marcus and Nathaniel that our tribe must have a bank that can issue currency and handle deposits. Whether it should have a triple issue or an unlimited one, I'm not yet sure. However, I think an unlimited issue would best serve our needs and would help us develop faster. I only offer this as my opinion. I have taken up a lot of your time, and I don't want to prolong the discussion. Therefore, I would like to hear the thoughts of Jacob, our trusted scribe.

Seth then sat down. Jacob then rose and spoke.

Chapter 3

My brothers, I rise now in response to Seth's call—not because I hope to offer anything new, since much has already been said, but simply to congratulate all of you for the significant position we have claimed before the world today. I fully support the idea of a Bank for issuing and depositing money, but I believe that a limited issue would be enough. While we may need more financial resources now, a few years of hard work and careful management will help our tribe grow in wealth and strength, and we will soon be able to adjust our needs to match what the bank can provide. Therefore, the bank's operations will be more sustainable and safer for our tribe in the long run. I won't speak much further, but I would like to hear from Isaac, a man whose experience and wisdom have been honed over the years. I now call upon Isaac to speak. Thank you for your attention.

Jacob then returned to his seat. Isaac stood up and said:

My beloved brothers, when I see men like Marcus, Nathaniel, Seth, Jacob, and Robert—who are well-known and respected among us—and when I listen carefully to their words, I feel that I should not take up your time with a long speech. I'm especially humbled by the kind things said about me, for which I offer my sincere thanks. But the questions before us are of great importance, requiring careful and thoughtful consideration. Although my opinions may be small in comparison to the ideas of others, I feel it is my duty to contribute them freely.

It has been said that I am an old man, having lived many years, and that I have seen time pass by. Whether those years have left me with wisdom that will be useful to you will be determined by the outcome of our discussions. I can only offer my thoughts, and whether they are wise or foolish, time will tell.

Now, to the matter at hand. We have come together to discuss matters that affect every part of our land. I have been pleased by Marcus's and Nathaniel's wise comments, Seth's passionate speeches, and the humble yet thoughtful words of Jacob, whom I think of as my son.

Now, my brothers, when I consider everything that has been said, I feel like someone standing alone in an empty hall, trying to make sense of it all. Marcus has pointed out that our tribe is rich in resources, that our land produces plenty, and that we have vast pastures and fields. But despite all this, there is one more thing we need to become a truly great tribe. Marcus has suggested that a bank with a half-million-dollar capital and the ability to issue money three times over will meet all our needs. Everyone here agrees with Marcus—'Give us a bank!' Nathaniel also supports the idea of a bank with a half-million-dollar capital and unlimited money issuance. Seth agrees with both Marcus and Nathaniel but does not take a firm stance on the issue of how much money should be issued. Jacob supports a bank but prefers limited issuance.

These different opinions represent a crucial issue, and it's my task to carefully consider them and decide what is best for us. After thinking carefully, I support the creation of a bank, but I disagree with the idea of a triple issue. I also oppose an unlimited issue, as well as a duplicate issue. Let me explain why.

First, a triple issue: If the bank starts with half a million dollars in reserves and issues 1.5 million dollars in bills that can be redeemed on demand, how could the bank possibly pay that amount if a financial crisis occurred? The bank would not have enough to cover the total issued amount. Even though the bank's debt could be backed by bills or foreign exchange, those would take time to mature and would not be immediately available for payment. If a large number of people tried to redeem their bills at once, the bank would not be able to cover the demand

and would likely collapse, which would cause more harm than good. Therefore, I oppose this plan.

Next, the unlimited issue: I have similar concerns. If the bank were managed by people with the same passions as us, they could be swayed by public pressure to issue more money than they should, especially during times of excitement or demand. This would lead to inflation and financial instability, harming the tribe. This is another reason I oppose the unlimited issue.

Now, the duplicate issue: Although this option seems less risky, it still carries dangers. We would still face many of the same problems, so I cannot support it either.

Instead, I propose a different plan. I suggest that the bank have a capital of $600,000, with a strict policy of issuing only as much money as it has in reserves—one dollar out for every dollar in. This would prevent the bank from taking reckless actions and ensure that the currency remains sound. While the bank's profits might not be large, they would be secure, and the risk of speculation and inflation would be reduced. This would allow for a stable and reliable market for our goods and protect the hardworking members of our tribe.

This is my honest opinion, and I hope you will consider it carefully as we move toward a decision that will shape the future of our tribe. Should we have a bank with a half-million-dollar capital and a triple, unlimited, duplicate, or unit issue? My proposal is for a capital of $600,000 and a unit issue, though I am open to adjusting the amount if necessary. Now, my brothers, I have finished, but I would like to hear Robert's views. Thank you for listening.

Isaac sat down. Robert rose and said:

My brothers, my ears have been open, and my mind has been engaged as I listened to the wise words of my fellow tribesmen. I must admit that I was pleased with Marcus's plan for a bank, but Nathaniel's idea seemed even better to me. Jacob presented good reasons for a duplicate issue, and Seth seems to agree with my views. But after hearing Isaac, whose experience and wisdom are beyond question, I find myself unsure of what to think.

I feel now very much like the woman that went into the fancy and variety dry good store, to choose for herself a calico dress. The merchant showed her one or two pieces of calicoes, with each of which she was well pleased, and either would have suited her. But the merchant being over anxious to sell two dresses instead of one, insisted that he should show her a variety of other pieces before she selected her dress—the consequence was, the woman saw so many pieces, that she could not for the life of her select a dress to suit her, and actually left without purchasing at all. I am in the same position. I want a bank, but I am torn between the different options for how much money it should issue. I hope we can agree on a plan that satisfies everyone and avoids dangerous pitfalls. Thank you, my brothers, for your kind attention.

Robert then sat down.

Chapter 4

After Robert finished speaking, the assembly fell into a thoughtful silence, reflecting on what had been said. Marcus, still hopeful, called on his fellow brethren for their opinions on the important matters at hand. He expressed his satisfaction with how well the discussion had gone, saying:

I am pleased to hear the views of my brethren. Isaac has taken a strong position, opposing the triple, unlimited, and duplicate issues of the bank. He suggests that the bank's issues should be limited to a one-to-one ratio: one dollar in for one dollar out, which would certainly be a safe banking method. However, I'm concerned that a bank based on such a cautious foundation might struggle to cover its operational costs and the transportation of precious metals. Still, I hope we can come to a consensus on this issue. Let's try to find common ground, so we can move forward together toward a goal that is important to all of us. I suggest that we take a vote on the issue of how much the bank should be allowed to issue. We will agree on the plan that the majority of the brethren support.

The question was put to the assembly: Should the bank issue a triple, unlimited, or unit amount of money? After the vote was taken, the duplicate issue was chosen. At that moment, a man named John D. Martin, a lawyer deeply versed in the law but not previously called upon by Marcus, stood and said, "May I have the honor of speaking for a moment?" Marcus nodded, allowing him to continue.

John began:

My brothers, I believe that the decision just made will greatly benefit us and will help advance our interests. This plan will assist in boosting our commerce and wealth. However, we still have an important task ahead of us that requires all of our wisdom. We must appeal to another tribe—one that lives under the same laws as we do—and convince them to support us in this endeavor. Since they claim equal representation with our tribe, we must approach them carefully and show them the mutual benefits of our plan. We must be wise, as the saying goes, 'wise as serpents and harmless as doves,' in order to win them over and disarm any suspicion they might have.

Additionally, I suggest that Marcus appoint three of the most wise and discreet members of our tribe to write an official letter to the rulers in the great city. This letter should explain our needs and make it clear to them that we deserve their support. The letter should also highlight our tribe's wealth, power, and importance. We will respectfully ask for the help and cooperation of the other tribes. I thank you, my brothers, for listening to me.

After John, sometimes called D. the lawyer, finished, another John, a farmer who owned many cattle and had many servants, stood up, eager to contribute to the discussion. Marcus responded, "Speak, John."

John then began:

My brothers, although Marcus had his reasons for selecting speakers earlier, we are now dealing with serious questions that require our deepest thoughts. The arguments presented by all of the speakers have been clear and well-reasoned, and I would feel neglectful if I didn't also add my voice to this important discussion. I want to express my support for the bank plan, which I believe will greatly improve our commerce and unlock the riches of our land, as Marcus has so eloquently described. But I agree with John D. (the lawyer) that we must be cautious. Our first steps are critical, as we must present our intentions carefully to the other tribes. They will scrutinize every word we say, looking for any hidden motives. As John D. said, we must be careful in how we approach them and make sure we appear as friends, not enemies.

I suggest that Jacob, Seth, and Isaac be chosen to draft our letter. Jacob is a skilled scribe, Seth has legal knowledge, and Isaac has the experience and wisdom needed to guide this process. I request that Marcus appoint these three to prepare the letter.

John then sat down. Marcus stood and appointed Jacob, Seth, and Isaac to write the letter, and once it was finished, they would bring it back to the assembly for everyone to hear.

Jacob, Seth, and Isaac stood and walked out of the assembly. A table was set up for Jacob to write, and he sat down, beginning to write: "That whereas…" But he quickly stopped, unsure of how to proceed. Seth suggested, "Put 'nevertheless' there next." Jacob paused again. Isaac then suggested, "Put 'notwithstanding to the contrary.'" Jacob read aloud what he had written: "That whereas, nevertheless, notwithstanding to the contrary." Isaac said, "That will do, but keep going."

Jacob asked Seth for help, saying, "I'm not sure how to continue. Could you write it?" Seth replied, "Money has always been a sensitive topic for me. While I've never hesitated to discuss it with my brethren at home, I'm reluctant to write about it so far from home. I think Isaac, with his experience, should write." Isaac, however, suggested that Jacob and Seth should write the letter and bring it to him for approval. But seeing that they were hesitant, Isaac agreed to write it himself and instructed Jacob to write down his words as he dictated.

Chapter 5

Isaac placed his spectacles on his nose and sat in deep thought for a moment. After a while, he said, "Jacob, write," and Jacob wrote as Isaac dictated.

To the tribe of Hugh Lawson White, from the mountains in the east, and to Ephraim Foster and Felix Grundy from the valley country in the center; the tribes of the great river in the west, in the land of David Crockett and Adam Huntsman, send this declaration and memorial, greeting:

We have heard, from this distant land, of your great nation that lives in the mountains in the east, where your mountains are rich in iron ore and salt. You have so much of both that you could cover our entire nation with iron on one side and salt on the other. We also know that your people in the valley country have large herds of animals—cattle, donkeys, horses, and servants—and that your land, when worked by the farmer, produces bountifully: corn, wheat, oats, and rye in abundance. Your granaries have overflowed, and you have invited neighboring tribes to help relieve you of your surpluses of gold, silver, and other goods.

Now, we, who belong to the same tribes as yours and are united by the same sun, wind, and soil, call you our brothers and wish to join you on equal footing. We wish to unite under one great sheltering wing, so that all the tribes in our great nation may share equal privileges and enjoy similar advantages.

With that in mind, we wish to say that our tribe is also large and far-reaching, stretching across the western land, from the rivers in the west, with the great river as our boundary. We too have a fertile valley, dotted with hills, rich with mines of wealth, while its surface provides generously to those who cultivate it. Yet much of the land remains untouched, waiting to be worked, its silence broken only by the occasional cry of wild creatures—doves, owls, panthers, and wolves—that roam the wilderness.

Our tribe also has great rivers, whose waters have never been disturbed by human voices or boats. These rivers have only carried serpents and wild birds, and have not yet borne the weight of a canoe. But, my brothers, we are proud to report that we have begun to build a small city on the banks of the great river, whose waves kiss the base of a mighty bluff. This city is just beginning to rise above the forest, and we are eager to use the river's flow to carry our commerce far and wide. All over this vast land, civilization is pushing forward, replacing the wild forest.

Now, my brothers, our tribe has gathered in a great convention to discuss how we can develop our resources and combat the untamed forces of nature. After a grand council, we have resolved to propose the following for your consideration and approval.

While we acknowledge the wealth and advantages of your tribe, we must assert that our resources are equal to yours. It is only because the necessary tools and resources have been withheld from us that we have not yet fully developed our land. We have not yet reclaimed all of our vast plains or turned them into gardens, but our tribe has awoken from its slumber and is now ready to work hard and industriously. We are determined to rise to the level of the other tribes in wealth and power.

We ask you, as the rulers of a great people, to look at our situation without bias and recognize the potential of our tribe. Just as the success of individual tribes benefits the nation as a whole, so too will the prosperity of our tribe help increase the wealth of the entire nation. Therefore, we petition you to grant us a "privileged monopoly" for a Bank of discount and deposit, with a capital of $600,000 and the ability to issue money in duplicate form. This privilege should last for thirty years. The capital should be divided into shares of one hundred dollars each, and when one-third of the capital is raised, the bank should be granted full privileges as if the entire capital had been raised. We request that the bank be located in our great city.

This grant, if approved, will rapidly develop our resources, open up trade, and allow us to be more generous and cooperative with other tribes. It will allow us to purchase their surplus goods and pay for them, creating mutual benefits for all. We have presented the facts as clearly as possible and now leave this matter in your hands, trusting that you will make a decision free from bias or prejudice. With great respect, your brothers in tribal bonds.

After submitting this memorial, the tribe agreed that it should be presented to the assembly for approval. Jacob, Seth, and the others returned to the assembly, where Marcus called upon Jacob to read the memorial. Jacob began, reading: "That whereas, nevertheless, notwithstanding to the contrary…"

Marcus interrupted, saying, "This is too verbose." Jacob explained that all the documents he had seen began with "That whereas," but Seth insisted that "nevertheless" was important, and Isaac agreed that the sentence wouldn't make sense without the phrase "notwithstanding to the contrary." After some back and forth, the memorial was read in its entirety and adopted by the assembly.

Chapter 6

Nathaniel then rose once again and said, "A new understanding has come to me, and I now see things more clearly than I have for years. It feels as though the fog has lifted from my eyes, and I can now see the path ahead of us. I am confident that the impressive and well-thought-out memorial we've just discussed will place our tribe in a high position among all the tribes of the land, and will convince even the most skeptical of our worth and the fairness of our demands." Nathaniel continued:

But while we have made significant progress in showing the value and strength of our tribe, we still face a tough battle. Our position will be challenged every step of the way by a determined and relentless opposition. We must now show our skills in diplomacy and strategy as we enter the territories of other tribes, as the idea of granting privileges outside their own boundaries will be new to them. Therefore, I suggest that we choose one among us who is most skilled in the art of persuasion to accompany the presentation of our memorial to the great rulers.

This person should emphasize our vast resources—our fertile land and abundance of production—along with our natural advantages in trade and navigation. They should make a strong appeal to the rulers, convincing them of our importance and the mutual benefits of supporting us. I also suggest we choose someone who excels in social interaction, to assist in dealing with the leaders of other tribes and help accomplish our goal.

Nathaniel then sat down. After Nathaniel finished, John D. (the lawyer) stood and said, "I fully support Nathaniel's suggestions, and I ask that someone nominate suitable candidates to fulfill the important role Nathaniel described." He then sat down. John, the farmer, stood and asked for permission to nominate. When granted, he said, "I nominate Marcus Winchester as the speaker to present the memorial to the rulers, along with an address that will emphasize our strengths. I also nominate Robert Lawrence who is the most skilled in social interaction, to help in dealing with the more hesitant leaders of other tribes. I trust the brethren will support and second my nominations." John then sat down.

The question was put to the assembly, and the nominations were unanimously approved.

Marcus rose and said:

I am deeply grateful for this honor and responsibility that has been placed upon me. I am humbled by the trust my brethren have placed in me, though I must admit I feel some uncertainty about the task ahead. To represent our tribe among strangers will be my first duty, followed by the challenge of facing the clever strategies of the other tribes. However, I am determined to raise our tribe's flag high, above all opposition, and to firmly plant our standard on solid ground among the other tribes. I hope to receive every possible piece of advice and support to ensure I am fully prepared to confront any objections and challenges. I am also thankful that you have appointed Robert to join me in this crucial task. I am confident that he will accept this honor, and together we will do our utmost to achieve the goals of our mission. My deepest thanks to you all.

Marcus then sat down. Robert stood and said, "I am honored, though surprised, by this appointment, as there are others with more experience and wisdom than I. Nonetheless, I will serve our tribe in any capacity, and I will do so with the full dedication that this role deserves." He then sat down.

Isaac Rawlings rose and said:

I am pleased with the choice of Marcus, as he has the capabilities to handle any difficulty that may arise. I have no doubt that he will successfully carry out the objectives of this mission. I also have confidence in Robert's ability to perform the role assigned to him with credit to himself and benefit to our tribe. However, I would like to offer a few suggestions for consideration.

Marcus has been a long-time member of our tribe and is well-respected for his judgment. But he has not had much experience with diplomacy and may, in a critical moment, fall prey to the tactics of more experienced negotiators. For example, he might approach a difficult situation with too much trust, like an unsuspecting fly walking into a spider's web. The fly, drawn in by the tempting glitter of the web, is unaware of the danger until it is too late. We must expect opposition, and when good principles fail, those who oppose us will likely resort to cunning schemes to trap Marcus.

Therefore, it is crucial that we support him with careful preparation. We should provide him with a strong, well-crafted speech to present to the rulers, so that our worth and importance are clear to them. This speech should leave a lasting impression and ensure that our tribe's value is recognized. We must arm Marcus with the tools he needs to succeed, and I suggest that three of our wisest brethren—myself, Nathaniel, and John the farmer—work together to draft this speech. This will give Marcus the best chance to succeed and ensure that our tribe's progress is cemented in the eyes of the rulers."

Isaac then sat down. After a brief discussion, the assembly agreed with Isaac's suggestion. Marcus appointed Isaac, Nathaniel, and John the farmer to write the speech. They then retired to begin their work.

Chapter 7

After Isaac, Nathaniel, and John, accompanied by Marcus, had gathered together, John suggested that Isaac should preside over their discussions. Nathaniel agreed with this suggestion, and Isaac took the seat at the head of the table. He then asked that Nathaniel sit on his right and John on his left. Since Marcus had been chosen unanimously as the speaker to present their memorial to the rulers, Isaac asked Marcus to rise and present the speech he intended to deliver to the rulers, while the others listened carefully. They would make note of any weaknesses or gaps in Marcus's arguments, style, or the facts he presented. If necessary, they could suggest any new points that might strengthen the speech, ensuring Marcus would be well-prepared when he addressed the rulers in the grand council. The group agreed, and Marcus rose to begin.

He asked, "Shall I address you as the grand assembly?" to which Isaac replied, "Certainly." Marcus then began:

Brothers, rulers, fathers, and wise men of all the tribes in our great nation, I stand before you as the humble representative of a great people living in a tribe in the far west, near the setting sun, on the fertile banks of one of nature's most majestic rivers. The advantages of this land are beyond description, and I come to present to you, on behalf of my people, the memorial of our needs, drawn up by our own hands in a grand council of all my brethren.

I am honored by the trust placed in me, and I accept the responsibility of delivering this sacred testament of our tribe's worth and our entitlement to the honors that we seek. Who among you, as you read through this memorial, detailing our greatness, wealth, power, and resources, can fail to feel admiration for us? It feels as though we are opening a new chapter in history, beginning afresh on a clean page.

When my brethren called me to be their leader in this effort, I must admit that although I knew our tribe's greatness, I had doubts when the task was assigned to 'write out a long epistle and memorial, and send it to the rulers for their review, so they may understand our needs and grant us their support.' I never doubted that we had the wisdom to create such a memorial, but I feared whether the simple words of the English language could fully capture the depth of our case and move others as we hoped.

But when my brethren read the memorial to me and to our gathered tribe, I was carried away by the eloquence and passion of their words. The opening lines of our memorial struck me deeply, and I felt as though I was swept away by the force of their arguments. As we spoke of our tribe's relationship with others, I could not help but feel the injustice that had been done to us, and I lamented that we had not raised our voices sooner to demand the fairness we deserve.

Our land, my brethren, is blessed with every beauty nature can offer. From our hills to our valleys, we are rich in the most picturesque landscapes. Our fields are abundant, our flowers fragrant, and the songs of our birds fill the air with joy. The beauty of our land is matched only by its productivity. Every species of tree and plant grows here, and the earth invites the farmer to sow his seeds, knowing his labor will be richly rewarded. Our rivers run cool and clear, filled with fish, and our great river, the Mississippi, flows majestically through our land, carrying with it the promise of prosperity.

These are only a few of the wonders of our land, and I must now turn to our tribe's commercial importance. With proper development, our tribe's agricultural and trading potential is unmatched. With the right resources and infrastructure, we could surpass all the other tribes in wealth and productivity.

I know this may seem like an overstatement, but let me assure you, with the same resources as others, our tribe would quickly become the second most prosperous in the land. We have a mild and healthy climate, perfect for growing the most valuable crops, and our land is capable of supporting both education and wealth. I envision a future where our tribe produces not only historians, statesmen, and philosophers, but also orators, artists, musicians, and poets. Our land will become renowned for its culture and the arts, just as the ancient groves of Arcadia are remembered.

Though this may not happen in our lifetimes, our children will see it come to pass. Can we, in good faith, stand before you and assert these claims? With boldness, I now present the core of our memorial: we ask that you grant us a bank with a capital of $600,000 with the privilege of issuing a duplicate currency. This bank should operate as a bank of discount and deposit, with a lease of thirty years, and the full rights to sue and be sued, along with any other safeguards you deem necessary to protect the interests of our tribe.

It may seem unnecessary to provide more arguments in support of our case, as we have already outlined our position clearly in our memorial. I respectfully ask that you consider this request, as it will not only benefit us but will also improve the resources and wealth of all the neighboring tribes.

I thank you for your patience in listening to my words, and I leave this matter in your capable hands, trusting that you will give it the consideration it deserves. With great respect, I now step down from this position of prominence, knowing that you are the best judges of our future.

Marcus then stepped down. Isaac, Nathaniel, and John then met to discuss Marcus's address. They agreed that it was a magnificent speech, with John remarking that it was "worthy of the finest orators of old." The convention was adjourned, with Marcus being thanked for his excellent delivery of the memorial, and the assembly wishing him well as he continued his important mission.

Chapter 8

After some time had passed, the day arrived for the gathering of all the great rulers from the various tribes. Marcus and Robert, preparing to say their goodbyes to their brethren and kin, were visited by many who wanted to wish them well and offer their blessings and advice before they left. Among those who came was Joseph, a merchant who had attended many of the meetings but had never spoken in the great assembly. He took Marcus by the hand, placed his other hand on his head, and blessed him, praying that Marcus would remain in good health, both physically and mentally, during his travels. Joseph further wished that if any mismanagement or disaster were to occur with the bank they were about to establish, Marcus would be guided with wisdom strong enough to persuade the great rulers to require that one dollar and twelve and a half cents in silver be securely placed in the bank's vaults for every dollar in paper currency issued, ensuring a strong safeguard against potential depreciation or loss of value in the currency.

Marcus, deeply moved, looked up to the heavens in quiet meditation and prayer, then nodded in agreement. Joseph left, and Marcus and Robert said their final goodbyes before setting off for the City of the Centre. After several days of travel, Marcus and Robert arrived safely at the city. They were in awe as they looked around at the wonders of the new city. As they walked, a towering spire caught Robert's attention, and he asked Marcus what it was. Marcus, unsure, speculated that it might be the tower from which the rulers drew wisdom and light from the sun, or perhaps it marked the spot where the sun stepped down as it rose in the morning. Robert preferred the latter explanation, noting that the sun always rises high before it descends but had never thought of it stepping upon a specific place in the center.

They continued walking and came upon a sign that read, "Private Entertainment Here." Marcus interpreted it as an invitation and suggested they go in and reserve a room, agreeing to pay for the meals they actually ate. He told Robert to keep track of the expenses to ensure they paid fairly. When they were shown to their room for the night, the host gave them a lighted candle, and they closed the door. Marcus then spoke to Robert about the possibility of being charged unfairly by the host and how they should keep track of everything, as an example of the "doctrine of equivalents." Robert asked if the landlord would charge extra for the use of candles, and Marcus said he wasn't sure, but he expected that he would. Robert suggested they put out the candle to save money since they could talk without much light.

Marcus smiled at this last suggestion of Robert. The two thought as one. He thought as well that they should lie down for the night; there being two beds. Robert questioned if the landlord should charge them each with lodging if they slept in the same bed. Marcus said he preferred sleeping separately until they could see the landlord, and learn his views upon the subject.

So each took a bed and slept soundly until morning, and when they met the landlord, Robert inquired into the matter, when the landlord answered, "it was a custom from time immemorial, as far back as he could trace his ancestors, where two persons slept in one room, to charge both with lodging, whether they slept separately or together."

From this time on, Marcus and Robert occupied separate beds. Robert then asked, "what was the custom of his family concerning lights?" To which the landlord also answered, that "in the early history of the world, before the invention of candles, he could find in none of the archives of his ancestors any precedent, making an extra charge for lights, and as he was not an innovator, upon ancient usages of customs, he should not now attempt to establish a rule upon this subject, therefore he would say to him, that lights were free." Robert then said to Marcus, that it must be upon the same principle of the sun lighting the world free.

Satisfied with the arrangements, Marcus and Robert decided to go out and see if they could find any of the great rulers of the nation. Robert was curious to see how great men looked, but Marcus, having already met Andrew Jackson himself, was not as eager. However, as they walked through the streets, Marcus spotted a man he recognized—Joseph McMinn, a leader from their tribe, who had previously served as one of the centurions among the rulers.

Joseph was pleased to see Marcus and asked why they had come so far. Marcus explained the purpose of their mission, and Joseph, listening attentively, offered to help them secure an audience with the rulers. He warned that such a request was highly unusual and would be a great honor if granted, as the right to speak before the council was a sacred privilege.

After some time, Joseph managed to convince a few of the rulers to grant Marcus an audience. They were initially shocked by the presumption of a tribe so far removed from the rest of the nation, but Joseph argued that his tribe was unfamiliar with parliamentary procedures and that their mission was of great importance. Reluctantly, the rulers agreed to allow Marcus to speak. Marcus waited patiently while Joseph found him and explained the details of the meeting. He advised Marcus to be ready when the assembly convened, as the rulers might reconsider their decision.

Marcus, now in the great hall, was invited to approach the speaker's stand. As he made his way to the front, all eyes were on him, and the assembly was filled with amazement at his boldness. The speaker sounded his mallet and motioned to Marcus to rise. When Marcus arose, he made a low bow and a long scrape back upon the floor with his right foot, righted himself, and delivered the address which he had previously delivered in presence of his brethren. At the conclusion of his speech, he handed the memorial to the speaker, took back his hat, and left the hall as quietly as he had entered.

The speaker, after a moment of stunned silence, called upon the assembly to discuss the proposal. James Iradell, a member of the tribe of Hugh, was the first to speak. James showing signs of hard respiration with puffs, rose to his feet making one grand ebullition, and opened, "men and brethren! after a veteran's service in the varied fields of human movements, this does certainly 'cap the climax' of all the high-handed, daring and unblushing presumptions, I have ever witnessed." He added, "I have often heard of the far-famed Tecumseh, and his daring exploits, but here has arisen a greater than he." James said it was monstrous indeed, that a tribe, living out of the pale of a common civilization, should have the unblushing impertinence to send those two before them. He demanded that they focus on taming the wilderness instead of seeking a bank.

After James's speech, the room fell silent again. Joseph then rose and spoke in defense of Marcus and his mission, urging the rulers to consider the request with the respect it deserved. He reminded them that this was the first and likely last request his tribe would make, and they should grant it as a sign of goodwill.

The speaker then asked the assembly to vote on whether the western tribe should be granted a charter for a bank, with the terms set out in their memorial. After a brief and tense moment, the proposal was approved by a small majority.

The order was made: the western tribe would be granted the bank, with the conditions outlined in the memorial. Robert and Nathaniel were appointed to handle the subscriptions and payments, and the bank would be required to ensure it could meet the terms for paper and silver issuance. The project was approved, and the tribe had achieved a significant victory.

Chapter Twenty Endnotes

1. Jesse, the "Scribe," edited by James E. Roper, *The Chronicles of the Farmers' and Merchants' Bank* (Memphis: Southwestern at Memphis, 1960), 2.
2. Bray Hammond, *Banks and Politics in America from the Revolution to the Civil War* (Princeton: Princeton University Press, 1957), 364–402.
3. Roper, *The Chronicles*, I.
4. Roper, *The Chronicles*, I.

FRANSIOLI & WILLIAMSON,

Importers, Wholesale and Retail Dealers in

CHINA, GLASS

---AND---

EARTHENWARE,

French and German Vases,

SILVER, SILVER PLATED,

GERMAN SILVER AND BRITANNIA WARE,

FINE TABLE CUTLERY,

188, MAIN ST., OPPOSITE THE APLUN HOUSE.

MEMPHIS, TENN.

☞ ALSO, Looking Glasses, Looking Glass Plates, Tea Trays, Parlor Lamps, Chandeliers, Girondoles &c. &c.

GEORGE PHILLER.   MYRON H. MILLER.

GEORGE PHILLER & CO.,

HAT AND CAP

Manufacturers, and Dealers

in all kinds of

HATS AND CAPS,

HATTERS' TRIMMINGS, FURS, &C.,

78, Front Row,

MEMPHIS, TENNESSEE.

Highest Cash Price paid for Beef Hides, Bees Wax, Furs, Peltry, &c.

From Rainey's Memphis City Directory, 1855/56

Chapter Twenty-one: Born Under a Bad Sign

Marcus Winchester loses it all

In literature, *peripeteia* refers to a pivotal moment in a story when a turning point occurs for the protagonist. Greek philosopher Aristotle is credited with coining the term, which is derived from a Greek word meaning "to change suddenly." This literary device is frequently seen in books, television, and films. Characters who experience *peripeteia* through a reversal of fortune are among the most compelling. Contemporary fictional characters such as Louis Winthorpe in *Trading Places*, the character played by Goldie Hawn in *Overboard*, the Rose family in *Schitt's Creek*, and the Bluth family in *Arrested Development* exemplify the riches-to-rags trope on screen, creating unforgettable comedic moments.

Of course, there is nothing humorous about reversals of fortune in real life. History is filled with stories of titans of business and industry who amassed great wealth only to face financial ruin. Notable examples include Walt Disney, Henry Ford, and Milton Hershey, all of whom filed for bankruptcy at some point during their remarkable careers. One wealthy businessman from Memphis experienced a reversal of fortune—twice.

Clarence Saunders transformed grocery shopping by introducing the self-service model through his Piggly Wiggly stores that were launched in Memphis. The first store opened at 79 Jefferson Avenue on September 6, 1916. Before his innovation, customers relied on clerks to retrieve their items, but Saunders designed a store where shoppers could pick up products themselves, making the process faster and more efficient. His idea took off, and by the early 1920s, Piggly Wiggly had grown into a massive enterprise with over one thousand stores nationwide with a combined revenue of $60 million. Saunders became incredibly wealthy, pouring his fortune into building a lavish pink marble mansion in Memphis that became known as the Pink Palace.

However, his success was short-lived. In an attempt to manipulate Piggly Wiggly's stock, he engaged in a financial maneuver that ultimately backfired, costing him his business and forcing him into bankruptcy. Unfazed, he quickly launched a new grocery chain called the Sole Owner Stores, which flourished until the Great Depression wiped out his second fortune. Despite these financial failures, Saunders remained a visionary in the industry, constantly searching for ways to innovate grocery retail.

His final major venture was Keedoozle, a fully automated grocery store concept inspired by vending machines. Customers would use a special key to select their items, which would then be retrieved and delivered via conveyor belts. Though ahead of its time, the technology of the era couldn't support Saunders's vision, and the project failed. Despite losing two fortunes, Saunders left a lasting legacy in the grocery industry, revolutionizing how people shop and shaping modern retail. His unfinished mansion, the Pink Palace, was eventually turned into a museum that is still serving the Memphis community today.

While he was not the financial equivalent of the great American titans of his day, Marcus Winchester's reversal of fortune was no less painful. The exact moment his financial troubles began is difficult to pinpoint. Similarly, the specific reasons for his financial downfall remain uncertain. Those few who have examined Winchester's life generally attribute his financial difficulties to a combination of factors, including the political climate of the era, the bursting of the real estate bubble following the Panic of 1837, and the hardening attitudes toward non-Whites during the first half of the nineteenth century.

James Davis, it has already been established, recorded incidents of the past in a way that merged fact with fiction. While entertaining, his stories cannot be relied on as historic accounts of events. However, they do sometimes provide clues. Davis attributed the initial cracks in Winchester's finances to "thieves and gamblers whose headquarters were at the Bell Tavern."[1]

According to Davis, the primary barriers between the bad guys, who included counterfeiting among their crimes, and the innocent residents of Memphis were Isaac Rawlings and Marcus Winchester. Davis wrote, "The most efficient means that the country people had of guarding against those sharpers was to deposit their money with Winchester or Rawlings, both of whom took particular pains to defeat the gentry by frustrating their schemes for making a living."[2]

In accounts by others, Winchester was credited with standing up to members of the Murrell gang. In a 1938 article about John Murrell in the *Commercial Appeal*, a reporter wrote, "Last of this bloodthirsty crew, and most infamous of the lot, was John Murrell who attempted to establish headquarters in the little river village of Memphis and was driven out by Marcus B. Winchester."[3]

John Murrell, also known as the Great Western Land Pirate, gained fame due to widespread belief that he led a large, region-wide gang called the Mystic Clan of the Confederacy. This supposed gang was rumored to include members of mixed-race communities, such as the Melungeons and Redbones. The gang's territory was said to stretch along the Mississippi River and the Natchez Trace. They were blamed for orchestrating slave rebellions across the South while robbing and killing hundreds of travelers.

Today, we know that if Marcus Winchester did chase the infamous John Murrell from Memphis, he was confronting a far less formidable con artist than was once suggested. The version of Murrell worthy of the nickname Great Western Land Pirate was a fictional creation of Virgil Stewart, who, in 1835, published a pamphlet under the pseudonym Augustus Q. Walton, Esq. The pamphlet, *A History of the Detection, Conviction, Life, and Designs of John A. Murrell, the Great Western Land Pirate*, spun a sensational tale alleging that Murrell and his gang had plotted to incite a massive rebellion among enslaved people throughout the South. According to the account, Murrell planned to exploit the resulting chaos to loot Southern landowners.

Those in West Tennessee who knew the Murrell family viewed the pamphlet's claims with skepticism, as they were familiar with the real John Murrell. Far from being the leader of a complex, multi-state gang, Murrell lived in Denmark, Tennessee, among a large extended family known for committing crimes such as counterfeiting, horse theft, and the occasional kidnapping of enslaved people. To those who knew him, the idea of John Murrell as the mastermind of a sophisticated criminal network capable of inciting a slave uprising was utterly absurd.

After being arrested and tried, Murrell was convicted, based in part on the testimony of Virgil Stewart. Stewart subsequently published the sensationalized account of Murrell's life and crimes under a pseudonym. In this pamphlet, he cast himself as the hero and Murrell as the villain.

Although Murrell's friends and neighbors in West Tennessee knew the story was pure fiction, thousands of White men and women across the South believed it. The tale sparked a wave of accusations and riots, with some individuals accused of belonging to the fictitious Mystic Clan of the Confederacy. Regardless of the fact that they were innocent, they were lynched. *The Niles Weekly Register* reported on some of the deaths in Mississippi: "The state of society is awful.... A bad feeling is getting up in several other places, and on many different accounts—but has burst out with the greatest force in Mississippi; where persons have been executed in an extraordinary manner."[4]

There is certainly merit to the idea that Marcus Winchester was among the very few that Memphis residents from all walks of life could trust with their money. According to James Davis, members of the Murrell gang in Memphis wanted to push Winchester out and did so by loudly expressing "virtuous indignation at the outrage he was perpetrating on society."[5]

According to Davis's account, gossip about Winchester's wife and children was spread until the necessary damage was done. Davis wrote, "From this source the slanders spread until the whole community seemed, with a few exceptions, infected, and Winchester found himself shunned and avoided by men indebted to him for various favors."[6] In Davis's narrative, Winchester finally had to stop venturing out in Memphis because it became too dangerous. Davis also noted that Winchester's biggest worry was the future of his children, who were already experiencing the impact of racism. It was true that Winchester was concerned about how race would impact his children as they became adults. He must have shared his concerns in a letter to Frances Wright in 1838. She replied, "I have always thought that if the slave question could once be settled our free colored population would, more especially in our extreme South become gradually and easily more incorporated with the white. At the present time, the least said on the subject the better."[7]

According to Davis's account, the strain of public attacks on his character and his fears for his children's safety weighed heavily on Winchester. Davis claimed that these pressures drove him to drink, ultimately leading to his financial ruin and death in poverty. There is no evidence, however, that indicates Winchester struggled with alcoholism. What is certain is that his marriage to Amarante Loiselle and their large family of mixed-race children provoked hostility in Memphis—an animosity that only deepened during the presidential campaign of 1836. At that time, national attention turned to the controversy surrounding Vice-Presidential candidate Richard Mentor Johnson of Kentucky, whose long relationship with Julia Chinn, an enslaved woman he treated as his wife and with whom he had two daughters, became the subject of vicious political attacks.

Andrew Jackson's Democratic Party ran against the Whigs that year, both seeking to rule in a country that was rapidly evolving. The Democratic Party, of which Marcus Winchester was an active member, championed a limited federal government, strict following of the constitution, and, above all, individual liberty—for White males. The Democrats of the antebellum era championed limited power in Washington, and in institutions like the Bank of the United States. They believed the "privileged elites" serving at the federal level would govern at the expense of ordinary citizens.

The Whigs, on the other hand, emerged as many Americans grew tired of the dominance and influence of Andrew Jackson and his followers. The Whigs emphasized the importance of a robust federal government in promoting economic development and national unity. Whigs were champions of federally funded improvements such as roads, canals, and railroads; protective tariffs to nurture American industry; and a reestablished national bank to stabilize the struggling economy. Their vision was pegged the "American System," and their objective was an interconnected nation.

Under Jackson's leadership, the Democratic Party aligned itself with Southern slaveholders by passionately embracing states' rights—a stance that effectively meant strong support for the institution of slavery. The Whigs were more ambivalent toward slavery with many in favor of the education and colonization schemes of activists like Frances Wright, while still claiming to oppose outright abolitionism.

The presidential election of 1836 was a defining moment for Tennessee politics as well. Tennessean Andrew Jackson had served two terms in office, governing from 1829 to 1837, and had personally selected Martin Van Buren as his successor and Richard M. Johnson of Kentucky as Van Buren's vice president. The Whigs, still a fledgling party, lacked a cohesive strategy for winning the presidency. At one point, they even considered Tennessee Congressman David Crockett as their candidate. However, after losing his 1835 congressional campaign to Adam Huntsman, Crockett famously declared that everyone could "go to hell," left Tennessee for Texas, and met his death at the Alamo.

Ultimately, the Whig's unsuccessful strategy involved running multiple regional candidates in the hope of splintering the vote and forcing the election into the House of Representatives.

For the Winchester family, opposition to one Whig candidate, William Henry Harrison, was personal. Harrison, James Winchester's old adversary, emerged as the most prominent Whig contender, appealing to voters in the West and North. Tennessean Hugh Lawson White was a popular Whig candidate in the South, Daniel Webster drew support in New England, and Willie Person Mangum of North Carolina garnered votes in the Carolinas.

The inclusion of Richard M. Johnson as the Democratic candidate for vice president, however, brought unwelcome scrutiny to Marcus Winchester and his family in Memphis. Despite a controversial personal life, Richard Johnson rose from the frontier to the national political stage through a combination of military heroism, charisma, and political skill. The son of early Kentucky settlers, Johnson came from a family active in politics and business. He taught himself law, and, in 1802, the twenty-two-year-old was admitted to the bar.

Johnson's political career began in the Kentucky legislature in 1804, and by 1806, he had been elected to the U.S. House of Representatives. A staunch supporter of Thomas Jefferson, Johnson was one of the War Hawks who ardently advocated for the War of 1812. When war broke out, Johnson returned to Kentucky, raised a regiment of volunteers, and led them into battle. His valor during the Battle of the Thames in 1813 earned him widespread recognition. At the time, he was publicly credited with killing Tecumseh, the renowned Shawnee leader, though modern historians largely dispute this claim.

After the war, Johnson shifted his focus to veterans' welfare, securing pensions for widows and orphans, and championing federally funded infrastructure projects. He also worked to abolish debtor's prisons and lower federal land prices to aid poor settlers. After losing reelection to the Senate, Johnson returned to the House in 1829, where he became a close ally of Andrew Jackson and a prominent figure in the Jacksonian Democratic Party. He chaired several committees, including those on military affairs and postal operations, and strongly defended mail delivery on Sundays, citing the separation of church and state.

Johnson's military legacy and his alignment with Andrew Jackson's political vision made him an appealing candidate for vice president alongside Martin Van Buren. However, his life embodied both the promise and contradictions of Jacksonian Democracy in antebellum America.

Like Isaac Rawlings, Richard Johnson openly lived with an enslaved woman whom he treated as his wife. Julia Chinn, a mixed-race woman enslaved by Johnson's father, had been sent to live at Johnson's Blue Spring Farm in 1812 when she was just fourteen. At the time, Johnson, then thirty, was a bachelor who had been more focused on his legal career than on starting a family. Their relationship quickly became intimate, and the couple soon had two mixed-race daughters, Imogene and Adaline. Johnson treated his daughters as if they were White, providing them with opportunities and privileges uncommon for their time.

Johnson's mother was likely among the first to learn of the relationship. Outraged, she demanded that her son sell Chinn and their daughters "before he got too attached." Ignoring his mother, he carried on and considered Chinn his wife until her death in 1833. Because, like Isaac Rawlings and Marcus Winchester, Johnson wielded significant power and wealth, most locals initially confined their disapproval to gossip whispered behind closed doors. However, as Chinn's biographer, Amrita Chakrabarti Myers, pointed out, true acceptance by most White individuals in their community remained elusive:

> The couple's younger daughter, Adaline, was excluded from attending a Fourth of July celebration alongside the country's

white women; area newspapers published angry editorials when Adeline married her white husband; and neighbors protested when Julia was seen riding in the family carriage, a marker of white ladyhood.[8]

Today, the Fourth of July picnic Myers referenced—and Johnson's response to the racism directed at his daughter—seems especially egregious. In 1832, Adaline Johnson, who was around sixteen years old, accompanied her father to a Fourth of July barbeque in Georgetown, Kentucky. As he took his place among others on stage, Adaline sat with other women and children underneath a tent set up to protect the audience from the hot sun. After Adaline sat down, several people left the tent and others complained. Johnson was informed by organizers that slaves were not allowed to sit with the Whites and that she would have to leave. Johnson escorted his daughter back to their carriage where she waited alone until after he gave his speech.[9]

Marcus Winchester was not a nationally prominent political figure, so public scrutiny and reactions to his marriage to Amarante were not as widely recorded as they were with the Johnson family. However, the vitriol directed at both families was the same. During the 1836 campaign, the Johnson family faced a media onslaught, even though Julia Chinn had died of cholera three years earlier, and both their daughters were married to successful White men and had children of their own. As Chinn's biographer noted, "As early as spring 1835, editorials, letters, cartoons, and songs attacking Julia, Richard, and their daughters appeared in newspapers throughout the nation. Although Julia was dead, the ghost of her memory, and the living examples of her mixed-race daughters, led to raging debates over the issue of amalgamation."[10] The editor of the *U.S. Telegraph* left no room for interpretation regarding his stance on the debate:

> It may be a matter of no importance to mere political automatons whether Richard M. Johnson is a white or a black man—whether he is free or a slave—or whether he is married to, or has been in connection with a jet-black, thick-lipped, odoriferous negro wench, by whom he has reared a family of children whom he has endeavored to force upon society as equals.[11]

Martin Van Buren secured a Democratic victory in 1836 with 170 electoral votes. Although Richard Johnson fell short of a majority in the Electoral College, the Senate confirmed him as vice president. Van Buren did not regard Johnson as a political partner and kept their relationship distant. Johnson was frequently excluded from meetings and wielded little influence on the administration's policies. Van Buren even dropped him from the Democratic ticket in the 1840 election, which Van Buren lost to James Winchester's nemesis, William Henry Harrison.

Meanwhile, in Memphis, Marcus Winchester's close connection to Andrew Jackson and his public support of Van Buren and Johnson made him a target for Whig newspapers such as the *Memphis Enquirer*. The publication ensured that the insults it hurled at Johnson regarding his mixed-race family were also directed at Winchester.

On September 4, 1837, the Memphis City Council even passed an ordinance making it illegal for a White man in Memphis to "keep a colored wife." It was likely around this time that the Winchester family moved outside the city limits of the town Marcus Winchester had essentially built from the ground up.

Winchester had worked to ensure the needs of Memphians were met by the town's proprietors and had provided leadership and protection for nearly twenty years. In the end, he was essentially run out of town. However, he did not run far. Marcus Winchester built a log cabin on the property he owned in present-day Midtown Memphis. It came to be known as Muscogee Camp. When Winchester's grandson, Clarence Nelson, died in 1947 at the age of ninety, his obituary mentioned that he had moved to Frayser fifteen years earlier but had previously lived at "The Old Winchester Place at Madison and Claybrook." This was likely the location of Muscogee Camp, where the Winchester family had relocated a century earlier.

Marcus Winchester likely read with great sadness the *Memphis Weekly Appeal* on October 27, 1843, that proclaimed, "How long will our citizens quietly permit free negroes to remain among us, demoralizing and ruining our slaves? . . . The truth is, the free negroes do more to injure our slaves than all the abolitionists in the world." The message was clear. Free Black individuals were not welcome in Memphis. Edward J. Carrell, editor of the *Memphis Daily Eagle*, expressed similar sentiments in 1849, declaring:

> We are convinced . . . the multiplying numbers of free negroes, is a serious evil in our community. We think it wise, just expedient, to forbid the residence of any free negro within the limits of our city or State. This class of population is immoral, unproductive, slothful and injurious to property—particularly slave property. It lives upon what is rotten and abominable in our social system, and stands as an unfailing cause of discontent, a dissatisfying contrast of the most utter indolence before our slave population.[12]

While public reaction to his mixed-race family contributed to Marcus Winchester's diminishing financial stability, other factors were also at play. A severe financial crisis, now known as the Panic of 1837, was caused by a combination of domestic and international factors. As it turned out, several of Andrew Jackson's economic policies implemented toward the end of his presidency proved especially detrimental to the economy. Two issues in particular caused significant damage—the dismantling of the Second Bank of the United States and the Specie Circular of 1836.

In 1833, Jackson directed his Secretary of the Treasury to remove federal funds from the National Bank and place them in various state banks, called "pet banks." This move significantly weakened the National Bank's power. In fact, two Treasury secretaries deemed the order so misguided that they refused to execute it, leading to their replacement. A third secretary, Roger B. Taney, eventually complied.

While a foolish decision, it would not be the worst of Taney's career. He later became one of the most consequential and controversial chief justices in American history. His infamous 1857 ruling in *Dred Scott v. Sandford* not only denied Black Americans citizenship but also invalidated congressional efforts to limit slavery's expansion. Far from calming the sectional crisis, the decision stiffened Southern resolve, inflamed Northern opinion, and propelled both regions toward ever more radical positions, widening the chasm that led to the Civil War.

Taney spent his final years condemned by abolitionists and vilified as the architect of a ruling that hastened the bloodiest conflict in American history. Historians often point to his death in 1864 as a symbolic turning point, marking the nation's final break from Andrew Jackson and the old, pro-slavery regime that had dominated the antebellum era.

Another damaging policy by Andrew Jackson, but actually implemented by the next administration, was the Specie Circular. The term came from the word "specie," which referred to hard money—gold and silver coins—rather than paper currency or banknotes. "Circular" referred to an official government order or directive. During the 1830s, cheap paper money issued by unregulated state banks had fueled a massive real estate bubble. Settlers and land speculators were buying huge amounts of land on credit, often with unstable banknotes. Jackson believed forcing people to use gold and silver would cool off this speculation and make transactions more stable.

It was a miscalculation that would have a long-term financial impact and trigger the Depression of the 1840s. Jackson's hard-money policy was too rigid and sudden, causing widespread economic disruption instead of stabilizing the financial system.

Meanwhile, in Europe, declining demand for American cotton—the South's most important export—and tighter monetary policies in Britain further strained the American economy. Cotton prices fell by twenty-five percent, creating a loss of confidence that caused widespread bank failures and a sharp contraction in credit. Thousands of banks collapsed—more than half of the banks in the United States—wiping out individual savings and paralyzing commerce.

Unemployment surged to over twenty-five percent, and wages declined significantly for those who could find work. The prices of land plummeted, ushering in the prolonged economic depression that lasted into the mid-1840s. Between 1837 and 1844, the total value of taxable property in Tennessee declined by approximately $16 million. Before the tide turned in 1845, the value of land fell by seventy-five percent, while the value of enslaved individuals across the state declined by seventy percent. In Memphis, where cotton was king, the decline in cotton prices rippled through the local economy, affecting businesses in every sector. Cotton that sold for around sixteen cents per pound in 1836 was sold for approximately five cents per pound in 1843.

It is ironic that Andrew Jackson first sent Marcus Winchester to the fourth Chickasaw bluff, launching his career as a businessman and land developer, then signed executive orders and implemented policies that essentially ended it.

Winchester seems to have hung on for as long as he could before he began selling property to pay his debts, sometimes at the order of the courts. In May 1842, he attempted to borrow money from John Claybrooke, explaining to him that without a personal loan, "his ferry hands and household servants must go on the block."[13] Instead, in September 1842, John Claybrooke purchased all Winchester's land, his interest in the ferry, and ten enslaved men and women including old Limus, who had ferried David Crockett across the Mississippi River as he left Tennessee for the last time. Marcus Winchester and his family continued to live at Muscogee Camp, and Winchester was able to buy that portion of his land back from Claybrooke at some point.

Change was also inevitable at the post office. Winchester had been serving the citizens of Memphis as postmaster from nearly day one. But because the role was a politically appointed one, it was only a matter of time before that was taken away as well.

Frank S. Latham was a former editor of the Whig *Enquirer* who was then editor of the *Fort Pickering Weekly American Eagle*. He had been railing against Winchester and the Memphis post office for years. Regarding Winchester's resistance to the efforts by a group of men wanting to move the post office closer to the center of town, Latham wrote in March 1842:

> But whether it will be removed or not remains to be seen. Major Winchester has had his way so long on so many matters—so long managed through others to exercise an overpowering influence in the affairs of Memphis, that he hates to yield without a stubborn and severe contest. So obnoxious has his course become that a large and highly respectable petition signed by many of our first citizens, always heretofore his friends, has been circulating for *his* removal and we hope the government *will* remove him.... He has had [the postmastership] ever since the office existed. He professes to believe "rotation in office" a democratic principle. He does not discharge his duties in person as required by the Department. He is President of a Bank, President of an Insurance Company, a Commission and Grocery Merchant, proprietor of a ferry, an extensive landholder and agent etc., etc., and *charity* at least urges he should no longer be burdened with the duties of an office discharged by *others* for twenty years.... We care not a pin were the office given another Democrat, so he be worthy of the trust.[14]

His professional challenges were minor compared to what he experienced at home. The death of his long-time friend, Isaac Rawlings, was not the only personal loss Marcus Winchester suffered in 1839. About a month before Rawlings's death, Amarante is thought to have died in New Orleans. There is an August 19, 1839, certificate of burial for a woman with her name who was "of about 30 years" who died at 8 a.m. Her residence was listed as 147 Royal Street, between St. Louis and Conti Streets. She was buried that same day in St. Louis Cemetery Number One, the oldest cemetery in New Orleans. Her grave is unidentified now and may lay underneath a nearby street.

If this was Marcus Winchester's wife, her death so far from her Memphis home raises many questions. If she and Marcus Winchester were legally married, why did the certificate of burial list her name as Amarante Loiselle rather than Amarante Winchester? Why was she in New Orleans in the first place? Had she moved there to escape the growing hostility toward free Black and mixed-race individuals? Marcus and Amarante's youngest daughter, Lisida, was born in 1839. Did Amarante Loiselle die in New Orleans giving birth to her? Was Marcus Winchester with her in New Orleans when she died?

They had family in the city, and Marcus visited often. His sister and brother-in-law, Maria and James W. Breedlove, were wealthy and influential residents of New Orleans. At the time of his death in 1868, the Breedlove family lived near Tivoli Circle at 294 St. Charles Street in New Orleans's First District.[15] Their home was bounded by St. Charles Avenue, Prytania Street, Clio Street, and Calliope Street in an area that is in today's Lower Garden District. The address 147 Royal Street, where Loiselle possibly died, was in the French Quarter, less than half-a-mile from the Breedlove's home on St. Charles Avenue. Whether they were living there when Loiselle died is unclear, but certainly a possibility.

Unless additional information is uncovered, circumstances around Loiselle's death—like her life—will remain a mystery. What is known is that Marcus Winchester became a widower with eight children. His youngest was a newborn, while his eldest, Laura, was just fourteen. The census of 1840 provides a small glimpse into his household of twenty-six individuals but also creates more questions than answers. Fourteen in his home were listed as enslaved, while twelve were free. There were only five White individuals who were under the age of twenty, so some of his children may not have been living with him at the time of the census. One male, likely Loiselle, was under five, while three White females, likely Lisida, Selima, and Valeria, were under five. There was one female in the household, likely Louise, who was between the ages of five and nine. His older children may have been living with friends or family at the time of the census, or they may have been away at school. Evidence indicates Selima went to school in Massachusetts when she was a little older. It is likely some of the twelve enslaved men and women living on his property were not owned by Winchester. In the tax records of 1838 and 1850, Winchester owned four enslaved individuals rather than twelve. It is possible some of those twelve enslaved individuals living at Muscogee Camp were working on Winchester's ferry or on the river in some other capacity. The census records six persons "employed in navigation of canals, lakes or rivers."

The 1850 slave schedule lists the ages and sexes of Winchester's four enslaved individuals: a male, age ninety, and three females ages twenty-eight, twenty-five, and ten. A ninety-year-old enslaved man would have been considered essentially worthless in the slave economy, so Winchester was likely caring for the man by providing a place for him to live. The man and the twenty-eight-year-old woman were recorded as Black, while the two younger girls were Mulatto. Their identities are unknown, but two of these enslaved individuals were likely Harry and Betsy, who Winchester would emancipate with a last-minute addition to his will.

It appears by the end of the 1840s, a decade after his wife's death, Winchester was still a major part of the Memphis business community. He was included in the planning committee for a welcome party for James K. Polk when the former president paid a visit to Memphis soon after he left the White House. In antebellum America, the arrival of a national figure like a former president was treated as both civic ritual and public entertainment. Memphians would have expected speeches, parades, receptions, banquets, and, often, an illuminated ball or fireworks display. Newspapers normally printed the full list of names of committee members, thereby advertising who ranked among the town's commercial, political, and social elite.

The March 22, 1849, issue of *The Memphis Daily Eagle* announced those who had been selected for the Committee of Reception and the Committee of Arrangements. Marcus Winchester's name appears among other Memphis notables including William C. Dunlap, Robertson Topp, Edwin Hickman, Samuel Tate, and John T. Trezevant.[16]

This particular visit by a former president, in March 1849, would be even more meaningful because Winchester considered Polk a close acquaintance, if not friend. It was part of Polk's post-presidential "farewell tour" of the southern states. He would be traveling through Alabama, Mississippi, and Louisiana before heading up the Mississippi River where a stop was planned in Memphis—his triumphant return to Tennessee after four years in the White House.

Polk's four-year presidency is widely regarded as one of the most successful and productive in American history, although it came with a price. Upon taking office in 1845, he announced just four goals: lower the tariff, restore the independent treasury, resolve the Oregon boundary, and obtain California—or at least a Pacific outlet—from Mexico. During his presidency, the United States acquired over a million square miles of territory, including present-day Arizona, Utah, Nevada, California, Oregon, Idaho, Washington, and parts of New Mexico, Wyoming, Montana, and Colorado. This expansion was realized through the annexation of Texas, the Oregon Treaty with Great Britain, and the Mexican Cession following the Mexican-American War. Domestically, Polk successfully lowered tariffs and established an independent federal treasury, fulfilling his major economic objectives.

It certainly did not look as though that would be the case during the election four years earlier. Polk had been a rising star in Tennessee politics but had faded from the spotlight after two consecutive defeats in the state's gubernatorial races. However, Polk was ambitious and let it be known he wanted to throw his hat into the ring for consideration as the Democratic candidate for president.

The front runner for that spot was someone who had done the job before. Martin Van Buren had occupied the White House as the eighth president of the United States from 1837 to 1841, and he was ready to return. The only problem was Van Buren had come out publicly against the immediate annexation of

Texas. Like others, he feared that annexation would provoke war with Mexico and intensify sectional tensions over slavery.

At the convention in Baltimore, neither Van Buren nor his main rival, Lewis Cass, secured the necessary two-thirds majority, leading to a deadlock. At the last minute, delegates turned to Polk. He was, after all, a former speaker of the house and Tennessee governor, whose expansionist vision aligned with the party's growing hunger for new land. Polk could also count on the endorsement of another Tennessean who championed Manifest Destiny at any cost—Andrew Jackson.

Jackson had been Polk's mentor for years. Polk was even given the nickname "Young Hickory," inspired by Jackson's own nickname, "Old Hickory," earned during the War of 1812. Jackson had also been a family friend of Polk's wife, Sarah Childress Polk. She was smart, well-educated, and an excellent hostess. Jackson thought she would make the perfect wife for a rising political figure. Jackson valued strong, politically savvy women and saw Sarah as an ideal partner for a rising politician. Jackson's instincts proved correct—Sarah Polk became a key advisor and supporter of her husband throughout his career, including during his presidency.

With the endorsement of Andrew Jackson, Polk emerged as the first "dark horse" candidate. As the 1844 campaign unfolded, Polk became the target of fierce political attacks from his Whig opponent, Henry Clay. The Whigs seized on Polk's obscurity, turning it into a rallying cry. "Who is James K. Polk?" became a mocking refrain in Whig newspaper articles and speeches.

The 1844 campaign also showcased a growing hostility in American politics. An abolitionist newspaper, the *Ithaca Chronicle*, published an excerpt from a book—later proven not to exist—by a German nobleman, Baron von Roorback. As it turned out, Roorback was also a complete fabrication. The excerpt described Roorback's supposed journey through the South, where he allegedly witnessed the mistreatment of a group of enslaved men and women. In the passage, he claimed to have watched in horror as forty enslaved individuals were branded with Polk's initials before being sold to traders and transported to Natchez, Mississippi, for resale.

The passage read, "Forty of these unfortunate beings had been purchased, I was informed, of the Hon. J.K. Polk, the present speaker of the House of Representatives; the mark of the branding iron, with the initials of his name on their shoulders distinguishing them from the rest."[17]

This false account backfired when it was exposed as a hoax and led to the coining of the term "Roorback," defined as a false or distorted report used to obtain political advantage over one's opponent. The list of presidential candidates who have faced Roorbacks over the years includes Grover Cleveland, accused of fathering an illegitimate child; Catholic Al Smith, falsely rumored to be overseeing the construction of a tunnel from Washington to the Vatican; Barry Goldwater, portrayed as mentally unstable; George W. Bush, alleged to have gone AWOL from the Texas Air National Guard; and Barack Obama, falsely accused of being born outside the United States.

Although Polk's Roorback was quickly uncovered and retracted, the question remained among those in the North and the South who were opposed to slavery. Could Polk, as a slaveholder, be trusted to lead a nation increasingly polarized? In the end, he narrowly defeated Clay, securing the presidency and reshaping the nation's future.

Sarah Polk transformed the role of first lady from mere hostess to strategist and power broker. She met privately with politicians, monitored the news for her husband, and influenced major policies, especially his expansionist agenda and the Mexican-American War. She also managed the enslaved laborers who sustained the Polk households and plantations—directly supervising those at the White House and overseeing, from a distance, those at Polk Place in Tennessee and on the family's plantation in Yalobusha, Mississippi.

As some had feared, Polk's aggressive expansionist policies also had significant drawbacks. His approach to acquiring Oregon risked conflict with Great Britain, and his failed diplomatic efforts with Mexico led to a controversial war that resulted in the deaths of around thirteen thousand American soldiers. While these actions resulted in substantial territorial gains, they also intensified the fight over slavery. Although the Civil War was still more than a decade away when he left office, Polk's inability to address the contentious issue of slavery in the newly acquired territories contributed to the growing divide between free and slave states. The failure to resolve these disputes deepened tensions, adding to the conditions that eventually led to the Civil War.

Aware of the contentious nature of slavery and the controversy sparked by the false story published in the *Ithaca Chronicle*, the Polks kept their purchases of enslaved individuals discreet during his presidency, particularly when purchasing enslaved children, some as young as ten, and separating them from their parents. The children and other enslaved Polk secretly purchased while in the White House were sent to work on his 920-acre cotton plantation in Yalobusha County, Mississippi, where he and his wife planned to retire.

During his campaign and presidency, Polk embodied the emerging ideology among enslavers that they were benevolent and paternalistic toward the people they enslaved. Much like Andrew Jackson, who positioned himself as a father figure to Native Americans and justified cruel relocation policies as measures for their protection and well-being, enslavers began arguing that slavery was essential for the survival of the enslaved. Many, including Polk, also defended their ownership of enslaved individuals by claiming they had merely inherited them from family members. It was easier on the conscience to convince oneself that one was simply providing slaves and their children who had been in the family for years with a clean and safe place to live in exchange for labor.

During his campaign for president, Polk made it clear that, if elected, he would serve only one term. It was a pledge he reiterated throughout his presidency and one that gave him an ability to govern without the concern of impacting another run for The White House. The next presidential election, held on November 7, 1848, occurred in the aftermath of the Mexican-American War. The Whig Party nominated General Zachary Taylor, a war hero, while the Democratic Party chose Senator Lewis Cass. A key issue during the election was the extension of slavery into the newly acquired territories. Despite enslaving hundreds, Taylor won the election, becoming the twelfth president of the United States. With a Whig in power, Marcus Winchester knew his time as postmaster in Memphis was coming to an end.

On March 28, 1849, the *Caroline E. Watkins* pulled up to the Memphis riverfront at 1 a.m. On board, Polk was very ill. In the days leading up to the stop in Memphis, he had dealt with fatigue and exhaustion that was so bad at times, he was unable to leave the steamboat to enjoy the festivities planned for him in the cities along the way like Natchez, Vicksburg, and Jackson. By March 25, he began to suffer with stomach and bowel problems. A few days earlier, a man died of cholera on Polk's boat. The former president wrote in his diary, "His body was put in a coarse, rough box, hastily nailed together & was entrusted to some wood choppers at a wood yard to be buried."[18] A few days later, after another night of restless sleep, he wrote, "I was no better this morning, and though I had no symptoms of cholera I began to be more concerned for my situation."[19]

The steamboat with the former president and first lady on board was not the only thing traveling along the Mississippi River. Believed to have first arrived on ships from England, cholera was slowly working its way upriver from New Orleans. The symptoms typically came on suddenly. Diarrhea, nausea, and vomiting first dehydrated the victim, then fluid loss led to lethargy, erratic heartbeat, sunken eyes, and dry and shriveled skin with a bluish tinge. Today, it is known cholera spreads when a bacterium in an infected person's feces contaminates food or drinking water by which it enters another victim's body, but that knowledge was still years away.

By the fall of 1849, there had been four hundred deaths out of twelve hundred cases in Memphis.[20] According to reports, most of the deaths were among "negroes and flatboat people who lived near the bluff."[21]

But cholera was not a worry on this day. A former president of the United States was returning to his home state of Tennessee. At daylight, a cannon was discharged, then around 8 a.m., the Polk's two nephews, who lived in Memphis, boarded the steamboat to meet with their aunt and uncle in advance of the welcoming committee.

Polk was still not feeling well, and he tried to talk his way out of having to attend the day's festivities. Polk wrote, "They insisted that Memphis was the first point in my own state which I had touched after an absence of more than four years, and that as extensive preparation had been made to receive me, that I should go on the shore if it was even for a short time."[22]

Polk joined the welcoming committee in a luxurious carriage, pulled by four striking gray horses adorned with decorative ornaments. The carriage proceeded up Main Street, descended to Front Row, then stopped to observe the navy yard. The group then rode down Front Row to the Gayoso House. Former Tennessee Whig senator Spencer Jarnagin was given the honor of presenting a short welcome address on behalf of the crowd gathered in front of the hotel.

After Jarnagin's comments, Polk rose from his seat in the carriage and addressed the crowd, many of whom were getting their first and only glimpse of a U.S. president. Afterward, Polk and his wife were escorted into the Gayoso House where he was taken to a large meeting room, where he shook hands and spoke with a large number of Memphis men for several hours. Sarah Polk was escorted to a separate room where, according to a newspaper account, "she received the compliments of several of her own sex."[23]

As soon as Polk felt he was able to get away without insulting his hosts, he and Sarah were taken back to the *Caroline E. Watkins*. A reporter who was there that day wrote of Polk's final moments in Memphis: "A few discharges of cannon; a few airs from the band, a few huzzas from the multitude; a few bows from Mr. Polk, and the boat glided away and the panoramic show sank back into the realities of life."[24]

It was obvious to anyone who saw him in Memphis that the former president was not well. Another reporter observed, "The James K. Polk of 1849 is not the James K. Polk of 1844—he is the shadow of his former self; but how he has changed!—pale, emaciated, tottering!—the apparent victim of bitter troubles!"[25]

Marcus Winchester, traveling back from Nashville, arrived in Memphis too late to join the welcoming party or the gathering that followed. He wrote his friend:

> Allow me to express to you my great regret that I did not reach town in time this morning to unite with my fellow citizens in

your reception. My disappointment is however in a great measure relieved, on learning, the good feeling by which your greeted, by men of all parties. You could not have failed to be gratified had you been present, and heard the sentiments which were uttered, at the collation, which took place, at the Gayoso, after your departure; but I fear, that you would not be as much pained, to learn the expressions of disappointment, which will flow from the fair lips, of our lady friends, at the soiráe to night, when they find that by your precipitated departure that you have deprived them of the opportunity of doing honor to Mrs. Polk.[26]

After he returned to the steamboat, Polk's health continued to decline. He wrote in his diary the following morning:

The Boat left, and I very soon felt the ill effects of the exertion through which I had imprudently gone. I found that the indisposition which had afflicted me for several days was increased. Nothing of interest occurred during the remainder of this day and night. Before reaching Memphis, three deaths of cholera had occurred on our Boat and there were other cases which had not proved fatal. I rested badly to-night.[27]

A little over two months later, on June 15, 1849, James K. Polk died at age fifty-three of cholera at his plantation in Nashville. Included in the provisions of his will was the stipulation that his enslaved people were to be freed upon the death of his wife. Sarah Polk lived more than forty more years, dying on August 14, 1891, twenty-six years after the end of the Civil War.

The political changes taking place in the country would have an impact on Marcus Winchester. A few years earlier, he had ignored a request from a group in Memphis to move the post office closer to where many of the new buildings were being built. After receiving many complaints, an agent from the Postmaster General's office arrived and agreed that the post office should be moved further south. Latham gleefully broke the news in the *Memphis Daily Eagle* on August 5, 1842: "So you're beaten for once in your life, Major, ain't you?"[28]

The location for the new post office was the south corner of Samuel Tait's row of elegant brick buildings that adjoined the Farmers' and Merchants' Bank. Being forced to move the post office was just the beginning of the end of Winchester's career as a successful business leader in Memphis. He had lost all his land, money, and the mother of his children. By the end of the 1840s, he also lost his job as postmaster.

Tennessee Democrat Cave Johnson, postmaster general under Polk, noted in a letter to the president in 1845 that he and Aaron Vail Brown had a visitor from Memphis pressing for Winchester's removal. He wrote, "Lucian Brown is here, pressing the removal of Winchester at Memphis. I have thought it prudent to decline interfering & I believe AVB also, for the reasons I have heretofore assigned."[29] Brown, another prominent Tennessee Democrat and close political ally of James K. Polk, was later appointed postmaster general under President James Buchanan.

Winchester was no doubt stubborn, and the time for a new postmaster in Memphis had likely come. But the real reason he was pushed out of his position can be found in a simple note written by Henderson King Yoakum, mayor of Murfreesboro and chair of the Tennessee Democratic Convention—Winchester's own party. On April 28, 1845, a few months after Polk was elected, Yoakum wrote to the new president, "It is not my business, but I think if you knew the moral standing of the postmaster here, you would give a tone to public virtue by turning him out. I have it from the best men in Memphis that he has been living in open adultery with a mulatto woman, and actually keeps one of his children, by her, in the post office."[30]

Chapter Twenty-one Endnotes

1. James D. Davis, *History of Memphis* (Memphis: Hite, Crumpton & Kelly, 1873), 74.
2. Davis, *History of Memphis*, 74.
3. "Bandits Preyed on Returning Flat Boatmen," *Commercial Appeal*, May 29, 1938, 41.
4. *Niles' Weekly Register*, August 8, 1835, 380.
5. Davis, *Memphis History*, 75.
6. Davis, *Memphis History*, 75.
7. William Randall Waterman, *Frances Wright* (New York: Longmans, Green and Co., 1924), 245.
8. Amrita Chakrabarti Myers, *The Vice President's Black Wife: The Untold Life of Julia Chinn* (Chapel Hill: University of North Carolina Press, 2023), 3.
9. Myers, *Vice President's Black Wife*, 118.
10. Myers, *Vice President's Black Wife*, 132.
11. Freeman Cleaves, *Old Tippecanoe: William Henry Harrison and His Time* (New York: Charles Scribner's Sons, 1939), 294.
12. *Memphis Daily Eagle*, November 8, 1849, 2.
13. Marcus Winchester to John Claybrooke, May 1, 1842, Claybrooke and Overton Papers, Addition 2, 1804–1903 (Tennessee State Library & Archives).
14. *Fort Pickering American Eagle*, March 8, 1842, 1.
15. "Died," *The New-Orleans Times*, January 12, 1868, 6.
16. "Public Meeting," *The Memphis Daily Eagle*, March 22, 1849, 3.
17. Samuel Blatchford, brief to the Superior Court of the City of New York in *Thurlow Weed v. James G. Bennett*, 1844.
18. James K. Polk, *The Diary of James K. Polk During His Presidency, 1845–1849*, ed. Milo Milton Quaife (Chicago: A. C. McClurg, 1910), 407.
19. Polk, *Diary*, 409.
20. John H. Ellis, "Businessmen and Public Health in the Urban South during the Nineteenth Century: New Orleans, Memphis, and Atlanta," *Bulletin of the History of Medicine* 44, no. 3 (1970): 205.
21. Ellis, "Businessmen and Public Health," 206.
22. Polk, *Diary*, 410.
23. "Reception of Mr. Polk," *The Weekly Memphis Eagle*, March 29, 1849, 3.
24. "Reception," *Memphis Eagle*, 3.
25. "Reception," *Memphis Eagle*, 3.
26. Marcus B. Winchester to James K. Polk, March 27, 1849, *Correspondence of James K. Polk Digital Edition*, ed. Michael David Cohen et al. (Charlottesville: University of Virginia Press, Rotunda, 2021).
27. Polk, *Diary*, 411.
28. *American Eagle* (Fort Pickering), August 5, 1842.
29. Cave Johnson to James K. Polk, February 3, 1845, *Correspondence of James K. Polk Digital Edition*, ed. Michael David Cohen et al. (Charlottesville: University of Virginia Press, Rotunda, 2021).
30. Henderson K. Yoakum to James K. Polk, April 28, 1845, *Correspondence of James K. Polk Digital Edition*, ed. Michael David Cohen et al. (Charlottesville: University of Virginia Press, Rotunda, 2021).

SCHWOOB'S RESTAURANT

And Ice Cream Saloon,

No. 22, ADAMS STREET.

TABLES SPREAD AT ALL HOURS

With the

Choicest Delicacies of the Season,

Business men, who are unable to dine at their residences, will find this a first-class

DINING SALOON.

Mr. Schwoob flatters himself that his reputation is too well known to the public, to need any lengthy advertisements.

ICE CREAM,

Refreshments and meals furnished at all hours, in the very best style and taste. A call from my numerous customers is solicited.

From Rainey's Memphis City Directory, 1855/56

Chapter Twenty-two: Love and Happiness

Marcus Winchester marries Lucy McLean

SCANDAL—Gossip is publicly whispering about the streets that a handsome young widow and a handsome middle-aged gentleman have silently absented themselves for certain purposes. The meddling jade says they will soon return like kindred drops, melted together. We wish them all the extatic felicity incident to such occasions. What a vixen Dame Twattly Gossip is! . . . We don't think it's none of our business nohow." *Nous verrons! Nous verrons!*[1]

Marcus Winchester's second marriage created enough sensation to be mentioned as a blind item in several Memphis newspapers. It was likely not lost on his family that his new White wife was described as "a handsome young widow," while Marcus Winchester was referred to as "a handsome middle-aged gentleman."

Winchester's new wife, Lucy Lenore Ferguson McLean Winchester, was born in 1823 in Kentucky. On October 6, 1839, she married Archibald "Arch" McLean, a successful Memphis businessman, at Calvary Episcopal Church. She was just sixteen, while he was twenty-nine.

McLean, a merchant who imported merchandise from Scotland for resale in the United States, worked closely with Marcus Winchester. On July 8, 1840, approximately nine months after their wedding, McLean made a new will in Baltimore, Maryland, just before departing for Europe on business. A few months later, he boarded the *Great Western* in Bristol for his return trip home via New York City. McLean never made it. On September 28, 1840, he died of consumption.[2] McLean was buried in The Green-Wood Cemetery in Brooklyn in a lot he did not own, and his grave was unmarked. His will was recorded in Shelby County on December 22, 1840.

In his will, McLean had appointed Marcus Winchester as one of the trustees of his estate. The other two were Memphis lawyer James T. Leath and William J. Ferguson of Washington, Mississippi, who was likely Lucy's brother or father. Before departing for Europe, McLean entrusted Winchester with cash, documents, and financial records related to his businesses. This introduces the possibility that when James Davis wrote that Thomas Hart Benton left money with Winchester to care for Amarante, Davis had conflated two stories. It was McLean who left money with Winchester to care for Lucy.

Lucy McLean inherited all her late husband's money and property after his debts were settled. As Winchester helped Lucy settle into widowhood, the two apparently became close, and the relationship developed into something more than a friendship.

Winchester married his friend's widow in Nashville on August 17, 1842, when she was nineteen, and he was forty-six. Marrying Winchester was an unusual choice for Lucy. Unlike many widows at the time who needed a man for financial support, she had a small inheritance and no children, giving her more options. Her marriage to Winchester also came with considerable complications. He was a man facing financial difficulties and remained deeply unpopular with some in Memphis because of his mixed-race family. Lucy would have been aware that the family had to live outside the city as a result. Additionally, she must have had reservations about becoming stepmother to Winchester's eight children, who, under the law, faced all the restrictions placed on the small number of free Black children and adults in Tennessee.

When the new Mr. and Mrs. Marcus B. Winchester arrived at Muscogee Camp from Nashville and crossed the threshold into their new home, they entered a household full of children: Laura (about fifteen), Robert Owen (fourteen, turning fifteen that month), Frances Wright (thirteen), Louisa (ten), Loiselle (seven), Valeria (five), and the youngest girls, Selina and Lisida, practically toddlers. Lucy was only a few years older than her eldest stepdaughter. Winchester's new wife and his oldest children essentially grew up together, and Lucy never had children of her own.

According to one visitor to the Winchester home, while it was not as elegant as the house Marcus and Amarante had built in town, Muscogee Camp was actually a nicer place to live. The visitor wrote, "It was a plain log house in a beautiful grove, and amid vines, arbors and summer blossoms, it seemed a delightful retreat from the dusty city."[3]

Through the years, Lucy's decision to marry Winchester resulted in racist behavior directed toward her from some in the community. Near the end of her life, she wrote to a friend:

> I recollect the prejudice, the bitter feeling manifested toward me, not because I had a drop of dark or African blood in my veins, but that I had once been the wife of Colonel Winchester, who had, at an early day married a wife who was, as the Memphis people would and often did say, was a 'little off color.' But a kinder, nobler-hearted woman never lived than the mother of his now living daughters.[4]

It is an irony worth noting that Amarante Loiselle was accused of "bewitching" Winchester into marriage, while it was actually his second wife who was conjuring up spirits. Early in the 1850s, Lucy raised eyebrows among some in Memphis—and adoration among others—when she began claiming the dead could speak through her. Hundreds of individuals, likely some responsible for driving Marcus and Amarante out of town in the first place, began making the journey out to Muscogee Camp to hear Lucy speak. They believed she was communicating with their dead relatives and sharing prophesies, while channeling the spirit of an ancient Native American chief.

About Lucy Winchester, spiritualist Jessie B. Ferguson wrote, "The shrines of the old saints were not more places of resort than was this quiet woodland home, where all classes and conditions of life, from the eminent statesman and clergyman of the nation to the humblest slave, received the bright evidences of human hope and man's immortality."[5]

An editor for the *Spiritual Telegraph* picked up a Memphis story in 1856 that described Lucy Winchester as "a lady of intelligence and a high sense of propriety."[6] The article reported that she "was entertaining and instructing every Sabbath afternoon large numbers of visitors with eloquent lectures—under, it is said, the influence of a Spirit of an Indian Chief who died some thousand or more years ago."[7]

It is not surprising that spiritualism—the belief that the spirits of the dead can communicate with the living through mediums—emerged as a religious and cultural movement in the mid-nineteenth century. Large families were the norm in the agriculture-heavy South, but one in six White babies died before their first birthday. Consequently, women bore many children, often at the cost of their own lives.

The babies who survived infectious diseases such as smallpox, yellow fever, cholera, and typhoid fever during their first year of life had a decent chance of living into their early forties—but rarely beyond that. Reaching the age of fifty meant beating the odds. Considering the poor sanitary conditions, rudimentary medical knowledge, lack of understanding about how diseases spread, hazards of daily living, and the risks associated with childbirth, it is remarkable that people lived as long as they did.

By the time men and women reached adulthood, most had experienced the deaths of numerous family members and close friends. Adults were also acutely aware that death could come for them at any moment. The question of what lay beyond the earthly realm was tantalizing, and for some, spiritualism offered an answer.

Even Robert Owen, Marcus Winchester's friend and his son's namesake, became a believer. It was a surprising turn for Owen, who had spent a lifetime claiming that all religions promoted false teachings. After a series of sittings in 1854, he embraced the Spiritualist movement and even believed he had communicated with Benjamin Franklin and Thomas Jefferson during séances.

Spiritualism, like abolitionism, the temperance movement, the Second Great Awakening, education reform, and women's suffrage, was part of the slow evolution taking place in American society during the antebellum period. Women, often the most active participants in Spiritualist circles, served as mediums and spiritual leaders, challenging the norms of the White patriarchal society that had been the cornerstone of the South since the first settlers crossed the Allegheny Mountains.

In 1855, Samuel Watson set out to prove Spiritualism and Christianity could coexist by engaging a group of prominent individuals to explore the phenomenon of spirit communication in Memphis. He published the results of his research in a book he titled *The Clock Struck One*. A minister who had been raised in a strict Methodist household, Watson arrived in Memphis in 1839. At the time, he thought spiritualism and the whole idea that people could talk to the dead was, in his words, "one of the vilest humbugs in the land of the 'isms.'"[8] That is, until 1854, when he began experiencing "spirit-rappings" for himself. He and his entire family would hear the sounds of knocking throughout their house. Watson's enslaved woman also lived with the family and had nursed three of his children who had died. She told Watson that she believed the knocking sounds were coming from his dead children and claimed she saw them frequently all through the house. Watson initially dismissed the claims as his enslaved woman being superstious.

One evening, the family was visited by Mary McMahon, daughter of

Reverend William McMahon, a leader in the Methodist denomination who was well known throughout Tennessee, Mississippi, and Kentucky. After hearing about the knocking sounds, Mary casually shared that she had experienced her own strange phenomenon. She explained she could sit down at a table with a pencil held gently by a pair of scissors in her hand. She could hold the pencil over a piece of paper in front of her and receive handwritten messages from the dead. Watson was skeptical, but curious. He quickly provided the materials she needed for a demonstration. The room grew quiet as McMahon seemed to enter a trance and began channeling the spirit of Watson's long-dead mother. According to Watson, she answered questions correctly that he thought rather than spoke aloud. The skeptic was made a believer. Watson eventually gathered a group of experts from various fields to explore the phenomenon of communication from the spirit world.

As part of their investigation, they paid a visit to Muscogee Camp to meet Marcus and Lucy Winchester so they could experience Lucy's growing abilities at conversing with the dead. While with the group, Lucy began channeling the spirit of one of the original settlers of Memphis who was evidently communicating from hell. Watson wrote:

> He said he was engaged in business there many years since; that he had cheated and defrauded the widow and the orphan, and that his children were then living off his ill gotten gains, while he was suffering indescribable agony for his conduct. He said he had occupied a high position in the community, and a member of three churches; but in all he was a hypocrite, and was now reaping the reward of his doings. He would rave as a maniac, and threaten death to us, if in his power to inflict it. Several times he called for water. It was the most fearful scene I ever witnessed, and such as I hope never to see again.[9]

It is unknown which early Memphis settler Lucy Winchester claimed she was channeling. Marcus Winchester was well acquainted with the Memphis men whose gains had been "ill-gotten," and he undoubtedly knew those he held responsible for tormenting his family over the years. If this particular early settler was among that group, Winchester may not have felt much sympathy when the man, speaking through Lucy, complained of "suffering indescribable agony for his conduct."

Chapter Twenty-two Endnotes

1. *American Eagle*, July 22, 1842.
2. David Dobson, *Scots in the USA and Canada, 1825–1875* (Baltimore: Clearfield, 2002), 70.
3. Thomas Low Nichols, *Supramundane Facts in the Life of Jesse Babcock Ferguson* (London: The Spiritual Lyceum, 1865), 142.
4. Samuel Watson, *The Clock Struck One* (New York: Samuel R. Wells, 1872), 187.
5. Nichols, *Supramundane Facts*, 144.
6. "Financial and Spiritual," *Spiritual Telegraph*, July 28, 1856, Vol. 5, no. 13, 101.
7. "Financial," *Spiritual Telegraph*, 101.
8. Watson, *The Clock Struck One*, 79.
9. Watson, *The Clock Struck One*, 124-125.

BORDLEY & SWAN,
DENTAL ROOMS,
ADAMS STREET,
OPPOSITE THE UNITED STATES HOTEL.

H. F. FARNSWORTH & CO.,
Wholesale and Retail
APOTHECARIES & DRUGGISTS
MEMPHIS, TENN.,
DEALERS IN

Drugs, Medicines, Chemicals, Paints,
OILS, DYE STUFFS, WINDOW GLASS,
DRUGGISTS' GLASS WARE,

Garden and Grass Seeds, Perfumery, &c. &c.,
A CHOICE ASSORTMENT ALWAYS ON HAND.

Every article warranted to be fresh and genuine, or to be returned.

R. A. PARKER & CO.,
GROCERS,
COMMISSION & FORWARDING
MERCHANTS
No. 6 Howard's Row, Memphis, Tenn.

☞ Special attention given to the Storage and sale of Cotton.

From Rainey's Memphis City Directory, 1855/56

Chapter Twenty-three: Berry Rides Again

Marcus Winchester attempts a comeback

Marcus Winchester had been knocked down, but he was not out. In the fall of 1844, he partnered with John S. Claybrooke, Anderson B. Carr, and Willoughby Williams Jr. to establish the Hopefield Real Estate Company. Seth Wheatley served on their board. Winchester knew all of them well. Long after Overton's death, John Claybrooke supported Winchester, whether by investing capital, backing his business opportunities, or purchasing property when Winchester had no other means of surviving.

Winchester and Carr had been in business together since Memphis's earliest days, running multiple general stores. Willoughby Williams Jr. was the son of a Revolutionary War officer. His stepfather, Joseph McMinn, had been the governor of Tennessee when Winchester first arrived at the bluffs, and he had lifelong ties to Sam Houston. Williams had served as sheriff of Davidson County before becoming president of the Bank of Tennessee in 1837.

The Hopefield Real Estate Company started with a sizable 5,250 acres of land just across the river from Memphis, some of which Claybrooke had purchased from Winchester to help him settle debts. The company also acquired another seven thousand acres along the Loosahatchie River, near what is today Arlington. According to historian James Roper, Winchester was in no position to contribute cash, so he offered 1,458 acres of his remaining Arkansas holdings in exchange for $11,660 worth of stock.[1] This was the last of Winchester's land, making the company's success absolutely vital.

Unfortunately, the land did not sell as well as expected, and when the inevitable tax bills came due, money to make the payment came up short.

Without a large enough payment, the land would be auctioned off for the debt. The other partners, however, were unwilling to invest additional funds. A bad situation was made even worse because money the company had deposited in The Farmers' and Merchants' Bank became inaccessible due to the bank's temporary closure. Though Winchester had no part in the bank's management, his old friend Seth Wheatley was serving as president. Wheatley and his wife, Mary, had become popular Memphis socialites, regularly hosting lavish gatherings in their luxurious Adams Street mansion purchased from Walter D. Dabney, another early Memphis land speculator.[2]

The good times didn't last. In 1845, Wheatley became embroiled in a financial scandal when he vastly overstated the bank's health. His reports portrayed the bank as solvent and thriving, but subsequent audits revealed a starkly different reality; it held just seven cents in specie for every dollar of its obligations. This was exactly what the Isaac Rawlings of Jesse the "Scribe's" *The Chronicles of the Farmers' and Merchants' Bank* had feared. Wheatley assured the board that $1.2 million in bills of exchange were in play and could be converted into cash in New Orleans within hours, and $377,000 in notes were due and fully collectible—assertions that subsequent audits conclusively proved false.

Wheatley was forced to resign under a cloud of suspicion. The bank trustee who first began loudly pointing out the bank's problems, Dr. Jeptha Fowlkes, wasted no time exposing what he alleged to be outright fabrications in Wheatley's reports. A new board was put into place, but there was worry that a run on the bank could only be delayed, not prevented. Those fears proved well-founded. On January 26, 1848, the sheriff served an injunction against the bank, making its problems public. Memphis residents panicked, rushing to withdraw their funds. A mob attempted to storm the bank, but the sheriff managed to restore order before anyone was hurt. Many, including Winchester on behalf of the Hopefield Real Estate Company, were unable to access their deposits in the bank.

Forced into reorganization, leaders at The Farmers' and Merchants' Bank began slashing its operations and scrambling to recover lost assets. Despite the turmoil, their efforts began to stabilize the institution, leaving it on firmer footing than it had been in years.[3]

After a two-year investigation, the state was prepared to return the bank to the board, with Fowlkes at the helm. However, some creditors and board members opposed the idea of Fowlkes as president of the bank. They hired Tennessee attorney and well-known politician Levin Hudson Coe to contest the action in court.

Coe was raised in Maury County, Tennessee, where he developed a lifelong friendship with James K. Polk. His father was a state senator, and he grew up in a family that was both affluent and politically active. Coe earned his law degree from the University of Pennsylvania. His brother, John, was among the soldiers in James W. Fannin's command who were killed in the Goliad Massacre during the Texas Revolution. According to family stories passed down through the years, Levin Coe spent a year traveling through Mexico in pursuit of Antonio López de Santa Anna, intending to assassinate him—a task at which he was obviously not successful.[4]

He returned to Tennessee, where he established a legal practice serving those in Bolivar, Somerville, and Memphis. Coe was elected to the Tennessee State Senate, where he served as speaker. In 1846, he moved permanently to Memphis with his wife and eight children, joining William T. Brown in an office on Main Street at Poplar Avenue. Coe was quick to anger, and he took his cases personally. During a public debate over Whig and Democratic policies, the discussion grew heated, and Coe, a Democrat, drew a pistol and shot Phineas T. Scruggs, a Whig. Coe was arrested but released when it became clear that Scruggs had suffered only minor injuries.

The case of The Farmers' and Merchants' Bank should have been a straightforward legal dispute, involving stacks of files and testimony that would lull most judges to sleep. Instead, it became a case about greed and revenge. Coe believed that Fowlkes and his associates were attempting to defraud the bank's creditors and shareholders. Coe also had personal issues with Fowlkes, and some thought Coe was using this case to hurt his nemesis. In an apparent effort to defend the case, protect their friend, and intimidate Coe, Alanson Trigg and other Fowlkes supporters circulated a letter warning Coe that if he persisted in his efforts, they would "take action."

When the next hearing convened, tensions in the courtroom were high. Coe claimed he feared for his life and told the judge that he believed he was in immediate danger. After the proceedings adjourned, Coe left and headed back to his office. At the corner of Main Street and Poplar Avenue, Trigg and four other men approached him. Whether Coe legitimately feared he was in danger or saw an opportunity for revenge in that moment will never be known. He drew one of the four pistols he was carrying and shot Trigg at close range, killing him almost instantly with a bullet through his heart. As Coe attempted to flee, another one of the men in the group shot him in the back. Coe was paralyzed immediately but lingered in agony for three months before he died on August 10, 1850.[5]

Seth Wheatley's situation had a much more favorable outcome. An investigation and trial into his mismanagement of the bank's funds took years, but he was ultimately found innocent of the charges. The verdict, covered in a Memphis paper, was also picked up in the March 3, 1855, edition of *The New York Times*:

> After a long, patient, and thorough investigation, aided by the ableist and most astute members of our bar on both sides, an intelligent special Jury, compose mostly of merchants and experienced businessmen, have rendered a verdict for the defendant, and thus furnished a complete vindication of the character of Mr. Wheatley from the imputations against it, of which this suit is all ever known in this community to give foundation to them. It cannot be otherwise than gratifying to the friends of Mr. Wheatley thus to know that the implicit confidence they have hitherto reposed in him has found no cause of disturbance from the trying ordeal to which it has been subjected; but, on the contrary, has been only the more justified as the scrutiny into his acts became close and severe.[6]

When the troubles with the bank began, Wheatley had left for Europe to get away from the scandal and returned in a "bad mental state." Bad state or not, Marcus Winchester needed his money, and he did not have time to wait. He visited his old friend at his farm south of Nonconnah Creek near today's Memphis International Airport. The two likely talked about old times, the death of Levin Coe, and the struggles to get a railroad in Memphis. By the time the evening ended, they had come to an agreement. Wheatley personally provided the money needed to pay the upcoming taxes, and in exchange, the matter of mismanaged Hopefield Real Estate funds would be dropped. Winchester rode twenty-five miles into the Arkansas bottoms with the money, reaching the tax collector in the middle of the night, hours before the payment was due.

The troubles around the Farmers' and Merchant's Bank of Memphis proved too significant to overcome. The bank Winchester willed into being with dramatic flair worthy of Shakespeare closed its doors for good in 1856. Seth Wheatley died at age forty-eight in 1858. His obituary noted, "some years ago, his naturally frail constitution gave way under the severe over-tax to which it had been subjected, and for several years thereafter he was a confirmed invalid, suffering from the most distressing ailments of the brain and nervous system."[7]

While Winchester was able to make the payment on the taxes for Hopefield land, many other obligations were missed—some of them personal. George Washington Winchester, Marcus's younger brother by twenty-six years, graduated from the University of Nashville around 1840. George had been only four years old when their father died, by which time Marcus was already established in Memphis. As a result, George grew up without getting to know Marcus well.

After completing his college education, George began studying law in Gallatin, Tennessee, though his true passion lay in writing. Before beginning a law practice, he took time off and worked on his writing career. In 1841, George married Malvina Gaines, and together they eventually had ten children.

Marcus had committed $1,500 to help George settle debts he had accumulated. However, when a lien was enforced in 1848, Marcus found himself unable to cover the obligation. George was forced to sell an enslaved man inherited from their father to satisfy the debt. Following the Civil War, George relocated with his family to Memphis, where he established a law practice and served as a Tennessee state legislator.

On September 15, 1855, Marcus Winchester and his family experienced a much worse tragedy than the loss of money or real estate with the death of a much-loved daughter and sister. Marcus's daughter, Selima Winchester, was just twenty-two when she died. It was the first death in their immediate family since Amarante had died years earlier. Selima had been just three years old when her mother died. According to Selima's obituary, she had lived in Cambridge, Massachusetts, since childhood. Although no information survives to explain why she lived there or who she lived with while growing up, the 1850 census shows Selima living as a boarder in the home of Elizabeth B. Manning. Winchester's daughter had only returned to Memphis months earlier, and it is unclear if she was visiting or had returned home to live.

Her obituary in the *Cambridge Chronicle* noted that when she left Massachusetts, she left behind "a large circle of acquaintances, in this city and in other places, to whom she had greatly endeared herself by the brilliancy of her intellect, her high and varied literary culture and attainments, her disinterestedness and warm affections, and the energy of her character."[8] She began feeling ill while at the home of one of her sisters, likely Frances, and the diagnosis confirmed the family's worst fear—yellow fever. Selima's obituary included details of her final days:

> A physician was subsequently called; but it was not known, till on vomiting after taking a Seidlitz powder the evening before she died, that she was attacked with the yellow fever. She repeatedly intimated to her father and sister a desire to make some communications respecting her Eastern friends, but before she could do so, she would seek into a stupor, and thus she continued to the last. Her sudden death has made a deep impression on friends whose sympathies were drawn towards her on account of her moral and intellectual worth and peculiarities of her circumstances

and condition.⁹

It is unknown what the writer of the obituary meant by the "peculiarities of her circumstances and condition."

From a letter written to Selima by her brother, Robert Owen Winchester, in 1850 when he was twenty-three, it is clear the two siblings were close and that Marcus Winchester had raised a young man who was intelligent and motivated.

James Davis remembered that growing up, Owen was extremely intelligent and "the sprightliest boy" he ever saw.[10] Davis wrote that Owen visited the newspaper where he worked and was able to read and discuss the stories in the paper as though he were many years older. At the age of twelve, Owen Winchester was impressing others with his ability to weigh and mark cotton, a highly respectable skill in Memphis at that time. For some, however, Owen Winchester's skills and abilities did not outweigh the darkness of his skin. It was in reference to Owen that Henry Yoakum wrote James K. Polk, "I have it from the best men in Memphis that [Marcus Winchester] has been living in open adultery with a mulatto woman, and actually keeps one of his children, by her, in the post office."[11]

In his letter to his sister, Owen shared his plans since he had quit working at the post office:

> Since leaving the post office, my time has been consumed with settling old business matters, leaving me little opportunity to write as often as I would like. I trust there will be a change in this regard in the future. As you have no doubt heard, I left the post office around the middle of October, as circumstances there were not entirely to my liking. I had intended to go to California, but, being unable to finalize certain necessary arrangements, I was compelled to postpone the trip for the present. However, do not think I have abandoned the idea—far from it. My mind is resolute on that matter. At present, my goal is to secure a position as a bookkeeper in one of the commercial houses in town. Business is slow, and clerks are abundant, making positions hard to come by. Still, I am unwilling to remain idle. Within the next two weeks, I hope to secure something suitable. Until then, my time has been better spent here than loitering about town.[12]

He also let her know others in the family were doing well and shared that Muscogee Camp was a charming place he believed would grow even more appealing with time. In closing, he provided a possible clue that Selima had some sort of medical issue, or perhaps he was just displaying brotherly concern when he wrote, "By the doctor's advice, I urge you to start using magnetic fluid rings as soon as you receive this letter."

Marcus Winchester's daughter, Laura, married John Nelson in 1844. By 1850, they were living across the river in Jasper, Arkansas. John, thirty, was recorded in the census as a farmer who owned 12,600 acres. Laura and John had four children at the time: a five-year-old, a three-year-old, and one-year-old twins. Over the course of their marriage, they had eight children, all of whom survived to adulthood. Their sixth child, Marcus Brutus Nelson—named after his grandfather—was born in 1855.

Marcus's daughter, Frances, married William Vance Jr. in 1846. Vance, originally from Belfast, Ireland, arrived in Memphis by way of New Orleans and farmed some of his father-in-law's Arkansas land. According to the 1850 census, the couple and their children also lived in Jasper, Arkansas. The names Frances gave the children she had by that time—Robert and Lucy—suggest a closeness to her family. Eventually, Frances and William had ten children, eight of whom lived to adulthood.

With the memory of Amarante fading, it appears the Winchester family was no longer the target of racial hostility. The writer of an article about Marcus Winchester that was included in the 1855 city directory of Memphis was clearly a friend. He wrote:

> We do not deem it necessary to write a full biographical sketch of Marcus Winchester. He is too well and favorably known in this community for us to say aught that would raise him in the estimation of his fellow-citizens, or add one laurel on his aged and honest brow. Nature has dealt kindly with him, and although in the "sear and yellow leaf" of life, his mind is as healthy and vigorous as in days of yore. Physically, he has been gradually failing for the past few years, but he still attends to business, and although now nearly sixty years of age, may be seen daily on our thoroughfares, with a cheerful smile and kind word for his many friends—and who is not one?[13]

Adjacent to the biography was an engraving of a photo of Winchester who looked at least twenty years older than his actual age—fifty-nine. Any animosity against Winchester from his fellow Memphis Democrats also seems to have faded with time, and he once again began performing duties as a civil servant. In 1851, he was nominated to run for Tennessee state legislator. While there was protest by county Democrats against a "city dweller" as a candidate, they were reminded he had, for several years, lived on a farm outside the city, even though he had an office in town. Winchester ran against Whig John Pope, an impressive contender.

A resident of Shelby County since 1832, Pope's passion was agriculture, although he was also president of the Union Bank. He was a major proponent of attracting a railroad to Memphis, and, at the Internal Improvements Convention held in Memphis in 1845, Pope delivered an impressive address on modern agriculture practices. He was a significant landowner and enslaver with five hundred acres of cotton land along present-day Jackson Avenue in the Highland Heights community. Winchester achieved a narrow victory receiving 1,490 votes to Pope's 1,474.

James Roper noted Winchester's one term as a state legislator was unremarkable with the exception of "a memorial submitted in behalf of temperance."[14]

Although Winchester was making a comeback, cash remained a problem. The few investments he still had were tied up in Arkansas land, leaving him reliant on charity at times. A few neighbors pitched in to purchase a used buggy so he could get into town for work, while an old friend from their Nashoba days, Richeson Whitby, gave them a horse to pull it.

At one point, Winchester wrote John Claybrooke, "I have 100 lbs. of bacon in my smokehouse, not an ounce of flour, and buy a bushel of corn meal at a time . . . but for the aid of $35 my wife got from the sale of strawberries, I really do not know how we should have got along."[15]

As it had been almost since the beginning, ferrying people, animals, and merchandise from the Memphis riverfront to Hopefield remained a persistent challenge. Throughout the years, Winchester navigated difficulties with Fooy's aging widow, various proprietors, John Overton Jr., John S. Claybrooke, a host of competitors, the Memphis city council, and others at different points in the 1840s and 1850s. Major issues included inexperienced pilots and enslaved men working on the ferries, high prices, irregular schedules, the absence of a modern steam-powered ferry, and disputes over ferry rights—it remained a problem he could not solve.

In the fall of 1849, Marcus Winchester was selected as a delegate to represent Memphis at the Great Transcontinental Railroad Convention in St. Louis. Presided over by Stephen A. Douglas, the event aimed to promote the construction of a railroad stretching from the Mississippi River to San Francisco. Winchester was among nine hundred men who gathered under the courthouse rotunda to hear the keynote address delivered by Senator Thomas Hart Benton. While many attendees were focused on the potential economic impact of railroads on their communities, Winchester was likely remembering a time more than twenty-five years earlier when Benton introduced Winchester to the girl who would become his first wife and mother to his children.

Benton advocated for a trade route that would connect San Francisco to New York, passing through St. Louis along the way. According to those who were there, he was in especially fine form that day as he gripped the podium and shouted:

> Let us beseech the National Legislature to build the great road upon the great national line which unites Europe and Asia—the line which will find on our continent the bay of San Francisco at one end, St. Louis in the middle, the national metropolis and great commercial emporium at the other end—the line which shall be adorned with its crowning honor, the colossal statue of the great Columbus, whose design it accomplishes, hewn from the granite mass of a peak of the Rocky Mountains, overlooking the road—the pedestal and the statue a part of the mountain, pointing with outstretched arm to the western horizon, and saying to the flying passengers, *there is the east—there is India!*

As he shouted the final line, Benton dramatically pointed toward San Francisco. His words and delivery were so iconic, they later inspired the sculptor of a statue commissioned in his memory. The statue, located in Lafayette Park in St. Louis, was created by Harriet Goodhue Hosmer and dedicated on May 27, 1868, ten years after Benton's death. It holds historical significance as the first public monument in the United States created by a woman and the first erected west of the Mississippi River. Inscribed on the front of the ten-foot-tall granite pedestal is Benton's quote: "There is the East, there is India."

St. Louis was far ahead of Memphis in railroads, paved streets, and architecture. When writer Lilian Foster visited Memphis in 1856, the city was beginning to show signs of the metropolis it would one day become, but progress was slow. She observed:

> If in railroads and manufactures Memphis is behind the age, she can boast of more banks and bachelors than any other city in the Union of its size. I am told there are twenty bachelors to one young lady, and at least a dozen banks, though there are very few bank bills in circulation that are redeemable here . . . Memphis is destined in a few years to be next in a commercial point of view on the Mississippi to St. Louis, and is now a fine city without much architectural style in building. It would be a great improvement to the place if her streets were graded and walks better paved. The reason for the delay, I am told is because they have no material of which to compose them, there being no rock within a hundred

miles of the city.[16]

The absence of rock posed a significant problem that would take years to resolve. Frances Trollope and her family were among many who lost their "shoes and gloves in the mire" while attempting to traverse the muddy terrain from their steamboat to the landing above. The Memphis riverfront consisted of rough, eroded sections of mud and silt, interspersed with treacherous pathways that were occasionally reinforced with wooden sidewalks. These makeshift walkways provided only limited access through the narrow and unstable strip of land along the river. However, the strong currents of the Mississippi River requently eroded any improvements, creating unreliable docking conditions for river traffic. The river's height sometimes fluctuated by as much as fifty feet between high and low water levels, making it difficult to address the problem effectively.

In response to these challenges, the city contracted John Loudon of Cincinnati to pave the wharf with limestone or granite cobblestones at an estimated cost of $83,000. Loudon sourced the stone from quarries in Illinois. Although the Civil War interrupted progress on the project, work resumed in 1866 and was finally completed in 1881.

The cobblestone landing was built almost entirely by immigrant labor—chiefly Irish refugees who fled the Great Famine of the late 1840s in search of work. They crowded into a settlement just south of Bayou Gayoso and along the Wolf River. They appeared so impoverished that their belts seemed to "pinch" their gaunt waists, earning the neighborhood the derisive nickname "Pinch-Gut," later shortened to the Pinch District. Thanks to the tireless efforts of these laborers, Memphis's riverfront was transformed into a durable, functional landing—portions of which still survive today.

Although Memphis's shallow, difficult-to-navigate riverfront hindered its ambitions as a transportation hub early on, this shortcoming paled beside its lack of rail service. By 1850, America was in the throes of a transportation revolution—cities with railroad connections surged ahead while Memphis was left behind.

The country's rail system had expanded to approximately nine thousand miles of track—a dramatic increase from just two decades earlier. Even more than steamboats had, railroads were transforming the nation's economy and connectivity.

At that time, railroads were predominantly concentrated in the Northeast and Midwest, where they linked cities to emerging industrial and agricultural centers. In contrast, the South's railroad network remained significantly underdeveloped, as the region relied heavily on waterways and maintained an economic focus on agriculture and slavery.

While John C. McLemore was creating the town he named Fort Pickering, he came up with a unique idea of how to attract a railroad at the same time. Investors were looking at running a train between LaGrange, Tennessee, and Memphis. John C. McLemore then offered one-half of the proceeds from sales of lots in his new town in return for the LaGrange and Memphis Railroad stopping there.

An 1843 map of Fort Pickering used to attract buyers shows a small park named Monument Square with a statue of Andrew Jackson as its centerpiece. The map also notes part of the riverfront was not suitable for commercial purposes but "would afford an excellent and safe Harbor at all seasons." While the statue of Andrew Jackson never came to fruition, the town was considered a success. Fort Pickering became home to a candy plant, a brewery, a boatyard, a school for girls, and the *American Eagle* newspaper. A train for Fort Pickering would have been the perfect addition.

On April 1, 1842, around sixty Memphians were selected to inaugurate the region's first railroad as others watched along the route. The train ran along four-and-a-half miles of track from its depot, which was located at the site of the former *Commercial Appeal* offices at 495 Union Avenue.

As the *Memphis Enquirer* reported, "a great portion of whom never before saw the like, witnessed the departure of Cars propelled by steam."[17] On May 1, 1842, Fort Pickering's newspaper, the *American Eagle*, gave its stamp of approval:

> Riding in a rail road car is the surest way we know of enjoying the fresh and invigorating country air, and a little the neatest way of bothering those tiny pests, though *tall* annoyers—the musquetoes. . . . we advise all, both ladye fair' and 'gentleman true' to try it. Tickets going and returning, both included, are set at 50 cents. Cheap enough, truly.[18]

Perhaps tickets were too cheap; just a few months after the train began rolling up and down the track, the county sheriff seized it due to the company's unpaid debts—and McLemore, once the biggest land speculator in Tennessee, was broke. He packed up what he could and headed to California in search of gold. In 1833, early Tennessee settler Memucan Hunt Howard was persuaded by Tennessee governor James D. Porter to write down some of his memories of the early years of Tennessee land speculation. He remembered McLemore's kindness and his financial decline:

> I knew Mr. McLemore well and was associated with him in

business for about ten years and had charge of the Land Office and Books mentioned a considerable part of that time, and know him to have been one of the most generous, kind hearted, benevolent men I ever knew, always in debt and "hard up" for money, always on the borrow and always sacrificing property whilst he had any. Once the owner of a large interest in both the Rice and Ramsey tracts of land of 5,000 acres each on a part of both of which Memphis situated. . . . His entire interest in the two tracts now worth millions of dollars, I suppose. And its generous philanthropic owner died at Memphis in indigent circumstances.[19]

In spite of the many railroad charters granted in Tennessee after 1831, the state could not boast of having an operating line until the Nashville & Chattanooga Railroad reached Chattanooga in 1854. The first rail connection linking the Atlantic Ocean to the Mississippi River arrived four years later, when the Memphis & Charleston Railroad opened in 1858. The Memphis business community was so elated to finally have transportation into and out of the city by rail that they held a two-day celebration called The Great Railroad Jubilee to mark the occasion.

Firefighters played a prominent role throughout the event, reflecting the early partnership between railroads and fire companies. Railroads gave fire brigades new mobility, a place in civic pageantry, and, through shared steam technology, a path to modern equipment. In return, the firemen protected railroad property, added spectacle to railroad promotions like the one in Memphis, and rushed to accidents, often aboard the very trains that sparked fires along the tracks they traveled.

Newspapers reported between fifteen to thirty thousand attended the first day of the Jubilee that featured bands, fireworks, speeches by Memphis dignitaries, and a large parade. Days of heavy rain had turned the streets to mud, but the two-mile procession of fire companies, carriages, and mounted riders were undeterred as they moved from Main Street to Court Square. Those in the parade passed under a large archway trimmed with evergreens and flowers that had been built across Main Street.

That evening, a dinner at the navy yard—described by one newspaper as the largest ever held in the South—set eight thousand places and served twenty-five thousand pounds of beef and mutton, four hundred chickens, and sixty pigs on a table nearly three-quarters of a mile long.[20] A fireworks display on the bluff opposite Madison Street—"the finest pyrotechnic display ever seen in Memphis," according to the press—ended the night for some.[21] Others continued to celebrate throughout the night.

The next morning, the *Memphis Daily Appeal* announced in bold type: "Imposing Procession of Military, Firemen, Councilmen and Citizens—Eloquent Speaking and Immense Enthusiasm." Its reporter wrote that "thousands upon thousands of spectators crowded the sidewalks, filled the streets, thronged the balconies and awnings, and displayed themselves at the windows of all the business houses and shops."[22]

After more speeches, steamboat rides, and competitions between the many fire departments in town, the second day concluded with the main event. Two large barrels—hogsheads in train jargon—of Atlantic Ocean water, shipped west in a freight car, were rolled to the wharf for the much-anticipated "Wedding of the Waters." Mayor Addison H. Douglass took the fire hose, gave the cue—"Pump!"—and as the seawater flowed into the Mississippi, a band's rendition of "Hail, Columbia" was barely audible above the crowd's cheers.

Memphis leaders like Samuel Tate, Robertson Topp, and John Robertson, whose years of work had brought the railroad to Memphis, were honored as "officers of the meeting." Missing, however, was Marcus Winchester, the city's earliest champion; he had not lived to see the railroad's arrival in Memphis.

Chapter Twenty-three Endnotes

1. James E. Roper, "Isaac Rawlings, Frontier Merchant," *Tennessee Historical Quarterly* 20, no. 3 (1961), 26.
2. "The Memphis of Forty-two Years Ago," *The Daily Memphis Avalanche*, April 3, 1881, 2.
3. *Journal of the House of Representatives of the State of Tennessee* (Knoxville: Jac. C. & Jno. L. Moses, 1848), 288–90.
4. Jeanne Crawford, "Levin Hudson Coe," *West Tennessee Historical Society Papers*, 1993, 65.
5. Perre Magness, "Politician Lived, Died by Bullets," *Commercial Appeal*, August 12, 1999, 10.
6. "Farmers' and Merchants' Bank Suit," *New York Times*, March 3, 1855, 2.
7. "Another Old Citizen Gone!," *Memphis Weekly Bulletin*, June 08, 1858, 2.
8. *Cambridge Chronicle*, vol. 10, no. 41, October 13, 1855, 3.
9. *Cambridge Chronicle*, 3.
10. James D. Davis, *History of Memphis* (Memphis: Hite, Crumpton & Kelly, 1873), 76.
11. Henderson K. Yoakum to James K. Polk, April 28, 1845, *Correspondence of James K. Polk Digital Edition*, ed. Michael David Cohen et al. (Charlottesville: University of Virginia Press, Rotunda, 2021).
12. Robert Owen Winchester to Selima Winchester, January 29, 1850, Ancestry.com.
13. W. H. Rainey, *Rainey's Memphis City Directory, 1855* (Memphis: D. O. Dooley & Co., 1855), 28.
14. Roper, *Winchester*, 26.
15. Marcus Winchester to Claybrooke, June 10, 1851, Tennessee State Library and Archives, *Claybrooke and Overton Papers*, Addition 2, 1804–1903.
16. Lillian Foster, *Way-Side Glimpses, North and South* (New York: Rudd & Carlton, 1859), 175-176.
17. Addie Lou Brooks, "Early Plans for Railroads in West Tennessee, 1830–1845," *Tennessee Historical Magazine* 3, no. 1 (1932): 35.
18. Brooks, *Way-Side Glimpse*, 35.
19. Memucan Hunt Howard, "Recollections of Tennessee," *The American Historical Magazine* 7, no. 1 (January 1902): 65-66.
20. "A Mammoth Dinner," *Vicksburg Whig*, May 20, 1857, 1.
21. "The Great Railroad Jubilee," *The Republican Banner*, May 5, 1857, 2.
22. "Great Railroad Jubilee," *Edgefield Advertiser*, May 13, 1857, 1.

HENRY TEST,
DRUGGIST AND APOTHECARY,
117 MAIN STREET, MEMPHIS, TENN.,
BETWEEN POPLAR AND EXCHANGE, (West Side.)

N. B.—Prescriptions carefully compounded at all hours of the day and night.

WHEATON,
MANUFACTURER,
AND WHOLESALE AND RETAIL DEALER IN

BOOTS, SHOES, LEATHER & FINDINGS,
75 FRONT ROW, MEMPHIS, TENN.

☞ Hats, Caps, Boots and Shoes, of the latest New York and European fashions, and every variety of style, adapted to the various wants of the public. Dealers from the country, and the public generally, are invited to examine our splendid stock of Goods.

R. B. HAWLEY & CO.,
WHOLESALE AND RETAIL
GROCERS & COMMISSION
MERCHANTS,
No. 77 FRONT ROW, MEMPHIS, TENN.

From Rainey's Memphis City Directory, 1855/56

Chapter Twenty-four: From Graceland to the Promised Land

Marcus Winchester dies with his harness on

On January 2, 1852, when he was fifty-five, Marcus Winchester suffered his first stroke but made a full recovery. He was staying at the Sewanee House on College Street in Nashville when it struck. The only lasting impact seems to have been that from then on, he dictated all his correspondence through Lucy. Within a month, he was back at work in his office at 40 Court Street. He continued his duties as a legislator and kept up the fight for better ferry service from Memphis to Hopefield. He had lost his portion of the Memphis ferry business when forced to liquidate and sell everything to John S. Claybrooke. Management of the ferry—or mismanagement as Winchester claimed—was turned over to John Overton Jr., who was only twenty-one. Young Overton used his own inexperienced enslaved men to run the ferry. Winchester questioned Claybrooke as to why Overton did not buy the men formerly owned by Winchester who had been running the ferry for years.

On behalf of the ferry company, Winchester also took possession of a new steam ferry and was given the honor of naming it. While others had turned their back on Frances Wright who died on December 13, 1852, in Cincinnati, Ohio, at the age of fifty-seven, Winchester did not. In her memory, he named the new boat *Nashoba*. Winchester also collaborated with Robert Brinkley on a proposed railroad that would run from Hopefield to Little Rock. By 1853, he was, once again, "embarrassed for want of funds, and in an extremely unpleasant position," as he wrote to Claybrooke.[1]

On the night of Marcus Winchester's second stroke on October 28, 1856, the Democratic Party of Memphis marched through the streets in support of presidential candidate James Buchanan. He was running against the first-ever nominee for the new Republican Party, John C. Frémont, and Whig Millard Fillmore. Winchester knew well the family of the Republican nominee. Frémont was married to Jessie Benton, a daughter of Thomas Hart Benton. She was an abolitionist, writer, and vocal political activist.

The presidential campaign of 1856 was one of the most divisive in American history because of the sectional tensions over slavery. Voters on both sides of the issue were focused on the expansion of slavery, with Northerners and abolitionists rallying behind Frémont and the new Republican Party's anti-slavery stance. Frémont's campaign slogan was "Free Soil, Free Labor, Free Speech, Free Men, and Fremont!" Buchanan's was "We Po'ked 'em in '44, We Pierced 'em in '52, and we'll 'Buck 'em' in '56." It referenced previous Democratic victors—James K. Polk in 1844 and Franklin Pierce in 1852—while playing on Buchanan's nickname, "Old Buck."

Southerners and many Northern conservatives feared that a Frémont victory would lead to the country breaking apart. Buchanan was a Pennsylvania Democrat who personally opposed slavery but believed the Constitution protected it where it already existed. He campaigned as the candidate of national unity, arguing that Republicans were extremists who would destroy the Union. The campaign was marked by intense mudslinging, with Democrats accusing Frémont—nicknamed "The Pathfinder" for his Western explorations—of being illegitimate and secretly Catholic, while Republicans painted Buchanan as a weak, pro-slavery puppet.

One of the campaign's most dramatic moments was the brutal caning of Senator Charles Sumner on the Senate floor by Representative Preston Brooks—an attack that came to symbolize the nation's widening divide. In the end, Buchanan won the election, largely due to Southern support and a split in the Northern vote, but his victory did little to calm the national crisis, as tensions over slavery continued to push the country toward civil war.

Winchester was, at the time, the oldest living resident of Shelby County. As he marched through a rainy Memphis with his fellow Democrats, it may have crossed his mind how much had changed since he first stood on the bluff nearly forty years earlier. While he had quickly come to know every one of the fifty or so people who lived on the bluff when he arrived, it was no longer possible to know every man, woman, and child living in Memphis. By 1830, the population grew to around three hundred, and by 1840, it had expanded to seventeen hundred.

A decade later, in 1850, Memphis was home to nearly nine thousand residents. New people were flowing into the city nearly every day throughout the 1850s, and by the census of 1860, the population more than doubled, hitting around twenty-two thousand. It was the first time Memphis was recorded as having more residents than Nashville. Along the entire length of the Mississippi River, only New Orleans and St. Louis were larger.

In Memphis, cotton was truly king. On the eve of the Civil War, more than 360,000 bales—worth almost $20 million—passed through the city in 1860, and an estimated 95 percent still moved by steamboat.[2] The cotton that passed through Memphis that year amounted to approximately one-fifth more than the entire crop actually grown inside Tennessee. Memphis had become the primary hub not only for Tennessee planters but also for large portions of North Mississippi, East Arkansas, and even Southwest Kentucky production. It moved down plantation roads and was ferried across the river for pressing, inspection, and sale.

The city was booming. Memphis had nine large banks, ten newspapers, twenty churches, public transportation via a car pulled by horses, public schools, colleges, seminaries, a new theater, a philharmonic, and all types of social clubs. The streets Winchester walked along during the Buchanan rally even had gas street lamps. That gathering of Democrats provided Winchester with a chance to speak with old friends and reminisce about those who had died young or settled further west It was the perfect ending to a long career spent looking after the interests of those who made Memphis home.

After he got into bed that night, Marcus Winchester had another stroke. He lingered a few days, long enough for his friends and family to say good-bye and for him to make a few additions to his will. He breathed his last on Sunday night, November 2, 1856, at age sixty. Death notices appeared in newspapers around the country with one noting he worked until the very end, dying with his harness on:

> DEATH OF MAJ. MARCUS B. WINCHESTER.—It is our painful duty to announce the death of this old and prominent citizen, who expired at his residence Sunday evening last, 2d inst., of paralysis. Maj. MARCUS B. WINCHESTER was born at Cairo, Sumner County, Tenn., about the year 1791. He was *aid de camp* to Gen. James Winchester, his father, in the War of 1812, who was appointed Brigadier General by Mr. Madison, in the Northwestern army. He was stationed at the River Raisin and was taken prisoner in the battle of Frenchtown on the 22d of January, 1813, was carried to Quebec and exchanged, when his father resigned and returned to his home in Tennessee. Soon afterwards, Maj. Winchester entered upon the study of the law at Nashville, but resolving to change his pursuit, he took up his abode on the

4th Chickasaw Bluff, now the seat of this city, in 1819, where he entered into mercantile pursuits in partnership with the late A. B. Carr. He was appointed Post Master of Memphis in 1822, which post he filled to the satisfaction of the Government and this community up to the year 1848, when he was removed by General Taylor on political grounds. He was the first Mayor of the city of Memphis and represented the county of Shelby in the Legislature of Tennessee in 1851. Major Winchester was, at the time of his death, the oldest inhabitant of Shelby County, white or black. He was charitable to a fault, of a warm and sympathizing heart, chivalrous bearing, and strict integrity, and died leaving not an enemy behind. He was in the Democratic procession last Tuesday and was stricken with paralysis the same evening. He may thus be said to have died "with his harness on."[3]

Friends and family were invited to depart from his home to attend his funeral at the Winchester Burying Ground. Carriages were made available for guests at the nearby livery stable of Newby and May. Members of the Memphis City Council attended his funeral as a group, then wore black mourning bands for thirty days. Predictably, no mention was made of Amarante, even though she was his first wife and the mother of his children.

Winchester had written his will in May 1850. To his twenty-nine-year-old widow, Lucy Winchester, he left watches, jewelry, household furniture, horses, hogs, cattle, and one-third of all his real estate. The remaining land was divided among his seven living children. He appointed John S. Claybrooke, whom he referred to as a "long, tried, and valued friend," and his son-in-law, William Vance Jr., as executors of his estate.

Hours before his death, Winchester amended his will to provide freedom for his remaining two enslaved individuals. He dictated the changes to Lucy: "I emancipate my slaves Harry and Betsy and direct my executors to take all proper steps in regard to them to make them free and secure their emancipation. I give Harriet C. Wray a five-acre lot in Hopefield, Arkansas, the lot to be selected by my Executors." This was the final matter of business he addressed before his death.

The role of Harriet C. Reinhardt Wray, the 36-year-old wife of James Richmond "Rich" Wray, in the life of the Winchesters remains a mystery, although this was possibly done to settle an existing debt. She had come to Memphis with her family as a twelve-year-old girl in 1832. Her connection to him is unclear, but she was evidently close enough to the family to warrant such a bequest. This is especially curious given that after Winchester's debts were settled, only three hundred acres of Arkansas land were left to divide among his seven living children.

All six of the children of Marcus and Amarante who married did so with White spouses. Laura married John Nelson and passed away in Memphis at age forty-one on Christmas Eve 1866. She was buried in Elmwood Cemetery. While no definitive proof exists, it appears Robert Owen Winchester eventually moved west but returned a few years later and settled in Arkansas, possibly in Sebastian County. Loiselle—who, as an adult, was frequently recorded as Loiselle—married Mary A. McNamara and became an evangelist. They had seven sons, one of whom was named Marcus Brutus. Loizelle would be the last surviving child of Marcus and Amarante, passing away in 1906 in West Memphis. He was also buried at Elmwood Cemetery.

Valeria Winchester married Robert Edgar Richards, and the couple had five children. She died on May 17, 1879, at the age of forty-three after "a protracted and painful sickness." According to her obituary, she and her family lived at "the old Winchester Place, two and one-half miles from Memphis on the Poplar Street Boulevard" at the time of her death.

Marcus Winchester owed much of his life and career to the Mississippi River. Sadly, nearly a decade after his passing, that same river claimed the life of his daughter, Frances Winchester Vance, in a tragic accident. On the afternoon of February 23, 1867, Frances boarded a flatboat at the foot of Washington Street with a small group. They were crossing the river from Memphis to Hopefield, where she lived with her large family.

Shortly after departing, the pilot lost control of the boat and collided with a coal barge, throwing all passengers into the cold, muddy water. Men working on the tugboat, *We Come to Stay*, attempted to rescue the victims. Two passengers managed to swim ashore, and six were rescued. Tragically, three individuals, including Fanny, drowned before they could be saved. A report of her death noted, "Mrs. Vance was the daughter of old General Winchester, of this city, and was loved and esteemed by all who knew her."

Lisida, the youngest of the Winchester's children, never knew her mother. Like Loiselle, she was too young when her mother died to have formed any lasting memories. Along with her younger siblings, she grew up at Muscogee Camp, with Lucy as her stepmother. As a young girl, Lisida surely overheard her father complain about the inefficiencies in ferry service between Memphis and Hopefield, where he had significant investments. On March 22, 1860, Lisida married Charles H. Organ at the home of her late father and stepmother, following her father's legacy in a way. Organ was a ferry pilot and the owner of a river steamboat. The couple had three children before Lisida passed away in 1867 at just twenty-nine years old. For many years, Charles Organ worked for the West Memphis Packet Company and became an iconic figure on the river.

His was so respected that one of Memphis's most renowned steamboats, the *Charles H. Organ*, was named in his honor. Built in 1897, the steamboat made daily trips from the foot of Court Square in Memphis to Hopefield, Mound City, and Wyanoke in Arkansas, as well as to President's Island in Tennessee. When Organ died at his daughter's home in 1914, all flags along the Mississippi River were flown at half-mast in his memory.

Both Laura Winchester Nelson and her family and Frances Winchester Vance and her family settled on Arkansas farmland belonging to Marcus Winchester, then purchased additional land on their own. In 1870, Frances and William gave their sons, Robert and Hopefield, six hundred acres of Arkansas land where the two brothers built a log cabin. In 1884, their brothers, Frank and Arthur, joined them, and together they laid out the town that became West Memphis, Arkansas.

In 1885, Robert Vance followed in his grandfather's footsteps when he was appointed the first postmaster of West Memphis. In 1892, the first bridge across the Mississippi River south of St. Louis, the Great Bridge—later known as the Frisco Bridge—opened, securing the future of West Memphis.

After the other Winchester children married and moved on to begin families of their own, Louisa remained at Muscogee Camp with Lucy and a house full of spirits.

Chapter Twenty-four Endnotes

1. James E. Roper, "Isaac Rawlings, Frontier Merchant," *Tennessee Historical Quarterly* 20, no. 3 (1961): 34.
2. Rob Robertson, "Fullen Dock Revives Shipment of Cotton via Mississippi Barges," *Memphis Business Journal* 26, no. 18 (August 27, 2004): 2.
3. "Death of Maj. Marcus Winchester," *Nashville Union and American*, November 09, 1856, 2.

A. LINDE,

MANUFACTURER OF

Guns & Pistols,

WITH ALL THE LATEST IMPROVEMENTS,

And dealer in

WATCHES,  **CLOCKS,**

GUNS, RIFLES, PISTOLS,

Silver-Ware and Equipments,

ACCORDEONS, CUTLERY,

GUNSMITHS' MATERIAL,

(Wholesale and Retail,)

No. 217, MAIN STREET,

(Opposite Odd-Fellows' Hall.)

MEMPHIS, TENNESSEE.

☞ New work done to order. Repairing done at shortest notice. ☜

From Rainey's Memphis City Directory, 1855/56

Chapter Twenty-five: Trying to Live my Life Without You

Lucy Winchester becomes a celebrity

In the years following Marcus Winchester's death, his wife, Lucy, and his daughter, Louisa, remained at Muscogee Camp and became minor celebrities within the growing Spiritualist movement. Lucy developed a close friendship with Jesse B. Ferguson, an early advocate for Spiritualism whose fame proved as fleeting as the movement itself. One early biographer described Ferguson's rise and fall:

> Like a meteor which flashes across the horizon, making a trail of glorious light behind it, and then suddenly disappearing and leaving nothing but darkness in its wake, Jesse B. Ferguson came above the horizon and shone as a great pulpit orator in the church of Christ at Nashville, Tenn., and then suddenly disappeared and dropped into obscurity.[1]

As a young man, Ferguson worked as an apprentice for a newspaper in Virginia and later for a book publisher in Baltimore. He returned to school and quickly received an education in the classics. By the age of thirteen, Ferguson had opened his own school, where he taught for several years. While a young man, he married Lucinda Vance and moved with his wife closer to her family in southern Kentucky.

It was there he converted to Christianity and began preaching and teaching. Ferguson was handsome, charismatic, and a talented orator and quickly rose to prominence as one of the most popular preachers in the South, drawing large crowds everywhere he preached. He was an outspoken advocate of slavery and often shared his opinions from the pulpit, making him especially popular among those who shared his philosophy. Ferguson even openly championed White supremacy, writing, "one comparatively civilized people, may hold another of absolutely inferior civic attainments, in hereditary bondage."[2]

After leading several revival meetings that drew standing-room-only crowds to the Church of Christ in Nashville, he moved his family there and began serving full-time as the head minister of the church. In 1844, he also became a writer and editor for *The Christian Magazine*. Ferguson was on track to becoming one of the leading religious figures of the nineteenth century when he changed his beliefs about a core tenet of the Christian faith: where do we go when we die?

In April 1852, Ferguson published an article interpreting the "spirits in prison" mentioned in 1 Peter 3:18-20:

> For Christ also hath once suffered for sins, the just for the unjust, that he might bring us to God, being put to death in the flesh, but quickened by the Spirit: By which also he went and *preached unto the spirits in prison*; Which sometime were disobedient, when once the longsuffering of God waited in the days of Noah, while the ark was a preparing, wherein few, that is, eight souls were saved by water.[3]

In his article, Ferguson argued that after death, everyone would be granted a second chance to accept Christ, ultimately leading to the salvation of all—a belief known as universalism. This was highly controversial within the early American evangelical church, particularly among those who embraced Calvinist doctrines of predestination and eternal damnation for the unsaved.

One fellow minister summed up the opinions of many when he wrote in a published letter, "I am truly sorry to see that Bro. Ferguson has got a maggot in his brain."[4] Another explained, "Few men have possessed as much conceit as he had. Of course, as he developed so much egotism, he lost his spirituality."[5] Still another wrote, "He does not claim to be a distinguished person, yet he is determined, at least, to be *notorious*. . . . We are in a quandary at which to be the most astonished, his boldness or his folly![6]

While most in his Nashville church and many in Middle Tennessee rejected Ferguson's theological shift, others—including a new audience—celebrated his beliefs. The final step in Ferguson's departure from traditional religious beliefs occurred when he published *Spirit Communion*, a book detailing his conversations with the dead through mediums. About one, he wrote:

> She always sees the Spirit while communicating; whether through

herself or others. Frequently, while engaged in her household duties, she receives a request from some Spirit-friend to give forth a communication. In such cases she sometimes refuses, and then, after her duties are over, will sit down and in a few moments, pour forth the wishes of her invisible visitants.[7]

While Ferguson's career as a traditional Christian preacher was over, he became sought after by those yearning to reconnect with deceased loved ones. In 1859, Ferguson was invited to deliver a series of lectures to an audience in Memphis. His hosts rented a large venue and secured a suite of rooms at the Worsham Hotel, located at the corner of Main and Adams Streets. It was the finest of Memphis's two luxury hotels, the other being the Gayoso House.

Ferguson, still his own biggest fan, was pleased after his first night in Memphis, writing to a friend, "The audience heard me with unabated interest for over two hours."[8]

One night, after he finished a two-hour lecture he titled "The Unity of Man in the Diversity of Human Manifestation," a group of men who were Masons and leaders in the city of Memphis showed up at his hotel room to meet the famous Spiritualist. James J. Worsham suggested the group take Ferguson out to Muscogee Camp and introduce him to Memphis's most popular medium, Lucy Winchester. They loaded into a carriage and made their way east through the dark night.

When they arrived, Lucy surprised the men by meeting them at the door and greeting Ferguson with more familiarity than anticipated considering it was their first time to meet. She invited the men into her home and welcomed them to participate in one of her séances. While her words are lost to history, Ferguson later wrote, "I am free to say I have never heard an address from mortal lips which I considered its equal either in thought, language, or manner."[9] Ferguson claimed he was so enamored with Winchester's "powers," he returned every day during the rest of his stay in Memphis.

Ferguson frequently encountered an unusual group gathered at Lucy Winchester's house, participating in her séances. At one such gathering, the group included Louisa Winchester, who served as a scribe; James E. Chadwick, an Englishman; Dr. Erasmus T. Rose, a physiologist; Dr. Young Allen Carr, a physician, early photographer, and author, who was married to Minerva Whitby, the daughter of Richeson Whitby; Arthur K. Taylor, a professor of anatomy; James Hart, a portrait artist; and Andrew Jackson Wheeler, the society editor of the *Commercial Appeal*.

After Marcus Winchester's death, Lucy set aside one room she called "The

World" and another she referred to as "The East Room." According to Ferguson, as the group gathered in The World, Lucy Winchester entered into a trance and began channeling a long-dead Native American chief. Through her, he answered questions on topics ranging from science and metaphysics to government and social issues. All the while, Louisa Winchester—who Ferguson noted was of superior intelligence and clearly came from a "high education culture"—furiously transcribed notes into one of many journals kept of the chief's words. After Lucy Winchester's death, the boxes of notebooks Louisa Winchester had worked on so diligently were given to Ferguson for safe keeping. Sadly, it seems the notebooks have been lost to history.

Lucy Winchester became close friends with Ferguson and his wife, Lucinda. He wrote, "From the day I met Mrs. Winchester til the day preceding her death, which took place November 1860, there was scarcely a mail that did not bring me a letter."[10]

In fact, if one believes Jesse Ferguson, it was his wife who heard Lucy Winchester's last words. Lucinda Ferguson was on her way to Nashville when she encountered Lucy, who said to her friend, "I shall live to bless you all."[11] Ferguson claimed they later discovered that when Lucy met Lucinda on the road to Nashville that day, she had already been dead over an hour.

In her will, Lucy left everything to Ferguson, who claimed she designated him as her sole heir and executor as a trust, of sorts, for "those who were likely to be defrauded out of their natural rights."[12] He must have been true to his word as "the Old Winchester Place" stayed in the Winchester family for at least two more generations.

Chapter Twenty-five Endnotes

1. H. Lee Bowles, *Biographical Sketches of Gospel Preachers* (Nashville: Gospel Advocate Company, 1932), 186.
2. Jesse B. Ferguson, *Address on the History, Authority, and Influence of Slavery* (Washington, DC: Smithsonian Institution, 1847), 25.
3. *The Holy Bible*, King James Version, 1 Peter 3:18–20.
4. *Millennial Harbinger*, July 1852, 414.
5. *Millennial Harbinger*, July 1852, 414.
6. "Furgusonism—No. 2," *Tennessee Baptist*, February 19, 1853, 3.
7. Jesse B. Ferguson, *Spirit Communion* (Parkersburg, WV: Globe Press, 1888), 41.
8. Thomas Low Nichols, *Supramundane Facts in the Life of Jesse Babcock Ferguson* (London: The Spiritual Lyceum, 1865), 141.
9. Nichols, *Supramundane Facts*, 143.
10. Nichols, *Supramundane Facts*, 145.
11. *Supramundane Facts*, 146.
12. *Supramundane Facts*, 145.

MEMPHIS MEDICAL COLLEGE.

This Institution will open on the FIRST OF OCTOBER, when each Professor will commence a Preliminary Course of Lectures, on subjects connected with his department, which, for want of time, cannot be fully taught in the regular course. This will occupy the whole month, and will be free of charge to the students and public.

The regular Lectures of this College will commence on the 1st of November, and will continue four months.

FACULTY:

AYRES P. MERRILL, M. D., Prof. of Principles and Practice of Medicine.
JOHN MILLINGTON, M. D., Prof. of Chemistry and Toxicology.
SOLON BORLAND, M. M., Prof. of Physiology and Pathology.
HOWELL R. ROBARDS, M. D., Prof. of Surgery.
ARTHUR K. TAYLOR, M. D., Prof. of Anatomy.
C. B. GUTHRIE, M. D., Prof. of Materia Medica and Pharmacy.
HERSCHEL S. PORTER, D. D., Prof. of Natural History and Geology.
LEWIS SHANKS, M. D., Prof. of Obstetrics and Diseases of Women and Children.
EMMETT WOODWARD, M. D., Demonstrator of Anatomy.

The Fee for the entire Course is $105, payable invariably in advance. Matriculation Fee, $5. Graduating Fee, $25. Anatomy and Dissection $10, to be taken once before graduating. Dissecting Room and Museum open 1st of October. The Chemical Course can be attended independently of the others on payment of $20.

CLINICAL INSTRUCTION is given twice a week at the Memphis Hospital, and a City Dispensary Clinique is held daily at the College at 8 o'clock in the morning, at which operations are performed and upwards of one thousand cases come before the students and are prescribed for and lectured upon daily by the Professors, during the session.

The College possesses an ample Anatomical Museum and complete and superb Chemical apparatus, with extensive samples of Materia Medica Minerals, &c.

Students desiring further information will address Prof. L. Shanks, M. D., or on arriving in the city call on him at his office, 137 Main st.

L. SHANKS, M. D., DEAN.

From Rainey's Memphis City Directory, 1855/56

Chapter Twenty-six: I Forgot to Remember to Forget

Marcus Winchester, Isaac Rawlings, and other early founders of Memphis are forgotten

Around 1915, Memphis attorney James H. Malone was on the hunt for legal documents on behalf of his client, the City of Memphis. It had been a little less than a hundred years since the Astoria Fur Company had moved west, donating their land on the fourth Chickasaw bluff and the building sitting on it to the city. As time passed, old documents were moved from one place to another, and a deed, if there ever was one, had been lost. There was a plan to turn the land into a greenspace that would be named Astor Park—changed to Tom Lee Park in 1954—but the city needed to make certain they actually owned it.

Malone was just the man for a job like this. He had been Memphis mayor from 1906 to 1910. Not only a civic leader, he was a dedicated historian and advocate for preserving the city's heritage. As a diversion during World War I, he had researched and written a pamphlet on the Chickasaw that was released during Memphis's centenary celebration in May 1919. Believing there was still more to be discovered, he continued working on the project, and in 1922, he released *The Chickasaw Nation: A Short Sketch of a Noble People*.

Alongside his brother, Walter—a judge known for penning a poem "Opportunity" that became very well known in its day—Malone worked out of a legal office on the eleventh floor of the Exchange Building overlooking Court Square.

In its earliest years, Court Square was the symbolic heart of the young city, but by the 1870s, civic leaders looked to it as the proper setting for expressing the city's ambitions, as they were rebuilding after the yellow fever epidemic and the Civil War. On May 27, 1876, with an audience of around five thousand, an ornate cast-iron fountain was dedicated, a gift from leading citizens and merchants. At its center stood Hebe, the cupbearer of the gods, her flowing robes and uplifted jug symbolizing youth and renewal.

A reporter from the Memphis *Public Ledger* observed that Miss Emma Etheridge, who was chosen to share a poem at the dedication, was "chaste in style and . . . dressed neatly and most becomingly . . . wore no jewelry, and beneath a straw hat trimmed with flowers and vines, looked like one of the divinities or woodland nymphs of the charmed spot."[1] Etheridge dramatically finished her poem with the words, ". . . and I bid the fountain's imprisoned waters break from their fetters, and mingle in freedom with the fragrance of the summer air." Then, as the reporter wrote, "jets of water sprang up from the fountain far into the sunlight and a beautiful rainbow formed amid the spray that fell back in a silvery shower that sparkled like diamonds."[2]

The fountain, designed by architect James B. Cook and cast by Heath & Livermore, became a centerpiece of downtown life. Around its iron basin, Memphians gathered on warm evenings, children splashed in its waters, and parades and public celebrations passed along its edges. Today, it remains a fixture in Court Square, the only one of the four original public squares laid out by Marcus Winchester and William Lawrence that survives in its historic form.

The square was an especially meaningful place for Malone who, at the end of his term as mayor in 1910, noted—perhaps tongue-in-cheek—"My greatest regret in leaving this office is missing the pleasure I have had in watching the pigeons and squirrels in this square. I am glad I have made it possible for them to be fed daily."[3]

As a last resort in Malone's search for the Astoria Fur Company deed, Malone climbed the dusty steps and opened the door to the belfry of the courthouse. As his eyes adjusted to the dark, he began picking through a few of the papers in a large stack of what looked like trash in the far corner. Few people then or now would have known what they had found, but Malone did.

He had stumbled upon more than one thousand pages from an old case on ferry privileges. *Pleasant Houston v. William Vance* had resulted in another of Marcus Winchester's depositions in legal battles over the use of Memphis riverfront property. William Vance was Winchester's son-in-law.

Malone was, of course, very familiar with Winchester's role in the history of Memphis. He included several references to Winchester in his book on the Chickasaw and was even responsible for having a painting of Memphis's first mayor created and hung with other mayoral portraits at city hall. About Winchester, Malone wrote:

> In the long series of litigations respect to these ferry privileges, the most important and, it may be added, the most intelligent witness,

was Maj. Marcus B. Winchester, the first mayor of the City of Memphis. Maj. Winchester was not an ordinary, but in many respects a remarkable man . . . [he] gives the only authoritative history of public property referred that I ever heard of.[4]

Through the years, Winchester testified in many cases about the proprietor's intent regarding Memphis's "promenade." In the case referenced in the introduction of this biography, *The Board of Mayor and Aldermen of South Memphis v. Wardlow Howard and James Kent Jr.*, it was affirmed that the river landing from what was then called "Union Street to what is now the north line of Beale Avenue" was indeed dedicated to public use as far back as 1829.

In that deposition, Winchester answered around four hundred questions. Because of his "advanced age" and impaired health, the court allowed him to write out his answers by hand on separate sheets of paper in advance, which were then transcribed into the official record.

While ferry privileges from Memphis to Hopefield, Arkansas, and back are a thing of the past, litigation over use of Memphis's valuable riverfront has continued to this day. In 2023, three heirs of the original proprietors, along with an organization called Friends for our Riverfront, filed suit in the Memphis Chancery Court—a court that focuses on fairness and equity over the letter of the law. Their goal was to alter the construction of the new Brooks Museum of Art in order to adhere to John Overton's original directive to Marcus Winchester. Ironically, the museum's previous location was in Overton Park—named in honor of John Overton in July 1902.

The group argued that the promenade, managed by the city through an easement, was intended to remain free of permanent construction. The site selected for the museum had previously been occupied by a fire station and a parking garage—uses the lawsuit contended had already departed from the proprietors' original intentions. The case remains unresolved at this time.

Marcus Winchester's last project, Hopefield, Arkansas, needs no protection, legal or otherwise—it no longer exists. In the spring of 1859, the trustees placed ads in newspapers in Tennessee, Arkansas, and Missouri, announcing The Hopefield Real Estate Company was "closing up business and selling out the town in lots, at public auction, to the highest bidder."[5] The railroad was a big part of their optimistic pitch:

> Hopefield is destined to be among the great cities of the west, situated, as it is, opposite the city of Memphis, Tenn., on the

western bank of the great Mississippi river at the eastern terminus of the Memphis and Little rock railroad, the only railroad in operation between St. Louis and New Orleans."[6]

Lest anyone had doubts about the future of Hopefield, they added, "the proprietors deem it unnecessary for them to say a word to show the public that Hopefield is bound to be the emporium where the commerce of the great eastern world will center."[7]

A small community had indeed formed there across from Memphis. It appeared as if the town had a chance to become, if not "the emporium where the commerce of the great eastern world will center," at least a town that could take advantage of its proximity to Memphis. Then came the Civil War.

Hopefield was burned to the ground by Union soldiers tired of being shot at from across the river. After the war, Hopefield was rebuilt and developed a reputation for having many more racetracks, saloons, and poolhalls than churches. It found its niche as the location for boxing matches, cockfights, horseraces, and other activities that had been banned across the river. For a time, it looked as though Hopefield was going to survive and perhaps even thrive. The town grew to include a wharf, many businesses of all kinds, a school, and a community of people who called it home.

Before there were bridges for trains to use to cross the river, The Rock Island line would ferry its boxcars across the Mississippi from Memphis to Hopefield. Once bridges for the trains were built, business in Hopefield declined until the Mississippi River finally put it out of its misery:

> The town began to fade but still stood. A rising river would overflow its banks and then run through the dirt streets of the town. The remains always would be straightened—always, until 1912 when the river left nothing. As the river began to move back towards its banks again, the land on which Hopefield was built caved in.[8]

According to one local story, the Hopefield postmaster showed up one morning in 1912 at the Memphis post office and laid his mail pouch and some supplies on the Memphis postmaster's counter. During the night, the Mississippi River had taken the Hopefield post office. "All that's left," he sighed, "is a house, a barn, and a chicken coop."[9]

Today, over 40,000 pass over the former site of Hopefield, Arkansas, each day as they cross the Hernando de Soto Bridge coming to or departing from Memphis. The vast majority of those people have never heard of Hopefield, Arkansas or Marcus Winchester.

Although long absent from the pages of Memphis newspapers, Marcus Winchester's name resurfaced unexpectedly in the summer of 2024. During the construction of a parking garage near St. Jude Children's Research Hospital, the crew unearthed a human bone on land that had been city property from 1895 until its sale to the hospital in 2018. Over the decades, the site had been repurposed again and again—first as a park, then as city stables, and later as a municipal garage where vehicles and heavy equipment were housed and serviced. The stables, erected around 1892, were built directly over Winchester's grave, almost certainly without knowledge of its presence.

According to Marcus's niece, Susan Winchester Powell Scales, it is doubtful a headstone ever marked the spot. Susan—daughter of Marcus's brother, George—kept the diary that preserved details about the later life of Marcus's mother. In a 1931 interview, she recalled that she and her husband, Dabney, had begun searching for her uncle's headstone as early as 1880. "We have never given up the search," she admitted, "but it seems hopeless."[10]

Isaac Rawlings nearly suffered the same fate. He was buried in the Raleigh Cemetery along with his brother and sister. After many years, his tombstone fell over, and with no descendants bothering to check, the location of his grave was eventually lost. In 1980, a group of local amateur historians with a passion for Shelby County history began searching for his headstone. One of them, identified as Mrs. W. A. Ericson, told a reporer, "Isaac's grave marker was one we shall never forget finding because we really struggled to dig and turn over the large slabs to check for an inscription."[11] Finally, they found a slab that had been broken in half, overturned, and partially covered with dirt. "We were elated when we saw it was Ike's grave marker!"[12] Chiseled on the marker, as instructed in Rawlings's will, they found the words:

Here lies the remains of
Isaac Rawlings
Born in Calvert County, Maryland
13th April 1788
And died in Memphis
19th Sept. 1839
Having lived 51 years and 5 months

Members of the crew who discovered the human bone while digging near St. Jude may have gazed across the fenced-in area where they were working and wondered if there were others—there were. Nearby stands a historic marker that identifies the site as the former location of the New Winchester Burying Ground. It reads:

> New Winchester Burying Ground was established in 1828 by deed from the original proprietors of Memphis. It occupied almost 11 acres within an area now bounded by Lane Ave. on the south, Danny Thomas Blvd. on the west, the old L&N Railroad tracks on the north, and Manassas St. on the east. Among those buried there were victims of the 1836 *Helen McGregor* steamboat disaster. It remained the city cemetery until 1874 but quickly deteriorated.

Had that crew gone back in time and visited the cemetery in those early years, they would have arrived to find a gate with a sign that proclaimed "Our Dead—1826." For a while at least, the cemetery was well cared for and included many headstones and monuments that provided a history of the city's first generation.

However, as wealthy families began burying their dead in new cemeteries further away from town, the Winchester Cemetery fell into neglect—and worse. It was later claimed by multiple eye witnesses that the night after some of the burials that took place there, coffins were unearthed, and the bodies were sold to the nearby medical college for students to use in their training.

In perhaps one of the most thoughtless actions by city officials, a road from Bull Run—now High Street—was cut through the west end of the cemetery to Raleigh Road. Once the work was completed, remnants of headstones, coffins, human bones, and items that had been buried with the dead were scattered across the area. Realizing what they had done, workers quickly dug a pit and reburied everything they could find, including headstones that identified the dead.

A reporter covering the incident noted that as he walked through the cemetery, he observed another section destroyed by "cattle, horses and hogs," with coffin ends protruding from the ground and on the verge of falling into the street.[13]

J. A. Ham never forgot his Winchester Cemetery story. Around 1899, as he walked along the west side of the road, he noticed a group of excited boys gathered near its edge. Approaching the group, he discovered they had found the exposed end of a metal casket with a glass top. Brushing away dirt with their hands, they could make out a man staring back at them. When Ham approached, one boy exclaimed, "Mister, we found a dead man." Ham wrote, "I stopped, and getting on my knees and properly shading with my hat, I could plainly see the head and shoulders of what seemed to be a fair-complexioned, dark-haired man of 35 or less."[14]

Some descendants moved the remains of their loved ones to other cemeteries—if there was anything left to move. After Shelby County purchased St. Peter's Cemetery with plans to use the property for the Memphis Medical College, an attempt was made to transfer the two thousand bodies buried there to Calvary Cemetery. Some of those buried at St. Peter's had already been re-interred there after being moved from the Winchester Cemetery. Now, they would be moved a third time. In 1896, a reporter covering that project wrote:

> Quite a number of graves were opened yesterday, but in most instances only a piece or two of bone, a button or other metal surfaces, or pieces of the coffin were found. One lot containing the graves of two adults and four children did not yield enough to fill a half-peck measure. From the grave of one adult were taken half a dozen pieces of skull, two portions of jawbones, still retaining the teeth, and a knuckle or two from the larger bones.... The four children's graves contained no more remains than could be held in a man's two hands. Among the articles found were two screws from the coffin and a small metal cross.[15]

By 1923, the Winchester Cemetery was in a state of "solemn desolation and wholesale desecration," according to *Commercial Appeal* reporter Lucile Webb Banks, who wrote an article that appeared under the headline "Graves of Memphis Fathers Lost in the March of Time." Banks wrote, "It hurts one to the heart to see this forgotten 'God's Acre,' where in distant days many of Memphis' first citizens were tenderly and reverently laid to rest."[16]

While there were still some headstones and monuments in place, many had been toppled over and broken or lay buried under years of dirt. As Banks explored the cemetery, she saw pieces of rotting wooden fences and stone posts formerly used to designate family plots. By then, they were scattered around, no longer marking anything but the passage of time. Some headstones were broken into pieces and lay far from the graves they once marked. Others had been thrown into a ditch running alongside the cemetery. Mules and horses belonging to the city, used to pull carriages, had been allowed to trample the graves. Letting them freely graze was less expensive than paying men to care for the grass and weeds that grew there.

Banks hoped if her fellow Memphians got to know those who were laid to rest in the cemetery, they might be more inclined to take better care of it. She wrote:

> Bear in mind, there is much in the lives of many of these first citizens of Memphis all of us should be proud to recall. When the story of the achievements of some of them is related let us hope public interest will be sufficiently awakened to have steps taken to shield their grass-covered graves from further pitiless defacement and entire obliteration.[17]

She pointed out that one of the first burials to take place in the cemetery was that of Thomas Sterne Trask, a Navy lieutenant who was a graduate of the United States Military Academy at West Point. Soon after graduation, Trask married Louisa Clark and was stationed in Memphis. He died at twenty-four years old at Fort Pickering on August 1, 1828. Two months after he was laid to rest, his son, Thomas Sterne Trask Jr., was born.

Other early graves in the cemetery belonged to victims of the explosion of the *Helen McGregor* on February 24, 1830. The steamboat, traveling from New Orleans to Louisville, made a brief stop in Memphis before continuing upriver. Shortly after departing, one of its boilers suddenly exploded, causing a tragic scene on the crowded boiler deck. Of the around 400 passengers on board, more than 50 were killed, though the exact number remains uncertain, as many passengers were strangers traveling far from home. Some just never returned.

Most of the casualties occurred on the boiler deck, where passengers had gathered. This disaster marked one of the most severe incidents involving a steamboat boiler at that time, although such explosions were not uncommon. Most of the graves of the victims of the explosion of the *Helen McGregor* were never marked.

Time and Mother Nature came together to protect one of the headstones. Virginia Kirk died in 1845 when she was thirteen years old. Shortly after she was placed into the ground and dirt covered her coffin, an acorn that had fallen into the soil sprouted and began to grow. Somehow, a small tree grew there undisturbed as the cemetery slowly disintegrated around it. By the time Lucile Banks visited in 1923, the tiny acorn had become a giant oak tree that enveloped the young girl's headstone, keeping it in place and undamaged beyond a few cracks from the pressure of the tree growing around it.

Others buried in the cemetery included Benjamin Fooy, who had established the first settlement across the river; William Lawrence, who first arrived in Memphis alongside Marcus Winchester; Memphis historian J. P. Young's half-sister, Emma J. Young, who died at just twenty; Henry Van Pelt, editor of the *Memphis Appeal*, and his wife, Catherine; Thomas Phoebus, editor of the *Memphis Advocate and Western District Intelligencer*; Thomas Frederick

Lennox, who migrated to Memphis from Scotland; Maria Allen Eaton, sister of John Eaton, the Tennessee politician who made a name for himself in Andrew Jackson's administration with the Petticoat Affair; Jacob Farrington and his wife and daughter; William Hilliard, a steamboat captain killed when its boiler exploded; and Agnes Hawthorne.

Hawthorne, who returned to Memphis from Natchez after her husband's death, was a founder of Memphis's First Presbyterian Church. The matriarch of a large family of children, grandchildren, and great-grandchildren died of pneumonia in 1870 at ninety-three at her home on Pigeon Roost Road. Her obituary noted:

> She knew Memphis before it was a village, and has witnessed its growth "out of the wilderness." Here her children, grand-children, and great grand-children were born; and here many of them live, respected and beloved by a large circle, the members of which will no doubt follow her remains on Wednesday evening at 3 o'clock to Winchester Cemetery, where she will be laid to rest with her kindred. A mother in Israel, a good woman, a revered parent and friend, has fallen.[18]

Barbara and Charles Grimm were buried there. According to their headstone, they both were born in 1791 and died in 1849. Near the Grimms' final resting place stood a large monument marking the grave of Caroline Jane, who died in 1844 at eight months old. Under her name was inscribed the name of Thomas Cowley, a Memphian from the Isle of Man who died on September 3, 1851. He was likely Caroline's grandfather.[19]

James Davis, who was responsible for much of the myth around Marcus and Amarante Winchester, had family buried in the Winchester Cemetery. He wrote, "In it a daughter and three grandchildren are buried, and there I expect my bones to finally rest.... I have another lot in the same yard, in which are the remains of my father, mother, grandmother, and other relations, some of whom were buried over forty years ago."[20] When Davis died, he did join his family. He was buried at Elmwood Cemetery.

In her research, Memphis anthropologist Midge Gurley uncovered the story of Joseph Blackburn, a clown who was buried in Winchester Cemetery in 1841 after dying aboard a steamboat. His funeral drew mourners from two different circuses, who led a parade from downtown to his graveside. Music for the procession was provided by Stickney's New Orleans Band.[21]

These were just a few of the thousands of early Memphis settlers buried in the Winchester Cemetery. Lucile Banks's theory that knowing those buried there would lead to more people caring about the cemetery proved incorrect, although there were periods of time when it looked like the Winchester Cemetery might be saved.

The Old Folks Society, the group focused on the early history of Memphis, was indignant about the treatment of the final resting place of those who came before. They purchased the cemetery intending to care for and protect it for future generations. As they discovered, writing about the early settlers was a lot less expensive and much easier than taking care of their graves. After a few years—and several Founder's Day picnics on the grounds—they got out of the cemetery business and deeded it to the city.

In 1896, the Memphis city council passed an act that provided funds for the care and protection of the cemetery. It called for the clean-up of the entire area and provided funds to pay a Civil War veteran, Lieutenant James M. Cusack, to manage it. Cusack was dedicated, even sleeping in the cemetery. Sometimes he slept in the large round receiving vault or, if it was a nice night, outside under the large oak tree that was wrapped around the headstone of Virginia Kirk. In previous years, at night, the cemetery became a place where some of Memphis's "thieves, gamblers, and prostitutes" camped, but under Cusack's watch, the cemetery remained empty at night. A *Commercial Appeal* story about Cusack noted, "The lieutenant has a double-barreled shotgun, which he finds a wonderful persuader to induce wayward persons to keep off the grounds of nights."[22] Cusack died in 1907 and was buried at Calvary Cemetery.

Decades passed. Residents continued complaining about the condition of the cemetery, city leaders came and went, and each administration continued the debate about the best solution. Also, without Cusack on guard with his double-barreled shotgun, vandals continued to damage what remained. Meetings and protests were arranged, and lawsuits were filed. At times, some of those buried in the cemetery were moved to Elmwood and other burial spots in Memphis, but no records were kept to record how many or who. Lieutenant Thomas Sterne Trask, one of the first to be buried in the Winchester Burying Ground, was reinterred at the National Cemetery in 1882, more than fifty years after his death.

As with the graves at St. Peter's Cemetery, very little remained of the young soldier to move. The manager of the National Cemetery charged with moving Trask shared he was only able to find a few scraps of Trask's walnut coffin and a dozen rusty nails that crumbled in his hands.[23] Trask's son had died of consumption in 1851, and his wife had died in 1861. His grave was moved at the request of his nephew, also named Thomas Sterne Trask, the last of his living relatives.

Susan Winchester Powell Scales had continued to fight for the cemetery, but by 1931 she realized that the dream of a tended burial ground, with headstones marking each grave, was long gone; the best she could hope for was a clean, well-kept park. At seventy-nine years old, she told a reporter for the *Memphis Press-Scimitar*, "I pray to God each day that He grant me life long enough to see the park before I die. I want to see the monument of all the names on it of the known dead buried there." Scales and one of her daughters spent a day writing down the names still visible on the tombstones and came up with a list of only fifty.

One year earlier, Mayor Watkins Overton, the longest-serving mayor in the history of Memphis and the great-great-grandson of John Overton, had given the final approval to turn what had been the Winchester Cemetery into a park. He acknowledged it would be appropriate to create a large monument in the park and include the names of all who had been buried in the cemetery since the beginning. But, he explained, no such list existed.[24] Soon after Scales's interview, the ground at the cemetery was leveled, any remaining holes were filled in and most of the remaining headstones were placed in a pile and ground into dust. Scales lived to see the park—she died in 1954 at age 101—but a monument of names was never produced.

The loss of the graveyard of Memphis's long-forgotten early settlers is unfortunate. Cemeteries create a unique biography for a city using architecture, sculpture, nature, and poetry. The headstones that ended up in ditches, were toppled over by vagrants, or were ground down into dust told stories that will now be forgotten. Madge Gurley noted:

> Gravestones were purposely made to convey information to future generations. Markers were dated and associated with known individuals. Other information was also conveyed, such as family relationships, religious beliefs, occupations, economic status, and ethnic heritage.... The destruction of the Winchester Burying Ground has eliminated a great deal of valuable information about the early history of Memphis, Tennessee.[25]

In September 2024, attorneys representing the American Lebanese Syrian Associated Charities, Inc. (ALSAC), the fundraising and awareness organization for St. Jude Children's Research Hospital, sent a registered letter to the executive director of the Tennessee Historical Commission. The letter, required by Tennessee code to gain access to property formerly designated as a cemetery, acknowledged forty-five additional sites were discovered in the former Winchester Cemetery that were identified as containing "human remains, grave shafts, or grave goods." The letter also included a copy of a complaint filed in chancery court formally requesting the termination of the Winchester Cemetery's designation as a burial ground. The request was contingent upon the reinterment of any human remains at Elmwood Cemetery with appropriate memorials erected at the site of reinterment. Additionally, ALSAC sought permission to repurpose the areas previously containing human remains for St. Jude campus expansion projects, including the construction of a parking garage.[26] Approval will no doubt be granted. In truth, the site stopped serving as a memorial more than a century ago, as the cemetery slipped into neglect and decline with few efforts made to protect it.

It is a reminder that we should honor our ancestors and those who made significant contributions before us by preserving and dedicating the physical spaces that reflect their legacies. Naming buildings, streets, and public landmarks after those who came before keeps their contributions alive in the everyday lives of future generations. Museums, exhibits, statues, and interpretive plaques and panels—and old cemeteries—provide educational opportunities, allowing communities to engage with history in meaningful ways. Repurposing old structures, rather than demolishing them, maintains a tangible connection to the past while integrating history into the present. By thoughtfully maintaining and protecting these spaces, we create lasting tributes that encourage reflection, respect, and appreciation for those who paved the way before us.

There are also other reasons to remember the past. As part of his philosophical exploration in his five-volume book, *The Life of Reason*, George Santayana, the Spanish-American philosopher, poet, and essayist, wrote in 1905, "Those who cannot remember the past are condemned to repeat it,"[27] Santayana believed there is a cyclical nature to human behavior, and ignorance of past failures leads to their recurrence. At the time, Europe and America were undergoing significant social and political changes, and Santayana recognized patterns of history repeating due to complacency, short-term thinking, and a failure to apply historical lessons. His hypothesis has repeatedly been proven true. The devastation of World War II was fueled in part by the failure to address unresolved grievances from World War I and the Treaty of Versailles. The 2008 global financial crisis echoed many of the same speculative excesses and weak regulatory oversight that had contributed to the Great Depression of the 1930s. More recently, public health officials have drawn parallels between the COVID-19 pandemic and earlier outbreaks like the 1918 influenza pandemic, where inadequate preparation and resistance to public health measures exacerbated the spread of disease.

Each case illustrates how neglecting the lessons of history allows the same mistakes to resurface, often with equally costly consequences. The writer of an 1876 Memphis obituary acknowledged the temporary nature of every individual's time on earth when he wrote, "One by one the old citizens who have seen Memphis emerge from a village to a city have faded from the earth, until few are left, and they too must soon follow, for the scroll of life, no matter how dotted with the brilliancy of achievement, rolls up and withers with the touch of time."[28]

Thanks to archivists, researchers, librarians, historians, and writers who dedicate themselves to accurately preserving the past, these individuals who "faded from earth" have not entirely "withered with the touch of time." The words penned in notebooks, typed on typewriters, and composed on computers by individuals like Lucile Banks, Midge Gurley, James Davis, Perre Magness, Paul Coppick, Arthur Webb, James Roper, John Keating, James H. Malone, John Preston Young, G. Wayne Dowdy, and even Jesse, the "Scribe" have helped ensure that the stories of Marcus Winchester and the men and women who built Memphis and made it home remain for future generations to discover.

Chapter Twenty-six Endnotes

1. "Court Square Fountain," *Public Ledger*, May 29, 1876, 3.
2. *Public Ledger*, May 29, 1876, 4.
3. William Thomas, "Ex-mayor Made Mark, But Never Got Marker," *Commercial Appeal*, February 8, 1991, 14.
4. James H. Malone, "History of Early Land Grants for Public Purposes in Memphis," *The Commercial Appeal*, March 21, 1915, 12.
5. "Immense Sale of Town Lots in Hopefield, Arkansas," *Little Rock True Democrat*, March 16, 1859, 4.
6. Little Rock True Democrat, March 16, 1859, 4.
7. Little Rock True Democrat, March 16, 1859, 4.
8. Walter Veazey, "Hopefield Has Fought A Long But Losing Match," *Commercial Appeal*, June 6, 1965, 35.
9. "Mississippi Devours Once Thriving Town," *Cape Girardeau Morning Sun*, October 20, 1916, 3.
10. "Winchester Park to Fulfil Dream for Granddaughter of City's Founder," *Memphis Press-Scimitar*, 1931, 1.
11. Paul Coppock, "He Once Was Lost," *Commercial Appeal*, February 19, 1980, 7.
12. Coppock, *Commercial Appeal*, 8.
13. "Protect the Dead," *Memphis Public Ledger*, April 26, 1875, 3.
14. J. A. Ham, "Winchester Cemetery," *Commercial Appeal*, January 13, 1931, 6.
15. "Remains of Two Thousand," *Commercial Appeal*, Dec 13, 1896, 7.
16. Lucile Webb Banks, "Graves of Memphis Fathers Lost in the March of Time," *Commercial Appeal*, April 8, 1923, 27.
17. Banks, *Commercial Appeal*, 27.
18. *Memphis Daily Appeal*, September 30, 1870, 1.
19. Alice Redden James, "The Winchester Cemetery," *Commercial Appeal*, January 10, 1909, 52.
20. "An Old Main's Plaint," *The Memphis Daily Appeal*, March 2, 1873, 4.
21. Gurley, "Abandoned," 2.
22. "Rescue from a Vandal Resort," *Commercial Appeal*, August 04, 1896, 5.
23. "A Soldier's Grave," *Memphis Public Ledger*, November 22, 1882, 4.
24. "Order Plans for New City Park," *Commercial Appeal*, April 18, 1931, 3.
25. Gurley, "Abandoned," 15.
26. *American Lebanese Syrian Associated Charities v. All Unknown Parties Having Any Interest in the Property Known as Old Burial Ground in Memphis*, Petition to Terminate Dedication and Use of Property as a Burial Ground, Chancery Court of Tennessee for the Thirteenth Judicial District at Memphis, filed August 30, 2024.
27. George Santayana, *The Life of Reason: Reason in Common Sense* (New York: Charles Scribner's Sons, 1905), 284.

Acknowledgment

I was first introduced to Marcus and Amarante Winchester while researching the life of David Crockett. The couple came to Crockett's aid after a business venture in which "the King of the Wild Frontier" attempted to navigate freshly cut barrel staves down the Mississippi River. His two flatboats ended up at the bottom of the river, and Crockett ended up naked and stranded on Paddy's Hen and Chickens, then a group of sandbars just north of Memphis. A passing steamboat came to the rescue and delivered him to the Winchesters. Crockett and Marcus Winchester became close friends, and it was Winchester who was the last to bid Crockett farewell as he departed Tennessee and headed to Texas.

Of course, much has been written about Crockett, but very little has been published about Marcus Winchester—and even less about his wife, Amarante Loiselle.

That made even minor bits of information all the more valuable.

My deepest thanks go to the Library of Congress; the National Archives; the Historical Society of Carroll County in Westminster, Maryland; the Gilder Lehrman Institute of American History; the West Tennessee Historical Society and their archives of the West Tennessee Historical Society Papers; the Memphis and Shelby County Room of the Memphis Public Library and Information Center; the Pink Palace Museum and Mansion; the Tennessee State Library and Archives; and the Research Department at the Ned R. McWherter Library at the University of Memphis.

Without the assistance of the many librarians and archivists at these institutions, who so generously guided my search, this book would not have been possible. Ginger Hadley, a direct descendant of Marcus and Amarante

Acknowledgment

Winchester who still calls Memphis home was instrumental in providing research about the family. The enthusiasm, direction, and advice of James Rout III, Shelby County historian, were also greatly appreciated.

Much appreciation goes to the leadership and staff of Historic Castalian Springs and Cragfont Mansion, Travellers Rest Historic House Museum, and Andrew Jackson's Hermitage for their work in sharing Tennessee's early history with thousands of residents and visitors to Nashville each year.

I am indebted to Jennifer Wildes Hunter, who applied her incredible editing skills to turn the rough draft of this book into something readable, and to Tom Martin, who lent his artistic talents to creating the cover design. My daughters, Alex and Liv, have grown up to be excellent proofreaders and sounding boards, for which I am deeply grateful. And last—but by no means least—love and appreciation to my smart and beautiful wife, Michelle, who endured many research trips and discussions about antebellum society in the southern United States. She also graciously accommodated her husband's late nights and early mornings writing draft after draft of this book.

I can thank my grandfather, Guy Lovelace, for my earliest memories of downtown Memphis. Our trips to Court Square to feed the pigeons and squirrels when I was a child planted seeds that grew into a love for the city.

Finally, to all those who have written letters, journals, newspaper articles, and books about Memphis and Tennessee history: I could not have shined a light on Marcus and Amarante Winchester without those who recorded stories of the past. Thank you for leaving behind a trail I could follow. I hope that those who are inspired to revisit Memphis's past in the future will find a crumb or two here that they can follow as they share the stories of all those who came before.

Appendix One: About the Chapter Titles

Each chapter title is a nod to Memphis's connection to music history, particularly blues, gospel, and rock 'n' roll. The city's diverse cultural landscape served as a melting pot where styles converged, giving rise to music in genres of all kinds. Memphis is often hailed as the home of the blues and the birthplace of rock 'n' roll, with landmarks like Beale Street, The Memphis Rock 'n' Soul Museum, Graceland, Sun Studio, and STAX Records playing a pivotal role in reminding visitors around the world of its significant contribution to the entertainment industry.

Introduction: "Going to Memphis"
Fresh from the momentum of his Sun-Studio breakthrough, Johnny Cash refashioned folklorist Alan Lomax's Parchman Farm work-chant "I'm Going to Memphis" into a hard-driving tale of chain-gang laborers dreaming of the Bluff City. The single "Going to Memphis" was issued by Columbia in September 1960. The song kept Memphis imagery in Cash's work even after he had relocated most of his recording sessions to Nashville.

Part One

Chapter One: "All American Boy"
Bobby Bare's talking-blues novelty "All American Boy" recorded as a Fraternity Records demo, was inspired by Elvis Presley's meteoric rise and 1958 Army draft. The single was issued under pal Bill Parsons's name and shot to number two on the U.S. pop chart, proving how strongly Presley's Memphis story gripped late-'50s pop culture.

Chapter Two: "Baby Let's Play House"
Elvis Presley took Arthur Gunter's 1954 blues tune and cut a rockabilly version of "Baby Let's Play House" in 1955 at Sam Phillips's Sun Studio. The song was recorded with Scotty Moore on guitar and Bill Black on bass. Presley's ad-libbed line about a "pink Cadillac" freshened the song's salacious call to "play house," or move in together. The single became Presley's first national hit, exporting the raw Memphis sound coast-to-coast.

Chapter Three: "We the People"
Booker T. Jones and Carl Smith wrote "We the People" as an empowerment

anthem for The Staple Singers's Stax breakthrough LP *Be Altitude: Respect Yourself*, released in February 1972. The track was cut during the album sessions split between Ardent Studios in Memphis and Muscle Shoals Sound Studios in Alabama. Stax executive Al Bell produced it and the famed Memphis Horns added their unique brass sound. Its refrain, "We the people, got to make the world go 'round," kept the group's civil rights message front-and-center even as their sound broadened beyond Memphis.

Chapter Four: "Good Morning Baltimore"

The first national tour of *Hairspray* played Memphis's Orpheum Theater early December 2004. Playing the role of Tracy Turnblad, Keala Settle, who later gained national fame in *The Greatest Showman*, performed "Good Morning Baltimore" in the opening number of that tour. The Orpheum Theater opened as the Grand Opera House in 1890 and joined the Orpheum vaudeville circuit in 1907. After it was destroyed by fire in 1923, a grand 2,300-seat replacement opened in November 1928, swiftly becoming Memphis's showcase movie and stage palace. Threatened with demolition decades later, it was rescued by the Memphis Development Foundation in 1977. The theater was closed for major restoration in 1982 and triumphantly reopened as the Orpheum Theater in January 1984, becoming the city's home for Broadway tours and concerts.

Chapter Five: "Trouble, Heartaches & Sadness"

Co-written by Ann Peebles and Don Bryant, "Trouble, Heartaches & Sadness" asks, "Trouble, heartaches, and sadness, why you always gotta knock on my door?" Willie Mitchell produced it at Royal Studios in Memphis with the Hi Rhythm Section. The song anchored Peebles's album *Straight from the Heart*.

Chapter Six: "Big River"

Johnny Cash wrote "Big River," a driving rockabilly tale of chasing a runaway lover "from St. Paul, Minnesota" down past Memphis to New Orleans. He cut it at Sam Phillips's Sun Studio in October 1957 with his Tennessee Two—Luther Perkins on guitar and Marshall Grant on slap bass. Released January 1958 as the flip side of "Ballad of a Teenage Queen," it climbed to number four on Billboard's country chart, spreading the raw Memphis Sun sound nationwide.

Chapter Seven: "Hello Memphis"

Arkansas-born rockabilly firebrand Sonny Burgess, one of Sam Phillips's original Sun stars, cut "Hello Memphis" during a 1985 session at Granny's Studio in Fulham, London; it appeared the next year on his LP *Raw Deal*. The lyric's opening line, "Hello Memphis, goodbye Birmingham," is a shout-out to

Memphis, the city that launched his career in 1956 at Sun Studio. The track is a heartfelt postcard from a Sun alumnus celebrating the city's rock-and-roll roots.

Part Two

Chapter Eight: "Chickasaw Special"

Harmonica ace Noah Lewis, a mainstay of Cannon's Jug Stompers, cut this train-imitating instrumental in Memphis on October 2, 1929, during Victor's field sessions at the Peabody Hotel. Released as "Chickasaw Special," it refers to the Illinois Central's *The Chickasaw* passenger train that linked St. Louis and Memphis. The take, solo harp over jug-band rhythm, remains one of the earliest to put the word "Chickasaw" on a recording.

Chapter Nine: "Memphis Blues"

Beale-Street bandleader W. C. Handy self-published "Memphis Blues," a rag-flavored 12-bar instrumental, in September 1912. It was adapted from his 1909 campaign tune "Mr. Crump," written for Memphis power-broker E. H. Crump. Bottling the sound Handy heard in Black dance halls along Beale Street, it is widely regarded as the first commercially successful blues sheet-music hit.

Chapter Ten: "Walking in Memphis"

Ohio-born singer-songwriter Marc Cohn wrote "Walking in Memphis" after a 1985 pilgrimage to Memphis where he soaked up Rev. Al Green's church, Graceland, Beale Street, and the W. C. Handy statue. Produced by Cohn and Ben Wisch for Cohn's debut album *Marc Cohn*, the piano-driven track evokes a Memphis vibe with lines like "Walking with my feet ten feet off of Beale." Issued March 1991, it became Cohn's signature hit reaching number thirteen on the Billboard Hot 100 and earning a Grammy Song-of-the-Year nomination the same year Cohn won Best New Artist.

Chapter Eleven: "Changes Comin' On"

Written by Buddy Cannon, Dean Dillon, and Jimmy Darrell, "Changes Comin' On" was cut at Nashville's Music Mill for Alabama's five-times-platinum LP *Mountain Music*. The song touches on 1960-70s milestones like Ford's Mustang, Vietnam, and Dr. King's dream before landing on its key Memphis line: "In Memphis, Tennessee, the King is gone," a nod to Elvis Presley's death in 1977.

Chapter Twelve: "Considering a Move to Memphis"

"Considering a Move to Memphis" was written by Rochester, New York, bandleader Chuck Cuminale (Colorblind James) and recorded for the group's self-titled debut LP *The Colorblind James Experience* in 1987. The lyric lists local Memphis landmarks, Graceland and Beale Street, and pledges to "shake hands with Gus Cannon," the iconic jug-band musician, presenting Memphis as a place of musical pilgrimage.

Chapter Thirteen: "That's How I Got to Memphis"
Country singer-songwriter Tom T. Hall wrote "That's How I Got to Memphis." Bobby Bare recorded the song in Nashville with producer Jerry Kennedy and released it as the single "How I Got to Memphis" on the Mercury label in August 1970. The lyric follows a man who travels to Memphis in search of a lost lover. The record spent sixteen weeks on Billboard's Hot Country Singles chart, peaking at number three in the week ending October 31, 1970.

Chapter Fourteen: "Memphis Bound Blues"
Ma Rainey and Her Georgia Band recorded "Memphis Bound Blues" in Chicago in August 1925. In the song, written by pianist-composer Thomas "Georgia Tom" Dorsey, Rainey sings about catching the train "down to Memphis" to reunite with her man. Paramount issued it that November as the B-side to "Rough and Tumble Blues." It is one of the earliest blues records to call Memphis by name, signaling the city's growing allure for musicians in the 1920s.

Chapter Fifteen: "Anywhere But Memphis"
Mark Wills recorded "Anywhere but Memphis" in Nashville for his platinum album *Wish You Were Here* in 1998. Written by Monty Criswell, Tony Martin, and Wills, the song opens with the narrator phoning his lover "from a pay phone down on Beale Street," only to admit that Memphis's ever-present blues intensify his heartache; he would rather be "anywhere but Memphis."

Part Three

Chapter Sixteen: "Tired of Being Alone"
Al Green wrote "Tired of Being Alone" and first cut it at producer Willie Mitchell's Royal Recording Studio in Memphis in late 1969. Mitchell shelved the take because the arrangement did not satisfy him. Green re-recorded the song at the same studio in early 1971, and Hi Records issued that version as a single in August 1971. Opening Green's 1971 album *Al Green Gets Next to You*, the track, driven by the Hi Rhythm Section's spare groove and Green's soaring falsetto, reached number seven on *Billboard's* R&B chart and number eleven on the Hot 100.

Chapter Seventeen: "I Am Somebody"

"I Am Somebody" was cut for Memphis-based Stax Records at its Studio A with producer Don Davis. The song turns Rev. Jesse Jackson's civil-rights chant, "I am somebody!," into a hard-grooving demand for dignity and the end of second-class treatment. Issued in September 1970, just two-and-a-half years after Dr. King's assassination in Memphis, the record climbed to number four for R&B and number thirty-nine for pop on Billboard's singles charts.

Chapter Eighteen: "Soul Man"

Isaac Hayes and David Porter, major Memphis hitmakers, penned "Soul Man" after the 1967 Detroit riots. The chorus's proud "I'm a soul man" is used to embrace African American identity as a badge of strength and resilience. The song was recorded by Sam Moore and Dave Prater and recorded at Stax Records. It was backed by Booker T. & the M.G.'s with Isaac Hayes and David Porter producing.

Chapter Nineteen: "Memphis in the Meantime"

John Hiatt wrote and recorded "Memphis in the Meantime" during a four-day session in February 1987 at Ocean Way Studio 2 in Hollywood. Produced by John Chelew and issued in May 1987 on Hiatt's LP *Bring the Family*. The lyric rejects slick Los Angeles polish in favor of Memphis rhythm and "a decent meal down at the Rendezvous." Although never released as a U.S. single, the cut became a concert staple and an enduring salute to Memphis's musical grit.

Chapter Twenty: "Memphis Money"

Connecticut singer-songwriter Richard Ferreira co-wrote "Memphis Money" with Nashville writer Mark Irwin and released it on his album *Somewhereville* in October 2002. The song's title frames Memphis as the place where a hustler expects to strike it rich and return home "rolling in Memphis money."

Chapter Twenty-one: "Born Under a Bad Sign"

Written by William Bell and Booker T. Jones, the song was recorded in May 1967 at Stax Studio. Booker T. & the M.G.'s and the Memphis Horns backed Albert King's signature Gibson Flying V. Released that summer as a single and as the title track of King's album *Born Under a Bad Sign*, it reached number forty-nine on Billboard's R&B chart and became a blues standard recorded by dozens of rock acts.

Chapter Twenty-two: "Love and Happiness"

Co-written by Al Green and Teenie Hodges, "Love and Happiness" was cut at Willie Mitchell's Royal Recording Studios during the 1972 sessions for *I'm Still in Love with You*. Mitchell produced with the Hi Rhythm Section, providing its signature groove. Released in the U.K. by London Records in April 1973 and later by Hi Records in the U.S. in the summer of 1977, the edited single reached number 104 on *Billboard*'s pop chart and number 92 on its R&B chart. The song's blend of gospel-inflected warmth and secular grit made it a soul classic—*Rolling Stone* placed it at number ninety-eight on its "500 Greatest Songs of All Time."

Chapter Twenty-three: "Berry Rides Again"

Steppenwolf's "Berry Rides Again" was cut in the fall of 1967 at American Recording in Studio City, California, and produced by Gabriel Mekler. It was issued as part of the band's self-titled debut album on January 29, 1968. Written by frontman John Kay, the track's driving guitar riffs and propulsive rhythm deliberately invoke Chuck Berry's pioneering style, offering both homage and continuation of Berry's rock-and-roll legacy. The lyrics include, "I left there in the mornin' and went back to Memphis, Tennessee."

Chapter Twenty-four: From "Graceland to the Promised Land"

Merle Haggard wrote and recorded "From Graceland to the Promised Land" as the sole single from his tribute album *My Farewell to Elvis*, issued October 3, 1977, on MCA Records. Produced by Fuzzy Owen, the song frames Elvis Presley's death at Graceland as a journey to the "Promised Land," blending country melody with gospel-tinged imagery. Released immediately after Presley's death, it climbed to number four on Billboard's Hot Country Singles chart, underscoring Haggard's role in honoring the legacy of the King of Rock 'n' Roll.

Chapter Twenty-five: "Trying to Live My Life Without You"

"Tryin' to Live My Life Without You" was written by Eugene Frank Williams and cut by soul singer Otis Clay at Royal Recording Studios in Memphis for Hi Records, with Willie Mitchell producing. Issued in December 1972, the record climbed to number 24 on Billboard's Hot Soul Singles chart and number 102 on the Bubbling Under chart in early 1973.

Chapter Twenty-six: "I Forgot to Remember to Forget"

Written by Stan Kesler and Charlie Feathers, the song was recorded by Elvis Presley on July 11, 1955, at Sam Phillips's Sun Studio in Memphis. The recording was backed by Scotty Moore on guitar, Bill Black on bass, and Johnny Bernero on drums, with Phillips producing. It was released August 20, 1955, as the flip side of "Mystery Train." It became Presley's first national number one, topping *Billboard*'s country charts in February 1956.

Appendix Two: Winchester Cemetery Records

The burial ground established in Memphis by Marcus Winchester after the death of his father in 1828 is referred to in newspaper articles, historical documents, and records as the New Winchester Burying Ground, Winchester Cemetery, and the Old Winchester Cemetery. The last burial there was in 1874.

The following names are included in the list of those buried in the Winchester Cemetery in the Find a Grave database as of August 2025.

Although Find a Grave is a crowd-sourced platform, it has become the single most comprehensive and readily accessible catalogue of interments for many historic cemeteries, including this one. However, every entry should be treated as a pointer rather than as an unquestioned fact.

William H. Abbott
unknown – 26 Feb 1856

William S. Abernathy
1829 – 24 Oct 1850

Henry S. Adair
unknown – 23 Oct 1865

Nancy Adair
unknown – 25 Oct 1869

Thomas Adair
unknown – 27 Nov 1866

Ann E. Adams
unknown – 7 Jun 1845

West Adams
1823 – 11 Oct 1867

Baby Aiken
Oct 1868 – 28 Nov 1868

Joel Akin
unknown – 15 Jun 1847

Martha M. Akin
unknown – 12 Jan 1851

Henry Alexander
unknown – 29 Dec 1847

James H. Alexander
unknown – 1849

James W. Alexander
1813 – 21 Feb 1846

Jesse Alexander
unknown – Oct 1845

Rebecca Ann Alexander
unknown – 5 Feb 1855

Child Allen
1869 – 26 Dec 1870

J. A. Allen
Jun 1855 – Jun 1855

Walter Allen
unknown – 13 Dec 1869

William F Allen
29 Feb 1808 – 28 Aug 1852

William S Allen
unknown – 28 Aug 1816

Henry W. Anderson
unknown – 21 Jun 1849

John Anderson
unknown – 9 Jun 1854

Thomas Andrews
unknown – 29 Aug 1866

Infant Apperson
Jul 1847 – 16 May 1848

Cora Armour
1848 – 25 Jul 1867

Willis Armour
unknown – 3 Jul 1867

Roberts Arters
1830 – 1 Jan 1849

E. E. Atkinson
unknown – 2 Oct 1865

Marie L Atkinson
unknown – 29 Sep 1850

Stephen B. Atkinson
unknown – 29 May 1855

Ann Greene Atwood
unknown – 16 Sep 1828

Infant Avery
Apr 1848 – 8 May 1848

John Avery
unknown – 8 Dec 1848

Dr. Nathan Avery
8 May 1792 – 5 Mar 1846

Rebecca Jones Rivers Avery
28 May 1793 – 30 May 1847

Charles W. Baccus
unknown – 7 Oct 1864

Harried N. Miller Badger
1826 – 19 Feb 1866

Annie Francis Bailey
unknown – 1 Sep 1868

Catherine Gwynne Bailey
1833 – 15 Jul 1876

Infant Bailey
2 Feb 1866 – 12 Feb 1866

Dr William T. Bailey
1826 – 7 Jul 1868

CPT Baker
1813 – 14 Jun 1858

James H. Bargar
unknown – 7 Feb 1852

Pricilla Barker
unknown – 29 Aug 1843

John l. Barnard
1856 – 26 Nov 1867

Nancy A. Barrow
unknown – 31 Mar 1867

Amelia Barry
unknown – 24 Jan 1867

Charles Barry
1848 – 8 Jun 1851

Martha Howell Adams Barry
3 Nov 1796 – 7 May 1845

Mary H. Barry
unknown – 8 May 1845

Valentine Derry Barry
1 Aug 1794 – 28 Apr 1853

William Bayliss
unknown – 7 Mar 1869

Edward Page Beadle
6 Sep 1808 – 24 Feb 1830

Elizabeth Ann Beattie
unknown – 24 Apr 1844

James Maryo Beatty
1831 – 22 Mar 1839

Child Beck
1845 – 10 Oct 1848

Delia D. Beck
unknown – 1 Oct 1848

Nancy Ann Bell
unknown – 1850

William Bellamy
unknown – 20 Nov 1852

Amelia Bender
unknown – 28 Aug 1861

Children Bender
1853 – 1856

John Bender
1810 – 21 Mar 1856

G. W. Benton
unknown – 10 Mar 1869

Henry Berger
unknown – 24 Aug 1869

Appendix Two: Winchester Cemetery Records

Mary W. Berryman
unknown – 14 Mar 1844

Alexander Betz
1843 – 14 Jun 1858

George Betz
unknown – 13 Jun 1858

J. P. Betz
1818 – 13 Jun 1858

Philip Betz
unknown – 13 Jun 1858

Willie Robert Jackson Bevan
unknown – 11 Sep 1870

Mary Jane Gatewood Bias
19 Jun 1814 – 1 May 1849

Joseph Biddluph
14 Feb 1807 – 11 Dec 1863

James Bishop
unknown – 7 May 1845

LTC William Wallace Bishop
28 Dec 1805 – 5 Feb 1865

Infant Black
unknown – 12 Jul 1870

Margaret Black
unknown – 8 May 1848

Joseph "Gentleman Joe" Blackburn
1809 – 26 Mar 1842

James Bledso
unknown – 24 Feb 1830

John Bley
unknown – 18 Feb 1863

Nicholas Block
unknown – 8 Oct 1863

Stephen Bond
unknown – Jul 1867

James B. Bone
unknown – 7 Mar 1853

Katie Boone
Jan 1874 – 15 Jul 1874

Thomas Booth
unknown – 14 Apr 1849

Elizabeth Buck "Eliza" Hart Borland
unknown – Jun 1840

Huldah G Wright Borland
1809 – 25 Aug 1837

John Green Bostick
30 Jun 1784 – Apr 1857

Mary Elizabeth Key Bostick
23 Oct 1784 – 11 Apr 1854

William E. Boswell
Birth and death dates unknown.

A. Bowen
unknown – 7 Feb 1870

Sammy Bowen
unknown – 21 Dec 1850

W. P. Bowers
Birth and death dates unknown.

Alfred P. Box
unknown – 17 Aug 1866

Peter Boyd
1821 – 9 Aug 1866

Bradshaw
unknown – 4 Mar 1870

Joseph Bradshaw
unknown – 20 Aug 1855

Nancy Bradshaw
unknown – 25 Jun 1850

William Bradshaw
1858 – 4 Nov 1867

Silas Braham
unknown – 9 May 1846

Infant Brassel
unknown – 5 Sep 1869

Solomon Breckinridge
1816 – 16 May 1841

Sebastian Brenner
unknown – 8 Apr 1860

Julia Brinkley
unknown – 4 May 1870

Jennie G. Brisbin
unknown – 31 Aug 1866

Sarah Brisbin
1832 – 26 Nov 1848

D. Brock
unknown – 22 May 1866

Mary Brock
unknown – 8 Jul 1867

E. V. Brooks
Jun 1863 – 3 Sep 1868

William F. Brotherline
26 Jul 1814 – 1 Feb 1852

Baby Brown
Dec 1846 – 22 Jun 1848

Jennie Brown
18 Aug 1861 – 29 May 1862

M. Brown
1840 – 15 Aug 1857

Rich P. Brown
unknown – 6 Oct 1856

H. L. Browning
1818 – 22 Apr 1858

John Bruce
Birth and death dates unknown.

Elizabeth Bruns
unknown – 7 Jan 1851

Fred Bruns
unknown – 5 Dec 1850

George Bruns
unknown – 3 Dec 1850

John F. Bruns
unknown – 10 Nov 1851

Joseph Bruns
unknown – Mar 1847

Thomas Bryant
1798 – 4 Sep 1848

Jane Buck
unknown – 25 Sep 1843

Silas Buck
unknown – 1867

M. Burnett
1806 – 20 Jan 1866

Wiley Burnett
1822 – 6 Sep 1850

Patrick Cain
1815 – 15 Oct 1850

John H. Campbell
1823 – 13 Jun 1858

Mary Campbell
Birth and death dates unknown.

Benjamin Henry Capps
12 Jan 1818 – 13 Jan 1870

Virginia F. Capps
unknown – 8 Feb 1867

Frank Y. Carlyle
1811 – 17 Feb 1866

Willie Carmichael
Jul 1872 – 29 Sep 1874

Carr
Birth and death dates unknown.

John Hudson Carr
unknown – 19 Jul 1849

Pitt Carr
1839 – 6 Jan 1866

Carroll
unknown – 23 Aug 1869

Peter Carroll
1814 – 13 Mar 1866

Male Carrot
unknown – 24 Feb 1830

S. Carson
unknown – 1 Oct 1855

Henry F. Carter
unknown – 6 Jul 1842

Jeff Cartwright
unknown – 27 Dec 1869

Angeline Cash
1873 – 7 Aug 1874

Susan A. Fleshart Causey
1827 – Mar 1850

William C. Causey
1817 – unknown

Dr Nathaniel Chaffee
unknown – 7 Nov 1864

Chandler
unknown – 8 Nov 1869

David H. Chapman
1838 – 28 Jul 1867

Florence Chapman
10 May 1866 – 25 Sep 1867

W. E. Chester
unknown – Apr 1841

Lizzie M. Chiles
unknown – 1864

Choate
unknown – 6 Aug 1862

Mary Bailey Christian
unknown – 17 Jul 1847

Dr Wyatt Christian
1799 – 15 Sep 1846

Sarah Church
Birth and death dates unknown.

Sallie C. Partee Clay
unknown – 1867

Appendix Two, Winchester Cemetery Records

Anthony Clopton
Dec 1875 – 23 Apr 1878

James W. Clopton
unknown – 29 Jul 1842

S. Ross Clopton
unknown – 1875

Infant Cobb
unknown – 13 Sep 1867

Jane Elizabeth Cobb
6 Dec 1810 – 6 May 1833

William Cobb
unknown – 13 May 1836

Mary E Haralson Cocke
1825 – 10 Jul 1846

Baby Cockrell
Dec 1846 – 19 Jun 1848

Rosa Cole
1843 – 2 Nov 1868

Louisa Coleman
unknown – 21 Mar 1870

Pamela Collier
1818 – 21 Dec 1858

S. Collier
unknown – 1 Apr 1869

J. C. Collins
unknown – 15 Feb 1847

Priscilla W. Collins
unknown – 9 Oct 1850

Louise Comstock
1847 – 15 Dec 1865

Mary Conden
unknown – 23 May 1869

Tinsly Connell
unknown – 25 Jun 1825

W. J. Connor
unknown – 7 Aug 1860

William B. Connor
1822 – 17 Jul 1848

John Cook
unknown – 11 Mar 1845

Marcus Cook
unknown – 4 May 1845

Mary Cook
unknown – 18 Jan 1867

Richard S. Cook
Birth and death dates unknown.

Robert Cook
7 May 1838 – 14 Dec 1844

Joseph Coones
unknown – 22 Apr 1868

Thomas Coontz
1829 – 31 Dec 1848

Bettie Cornwell
unknown – 11 Jan 1856

Abraham Allen Cos
1812 – 16 Jul 1869

Mary Alcorn Cowden
1 Apr 1757 – 1841

Caroline Jane Cowley
Nov 1843 – 11 Jul 1844

Thomas Cowley
1776 – 3 Sep 1851

Thomas Cowperthwait
unknown – 1 Jun 1859

Euphemia Theresa Cox
unknown – 1 Apr 1842

J. N. Craft
unknown – 15 Nov 1849

John B. Creed
unknown – 6 Feb 1864

Sarah F. "Sallie" Lewis Crockett
Jan 1836 – 14 Feb 1856

Crosson
unknown – 4 Jun 1870

John Crowell
1836 – 25 Apr 1867

Child Cubbins
Apr 1850 – 20 Jul 1851

Mary Ann Cubbins
Jan 1849 – 15 Sep 1850

R. Cubbins
unknown – 22 May 1851

Frank P. Cummings
1838 – 20 Sep 1866

Child Cuneo
unknown – 14 Nov 1867

Nancy Jane Currin
1786 – 1 Nov 1850

Silas Curtis
1845 – 23 Sep 1866

Mary Catherine Dacus
1825 – 3 Oct 1852

Milbre Dalton
unknown – 18 Dec 1862

James A Daniel
unknown – 17 Mar 1861

Robert Saule Daniel
1845 – 30 Jan 1855

Infant Daugherty
unknown – 5 Apr 1860

William L. Daugherty
1831 – 14 Aug 1855

Dardy Davenport
1788 – 14 Aug 1878

Elizabeth L. "Lizzie" Coates Davenport
1807 – 1880

John C. Davenport
1804 – 26 Nov 1855

William Walton Davidson
1832 – 12 Jun 1869

Archa Davis
1839 – 25 Apr 1870

Daughter Davis
Birth and death dates unknown.

Dr. Eli Simon Davis
1784 – 1849

Jane Davis
unknown – 10 Jun 1854

June Davis
1792 – 9 Jul 1834

Child Dayton
Nov 1846 – 26 Jun 1848

Emanuel DeGeneres
1848 – 13 Jun 1858

John Delaney
unknown – 24 Feb 1830

L. E. Dennis
1840 – 1 May 1870

Mary Devine
1812 – 1865

Mary Sidney Diamond
unknown – 14 Jul 1853

J. "Mother" Dick
Birth and death dates unknown.

Ben Dickerson
unknown – 29 Aug 1867

Infant Doll
Jul 1858 – 30 Dec 1858

Louise Doll
Birth and death dates unknown.

James Dorris
10 Sep 1826 – 13 Jun 1858

Samuel Douglass
unknown – Sep 1829

Camilla F. DuBose
unknown – Jan 1867

Henry R. Dunn
1840 – 2 May 1866

J. Dunn
unknown – 24 Feb 1830

Josephine Boharnais Dunn
1844 – 22 Dec 1845

A. Dunscomb
unknown – 14 Jun 1870

Asa Purnell Dupuy
1833 – 6 Apr 1862

Oliver Everett Durivage
1814 – 21 Feb 1861

Maria Allen Eaton
5 Aug 1797 – 18 Jul 1832

Christine Eckerle
unknown – 19 Aug 1863

Daniel Eckerle
unknown – Dec 1861

Emma Eddy
unknown – 28 Nov 1861

Rebecca Edgar
unknown – 11 Nov 1845

Infant Edgerly
Dec 1847 – 15 Jun 1848

Charles Edwards
Birth and death dates unknown.

Archie Elam
Birth and death dates unknown.

Ann Elliot
unknown – 10 Aug 1867

Ann T. Elliot
unknown – 24 Apr 1854

Elizabeth Elliot
unknown – 30 Apr 1854

Nicholas Elliot
1804 – 4 Jan 1849

William Elliot Sr.
unknown – 26 Nov 1845

Benjamin Enloe
Oct 1856 – 28 Dec 1856

Joan Enloe
unknown – 9 Apr 1856

Appendix Two: Winchester Cemetery Records

Child Epps
unknown – 10 Jul 1866

Joseph "French Joe" Etchevarne
1817 – 27 Jul 1866

Darius Durham Evans
Birth and death dates unknown.

George Evans
unknown – 21 Nov 1866

William Ewing
unknown – 24 Feb 1830

William Ezell
27 Jan 1817 – 9 Jul 1866

Infant Falls
24 Dec 1868 – 24 Dec 1868

Infant Falls
Mar 1866 – 13 Apr 1866

Child Farrington
1835 – 12 Jun 1848

Emma McGehee Farrington
unknown – 12 Nov 1847]

Gen Jacob F. Farrington
May 1812 – 28 Jan 1851

Madison J. Farrington
1829 – 15 Jun 1863

Grace Farris
unknown – 24 Sep 1850

John Farris
unknown – 12 Aug 1850

John A. Farrow
1812 – 23 Jul 1866

Mary Ann Patterson Faucette
1 Mar 1813 – 11 Apr 1844

Robert A. Feeney
unknown – 23 Sep 1823

Dewis Felts
unknown – 20 Jan 1872

James E. Felts
1812 – 29 Jun 1866

E. T. Ferguson
unknown – 17 Aug 1866

Jennie Field
Birth and death dates unknown.

Cora Fields
unknown – 30 Aug 1866

Erastus Fillington
unknown – 7 Aug 1853

Frances M. Fisher
unknown – 7 Sep 1838

Wesley Fisher
unknown – 27 Oct 1870

William H. Flesheart
1840 – 17 Nov 1866

Dolly Flint
unknown – 19 Dec 1866

Noble Bruce Ford
unknown – 19 Feb 1866

Thomas Ford
1833 – 24 Feb 1866

Mary Foster
unknown – 5 Jan 1841

S. R. Foster
unknown – 4 Feb 1870

Granville Fowler
1826 – 1 Oct 1861

Infant Fowler
30 Mar 1860 – 2 Apr 1860

Unknown Name Fowler
unknown – 28 Aug 1850

Dr Jeptha Fowlkes
1808 – 2 Jan 1864

Joseph Lee Fox
Jul 1865 – 12 Jan 1866

Annie Frank
1864 – 19 May 1872

Ida Frank
1870 – 18 May 1872

Joseph Frank
unknown – 26 Aug 1849

Josephina Frank
unknown – 26 Jan 1850

Meenie Frank
1859 – 19 May 1872

Paul Frank
1862 – 19 May 1872

George W. Frazer
unknown – 18 Jul 1867

Francis French
1800 – 8 May 1848

Emma Frey
unknown – 27 Jan 1857

William Frey
unknown – 30 May 1864

Dora Fritz
unknown – 20 Jul 1869

William Fritz
unknown – 11 Sep 1870

M. Frymaire
unknown – 29 May 1867

Child Fuller
unknown – 30 Aug 1869

Child Ganter
unknown – 4 Oct 1867

Wade Garrett
unknown – 26 Sep 1866

Sarah Elizabeth Garrison
1838 – 26 Oct 1841

William B. S. Garrison
1813 – 1 Jan 1849

Adaline Gates
unknown – 9 Sep 1866

Lebitha F. Gates
unknown – 13 Sep 1866

Jane Warwick Gatewood
27 Apr 1779 – 27 Jul 1839

Mary Gatewood
25 May 1779 – 27 Dec 1838

Ida George
unknown – 13 Jun 1867

Willie Getz
unknown – 1 Sep 1866

A. D. Gibbs
unknown – 19 Dec 1853

Isabella Gibbs
unknown – 27 Feb 1845

Julia Gibbs
unknown – 9 Aug 1860

Mary Palmer Gibbs
unknown – 7 Jul 1860

Catherine Fowlkes Gibson
unknown – Sep 1846

Katharine J. Van Pelt Gibson
unknown – 1 Sep 1846

Martha Ann Mitchell Gibson
unknown – 13 May 1845

Mary Albe Able Gibson
unknown – 30 Apr 1850

Sarah Gibson
unknown – 23 Aug 1857

G. B. Giles
unknown – 24 Feb 1830

John Gleary
1820 – 12 Oct 1850

Patrick Gleary
1820 – 12 Oct 1850

Archibald M. Glenn
28 Feb 1833 – 20 Apr 1867

A. Goad
unknown – 31 Jan 1870

Nancy Goad
unknown – 17 Jun 1870

Ephraim Goble
unknown – 24 Feb 1830

Anne E. Goddard
unknown – 3 Sep 1847

Child Godsey
unknown – 12 Oct 1867

Emmons Godsey
1826 – Jun 1873

Sam L. Godwin
unknown – 1 Feb 1849

Sons Goldsmith
unknown – 11 Jan 1844

Elizabeth Sibley Goode
1835 – 17 Jan 1861

M. A. Gorman
1872 – 15 Aug 1874

Sophia Amanda Graham
unknown – 7 Jan 1861

Cpl. William A.H. Graham
11 May 1839 – Dec 1864

Amanda Grahan
unknown – 9 Nov 1845

Philip Graner
1823 – 13 Jun 1858

Louis Grau
unknown – 1866

William Graves
unknown – Nov 1844

Dr George C. Gray
unknown – 19 Sep 1866

Maria Gray
1818 – 10 Sep 1866

Baby Gridley
13 Nov 1854 – 14 Nov 1854

Child Gridley
1847 – 13 Oct 1852

Appendix Two, Winchester Cemetery Records

Child Gridley
1850 – 13 Oct 1852

Mary Gridley
1818 – 29 Jul 1856

Mary E. Griffin
1861 – 30 Aug 1867

Sally R. Griffin
May 1874 – 9 Nov 1874

Barbara Grimes
1791 – 1849

Charles Grimes
unknown – 1849

Charles Grimm
1786 – 30 Dec 1851

James Grundy
unknown – 9 Sep 1870

Child Gumbinger
unknown – 8 Jan 1870

Infant Gusmani
unknown – 30 Jul 1867

Henrietta Luscher Gutherz
1820 – 15 Jul 1870

Parmelia Gwynne
unknown – 20 Mar 1851

Cora Haisten
unknown – 13 Oct 1868

Thomas S. Haisten
1838 – 20 Aug 1866

Gideon E. Hallett
1810 – 23 Oct 1840

Robert H. Hamilton
unknown – 12 Jul 1831

Child Hampe
unknown – 8 Nov 1867

Richard Hancock
unknown – 24 Feb 1830

John Hanke
1838 – 12 Dec 1866

Elisha Hanlan
unknown – 4 Oct 1857

Greene D. Haralson
1828 – 22 Mar 1850

Catherine Jane "Kate" Hardaway
unknown – 27 Jan 1845

James Paine Hardaway
1799 – 23 Jul 1846

John Paine Hardaway
unknown – Mar 1849

Lemuel Paine Hardaway
1814 – 1849

Edith Hardin
1800 – 19 Nov 1853

Francis Hardin
1852 – 22 Jun 1867

Alfred Hardy
unknown – 9 Jun 1863

Samuel P. Hardy
unknown – 9 Nov 1866

William F. Hardy
unknown – 3 Jul 1863

John Harris
unknown – 20 Aug 1866

Emma Harrison
unknown – 24 Jul 1868

Edwin A. Harsson
1819 – 1868

Eliza A. Harsson
unknown – 1868

William Harsson
unknown – 1868

Royal G. Hart
unknown – 10 Sep 1839

Willie Hartz
28 Feb 1862 – 8 Mar 1862

Jane Harum
unknown – 16 Apr 1853

Asa G. Harwood
1834 – 20 Sep 1866

Judah Hasper
1810 – 19 Apr 1867

Durant Hatch
1785 – 5 Nov 1845

John H. Hathaway
1778 – 27 Oct 1853

Susan M Haw
1834 – 29 Aug 1850

Child Hawkins
unknown – 7 Jun 1868

Henry J. Hawley
unknown – 4 Aug 1857

Hezekiah Hawley
18 Feb 1782 – 2 Mar 1859

Mary Rose Hawley
unknown – 25 May 1852

Agnes Price Hawthorne
17 Mar 1777 – 8 Nov 1869

Hugh Hawthorne
unknown – 8 Nov 1869

John W. Hawthorne
1805 – 10 Dec 1869

Margaret Miller Hayne
1836 – 7 Feb 1863

Catherine Hearth
unknown – 6 Oct 1866

Charles F. Heidel Jr.
1817 – Aug 1857

Catherina Hein
unknown – 1842

Daniel Littleton Henderson
26 Dec 1790 – 5 Apr 1857

Mary King Findlay Henderson
17 Dec 1799 – 20 Nov 1854

Rev. Singleton J. Henderson
7 Mar 1815 – 11 Sep 1852

Jonathan Hendy
1842 – 1871

Baby Hewitt
Apr 1848 – 8 May 1848

Sammuel Hicks
1860 – 25 Sep 1868

Andrew Patton Hill
1858 – 29 Jan 1861

Child Hill
unknown – 3 Oct 1869

James Hill
1845 – 16 Dec 1866

Matilda Hill
Birth and death dates unknown.

Mattie May Hill
unknown – 1863

Thomas P. Hill
unknown – 24 Feb 1849

William Hill
unknown – 8 Oct 1866

Wyatt M. Hill
1834 – 16 Oct 1860

W. H. M. Hilliard
unknown – 9 Apr 1832

Montilus Hines
unknown – 21 Dec 1848

Sarah Church Hines
unknown – 1860

Zachariah Hite
1800 – 1840

Anna Eliza Hobbs
1822 – Jul 1841

Infant Hobbs
1841 – Jul 1841

Isaac Holcombe
Birth and death dates unknown.

Mirfield Holroyd
unknown – 6 Oct 1866

Infant Holst
Nov 1847 – 22 May 1848

Robert E. Holt
21 Mar 1842 – 30 Mar 1842

Mollie Kate Hood
16 Jun 1864 – 17 Sep 1866

George Hook
May 1831 – 16 Sep 1866

Dr John J. Hooks
1820 – Jun 1868

Rowland M. Horsley
1814 – 9 Mar 1857

Luther Houston
unknown – 23 Jun 1844

Child Howard
unknown – 24 Aug 1869

William D. Howard
unknown – 13 Jun 1858

Child Hufman
Mar 1847 – 22 May 1848

Terry Huly
1823 – 15 Nov 1848

James A. Hume
1856 – 20 Apr 1866

Ann Hunter
1807 – 28 Jul 1867

Dr. Benjamin Lawrence Hynes
20 Nov 1803 – 19 Sep 1828

William Irvine
unknown – Aug 1828

Child Jackson
1840 – 15 May 1848

John Jackson
1812 – 22 Mar 1859

Appendix Two: Winchester Cemetery Records

Mary Elivira Lamb Jackson
20 Nov 1828 – 28 Aug 1847

Rebecca E. Jackson
1848 – 4 Oct 1866

Child James
unknown – 6 Aug 1867

Eliza J. James
unknown – 24 Sep 1834

Elizabeth James
9 Aug 1838 – 6 Jan 1840

Henry F. James
1797 – 1834

James James
9 Jul 1838 – 6 Jan 1840

Louisa H. James
unknown – 1855

Martha A. James
1827 – 12 Dec 1834

Thomas R. James
unknown – 1 Oct 1834

Virginia James
25 May 1835 – 8 Dec 1836

William R. James
unknown – 1848

Maria Jay
1800 – 14 Nov 1870

Joshua T. Jefferson
1816 – 11 Apr 1842

Maximillian M. Jehlen
unknown – 14 Feb 1867

Albert Jenkins
1835 – 26 Oct 1867

Oscar D. Johns
1835 – 20 Apr 1857

Johnson
unknown – 13 Jul 1866

Ellsworth Johnson
Jun 1862 – Sep 1862

Infant Johnson
22 Jun 1860 – 24 Jun 1860

James W. Johnson
Apr 1853 – 21 Oct 1853

Kathryn Kerbaugh Johnson
1822 – 3 Sep 1862

Narcissa L. Johnson
unknown – Oct 1853

Samuel W. Johnson
1836 – 3 Sep 1866

Zachariah Joiner
1793 – 5 Jun 1848

Adeline Boaz Jones
Birth and death dates unknown.

Ann Eliza Jones
Birth and death dates unknown.

Charles Jones
Birth and death dates unknown.

David Jones
Birth and death dates unknown.

David "Uncle Punch" Jones
1805 – 29 Aug 1875

Dudley Jones
unknown – 3 Sep 1866

Frank R. Jones
1832 – 13 Jun 1858

Dr. George F. Jones
1819 – 1866

Granville Jones
Birth and death dates unknown.

Ida Lavenia Jones
31 May 1866 – 8 Jun 1866

Jefferson Jones
unknown – 24 Jan 1868

John Lewis Jones
29 Dec 1815 – 15 Mar 1864

Lucy Adeline Jones
Birth and death dates unknown.

Marcus Jones Jr.
Birth and death dates unknown.

Margaret A. Jones
1861 – 24 Sep 1866

Patton Jones
unknown – 17 Aug 1867

Solomon Jones
unknown – 24 Feb 1830

William Jones
Birth and death dates unknown.

Thomas Watson Jordan
1838 – 1 Apr 1866

L. Joyner
unknown – 27 Jun 1870

MAJ Hiram Kaine
unknown – 26 Dec 1853

George Kane
unknown – 13 Sep 1866

James Kane
unknown – 1871

T. L. Keefer
unknown – 12 Jan 1871

J. R. Keel
1833 – 7 Jun 1852

James Thomas Keel
1847 – 13 Jun 1855

Louisa C. Grace Keel
1826 – 19 Jun 1860

B. Keeling
unknown – 10 Oct 1870

John "Johnny, the Miller" Keho
unknown – 18 Sep 1866

James A. Kehoe
unknown – 19 Mar 1872

Dennis Keif
unknown – 14 Nov 1870

Catherine Kempf
1830 – 28 Oct 1874

Child Kempf
unknown – 1870

Henrich "Henry" Kempf
1823 – 12 Jan 1878

Kimbrough
unknown – 1829

James Kimbrough
unknown – 31 Mar 1833

Matilda Johnson King
1843 – 24 Feb 1866

Virginia Kirk
1831 – 17 May 1845

Martin Kirsh
unknown – 9 Jul 1867

Alvin G. Knapp
1816 – 6 Jun 1860

Child Knapp
1848 – 25 Nov 1851

Caroline Krafft
unknown – 15 Apr 1862

August Kraft
Oct 1864 – 24 Apr 1866

Lawrence Kraft
1804 – 3 Sep 1868

E. Lake
1815 – 14 Nov 1875

G. W. Lamphier
unknown – 5 Mar 1845

Virginia Woodward Lamphier
1826 – 26 May 1848

Jeremiah Land
1815 – 31 Aug 1860

Paul Y. Land
unknown – 4 Sep 1858

Sarah E. Henry Land
unknown – 2 Oct 1866

Albert Lane
unknown – Sep 1862

John Langtrey
1815 – 5 Apr 1842

G. W. Lanphier
unknown – 5 Mar 1845

Virginia Woodward Lanphier
unknown – 26 May 1848

Polly Latner
1793 – 25 Oct 1866

William H. Laughlin
1830 – 22 Jun 1861

William S. Laurance
Jun 1850 – 11 Sep 1850

Victoria A. Krafft Laux
1846 – 17 Apr 1868

Albert S. Lavensen
1867 – 11 Oct 1867

Michael Lawler
1831 – 30 Jan 1866

James H. Lawrence
24 Aug 1802 – 13 Dec 1845

William Lawrence
27 Mar 1798 – 11 Apr 1830

John Lee
1848 – 1 Jul 1873

Robert Lee
Apr 1866 – 2 Oct 1867

Arthur S. LeMeair
2 Dec 1867 – 3 Mar 1868

Child Lemon
13 Aug 1850 – 13 Jun 1860

Thomas Frederick Lennox
1810 – 15 Oct 1849

Thomas E. Lewis
unknown – 14 Oct 1863

Lucinda C. Morrison Lide
1824 – 5 Oct 1867

Mary L. Lide
1853 – 2 Nov 1867

Oscar H. Lide
1821 – 27 Oct 1867

A. Linde
unknown – 3 Sep 1870

W. Linsley
unknown – 30 Aug 1870

Child Little
unknown – 1 Jun 1868

Gus Little
unknown – 10 Apr 1866

Elizabeth Littlefield
1807 – 11 May 1851

Henry A. Littleton
unknown – 7 Oct 1873

John W. Lodge
1828 – 13 Jun 1858

Bias Moon Lofland
unknown – 26 Jan 1841

Francis B. Lofland
unknown – 12 Feb 1841

Catherine W. Loftin
1796 – 3 Jun 1852

Edward Loftland
1818 – 7 Sep 1867

Thomas Logan
1798 – Aug 1848

Laura Long
unknown – 14 Aug 1866

Jesse A. Looney
unknown – Jan 1845

Thomas Lucas
unknown – 19 Aug 1869

A. Lumpkins
unknown – 22 Apr 1870

Josephine Lunsford
Sep 1873 – 7 Aug 1874

A. Lyons
1800 – 4 Jul 1855

Jacob F. Mackey
unknown – 21 Jun 1871

Louis Macklin
unknown – 1 Jul 1869

W. G. Maddox
Birth and death dates unknown.

William M. Maddox
Birth and death dates unknown.

Augustin Magdalon
1822 – 19 Jun 1848

Julie Maier
1856 – 26 Oct 1857

Infant Malone
Dec 1847 – 15 Jun 1848

Unidentified Black Man
unknown – 13 May 1866

Sarah H. Manning
19 May 1807 – 25 Jul 1851

Henry L. Marks
unknown – 8 Nov 1870

Peter Marsant
1818 – 27 Dec 1848

Emma Ann Martin
unknown – 3 Oct 1847

Martha Ann Martin
unknown – 27 Oct 1856

Sophia Mason
1868 – 11 Feb 1869

Joseph S. Maus
unknown – 19 Aug 1849

J. G. McBain
Oct 1865 – 24 Aug 1866

Charles McBride
1837 – 10 Jan 1866

John McCarthy
unknown – 12 Aug 1866

Fanny McClure
22 Dec 1840 – 2 Feb 1872

Child McConnico
unknown – 4 Jul 1869

Philip McCormick
1838 – 3 Sep 1866

Silas McCracken
unknown – 22 Aug 1866

William M. McCullough
1828 – 9 Mar 1874

Child McDaniel
May 1847 – 12 Jun 1848

A. McDonald
1856 – 9 Aug 1877

Alexander McElherin
1833 – 9 Jul 1859

Margaret McFee
unknown – 30 Oct 1867

Jonathan McGeary
unknown – 16 Mar 1867

Thomas McGee
1828 – 13 Jun 1858

Henderson McGowan
1824 – 15 Jul 1852

Louis McGowen
unknown – 3 May 1868

Katie McGrath
1 Feb 1859 – 13 Sep 1866

Henry McGuire
unknown – 2 Nov 1857

R. R. McKinney
1820 – 22 Nov 1866

Elizabeth McLeroy
unknown – 20 May 1846

Thomas D. McMahon
1840 – 2 Jan 1866

Robert McMillan
1826 – 9 Aug 1850

Sarah L. McMullen
1803 – 28 Oct 1850

Elizabeth L. McMurry
Birth and death dates unknown.

John M. McNeill
1823 – 4 Aug 1848

William C. McNinch
1806 – 6 Jun 1851

Eliza McPherson
unknown – 14 Nov 1843

John McPherson
1827 – 23 Sep 1847

Frances Anthony McWilliams
1791 – 12 Oct 1864

John Harvey Means
30 May 1826 – 23 Mar 1855

Rachel Henderson Means
1823 – 27 Feb 1851

Rachel Means
unknown – 9 Oct 1846

John H. Mendelar
1836 – 1867

Sally Merriman
unknown – 31 May 1870

Mary Mhoon
1858 – 3 Oct 1878

Elizabeth Miles
unknown – 31 Dec 1841

Cynthia Tennant Hamilton Miller
1802 – 2 Jun 1846

E. Miller
1801 – 13 Apr 1851

Elizabeth Miller
1833 – 4 Jul 1851

George Miller
Mar 1802 – 23 Aug 1873

H. Miller
Feb 1862 – 3 Sep 1868

Ward W. Miller
1817 – 8 Apr 1852

Child Mindler
unknown – 4 Mar 1867

Calvin Mitchell
unknown – 14 Sep 1866

Child Mitchell
unknown – 5 Jan 1870

George M. Mitchell
unknown – 2 Feb 1866

Alfred Moore
1802 – 1865

Alfred "Al" Moore
1843 – 1861

Franklin M. Moore
1833 – 27 Jul 1873

George Moore
1835 – 24 May 1857

William S. Moore
1822 – 28 Sep 1866

Infant Moreland
9 Feb 1868 – 9 Mar 1868

Samuel T. Morgan
19 Oct 1826 – 8 Apr 1853

William C. Morgan
1836 – 4 Jan 1866

William R. Morgan
unknown – 3 Dec 1852

Child Morris
1851 – 20 Jan 1856

Child Morris
1852 – 7 Aug 1854

David Morrison
unknown – 16 Sep 1852

Appendix Two: Winchester Cemetery Records

Child Mosby
unknown – 15 Oct 1870

Clara Mosby
unknown – 21 Jul 1870

William H. Mower
1834 – 1 Mar 1866

George D. Moyers
1860 – 8 Jul 1866

Samuel Muller
unknown – 15 Mar 1854

Eliza Munson
unknown – 8 Mar 1847

James S. Murphy
unknown – 27 Sep 1867

Ophelia Murray
11 Jul 1849 – 24 May 1852

Margaret Nelson
unknown – 18 Feb 1870

Seth M. Nelson
8 Dec 1804 – 26 Mar 1843

James W. Newby
unknown – 14 Oct 1848

Elizabeth "Lizzie" Brown Newell
unknown – 20 Apr 1868

Laura H. Newport
unknown – 8 Mar 1870

Mary C. Nichols
Apr 1857 – 4 Jun 1857

Walter Nichols
22 Dec 1809 – 31 May 1847

James M. Norfleet
1810 – 12 Dec 1840

Charlotte Norman
1803 – 7 Jul 1854

C. H. Norris
unknown – 14 Nov 1867

Sarah Mariah Carroll Norris
1816 – 26 Jul 1874

Son Norris
unknown – 3 Oct 1867

Harriet J O'Cain
1848 – 20 May 1854

Child O'Haver
1851 – 20 May 1852

Francis Olden
unknown – 9 Jun 1867

Joseph A. Orr
unknown – 18 Dec 1856

Catherine Paine Owen
unknown – 1842

Mary Elizabeth Owen
unknown – 16 Feb 1870

Frances Palmer
15 Sep 1846 – 4 May 1848

A. G. Park
unknown – 3 Feb 1859

Richard Parker
unknown – 31 Mar 1867

Thomas Parron
unknown – 1836

Mary J. "Mollie" Freeman Parrott
1855 – 18 Feb 1874

L. K. Patrick
unknown – Jun 1847

Robert G. Patrick
unknown – Jun 1847

Lucy Patter
unknown – 8 Nov 1835

M. J. Pattison
1867 – 19 Sep 1868

Sallie Patton
Birth and death dates unknown.

Christian Pender
unknown – 1867

Alphise Peplow
1849 – Jun 1849

Mary Wills Perryman
unknown – Mar 1841

Thomas B. Phoebus
1805 – 11 Sep 1838

George Pitcher
unknown – 17 Oct 1842

Cesario Bias Pittman
1846 – 16 Oct 1858

Isaac M. Pittman
1844 – 20 Oct 1867

Thomas Pittman
unknown – 1 Jun 1856

Thomas Pittman Jr.
1818 – 24 Mar 1849

Richard Polk
Birth and death dates unknown.

Robert Polk
1841 – 11 Feb 1869

E. Porter
Birth and death dates unknown.

Sarah Porter
unknown – 1855

Thomas J. Porter
1803 – 30 Aug 1843

Child Poston
unknown – 19 Aug 1867

Child Potter
unknown – 5 Mar 1867

Columbus Potts
1853 – 19 Sep 1866

Mary A. Powell
1828 – 9 Sep 1853

Rebecca T. Powell
Jan 1852 – 30 Sep 1853

Abby Prescott
1811 – 10 Feb 1852

Hannah Prescott
15 Apr 1794 – 19 Jan 1848

Jedekiah Prescott
unknown – 13 Nov 1859

Josiah Prescott
1821 – 31 Oct 1858

Sarah Prescott
unknown – 22 Oct 1840

Sylvester Prescott
unknown – 14 Nov 1849

Child Preston
unknown – 15 Dec 1867

Child Preston
unknown – 9 Mar 1867

Henry Price
1835 – 26 Apr 1867

Nora Sullivan Province
1848 – 10 Oct 1870

Mary Quarmby
unknown – 31 May 1866

Adam Rankin
unknown – 7 Oct 1836

Fredrick Rapp
Jul 1860 – 13 Nov 1861

Xavier Rauch
1818 – 13 Jun 1858

Sarah Ray
unknown – 13 Jan 1870

Child Read
unknown – 1868

J. Reaves
unknown – 24 Feb 1830

Child Reckord
unknown – 16 Dec 1867

James Thomas Reed
unknown – 3 Jun 1855

Susan A. Reed
unknown – 11 Mar 1845

Susan E. Reed
unknown – 23 Dec 1859

Child Reeder
unknown – 20 Oct 1866

James Reid
unknown – 18 Aug 1867

Martha Reid
Birth and death dates unknown.

Mary Reid
1796 – 19 Aug 1833

Thomas Reid
Birth and death dates unknown.

Dr. Charles Emanuel Reinhardt
23 Jan 1795 – 4 Nov 1847

Frank Reudelheuber
unknown – 19 Dec 1866

Josephine Rhodes
1838 – 1 Apr 1854

Child Rice
unknown – 14 Jun 1867

Richards
unknown – 31 Aug 1867

E. A. Richards
unknown – 26 May 1867

Infant Riddick
15 Feb 1869 – 15 Feb 1869

Ridgeway
1825 – 19 Oct 1850

Infant Ridgeway
13 Oct 1850 – 13 Oct 1850

Agnes Riggs
Jun 1853 – 1 Jul 1854

Molly Riggs
Jun 1853 – 1 Jul 1854

Mathew Riley
1834 – 13 Jun 1858

Child Ringwald
unknown – 19 Dec 1866

Child Ringwald
unknown – 19 Dec 1866

Lucinda Ringwald
unknown – 19 Dec 1866

Wile Roberts
unknown – 7 Nov 1833

Charles N. Robinson
unknown – 16 Nov 1868

Child Robinson
Jan 1846 – 1 May 1848

Susan Robinson
Jan 1874 – 13 Jul 1874

Eliza Rodgers
unknown – 13 Feb 1869

Walter M. Rogers
unknown – 4 Jun 1867

Ann S Rollins
1847 – 4 Oct 1850

J. H. Roper
unknown – 7 May 1870

Ann Rose
Jul 1845 – 17 Aug 1845

John Rose
1827 – unknown

Kittie Ross
unknown – 3 Apr 1868

Willie Rounds
1860 – 19 Sep 1866

Child Ruffin
unknown – 27 May 1868

George Russell
1836 – 31 Jul 1866

M. B. Rutledge
1823 – 19 Dec 1867

Joseph Ryan
1806 – 13 Jun 1858

Thomas Ryan
1858 – 25 Jun 1868

John Saalfrank
unknown – 16 Jun 1869

George W. Saffarans
unknown – 21 Feb 1864

Annie K. Salziger
Jan 1868 – 5 Jul 1868

Child Salziger
unknown – 31 May 1868

George Salziger
unknown – 21 Nov 1866

Henry G. Salziger
unknown – 1867

Rosa P Sangier
unknown – 17 Oct 1862

Florence Sappington
Nov 1842 – 15 Sep 1845

Dr Mark Brown
Sappington Jr.
unknown – 28 Aug 1852

Mary Sappington
unknown – 1852

Susannah Sappington
1779 – 19 Jun 1838

Ellen Saunders
unknown – 19 Aug 1870

Lockey Trigg Saunders
1 Jun 1779 – 27 Aug 1840

Napoleon B Saunders
1820 – 28 Feb 1858

Otto Saupe
1867 – 16 Jul 1876

Sarah Schabel
unknown – 22 Aug 1837

Charlotte Schad
unknown – 20 Jun 1849

Dorothee Schad
unknown – 2 Jun 1849

Child Schurmeyer
unknown – 17 Jul 1866

Henrietta Scott
unknown – 2 Nov 1870

Child Seay
unknown – 22 Dec 1868

A. J. Selby
unknown – 22 Aug 1866

George W. Sexton
1835 – 17 Nov 1866

George W. Sharpe
unknown – 19 Feb 1851

William Shead
1790 – 2 Sep 1850

Caroline Shelton
unknown – 18 Sep 1843

William H. Shelton
unknown – 11 Jul 1833

Shirley
1803 – 31 Dec 1850

Sarah A. Sibley
1806 – 15 Mar 1873

Henry Sickel
unknown – 6 Dec 1855

Joseph Simonds
1841 – 13 Sep 1858

Mary A. Simpson
unknown – 10 Mar 1870

Thomas W. Slover
22 Apr 1856 – 22 Jul 1856

John S. Small
1836 – 16 Jun 1851

William Thomas Smedley
10 Nov 1832 – 1 Nov 1850

Albert G. Smith
unknown – 18 May 1849

Child Smith
unknown – 4 Jan 1870

Fielding C. Smith
unknown – 28 Jun 1844

H. H. Smith
unknown – 20 Jun 1844

Infant Smith
unknown – 19 Jul 1878

James D. Smith
3 May 1833 – 4 Mar 1916

COL John Smith
1765 – 1851

Jonathan G. Smith
unknown – 6 May 1851

Mary Smith
unknown – 4 Oct 1876

Mary Smith
unknown – 9 Sep 1869

Thomas O. Smith Jr.
unknown – 25 Apr 1872

Thomas Othello Smith
1838 – 1869

William R. Smith
unknown – 15 Jun 1867

Infant Smoot
Sep 1847 – 8 May 1848

Horace Spickernagle
21 Mar 1829 – 18 Jul 1855

M. Spickernagle
Oct 1866 – 28 Sep 1868

William Spickernagle
unknown – 12 Jul 1845

Spittle
Sep 1854 – 20 Jul 1855

Sarah Ann Spittle
Oct 1850 – 28 Jul 1851

Leonia Staily
unknown – 8 Jul 1868

Francis Epps Stainback
1830 – 1864

Benjamin Stanton Jr.
unknown – 15 Sep 1846

Hallowell Stanton
1844 – 10 Dec 1846

Jeptha Fowlkes Stanton
1835 – 30 Jul 1837

Richard Stanton
1789 – 13 Nov 1846

Walter Scott Stanton
unknown – May 1839

William Stanton
unknown – 21 Oct 1847

Starke
31 Aug 1856 – 4 Sep 1856

B. A. Stedman
unknown – 4 Feb 1866

Child Stephenson
1859 – 31 Aug 1868

Susan C. Stephenson
Birth and death dates unknown.

Child Stewart
unknown – 26 Jun 1869

Cpt. James Stewart
Birth and death dates unknown.

Robert F. Stewart
unknown – 6 Sep 1835

William Stockwell
27 Jun 1796 – 24 Feb 1830

Joseph Stone
1835 – 29 Jul 1860

Eveline W. Curren Strange
unknown – 22 Jul 1842

Jesse Alloway Strange
1798 – 21 Aug 1856

Apolnia Strehl
8 May 1793 – 13 Jul 1849

William H. Sugg
unknown – 6 May 1865

Samuel C. Suit
1820 – 4 Nov 1859

Appendix Two: Winchester Cemetery Records

Caroline Summerville
Birth and death dates unknown.

Bazil D. Talbot
1806 – 24 Feb 1830

Rachel Tarlton
1793 – 6 Feb 1871

James Tate
1826 – 31 Jul 1852

Lucy Taylor
unknown – 14 Jun 1868

Oscar Taylor
unknown – 8 Apr 1867

Oscar Taylor
unknown – 10 May 1868

C. Thomas
1835 – 19 Dec 1867

Child Thomas
unknown – 26 Oct 1868

Frances A. Walker Thomas
unknown – 16 Dec 1846

James B. Thompson
1830 – 13 Jun 1858

James R. Thompson
unknown – 5 Feb 1865

James W. Thompson
unknown – 18 Aug 1853

Elmira Thurman
unknown – 1 May 1872

Ebenezer Titus
Mar 1802 – 1851

James Titus
unknown – 1854

William E. Titus
1806 – Nov 1832

Edward Sharp Tod
22 Jun 1815 – 9 Apr 1855

Emma R. Hall Tod
1828 – 11 Mar 1857

Edward S. Todd
Birth and death dates unknown.

Ward Todd
Birth and death dates unknown.

Orpah Hansborough Toncray
unknown – 1848

Dr. Silas Tracy Toncray
1795 – 11 Feb 1847

Caroline A. Trader
unknown – 1846

Mary Frances Pamplin Trader
1822 – 1849

William Trader
unknown – 1860

John G. Trantwein
unknown – 1 Apr 1867

Trapp
1804 – 15 Jan 1849

Lieut. Thomas S. Trask
unknown – 29 Jul 1828

John G. Trautwine
unknown – 7 Aug 1867

Elizabeth Marion Cocke Trezevant
1809 – 6 Mar 1845

Georgiana Trezevant
1837 – 7 Jun 1845

Johnathan P. Trezevant
Birth and death dates unknown.

Dr. Lewis Cruger Trezevant
11 Jun 1804 – Nov 1844

Louisa Trezevant
Birth and death dates unknown.

Theodore P. Trezevant
20 Apr 1851 – Nov 1852

Lue Trotter
1841 – 27 Aug 1866

William Shiloh True
13 Nov 1819 – 4 Jul 1853

William Shiloh True
13 Nov 1819 – 4 Jul 1853

Charles Carver Tucker
1797 – 2 Oct 1834

P. H. Tucker
unknown – 1 Jul 1853

William Tucker
1824 – 7 Jan 1849

W. M. Tugman
Dec 1849 – 24 Aug 1850

W. G. Tunnage
1813 – 30 Dec 1848

Judge William B. Turley
1798 – 28 May 1851

Samuel Turner
1831 – 5 Oct 1867

Sarah Turpin
unknown – 28 Jul 1860

Elizabeth Underhill
unknown – 4 Jul 1864

Child Underwood
1843 – 19 Jun 1848

Infant Unidentified
Mar 1848 – 8 May 1848

Augustus Unknown
unknown – 19 Dec 1866

Jack Unknown
unknown – 24 Feb 1830

Lucy Unknown
unknown – 19 Dec 1866

Philip Unknown
unknown – 19 Dec 1866

Tom Unknown
unknown – 19 Dec 1866

Walter Unknown
unknown – 19 Dec 1866

Cornelius V. Van Campen
unknown – 13 Mar 1862

Aaron Van Hook
unknown – Jun 1850

A. Van Meeter
unknown – 24 Feb 1830

Henry Van Pelt
22 Feb 1798 – 23 Apr 1851

H. C. Varrelman
unknown – 17 Sep 1853

Son Vaulx
unknown – 14 Jul 1867

George Veary
unknown – 3 Dec 1857

George B. Vincent
1825 – 3 Oct 1851

Dr. John Peter Wagnon Jr.
8 Nov 1789 – 30 May 1842

Emily Waldron
unknown – 26 Nov 1869

Baby Walker
Dec 1847 – 12 Jun 1848

Betsy Walker
unknown – 10 Oct 1867

Malvina Walker
1853 – 31 Jul 1866

Children Ward
unknown – 1867

Elizabeth L. Saunders Ward
1812 – Apr 1837

William A. Ward
9 Mar 1841 – 19 Jul 1874

Anna Ware
1861 – 28 Sep 1866

Eveline Chandler Warner
unknown – 29 Sep 1869

Lucinda Water
unknown – 22 Dec 1863

Susan Watkins
1806 – 30 Sep 1854

Susanna Watkins
unknown – 30 Sep 1854

George W. Watson
unknown – 14 Dec 1860

Peter Stuart Watson
1821 – 14 Jun 1847

Tiffey Watson
unknown – 14 Jun 1868

Margaret I. Waymon
unknown – 23 May 1857

Child Weise
unknown – 21 Aug 1870

Chester Welch
unknown – 30 Apr 1870

William Wharum
1815 – 21 Oct 1850

Mary Wheelock
1855 – 1 Mar 1859

Andrew Wherry
1785 – 1 Apr 1834

Elizabeth Strait Wherry
1 Jan 1776 – 1860

A. White
1867 – 16 Sep 1868

Adaline White
Birth and death dates unknown.

Jane A. White
1827 – 6 Nov 1868

Child Whitfield
1846 – 22 May 1848

Joseph Stanfield Whitmore
1846 – 13 Sep 1868

William Alexander "Billie" Whitmore Sr.
24 Feb 1838 – 1 Mar 1867

Appendix Two, Winchester Cemetery Records

Sarah Whitsett
1782 – 8 Dec 1853

W. W. Whitsett
unknown – 1876

Child Whitsitt
Feb 1847 – 12 Jun 1848

Elizabeth Jane "Eliza" Whitsitt
unknown – 2 Feb 1888

James S. Whitsitt
1773 – 1836

Jane Harden Whitsitt
unknown – 2 Apr 1876

Sarah Whitsitt
1782 – 1853

Sarah Whitsitt
unknown – 20 Aug 1837

Wilie H. Whitsitt
unknown – 28 Sep 1871

William James Whitsitt
unknown – 5 Mar 1862

William Wiley Whitsitt
1802 – 28 Oct 1853

Catharine Fletcher Whittier
1795 – 24 Apr 1870

Thomas Wiatt
1818 – 12 Jan 1840

Catharine W. Willett
1823 – 9 Oct 1873

Albert Williams
Birth and death dates unknown.

Australia Williams
29 May 1859 – 29 Nov 1860

Child Williams
1841 – 15 Jun 1848

Josephine Williams
1836 – 20 Jul 1867

Nancy Webb Williams
unknown – 15 Feb 1868

Sarah Williams
unknown – 1834

Sarah E. Williams
unknown – 5 May 1863

Warner W. Williams
1823 – 31 Jul 1848

J. L. Williamson
unknown – 7 Nov 1871

Lizzie B. Wills
1854 – 7 Oct 1873

Baby Wilson
Dec 1846 – 19 Jun 1848

Francis Wilson
unknown – 1 Nov 1863

Infant Wilson
10 Feb 1868 – 21 Feb 1868

Jane Tarlton Wilson
unknown – 1838

Joseph C. Wilson
1824 – 2 May 1868

Mary Emma Wilson
unknown – 22 Jun 1861

Matilda Wilson
Birth and death dates unknown.

Samuel Wilson
1798 – 3 Jul 1848

Willie K. Wilson
unknown – 19 Jul 1863

MAJ Marcus Brutus Winchester
28 May 1796 – 2 Nov 1856

Infant Winston
Feb 1868 – 1 Nov 1868

Child Wise
Feb 1858 – 1 Aug 1859

John A. Wise
1816 – 20 Apr 1866

Emil G. Wolf
unknown – 12 Aug 1857

Unidentified Black Female
1828 – 3 Jul 1848

Amelia C. Wood
unknown – Oct 1865

Ann Wood
1827 – 7 Aug 1867

John W. Wood
1828 – 13 Aug 1878

Wright Wood
1857 – 18 Aug 1878

Frank Woods
1851 – 31 Dec 1874

Jane Woods
1843 – 16 May 1860

Micajah Woods
unknown – 1862

Baker Woodward
unknown – 1829

G. W. Woolcott
unknown – 30 Aug 1868

John P. Wortham
Birth and death dates unknown.

Alexander J. Wright
1812 – 26 Sep 1833

Benjamin Wright
unknown – 10 May 1858

Elizabeth Wright
Birth and death dates unknown.

Jonathan Wright Jr.
1816 – 1 Oct 1855

Samuel C. Wright
unknown – 15 Sep 1847

Child Wynsberry
unknown – 28 Jul 1866

Almarion Young
unknown – 23 May 1854

Emanuel Young
unknown – 30 Nov 1831

Emma J. Young
15 Oct 1836 – 23 Jul 1856

Lewis Young
unknown – 24 Feb 1830

Sam Young
unknown – 1851

A Portion of Address by Judge C. F. Vance at the Winchester Cemetery, July 1882

We have met here for the purpose of decorating the graves of our fathers. Here lie the bodies of Robert Lawrence, Littleton Henderson, Anderson Carr, M. B. Winchester, W. D. Ferguson, Nathaniel Anderson, the Allens, the Armours, the Lawrences, the Kerrs, the Prescotts, the Morgans, the Parks, the Remberts, the Saffarans, the Strattons, the Searcys, the Stewarts, the Shelbys, the Smiths, the Taylors, the Trezvants, the Triggs, the Thompsons, the Walkers, the Watkins, the Webbs, the Wheatleys, the Wrights, the Whites, the Youngs, the Bettises, the Montgomeries, the Davises, and others identified with the history of Memphis.

Their graves were neglected! Yes, this old and venerable resting place of our earlier dead was sadly overlooked. The fences, the grounds and the graves of a cemetery which should be so dear to the memory of our citizens went to decay. Even streets were opened over the graves of our fathers. Slabs and tombs were cut off and thrown out from the course of the street.

These moss-grown monuments stand like so many solemn sentinels over their ashes, and admonish you to revere their memories. Let not decay and desolation wipe out these mementoes, but do your duty to the memory of the dead.

Bibliography

Abernethy, Thomas Perkins. *From Frontier to Plantation: A Study in Frontier Democracy.* Chapel Hill: University of North Carolina Press, 1932.
"The Aborigines of West Tennessee." *Old Folks Record*, no. 4 (January 1874): 179.
Adamiak, Stanley J. "A Naval Depot and Dockyard on the Western Waters: The Rise and Fall of the Memphis Naval Yard, 1844–1854." *International Journal of Naval History* 1, no. 1 (April 2002): 5.
"Address of Judge Q. K. Underwood." *Old Folks Record* 12 (September 1875): 532.
American Lebanese Syrian Associated Charities v. All Unknown Parties Having Any Interest in the Property Known as Old Burial Ground in Memphis, Petition to Terminate Dedication and Use of Property as a Burial Ground. Chancery Court of Tennessee for the Thirteenth Judicial District at Memphis, filed August 30, 2024.
Anderson, Douglas. "G. W. Winchester of Bledsoe's 'Lick'." *Nashville Banner*, August 16, 1925.
"Another Old Citizen Gone!" *Memphis Weekly Bulletin*, June 8, 1858.
Atherton, William, Elias Darnell, and E. A. Cruikshank. Massacre on the River Raisin: Three Accounts of the Disastrous Michigan Campaign During the War of 1812. East Yorkshire, UK: Leonaur Books, 2013.
Auricchio, Laura. *The Marquis: Lafayette Reconsidered.* New York: Alfred A. Knopf, 2014.
Ayers, Edward L. *American Visions: The United States, 1800 – 1860.* New York: W. W. Norton and Company, 2023.
Bailey, Francis. *Journal of a Tour in Unsettled Parts of North America in 1796 & 1797.* London: Baily Bros., 1856.
Baldwin, Leland D. *The Keelboat Age on Western Waters.* Pittsburgh: University of Pittsburgh Press, 1980.
"Bandits Preyed on Returning Flat Boatmen." *The Commercial Appeal*, May 29, 1938.
Banks, Lucile Webb. "Graves of Memphis Fathers Lost in the March of Time." *The Commercial Appeal*, April 8, 1923.
Barker, Eugene, ed. Annual Report of the American Historical Association for the Year 1919: The Austin Papers. 3 vols. Vol. 1, Part 2. Washington, D.C.: Government Printing Office, 1924.
Barry, Richard H. Letter to Marcus B. Winchester, April 14, 1833. Tennessee State Library and Archives.
Bassett, John Spencer, ed. *Correspondence of Andrew Jackson.* 7 vols. Washington, D.C.: Carnegie Institution of Washington, 1926.
Bederman, Gail. "Revisiting Nashoba: Slavery, Utopia, and Frances Wright in America, 1818–1826." *American Literary History* 17, no. 3 (2005): 454.
Bell, Richard. *Stolen.* New York: Simon & Schuster, 2019.

Bibliography

Blair, E. P. "The Real Rachel Jackson." *Nashville Tennessean*, September 6, 1936.
Bond, Beverly G., and Janann Sherman. *Memphis in Black and White*. Charleston, SC: Arcadia Publishing, 2003.
Botkin, B. A., ed. *A Treasury of Mississippi River Folklore.* New York: Crown Publishers, 1955.
Bowles, H. Lee. *Biographical Sketches of Gospel Preachers*. Nashville: Gospel Advocate Company, 1932.
Brands, H. W. *Andrew Jackson: His Life and Times*. New York: Doubleday, 2005.
Brooks, Addie Lou. "Early Plans for Railroads in West Tennessee, 1830–1845." *Tennessee Historical Magazine* 3, no. 1 (1932): 35.
"Businessmen and Public Health in the South." *Bulletin of the History of Medicine* 44, no. 3 (1970): 197–212.
Calhoun, John C. "Speech on the Reception of Abolition Petitions," February 6, 1837. In *The Works of John C. Calhoun*, edited by Richard K. Crallé, vol. 2, 630. New York: D. Appleton and Company, 1853.
The Cambridge Chronicle 10, no. 41 (October 13, 1855): 3.
"Career of Fannie Wright in West Tennessee." *The Tennessean*, December 25, 1901.
Carr, John. *Early Times in Middle Tennessee*. Nashville: E. Carr, by E. Stevenson & F. A. Owens, 1857.
Carrel, Edward J. *The Memphis Daily Eagle*, November 8, 1849.
Carroll, Mary S. "Tennessee Sectionalism." PhD diss., Duke University, 1931.
Cassedy, Charles. Letter to Maria Breedlove regarding a biography of her father, James Winchester. *Correspondence*. The Gilder Lehrman Institute of American History, GLC06997.77. Accessed through Adam Matthew, *American History, 1493–1945* (Marlborough, UK).
Cassedy, Charles. Letter to Maria Breedlove regarding a biography of her father, James Winchester. *Correspondence*. The Gilder Lehrman Institute of American History, GLC06997.77. Accessed through Adam Matthew, *American History, 1493–1945*.
Chambers, William Nisbet. *Old Bullion Benton*. Boston: Atlantic–Little, Brown and Company, 1956.
Cheathem, Mark. "The Evolution of the Enslaved Community at Andrew Jackson's Plantations, 1790s–1840s." Paper presented at the BrANCH Conference, Newcastle-upon-Tyne, Fall 2012.
Clark, Thomas D. "The Jackson Purchase: A Dramatic Chapter in Southern Indian Policy and Relations." *Jackson Purchase Historical Society Journal* 45, no. 1 (1988): 307.
Clayton, William W. *History of Davidson County, Tennessee, with Illustrations and Biographical Sketches of Its Prominent Men and Pioneers*. Philadelphia: J. W. Lewis & Co., 1880.
Cleaves, Freeman. *Old Tippecanoe: William Henry Harrison and His Time*. New York: Scribner's, 1939.
Clements, Paul. *Chronicles of the Cumberland Settlements, 1779–1796*. Nashville: Private Printing, The Foundation of Jennifer and William Frist and Paul Clements, 2012.
Clifton, Frances. "John Overton as Andrew Jackson's Friend." *Tennessee Historical Quarterly* 11, no. 1 (1952): 30.
Cobb, James C. *A Way Down South: A History of Southern Identity*. Oxford: Oxford University Press, 2005.
Cohn, David L. *The Life and Times of King Cotton*. New York: Oxford University Press, 1956.
Coke, Fletch. *Dear Judge: Selected Letters of John Overton of Travellers' Rest*. Nashville: Travellers' Rest Historic Museum House, 1978.
Coppock, Paul. "He Once Was Lost." *The Commercial Appeal*, February 19, 1980.
Corlew, Robert E. *Tennessee: A Short History*. Knoxville: University of Tennessee Press, 1989.
Cox, Anna-Lisa. *The Bone and Sinew of the Land: America's Forgotten Black Pioneers and the Struggle for Equality*. New York: Public Affairs, 2018.
Cozzens, Peter. A Brutal Reckoning: The Creek War and the Epic Story of Red Stick Defeat. New York: Vintage Books, 2023.
Cramer, Zadok. The Navigator. Pittsburgh: Cramer, Spear and Eichbaum, 1814.
Crawford, Jeanne. "Levin Hudson Coe." *The West Tennessee Historical Society Papers* (1993): 65.
Crockett, David. *A Narrative of the Life of David Crockett, of the State of Tennessee*. Philadelphia: E.L. Carey and A. Hart, 1834.
———. "David Crockett's Circular," February 28, 1831. Rare Books Division, Library of Congress.
———. *Autobiography of David Crockett*. New York: Charles Scribner's Sons, 1923.
"Cumberland House." *Memphis Daily Appeal*, December 2, 1868.
Cuming, Fortescue. *Sketches of a Tour to the Western Country, Through the States of Ohio and Kentucky.*

Pittsburgh: Cramer, Spear & Eichbaum, 1810.

Curtis, Joe. "Memphis Wharfage Fee Fight Was Long and Hard Battle, Finally Won by Tobias Wolfe." *The Commercial Appeal*, October 19, 1941.

Darnell, Elias. *Massacre on the River Raisin*. Leonaur: United Kingdom, 2013.

Davis, David Brion. *Antebellum American Culture*. Lexington, MA: D.C. Heath and Company, 1979.

Davis, James D. *History of Memphis*. Memphis: Hite, Crumpton & Kelly, 1873.

———. "Old Times." *The Commercial Appeal*, January 16, 1871.

Davis, Reuben. *Recollections of Mississippi and Mississippians*. Boston and New York: Houghton, Mifflin and Company, 1889.

De Bow's Review 19 (September 1855): 363.

Dearborn, Henry. Letter to James Wilkinson, September 6, 1806. Records of the Bureau of Indian Affairs, Record Group 75, vol. D, 151. National Archives.

"Death of Maj. Marcus Winchester." *Nashville Union and American*, November 9, 1856.

"Death of Major Winchester of New Orleans." *New Orleans Times-Picayune*, November 11, 1856.

DeRosier, Arthur H. *The Removal of the Choctaw Indians*. Knoxville: The University of Tennessee Press, 1999.

DeWitt, John H. "General James Winchester, 1752–1826." *Tennessee Historical Magazine* 1, no. 2 (1915): 87.

"Died." *The New-Orleans Times*, January 12, 1868.

Dodson, David. *Scots in the USA and Canada, 1825–1875*. Baltimore: Clearfield, 2002.

Dougan, James. *Memphis*. Images of America. Charleston, SC: Arcadia Publishing, 1998.

Dowdy, G. Wayne. *Enslavement in Memphis*. United States: History Press, 2021.

Durham, Walter. *James Winchester: Tennessee Pioneer*. Gallatin: Sumner County Library Board, 1979.

Eckert, Allan W. *Johnny Logan: Shawnee Spy*. Boston: Little Brown and Company. 1983.

Eckhardt, Celia Morris. *Fanny Wright, Rebel in America*. Cambridge: Harvard University Press, 1984.

Egerton, John. *Visions of Utopia*. Knoxville: University of Tennessee Press, 1977.

Ehle, John. *Trail of Tears: The Rise and Fall of the Cherokee Nation*. New York: Doubleday, 1988.

"Eliza Lawrence." *Old Folks Record*, no. 7 (April 1875): 333.

Elmwood Cemetery Biographical Sketches. "Seth Wheatley," 1874.

Elting, John R. *Amateurs, to Arms!: A Military History of the War of 1812*. Boston: Da Capo Press, 1995.

"Executor's Sale." *Republican Banner*, June 19, 1844.

"Farmers' and Merchants' Bank Suit." *The New York Times*, March 3, 1855.

Farrell, Louis. *Descendants of William Winchester*. Washington, D.C.: Self-published, 1933.

Feldman, Jay. *When the Mississippi Ran Backwards: Empire, Intrigue, Murder, and the New Madrid Earthquakes*. New York: Free Press, 2005.

Ferguson, Jesse B. *Address on the History, Authority, and Influence of Slavery*. Washington, D.C.: Smithsonian Institution, 1847.

———. *Spirit Communion*. Parkersburg, WV: Globe Press, 1888.

"Furgusonism—No. 2." *Tennessee Baptist*, February 19, 1853.

"Financial and Spiritual." *Spiritual Telegraph* 5, no. 13 (July 28, 1856): 101.

Finger, John R. *Tennessee Frontiers: Three Regions in Transition*. Bloomington: Indiana University Press, 2001.

Finkelman, Paul. *Slavery and the Founders: Race and Liberty in the Age of Jefferson*. Armonk, NY: M.E. Sharpe, 2001.

Flint, Timothy. *Recollections of the Last Ten Years, Passed in Occasional Residences and Journeyings in the Valley of the Mississippi*. Boston: Cummings, Hilliard, and Co., 1826.

Ford, Lacy K. *Deliver us from Evil: The Slavery Question in the Old South*. Oxford: Oxford University Press, 2009.

Foreman, Grant. *Indian Removal: The Emigration of the Five Civilized Tribes*. Norman: The University of Oklahoma Press, 1974.

Fort Pickering American Eagle, March 8, 1842.

Fossick, George L. "The Old Bell Tavern." *The Commercial Appeal*, November 28, 1915.

Foster, Lillian. *Way-Side Glimpses, North and South*. New York: Rudd & Carlton, 1859.

Bibliography

Genovese, Eugene D. *The Mind of the Master Class: History and Faith in the Southern Slaveholders' Worldview*. Cambridge: Cambridge University Press, 2005.

Gilje, Paul A. "'Free Trade and Sailors' Rights': The Rhetoric of the War of 1812." *Journal of the Early Republic* 30, no. 1 (2010): 23–52.

"Going, Going, Gone." *Memphis Daily Appeal*, January 13, 1876.

"Great City Now Stands on Chickasaw Bluffs." *The Tennessean*, July 26, 1910.

"The Great Railroad Jubilee." *Edgefield Advertiser*, May 13, 1857.

Gray, John W., M.D. *The Life of Joseph Bishop*. Nashville: Self-published, 1858.

Gurley, Midge H. "Abandoned, Abused, and a Municipal Pariah: The Life and Death of Winchester Burying Ground." *The West Tennessee Historical Society Papers* (2018): 1.

Hacker, J. David. "A Census-Based Count of the Civil War Dead." *Civil War History* 57, no. 4 (December 2011): 307–48.

"Half Forgotten Pages in the History of Memphis." *The Commercial Appeal*, December 12, 1909.

Ham, J. A. "Winchester Cemetery." *The Commercial Appeal*, January 13, 1931.

Hammond, Bray. Banks and Politics in America from the Revolution to the Civil War. Princeton, NJ: Princeton University Press, 1957.

Harkins, John E. *Metropolis of the American Nile*. Woodland Hills, CA: Windsor Publications, 1982.

Harrell, John M. "James Winchester." *Tennessee Historical Quarterly* 18, no. 3 (1959): 311

Haywood, John. The Natural and Aboriginal History of Tennessee. Nashville: Printed by George Wilson, 1823.

Heiskell, Samuel Gordon. *Andrew Jackson and Early Tennessee History*. Nashville: Ambrose Printing Co., 1918.

Hill, Raymond S. "Memphis Theatre, 1836–1846." *The West Tennessee Historical Society Papers* 9 (1955): 48.

History of Sangamon County, Illinois: Together with Sketches of Its Cities, Villages and Townships. Chicago: Interstate Publishing Company, 1881.

Hofbauer, Adam. "The Lost Films of the 1840s: The Mississippi River and the Tradition of Proto-Cinema." *Bright Lights Film Journal*, April 30, 2013.

Hoss, E. E. "Elihu Embree, Abolitionist." *The American Historical Magazine* 2, no. 2 (1897): 117.

Howard, Memucan Hunt. "Recollections of Tennessee." *The American Historical Magazine* 7, no. 1 (January 1902): 65–66.

Hoyt, William Henry. *The Papers of Archibald D. Murphey*. Raleigh: E. M. Uzzell & Co., State Printers, 1914.

Hudson, Henry A., Jr., USNR. "Marcus Winchester and Early Memphis Postal History." *Ansearchin' News* (Winter 1997): 22.

Hughes, Cleo A. "Speculation and Settlement in West Tennessee." M.A. thesis, George Peabody College for Teachers, June 1, 1968.

Hutchison, John. "Building Was There When Megeveny Came." *The Commercial Appeal*, January 8, 1939.

"Immense Sale of Town Lots in Hopefield, Arkansas." *Little Rock True Democrat*, March 16, 1859.

"Indians Got Drunk." *The Commercial Appeal*, December 25, 1898.

Jackson, Andrew. Letter to James Winchester, April 13, 1819. *James Winchester Correspondence*. Archives Division, Tennessee State Library and Archives.

———. Letter to John Coffee, April 1832. In *Correspondence of Andrew Jackson*, edited by John Spencer Bassett, vol. 4, 430. Washington, DC: Carnegie Institution, 1929.

———. "Second Annual Message to Congress," December 6, 1830. In *A Compilation of the Messages and Papers of the Presidents, 1789–1897*, edited by James D. Richardson, vol. 2, 519–20. Washington, D.C.: Government Printing Office, 1896.

Jackson Purchase 150 Years, A Sesquicentennial. Mayfield, KY: The Mayfield Messenger, 1969.

James E. Arsenault & Co. Brief submitted by attorney Samuel Blatchford to the Superior Court of the City of New York, 1844, in the libel case of *Thurlow Weed vs. James G. Bennett*.

James, Alice Redden. "The Winchester Cemetery." *The Commercial Appeal*, January 10, 1909.

James, Marquis. *The Life of Andrew Jackson*. New York: The Bobbs-Merrill Company, 1938.

Bibliography

Jefferson, Thomas. Letter to Governor William Henry Harrison, February 27, 1803. In *The Territorial Papers of the United States, vol. 7, The Territory of Indiana, 1800–1810*, edited by Clarence E. Carter, 90–92. Washington, D.C.: Government Printing Office, 1939.

Jesse, the "Scribe." Edited by James E. Roper. *The Chronicles of the Farmers' and Merchants' Bank*. Memphis: Southwestern at Memphis, 1960.

John, Richard R. *Spreading the News: The American Postal System from Franklin to Morse*. Cambridge, MA: Harvard University Press, 1995.

Johnson, Cave. Letter to James K. Polk, February 3, 1845. In *Correspondence of James K. Polk Digital Edition*, edited by Michael David Cohen et al. Charlottesville: University of Virginia Press, Rotunda, 2021.

Journal of the House of Representatives of the State of Tennessee. Knoxville: Jac. C. & Jno. L. Moses, 1848.

Journal of the Proceedings of the Southwestern Convention: Began and Held at the City of Memphis, on the 12th November, 1845. Memphis: Southwestern Convention, November 15, 1845.

Kanon, Tom. *Tennesseans at War, 1812–1815*. Tuscaloosa, AL: University of Alabama Press, 2014.

Keating, John M. *History of Memphis, Tennessee*. Syracuse, NY: D. Mason & Co., 1888.

King, Edward. *The Great South*. Hartford: American Publishing Company, 1875.

Kinnaird, Lawrence. *Spain in the Mississippi Valley, 1765–1794*. In *Annual Report of the American Historical Association for the Year 1945*, vol. 2, pt. 1, 317. Washington, D.C.: U.S. Government Printing Office, 1949.

Koch, Alexander, Chris Brierley, Mark M. Maslin, and Simon L. Lewis. "Earth System Impacts of the European Arrival and Great Dying in the Americas after 1492." *Quaternary Science Reviews* 207 (2019): 13–36.

Kriebel, Bob. "Battle of Tippecanoe through Harrison, Indians' Eyes." Journal & Courier (Lafayette, IN). Accessed March 24, 2024.

Lafayette, Marquis de. Letter to George Washington, March 17, 1790. In *The Papers of George Washington, Presidential Series*, vol. 5, edited by Dorothy Twohig. Charlottesville: University Press of Virginia, 1996.

Langguth, A. J. *Union 1812: The Americans Who Fought the Second War of Independence*. New York: Simon & Schuster, 2006.

Lane, Margaret. *Frances Wright and the Great Experiment*. Manchester: Manchester University Press, 1972.

"Last Rites Today." *The Tennessean* (Nashville, TN), December 13, 1903.

"The Late Robertson Topp." *Memphis Daily Appeal*, June 14, 1876.

Lawrence, William. Letter to John Overton, June 4, 1819. *William Lawrence Correspondence*. Archives Division, Tennessee State Library and Archives.

———. Will, January 17, 1830. *Shelby County, Tennessee, Will Books 1830–1862*, no. 1. Shelby County Archives.

Leavitt, Joshua. Remarks at an anti-slavery convention, London, 1843. Quoted in David S. Heidler and Jeanne T. Heidler, *David Farragut: Union Admiral*. Santa Barbara, CA: ABC-CLIO, 2010.

Lewis, Henry. *The Valley of the Mississippi Illustrated*. Dusseldorf: Arnz & Comp., 1857.

"Lewis' Panorama of the Mississippi." *National Intelligencer and Washington Express*, April 8, 1850.

Linklater, Andro. *Measuring America: How the United States was Shaped by the Greatest Land Sale in History*. New York: Penguin Group, 2003.

Lives on the Mississippi: Literature and Culture along the Great River from the Collections of the St. Louis Mercantile Library Association. St. Louis: St. Louis Mercantile Library at the University of Missouri–St. Louis, 2010.

Loller, Travis. "'A Whole Lot of People Upset by This Study': DNA & the Truth About Appalachia's Melungeons." *The News Leader* (Staunton, VA), March 8, 2021.

"Lots in Memphis." *Memphis Advocate and Western-District Intelligencer*, February 23, 1828.

Ludlow, N. M. *Dramatic Life, As I Found It*. St. Louis: G. I. Jones and Company, 1880.

Madison, James. "Message to Congress, June 1, 1812." In The Writings of James Madison, edited by Gaillard Hunt, 161. New York: G.P. Putnam's Sons, 1901.

Magness, Perre. "Founders Had Eye on Quick Profits." *The Commercial Appeal*, July 21, 1988.

———. "Methodists Helped Tame Rivertown." *The Commercial Appeal*, November 22, 1992.

———. *Past Times: Stories of Early Memphis*. Memphis: Parkway Press, 1994.
———. "Politician Lived, Died by Bullets." *The Commercial Appeal*, August 12, 1999.
Malone, James H. "History of Early Land Grants for Public Purposes in Memphis." *The Commercial Appeal*, March 21, 1915.
"A Mammoth Dinner." *Vicksburg Whig*, May 20, 1857.
Mass, John R. *Defending a New Nation, 1783–1811*. Washington, D.C.: Center of Military History, 2023.
McAfee, Robert B. *History of the Late War in the Western Country*. Bowling Green: Historical Publications Company, 1919.
McCallie, Ellen Douglas Jarnagin. "Early Advocate Women's Rights." *The Chattanooga News*, November 10, 1914.
McCormack, Edward Michael. *Slavery on the Tennessee Frontier*. Nashville: Tennessee American Revolution Bicentennial Commission, 1977.
McDermott, John Frances. *The Lost Panoramas of the Mississippi*. Chicago: The University of Chicago Press, 1958.
McGee, G. R. *A History of Tennessee from 1663 to 1914*. New York: American Book Company, 1899.
McPherson, James M. *Battle Cry of Freedom: The Civil War Era*. New York: Oxford University Press, 1988.
Memphis City Directory. "Maj. M.B. Winchester." Memphis: D.O. Dooley & Company, 1855.
"Memphis First Brick Home Goes to Make Way for Auto." *The Commercial Appeal* (Memphis, TN), August 10, 1930.
"Memphis Had a Rival Then." *The Commercial Appeal*, August 5, 1894.
"The Memphis of Forty-two Years Ago." *The Daily Memphis Avalanche*, April 3, 1881.
Mills, John. Letter to cousin Gilbert, May 19, 1807. *John Mills Letters*. Department of Archives and History, Louisiana State University.
"Minister Has Troubles." *The Commercial Appeal*, December 9, 1926.
Minutes of House of Burgesses, 1730–35. Box 2, bundle: S.C., 9, Parish Transcripts, N.Y. Historical Society. Quoted in Winthrop D. Jordan. *White over Black: American Attitudes Toward the Negro, 1550–1812*. Chapel Hill: University of North Carolina Press, 1968.
"Mississippi Devours Once Thriving Town." *Cape Girardeau Morning Sun*, October 20, 1916.
Mooney, Chase C. *Slavery in Tennessee*. Westport, CT: Negro Universities Press, 1957.
Moore, Gary. "Memphis Belle." *Memphis Magazine*, May 1943.
"Movie Built Around Jackson OK'd by Censors." *The Nashville Banner*, September 4, 1936.
Myers, Amrita Chakrabarti. *The Vice President's Black Wife: The Untold Life of Julia Chinn*. Chapel Hill: The University of North Carolina Press, 2023.
"The Name of Memphis." *The Commercial Appeal*, December 9, 1926.
Nashville Clarion, April 7, 1812
"New Music." *The Memphis Daily Eagle*, April 20, 1848.
Nichols, Thomas Low. *Supramundane Facts in the Life of Jesse Babcock Ferguson*. London: The Spiritual Lyceum, 1865.
Niles' Weekly Register, August 8, 1835.
Northup, Solomon. *Twelve Years a Slave*. Auburn: Derby and Miller, 1853.
Nugent, Frank. "The Screen." *The New York Times*, September 5, 1936.
"Obituary." *National Banner and Nashville Whig*, August 5, 1826.
"The Old Folks." *Memphis Daily Appeal*, June 18, 1871.
Old Folks Record, no. 1 (October 1874): 1.
Old Folks Record, no. 12 (September 1875): 533–34.
"Old Folks at Home." *Memphis Daily Appeal* (Memphis, TN), July 26, 1867.
"Old Landmarks in Memphis." *Memphis Avalanche*, May 27, 1888.
"An Old Man's Plaint." *The Memphis Daily Appeal*, March 2, 1873.
"Old Times." *Memphis Daily Appeal*, June 18, 1871.
Oldschool, Oliver. "Memphis, A New Town on the Mississippi." *The Port Folio* 9, no. 1 (1820): 489–94.
"Order Plans for New City Park." *The Commercial Appeal*, April 18, 1931.

Overton, John. Letter to James Winchester, April 4, 1823. *James Winchester Correspondence*. Archives Division, Tennessee State Library and Archives.

———. Letter to James Winchester, January 21, 1828. *James Winchester Correspondence*, Archives Division, Tennessee State Library and Archives.

———. Letter to James Winchester, October 15, 1820. *Winchester Papers*. Tennessee State Library and Museum.

———. Letter to James Winchester, October 25, 1818. *James Winchester Papers, 1787–1953*. Tennessee State Library and Archives.

"Paralysis Cured." *Public Ledger*, October 27, 1870.

Pardon, James. *Life of Andrew Jackson*. Vol. 1. New York: Mason Brothers, 1861.

Parker, Allison M. "'What We Do Expect the People Legislatively to Effect.'" In *Women and the Unstable State in Nineteenth-Century America*, edited by Alison M. Parker and Stephanie Cole, 62–63. College Station, TX: Texas A&M University Press, 2000.

Parrington, Vernon Louis. *The Colonial Mind*. New York: Harcourt, Brace and Company, 1927.

Patrick, James. *Architecture in Tennessee*. Knoxville: The University of Tennessee Press, 1981.

Perkins, Alice J. G., and Theresa Wolfson. *Frances Wright, Free Enquirer: The Study of a Temperament*. New York: Harper & Brothers, 1939.

Perkins, J. G., and Theresa Wolfson. *Frances Wright: Free Enquirer, The Study of a Temperament*. Philadelphia: Porcupine Press, 1972.

Phelan, James. *History of Tennessee: The Making of a State*. Boston: Houghton, Mifflin and Company, 1888.

Pittsburgh Weekly Gazette (Pittsburgh, PA), March 12, 1813.

Poinsatte, Charles. *Outpost in the Wilderness: Fort Wayne, 1706–1828*. Allen County, IN: Fort Wayne Historical Society, 1976.

Post Office Department, Letters Sent, Book 0-2 (August 13, 1845), 458.

Proceedings of the Seventh Annual Meeting of the Bar Association of Tennessee. Nashville: Marshall & Bruce C., 1899.

"Proposals for Publishing in Memphis, Tennessee." *The Memphis Advocate and Western District Intelligencer*, October 30, 1832.

"Protect the Dead." *Memphis Public Ledger*, April 26, 1875.

"Public Meeting." *The Memphis Daily Eagle*, March 22, 1849.

Putnam, Albigence Waldo. *History of Middle Tennessee*. Nashville: A. A. Stitt, Southern Methodist Publishing House, 1859.

Quaife, Milo Milton. *James K. Polk's Diary*. Chicago: A. C. McClurg & Co., 1910.

Raboteau, Albert J. *Slave Religion: The "Invisible Institution" in the South*. Oxford: Oxford University Press, 2004.

Rainey, W. H. *Rainey's Memphis City Directory, 1855*. Memphis: D.O. Dooley & Co, 1855.

Rawlings, Isaac. Will. *Shelby County Will Books, 1830–1862*. Tennessee, U.S., Wills and Probate Records, 1779–2008. Accessed November 20, 2024. Ancestry.com.

Rawlings, J. J. *Miscellaneous Writings and Reminiscences of J. J. Rawlings*. Memphis: United Charities, 1896.

"Reception of Mr. Polk." *The Weekly Memphis Eagle*, March 29, 1849.

"A Relic of the Olden Time." *The Memphis Daily Avalanche*, April 29, 1859.

"Remains of Two Thousand." *The Commercial Appeal*, December 13, 1896.

Remini, Robert V. *Andrew Jackson*. New York: Harper Perennial, 1966.

"Rescue from a Vandal Resort." *The Commercial Appeal*, August 4, 1896.

Roark, Eldon. "A New Look into the Past." *The Memphis Press-Scimitar*, March 30, 1953.

Robertson, Rob. "Fullen Dock Revives Shipment of Cotton via Mississippi Barges." *Memphis Business Journal* 26, no. 18 (August 27, 2004): 2.

Roosevelt, Thomas. *American Statesman: Thomas Hart Benton*. Boston: The Riverside Press, 1886.

Roper, James E. "Isaac Rawlings, Frontier Merchant." *Tennessee Historical Quarterly* 20, no. 3 (1961): 266–69.

———. "Marcus B. Winchester, First Mayor of Memphis." *Tennessee Historical Quarterly* 18, no. 1 (1959): 7.

Bibliography

———. "Marcus Winchester and the Earliest Years of Memphis." *Tennessee Historical Quarterly* 21, no. 4 (1962): 327–328.

———. "Paddy Meagher, Tom Huling, and the Bell Tavern." *West Tennessee Historical Society Papers*, no. 31 (1977): 13–15.

Roper, James. *The Founding of Memphis, 1818–1820*. Memphis: The Memphis Sesquicentennial, Inc., 1970.

Rothman, Joshua D. *Flush Times and Fever Dreams: A Story of Capitalism and Slavery in the Age of Jackson*. Athens: University of Georgia Press, 2001.

Santayana, George. *The Life of Reason: Reason in Common Sense*. New York: Charles Scribner's Sons, 1905.

Scales, Susan Winchester Powel. *My Mother, A Biography*. Unpublished manuscript, 1950.

Sealsfield, Charles. *The Americans as They Are*. London: Hurst, Chance & Co., 1828.

Seigenthaler, John. *James K. Polk*. New York: Time Books, 2003.

Semmes, John E. *John H. B. Latrobe and His Times, 1803–1891*. Baltimore: The Norman Remington Co, 1917.

Semmes, Raphael. *Baltimore as Seen by Visitors, 1783–1860*. Baltimore: Maryland Historical Society, 1953.

Shackford, James Atkins. *David Crockett: The Man and the Legend*. Chapel Hill: University of North Carolina Press, 1956.

Shelton, Emma. *William Winchester, 1711–1790*. Carroll County, MD: Historical Society of Carroll County, Maryland, 1993.

Sioussat, George L. "Memphis as a Gateway to the West." *Tennessee Historical Magazine* 3, no. 1 (March 1917): 4.

Smith, Sol. *Theatrical Management in the West and the South for Thirty Years*. New York: Harper & Brothers, 1868.

Smith, Thomas. Letter to W. W. Worsley, November 7, 1812. State Historical Society of Wisconsin Library, Draper MSS, Kentucky Papers, 5CC69.

"A Soldier's Grave." *Memphis Public Ledger*, November 22, 1882.

The South: A Collection from Harper's Magazine. New York: Gallery Books, 1990.

St. Louis Weekly Reveille, September 6, 1849. 4.

Stampp, Kenneth M. *The Particular Institution: Slavery in the American South*. New York: Alfred E. Knopf, 1936.

Starrs, James E., and Kira Gale. *The Death of Meriwether Lewis: A Historic Crime Scene Investigation*. Omaha: River Junction Press, 2009.

Tebbel, John and Keith Jennison. *The American Indian Wars*. Edison, NJ: Castle Books, 2003.

Thomas, William. "Ex-mayor Made Mark, But Never Got Marker." *The Commercial Appeal*, February 8, 1991.

Tocqueville, Alexis de. *Democracy in America*. London: Saunders and Otley, 1835.

———. *Memoir, Letters, and Remains of Alexis de Tocqueville*. Vol. 1. Cambridge: Macmillan and Co., 1861.

Tracy, Ebenezer Carter. *Memoir of the Life of Jeremiah Evarts*. Boston: Crocker and Brewster, 1845.

Travellers Rest. *A Past Uncovered: The Story of the Enslaved People of Travellers Rest*. Nashville, TN, October 19, 2025.

Trollope, Anthony. *Autobiography of Anthony Trollope*. New York: Dodd, Mead & Company, 1905.

Trollope, Frances. *Domestic Manners of the Americans*. New York: Alfred A. Knopf, 1949.

Underwood, Quincy K. "Address of Judge Q. K. Underwood." *Old Folks Record*, no. 12 (September 1875): 531–32.

Van Buren, Martin. "Second Annual Message." December 3, 1838. In *The American Presidency Project*, edited by John T. Woolley and Gerhard Peters. Santa Barbara, CA: University of California at Santa Barbara.

Veazey, Walter. "Hopefield Has Fought A Long But Losing Match." *The Commercial Appeal*, June 6, 1965.

Wade, Richard C. *The Urban Frontier: The Rise of Western Cities, 1790–1830*. Cambridge, MA: Harvard University Press, 1959.

Waldran, William B. "Anniversary Address of W. B. Waldran." *Old Folks Record* 1 (December 1874): 100.

Waldstreicher, David. *Slavery's Constitution: From Revolution to Ratification*. New York: Hill and Wang, 2009.
Walker, William A. "Martial Sons: Tennessee Enthusiasm for the War of 1812." *Tennessee Historical Quarterly* 20, no. 1 (1961): 31.
Wallace, David Duncan. *The Life of Henry Laurens*. New York: G. P. Putnam's Sons, 1915.
Warner, Michael. "Publics and Counterpublics (Abbreviated Version)." *Quarterly Journal of Speech* 88, no. 4 (2002): 413–25.
Washington, George. Letter to the Commissioners to the Southern Indians, August 29, 1789. Founders Online, National Archives. Accessed February 9, 2025. Originally published in *The Papers of George Washington, Presidential Series*, vol. 3, 15 June 1789–5 September 1789, edited by Dorothy Twohig, 551. Charlottesville: University Press of Virginia, 1989.
Waterman, William Randall. *Frances Wright*. New York: Longmans, Green & Co., 1924.
Watson, Samuel. *The Clock Struck One, and Christian Spiritualist*. New York: Samuel R. Wells, 1872.
Watson, Samuel. *The Clock Struck One*. New York: Samuel R. Wells, 1872.
Webster, Daniel. "Seventh of March Speech," March 7, 1850. In *The Works of Daniel Webster*, vol. 5, 344. Boston: Little, Brown and Company, 1853.
Weeks, Linton. *Memphis: A Folk History*. Little Rock: Parkhurst Publishers, 1982.
West, Audrey. "Historian Says Memphis Neglects Its Past." *The Memphis Press-Scimitar*, May 25, 1977.
"Where Weary Travelers of Yesterday Found Rest in Memphis." *The Commercial Appeal*, January 1, 1940.
"Will of Duke W. Sumner." *Tennessee, U.S., Wills and Probate Records, 1779–2008*, Davidson County. Accessed November 7, 2024. Ancestry.com.
"William Mizell – Chickasaw Indian Interpreter, Trader and Trapper." Ancestry.com. Uploaded by Pearcy, August 11, 2009. Accessed December 2, 2024.
Williams, Edward III. *Early Memphis and Its River Rivals*. Memphis: Historical Hiking Trails, reprinted from *The West Tennessee Historical Society Papers* 22 (1968).
Williams, Frank. *Tennessee's Presidents*. Knoxville: University of Tennessee Press, 1981.
Williams, Joseph S. *Old Times in West Tennessee*. Memphis: W. G. Cheeney, 1873.
Winchester Revolutionary War Account Book, 1779–1804. Accessed on Case Antiques Auctions & Appraisals.
Winchester, James. *Letter of Condolence to David Winchester*. 1752–1826. GLC06997.55. The Gilder Lehrman Institute of American History. Accessed through Adam Matthew, *American History, 1493–1945*.
Winchester, John. *The Clarion and Tennessee State Gazette*, July 8, 1817.
Winchester, Marcus B. Letter to James K. Polk, March 27, 1849. In *Correspondence of James K. Polk, Digital Edition*, edited by Michael David Cohen et al. Charlottesville: University of Virginia Press, Rotunda, 2021.
———. Deposition, September 15, 1851. *The Mayor and Aldermen of South Memphis v. Wardlow Howard and Joseph Kent*. Benjamin L. Hooks Central Library, Memphis and Shelby County Room.
———. Letter to John Claybrooke, June 10, 1851. *Claybrooke and Overton Papers, Addition 2, 1804–1903*. Tennessee State Library and Archives.
———. Letter to John Claybrooke, May 1, 1842. *Claybrooke and Overton Papers, Addition 2, 1804–1903*.
———. Letter to John Overton, January 15, 1826. *John Overton Correspondence*, Archives Division, Tennessee State Library and Archives.
———. *Map of Ohio and Letter from Marcus Winchester to His Sister* [map]. The Gilder Lehrman Institute of American History, GLC06997.18. Available through Adam Matthew, *American History, 1493–1945* (Marlborough, UK).
———. *Will of Marcus B. Winchester*, case no. 1730, 1857. In *Loose Probate Papers, Folders 1–2014, 1857*. Shelby County Probate Records. Shelby County Archives, Memphis, Tennessee.
"Winchester Park to Fulfil Dream for Granddaughter of City's Founder." *Memphis Press-Scimitar*, 1931.
Winchester, Robert Owen. Letter to Selima Winchester, January 29, 1850. Ancestry.com.
Winchester, William. *Letter to James Winchester*, August 25, 1810. GLC06997.13. The Gilder Lehrman Institute of American History. Accessed through *American History, 1493–1945*. Marlborough, UK: Adam Matthew Digital.

Bibliography

Wooldridge, John. History of Nashville, Tennessee. Nashville, TN: Published for H. W. Crew by the Publishing House of the Methodist Episcopal Church, South, 1890.

Wright, Frances. *A Plan for the Gradual Abolition of Slavery in the United States, Without Danger or Loss to the Citizens of the South*. Baltimore: Benjamin Lundy, 1825.

———. *Course of Popular Lectures, as Delivered by Frances Wright; with Three Addresses on Various Public Occasions, and a Reply to the Charges Against the French Reformers of 1789*. New York: Office of the Free Enquirer, 1829.

———. Letter to Timothy Pickering, July 1, 1796. Founders Online, National Archives. Accessed February 9, 2025. Originally published in *The Papers of George Washington, Presidential Series*, vol. 20, 1 April–21 September 1796, edited by David R. Hoth and William M. Ferraro, 349–50. Charlottesville: University of Virginia Press, 2019.

———. *Views of Society and Manners in America: In a Series of Letters from That Country to a Friend in England, During the Years 1818, 1819, and 1820*. New York: E. Bliss and E. White, 1821.

Yoakum, Henderson K. *Letter to James K. Polk*, April 28, 1845. In *Correspondence of James K. Polk Digital Edition*, edited by Michael David Cohen et al. Charlottesville: University of Virginia Press, Rotunda, 2021.

Young, J. P. *Standard History of Memphis, Tennessee*. Knoxville, TN: H. W. Crew & Co., 1912.

This book is set in Adobe Caslon Pro, a modern digital revival of William Caslon's eighteenth-century typeface, renowned for its clarity, elegance, and historical resonance.

Index

A

Abbot, William 192
Adams, John Quincy 27, 39, 154–56, 203
Alexander, Adam 203
Alleghany (steamship) 227
American Fur Company 150
American Lebanese Syrian Associated Charities, Inc. 321
American Revolution 196, 206
American Sound Studio 220
America's Distribution Center 223
Anderson, Mildred Moon 191
Anderson, Nathaniel 190–91, 231, 236, 238–39, 240, 244–45, 246, 248, 251, 345
Andrews, Joseph F. 216
Angel, Hamp 117
Ardent Studios 220
Arkansas River 215
Astoria Fur Company 311–12
Astor Park 311
A Tale of Freedom 138
Atwood, N. B. 127

Auction Square 96–97
Auction Street 96, 117
Austin, Stephen F. 22

B

Baily, Francis 55
Ballio, Paul 76
Bank of Tennessee 283
Banks, Lucile Webb 317–18, 324
Barbara (enslaved) 178
Baribeau, Adrien 174
Baribeau, Perry 174
Baribeau, Pierre 173–75
Baribeau, Therese 174
Baribeau, Victoire Loiselle 174–75
Barry, H. L. 160
Barry, Mary 160
Barry, Richard 160
Battle of Alamance 20
Battle of Horseshoe Bend 66, 132
Battle of King's Mountain 105
Battle of the Thames 258
Bayou Gayoso 105, 128, 292
B.B. King Boulevard 217, 219
Bean, Elizabeth 106
Bean, Jesse 105–6
Bean, Joab 105

Bean, Lydia 105
Bean, Russell 105
Bean's Creek 106
Bean Station 106
Bean, William 105
Bean, William Jr. 105
Beaumont, Gustave de 84, 131
Beecher, Catherine 194
Beecher, Henry Ward 194
Bell Tavern 89, 108, 114, 159, 219, 254
Bell, William 178
Benton, Elizabeth McDowell 172
Benton, Jesse 171
Benton, Thomas Hart 166, 168, 171–73, 175–76, 276, 290–91, 298
Bergen, John 158
Berry, Richard H. 159
Betis, John 112
Betsy (enslaved) 300
Bettis, Mary Jane 112
Bettis, Sally 112
Bettis, Sarah Patterson 112
Bettis, Tillman "Till" 112
Bettis, William 112–13
Blackburn, Joseph 319
Black, George Gabriel 18
Black, John 18
Black, John Jr. 18
Black, Mariah Susan Gibson

Index

18
Bledsoe's Creek 12, 14, 18, 20
Blount, William 9, 13
Blue Ruin Tavern 109, 219
Bondi, Barrymore 157
Bondi, Beulah 157
Borlon, Solon 110
Botta, Carlo 137
Boucher, Joshua 205
Boulton, Annice 112
Boyd, Ruthie Ann (enslaved) 178
Boyer, Jean-Pierre 195
Breedlove, James Waller 22, 43, 47, 165, 185, 195, 196, 263, 264
Brinkley, Ann Overton 160
Brock, Isaac 40
Brooks Museum of Art 313
Brooks, Preston 298
Brown, Aaron Vail 271
Brown, Daniel R. 107
Brown, Eliza 107
Brown, James 96
Brown, Lucian 271
Brown, Samuel 96, 113
Brown, Samuel R. 107
Brown, William T. 285
Buchanan, George 32
Buchanan, James 271, 298–99
Bullard, Joseph 74
Burgin, Abner 136
Burr, Aaron 173
Bush, George W. 267
Butler, Robert 68–69

C

Cage, William 22, 93
Cairo, Illinois 85
Cairo, Tennessee 22, 33, 82–83, 85, 92, 152, 184, 299
Calhoun Building 220
Calhoun, John C. 26, 68, 95, 111–12, 203, 220–21, 223
Calhoun Street 221
Calvary Cemetery 317, 320
Calvary Episcopal Church 177, 220, 275
Campbell, George Washington 36
Cannon, Patty 205

Caroline E. Watkins (steamboat) 268
Carr, Anderson B. 92–93, 95–96, 110, 113, 116, 184, 283, 300
Carrell, Edward J. 260
Carr, John 47
Carroll, William 48, 171
Carr, Overton 92, 107
Carr, Thomas 92, 95–96 113–14
Carr, Young Allen 307
Carter, Thomas D. 113
Cassedy, Charles 46–47, 82, 151–52
Cass, Lewis 265–66
Catfish Bay 128
Cavelier, René-Robert, Sieur de La Salle 53
Chadwick, James E. 307
Chapman's Theatrical Steamboat 220
Charles H. Organ (steamboat) 302
Cherokee 4, 12, 54, 66, 125, 131–34, 136
Cherokee Nation v. Georgia 133
Cherokee Phoenix 133
Chesapeake 26
Chickasaw 2–4, 12, 36, 40, 51–57, 61–62, 65, 68–69, 73–78, 81–82, 86, 91, 93–95, 97, 101, 116, 125–26, 132, 143, 148, 169, 209, 218–19, 222–23, 262, 300, 311–12
Chickasaw Old Town 69
Chickasaw Street 97, 116
Chinn, Julia (enslaved) 256, 258–59
Chinubby 77
Choctaw 12, 40, 52, 125, 132, 134, 145
Chronicles of the Farmers' and Merchants' Bank 233–34, 284
Chucalissa 52
Cincinnati Bazaar 192
City Hotel 136
Civil Rights Act of 1964 197
Civil War 112, 150, 160, 182, 197, 202, 226, 261,

267, 270, 287, 292, 299, 311, 314, 320
Claiborne, William C. C. 73
Clark, George Rogers 91
Clark, William 57, 75, 173
Claybrooke, John S. 160–61, 165, 262, 283, 290, 297, 300
Claybrooke, Mary Ann Perkins 161
Clay, Henry 26, 111, 140, 222, 266, 267, 333, 335
Cleveland, Grover 222, 267
Cobblestones 292
Coe, Hudson Levin 284, 286
Coe, John 285
Coffee, Elijah 108–09
Coffee, John 66, 78, 108–09, 133, 155, 221
Coffin, Long Tom 220
Colbert, George 77
Colbert, James Jr. 94, 95
Colbert, James Logan 91, 209
Colbert, Levi 77
Colbert, Sally 209
Colbert's Ferry 93, 94
Commerce Street 177
Commercial Hotel 220
Cook, James B. 312
Cooper, James Fenimore 220
Cooper's Mercantile 135
Coppock, Paul 323
Cornwallis, Charles 8
Corrupt Bargain 154
Cotton Exchange 108, 121
Cotton Exchange Building 108
Court Square 97, 109–10, 294, 302, 311, 327
Court Street 217
Cowley, Thomas 319
Cragfont 2, 17–18, 21, 28, 44–45, 47, 67, 92, 151–53
Creek 10, 12, 14, 18, 20, 48, 65, 67, 106, 116, 132, 187, 207, 219, 253, 286
Crockett, David 48, 115–16, 125, 128–36, 158, 243, 257, 262, 326, 336,
Cumberland River 22, 62,

357

83
Cuming, Fortescue 56–57,
Curtis, Joe 225
Cusack, James M. 320

D

Dabney, Walter D. 147, 284
Dakin, James 222
Dakota 174
D'Arusmont, Frances Sylva 197
D'Arusmont, Guillaume Phiquepal 195, 197
Davis, James 2, 7, 105, 112, 126, 130, 135, 168–69, 177–178, 203, 216, 226–27, 233, 254, 256, 276, 288, 319, 323
Davis, Joseph L. 127
Davis, Ruben 117
Davis, William A. 113
Dean, William 113
Declaration of Independence 40, 181
Democratic Party 112, 126–27, 154, 231, 256, 257–60, 263, 265, 268, 271, 285, 289, 297, 298–300
De Soto, Hernando 52, 106, 315
Desoto Insurance Company 121
Devil's Elbow 86
DeWitt, John H. 48, 157
Dillahunty, Lewis 116
Dolly (enslaved) 208
Domestic Manners of the Americans 107, 192
Dougherty, John R. 127
Douglass, Addison H. 295
Dred Scott v. Sandford 261
Dunlap, William C. 265
Durham, Walter T. 22, 27–28, 42, 199

E

Earl, Ralph E. W. 47, 126, 157, 221
East Parkway North 97
Eaton, John 154–57, 319, 336
Eaton, Maria Allen 319

Eaton, Peggy 157
Edward (steamboat) 190
Elmwood Cemetery 153, 301, 319, 320, 322
Emancipator 189
Embree, Elihu 187, 189
Enterprise (steamboat) 183
Epps, Edwin 205
Etheridge, Emma 312
Evarts, Jeremiah (William Penn) 108
Exchange Square 36, 97, 108, 121, 311

F

Fannin, James W. 285
Fanny (enslaved) 208
Farmers' and Merchants' Bank 128, 210, 218, 233–34, 270, 284–85
Farrington, Jacob 319
F. A. & T. Young 116
Federalist Party 27
Ferguson, Jesse B. 277, 305–07, 309
Ferguson, Lucinda 308
Ferguson, William J. 276
Fillmore, Millard 222, 298
First Presbyterian Church 319
Flatboatmen's War 225
Flavio, Philip 220
Flint, Timothy 224
Flower, George 137, 141, 188, 189
Flynn, Barney 108
Fooy, Benjamin 54, 56, 90, 91, 105, 153, 223, 290, 318
Fort Malden 39, 44, 45
Fort Pickering 56, 57, 58, 63, 73, 75, 82, 86, 221, 223, 262, 293, 318
Fort San Fernando 54, 55, 105
Fort Tuckahoe 12, 13
Foster, Ephraim 243
Fowler, John W. 216
Fowlkes, Jeptha 284–85, 337, 342
Franklin, Benjamin 53, 82, 106, 160, 278, 298, 340
Franklin County 106

Frémont, Jessie Benton 298
Frémont, John C. 172, 298
French and Indian War 8
French Revolution 82, 138, 139, 196
Frenchtown 43, 45–46, 299
Friends for our Riverfront 313
Frisco Bridge 302
Front Street 54, 97, 106, 108, 177
Fulton, Robert 183
Furness, Horace Howard 233

G

Gaines, P. G. 110
Gallatin, Tennessee 14, 287
Gayoso de Lemos, Manuel Luis 54, 58, 96, 105, 128, 222
Gayoso House 222, 226, 269, 270, 307
George (enslaved) 208
Gibson, Gideon 4, 19
Gibson, Gideon Jr. 19, 20
Gibson, Jordan 18, 20
Goldwater, Barry 267
Goliad Massacre 285
Grace, Catherine 105
Grace Delphia (enslaved) 208
Graham, Frank 216
Graham, George 65, 121, 127, 216, 337
Graham, George F. 127
Graham, Joseph 121
Great Depression 322
Great Transcontinental Railroad Convention 290
Great Western Land Pirate 86, 255
Great Western (steamship) 275
Greenlow v. Rawlings 210
Grimm, Barbara 319
Grimm, Charles 319
Grundy, Felix 26, 154, 243, 338
Gunter, Edmund 94
Gunter's chain 94

H

Haiti 143, 195, 196–197
Haitian Revolution 195
Hall, Aaron 206
Hall, James 206
Hall, Jude 204, 206
Hall of Science 194
Hall, William 20, 206
Hamilton, Alexander 27, 117, 173
Ham, J. A. 316, 317
Handy, W. C. 220
Hannah (enslaved) 177, 209, 211
Hardeman Academy 160
Hardeman's Cross Roads 160
Harpeth Union Male Academy 160
Harrison, William Henry 20, 40–47, 66–67, 257, 260, 338
Harry (enslaved) 300
Hart, James 307
Hart's Saloon 135, 220
Hatchie River 53, 94
Hatley, J. 116
Hawthorne, Agnes Price 218, 319
Hawthorne, Hugh 218
Heath & Livermore 312
Helen McGregor (steamboat) 188, 316, 318
Henderson & Fern 177
Henry (enslaved) 208
Hermitage 17–18, 82, 157, 159
Hernando de Soto Bridge 106, 315
Hervieu, Auguste 190–192
Hickman, Edwin 136, 225, 265
Highland Heights 290
High Street 316
Hilliard, William 319
Hill, Mary 107
Hinds, Dick 216–17
Hogg, Samuel 159
Hooker, Isabella Beecher 194
Hook, John 127
Hopefield, Arkansas 297, 301, 313, 315
Hopefield Real Estate Company 4, 283–84, 286, 313
Hosmer, Harriet Goodhue 291
Hoss, Elijah E. 202
Hotchkiss, Katherine Winchester (aunt) 150–51
Houston, Sam 48, 67, 139, 222, 283, 312
Howard, Memucan Hunt 293
Huling, Tom 89
Hull, William 39–41, 45
Hume 32
Hunter, Alberta 220
Huntsman, Adam 243, 257
Huran (steamboat) 134

I

Indian Removal Act of 1830 130
Internal Improvements Convention 290
Iradell, James 250
Irwin, William 113
Island Thirty-Seven 86
It's a Wonderful Life 157

J

Jackson, Andrew 1, 3, 10–11, 18, 22, 26, 46–48, 58, 62–63, 65–66, 68–69, 73, 76, 77–78, 81–82, 92–93, 95, 97, 111–13, 116, 130, 132–34, 137, 139, 142, 144, 154–60, 166, 168, 171–72, 183–85, 203, 221, 232, 235, 250, 256–58, 260–62, 266–67, 293, 307, 319
Jackson (enslaved) 208
Jackson Purchase 3, 62, 65, 77
Jackson, Rachel 10–11, 18, 47, 69, 155–57, 219, 221, 340, 343
Jackson Street 97, 106
James, Bettis 112
Jane, Caroline 319
Jarnagin, Ellen Douglas 142
Jarnagin, Spencer 142, 269
Jefferson Street 220
Jefferson, Thomas 39, 56, 62, 66, 73, 97, 112, 139, 173, 253, 258, 278
Jenner, Edward 149
Jesse, the "Scribe" 233–34, 323
Jim (enslaved) 208
Joab, Bean 106
John (enslaved) 208–09
John Quincy Adams (steamboat) 195
John Rice Grant 2, 54, 61
John Sevier's Riflemen 105
Johnson, Adaline 258–59, 337, 343
Johnson, Cave 271
Johnson, Imogene 258
Johnson, Richard Mentor 256–260
Johnson, Robert 19
Joliet, Louis 52, 58, 222

K

Kaskaskia 174
Kearney, H. G. 110
Keating, John 323
Keedoozle 254
Kennon, Robert L. 205
King, B. B. 220
Kirk, Virginia 318, 320, 339
Knickerbocker and Wright 105

L

Ladies Hermitage Association 157
Lafayette, Marquis de 41, 112, 138–39, 142, 195, 291
Lafayette Square 112
Latham, Frank S. 262
Laurens, Henry 19, 23
Lawrence, Eliza 217–18
Lawrence, Robert 135–36, 177, 218, 231, 236, 239, 240–41, 245, 248–49, 251, 345
Lawrence, Thomas 218
Lawrence, William 81, 83, 90, 96, 107, 110, 113, 115, 116, 137, 169, 217–18, 231–32, 312, 318, 339
Lea, John M. 159
Leath, James T. 276
Leavitt, Joshua 186

Lennox, Thomas Frederick 319
Lewis and Clark Expedition 57, 173
Lewis (enslaved) 208
Lewis, Henry 213, 214
Lewis, Meriwether 57, 75
Lewis, William 43
Lewis, William B. 155
Limus (enslaved) 135, 136, 262
Livingston, Robert 183
Logan, Johnny 67, 91, 209, 340
Longacre, James Barton 221
Loosahatchie River 177, 283
Loudon, John 292
Louisiana Purchase 90, 173–74
Love, Thomas William 209
Lowes Vendome Theater 157
Ludlow, Noah 84–86
Lundy, Benjamin 189

M

Madison, James 26–27, 35, 39, 73, 93, 97, 139–40
Madison Street 220
Magevney, Eugene 109–10
Magness, Perre 83, 323
Main Street 97, 108, 116, 177, 216, 220, 233, 269, 285, 294
Malaria 55, 148, 187, 193, 217
Malone, James H. 2, 311–12, 323
Malone, Walter 311
Mangum, Willie Person 257
Manifest Destiny 266
Manning, Elizabeth B. 287
Manning, John M. 110
Manumission Intelligencer 187
Maria (enslaved) 208
Market Square 97, 177
Market Street 135
Marquette, Jacques 52–53, 58, 222
Martin, John D. 241–42, 245
Martin, William 13–14, 20

Mary (enslaved) 208
Matilda (enslaved) 182, 208
May, Andrew Jackson 160
May, Francis 95
McAfee, Robert B. 45–46
McClellan, W. B. 110
McCool, Neil 135
McDowell, James 172
McLean, Archibald "Arch" 275–76
McLean, C. D. 136
McLemore, John C. 63, 93, 117, 153, 217–18, 293
McMahon, Mary 278–79
McMahon, William 279
McMinn, Joseph 250, 283
Meagher, Paddy 89, 91–92, 105, 113–15, 169
Meagher, Sally 105
Meagher's Landing 105, 114
Meazels, Jack 125
Meigs, Return J. 45, 66
Memphis Advocate 3, 107, 109–11, 116, 319
Memphis Advocate and Western District Intelligencer 110
Memphis Businessmen's Club 191
Memphis Centenary Celebration 311
Memphis & Charleston Railroad 294
Memphis City Council 300
Memphis First United Methodist Church 109
Memphis Gazette 110
Memphis Marine and Fire Insurance Company 177
Memphis Medical College 317
Memphis Methodist Episcopal Church 223
Memphis & Ohio Railroad 227
Memphis Pyramid 106
Memphis Thespian Society 219
Memphis Tourism 220
Memphis Wharf Company 177, 210
Mero District 9–10
Métis 174

Mexican-American War 265, 268
Michigan Territory 39–40, 43, 44, 76
Minerva (enslaved) 208
Missouri River 150, 174
Mizell, William 74–5, 78
Moon, Jacob N. 178, 236, 238–39, 242, 244
Moore, Ellick 13
Morgan, Charles 20
Morgan, John 20
Mound Builders 51
Mount Vernon 138–39
Mt. Olivet Cemetery 160
Murphey, Victor Moreau 106–07
Murrell, John 86, 254–56
Muscogee Camp 169, 260, 262, 264, 276–77, 279, 288, 301–02, 305, 307
Mylne, James 137
Mystic Clan of the Confederacy 255

N

Nancy (enslaved) 185
Nashoba 142–43, 187–97, 290, 297
Nashoba (steamferry) 297
Nashville & Chattanooga Railroad 294
Nashville Junto 154–57
Natchez 11, 54, 63, 84, 95, 102, 155, 175, 190, 218, 225, 255, 266, 268, 319
Natchez Trace 255
Nathaniel Anderson 116, 190, 191, 231, 236, 345
National Cemetery 320
National Labor Union 197
Navy Yard 226, 227, 269
Neely, William D. 127
Neil McCool's Saloon 135
Nelson, John (son-in-law) 289, 301
Nelson, Marcus Brutus (grandson) 289
Nelson, Seth M. 216
New Harmony 140–41, 144, 188–89, 192, 195
New Madrid Earthquake 183
New Orleans (steamboat)

183
New Orleans Steam Packet Company 121
Nile 82–83, 102
Nineteenth Amendment 197
Nonconnah Creek 286
Northup, Solomon 204–05
Northwest Ordinance of 1787 13, 181
Northwest Territory 40–42

O

Obama, Barack 267
Ohio River 67, 85, 174, 181, 218
Old Folks of Shelby County 148, 169, 320
Old Folks Record 169–70
Old Folks Society 148, 320
Oldschool, Oliver 101
Organ, Charles H. (son-in-law) 301
Osage 174
Overton, Anne Coleman 95
Overton, Elizabeth Belle 95
Overton, John 1, 3, 9–11, 17–18, 26, 46, 61–63, 73, 78, 81–82, 90, 92–93, 95–98, 101, 105, 107, 110–11, 113, 117, 119–21, 127, 130, 144, 149, 153–61, 165–66, 171, 182, 184–85, 216–17, 221, 223–24, 283, 290, 297, 313, 321
Overton, John Jr. 95, 160, 290, 297
Overton, Mary McConnell White May 95, 160
Overton Park 313
Overton, Samuel 160
Overton, Sarah Claybrooke 160
Overton Street 105, 216
Overton, Watkins 321
Owen, Robert 140, 188, 192, 278
Owen, Robert Dale 188

P

Paddy's Hen and Chickens 36, 91, 102, 129

Paine, Thomas 137
Panic of 1837 4, 232, 254, 261
Panorama of the Mississippi River 213–14
Patsey (enslaved) 204
Patterson, Dury 112
Patton, William 136
Pelt, Van 110, 319, 337, 343
Perkins, John 113
Person, Thomas H. 67
Peter (enslaved) 208
Peterkin, Thomas 74
Petticoat Affair 157, 319
Peyton, Robert 14
Phelan, James 126, 128
Philadelphia's city plan 96
Phillips, Sam 220
Phoebus, Thomas 110–11, 319, 341
Pickering, James 56–57, 63, 73, 75, 82, 86, 92, 221–23, 262, 293, 318
Pierce, Franklin 298
Pigeon Roost Road 319
Piggly Wiggly 253–254
Pinch District 128, 292
Pink Palace Museum 110, 254
Pitts, James 116
Plum Point 86
Polk, James K. 154, 222, 264–71, 285, 288, 298, 341
Polk, Sarah 266, 269–70
Pompey (enslaved) 207
Pope, Alexander 116
Pope, John 208
Poplar Avenue 97, 106, 219, 221, 285
Porter, James D. 293
Porter, Joseph B. 96
Powell, George Gabriel 19
President's Island 36, 102
Presley, Elvis 220
Prince (enslaved) 184
Procter, Henry 43–45
Prophetstown 41
Prophet, the 41
Prudhomme, Pierre 53
Purnell, John 205
Putnam, Albigence W. 26, 29

Q

Quadroon balls 167

R

Raleigh 121, 131, 209, 225, 315
Raleigh Cemetery 209, 315
Ramsey Tract 294
Rawlings Choice 210
Rawlings, Isaac Jr. ("Old Ike") 75–76, 121, 125–128, 166, 176–177, 184, 203, 208–211, 215, 217, 220, 231, 236, 239, 242, 245, 246, 248, 254, 258, 263, 284, 311, 315
Rawlings, Joseph J. 115, 119, 121, 125, 147, 177, 211, 215, 248
Rawlings, Juliet 177, 209
Rawlings, Susanna 209
Rawlings, Thomas J. 126, 177, 210
Rawlings, William Isaac 177, 208, 210, 211
Rayland, Nathaniel 216
Red River 215
Red Sticks 67
Reelfoot Lake 86, 118
Regulator Movement 19–20
Revolutionary War 3, 8, 9, 12, 17, 25, 32, 39, 40, 54, 105, 283
Rice, Elisha 61–62
Rice, John 2, 54, 61
Rice Tract 294
Richardson, James 142, 188–189, 193
Richards, Robert Edgar 301
Ridley, William 20
River Raisin 43–46, 48, 299
Robards, Lewis 10, 11
Roberts, Isaac 53–54, 334, 342
Robertson, John 295
Robertson, Topp 222
Rock Island Line 314
Roorback 266, 267
Roorback, Baron Von 266
Roosevelt, Theodore 172, 215–16, 222
Roper, James 323
Rose, Erasmus T. 307

361

Roundhead, Chief 43–44
Rousby Hall 210
Royal Studios 220
Russell, Gilbert C. 57–58, 105, 342
Rust, Esther 192

S

Sabine Hill 113
Santa Anna, Antonio López de 285
Sarah (enslaved) 178
Saunders, Clarence 253–254
Scales, Dabney 315
Scales, Susan Winchester Powell (niece) 152, 321
Scruggs, Phineas T. 285
Second Bank of the United States 232, 261
Second Bayou 153
Second Street 109
Seely, Samuel 94–95
Seminole 12, 132
Shelby, Isaac 3, 113
Shelby Street 97
She Stoops to Conquer 219
Shreve, Henry Miller 183
Sinclair, Cornelius 204–205
Smallpox 149
Smith, Al 267
Smith, Graeme McGregor 157
Smith, Solomon "Old Sol" 219
Smith, William R. 153
Society of the Cincinnati 9
South Memphis 221, 223
Southwestern Convention 222
Specie Circular 261
Spicer, Robert M. 208
Spicer, Winifred 208
Spickernagle, William 128, 225
Spiritualism 278, 305
Stampp, Kenneth 202
State of Tennessee v. Meagher 114
Stax Records 220
St. Charles Hotel, New Orleans 222
Steele, Elizabeth 20
Stewart, Thomas 118
Stewart, Virgil 255

Stickney's New Orleans Band 320
St. Jude Children's Research Hospital 125, 315–16, 322
St. Louis Cemetery Number One 263
St. Louis King of France Cemetery 174
Stowe, Harriet Beecher 194
St. Peter's Catholic Church 110, 317, 320
St. Peter's Cemetery 317, 320
Stuart, Charles 203
Sultana (Steamboat) 91
Sumner, Charles 298
Sumner County, Tennessee 12, 14, 62, 67, 299
Sumner, Duke William 207
Sun Studio 220
Supreme Court 36, 97, 133, 134

T

Tancray, Rachel 219
Taney, Roger B. 261
Tariff of 1828 111
Tate, Samuel 265, 295
Taylor, Arthur K. 307
Taylor, Landon 113
Taylor, Mary Patton 113
Taylor, Nathaniel 113
Taylor, Thomas 113
Taylor, William Dabney Strother 56
Taylor, Zachary 56, 57, 214, 222, 268, 300
Tecumseh 40–41, 67–68, 250, 258
Tennessee Democratic Convention 271
Tennessee General Assembly 113, 203
Tennessee Historical Magazine 48, 123, 228
Tennessee Society for Promoting the Manumission of Slaves 187
Tennessee State Constitutional Convention 203
Tenskwatawa 41

Texas Revolution 285
The Board of Mayor and Aldermen of South Memphis v. Wardlow Howard and James Kent Jr. 313
The Genius of Universal Emancipation 189
The Gorgeous Hussy 156
The Great Railroad Jubilee 294
Third Street 219
Thirteenth Amendment 197
Tinkle, Lindsey 136
Tippecanoe 41
Tipton, Jacob 113, 117
Tipton, Lorina Taylor 113
Tishomingo 77
Tocqueville, Alexis de 131
Tom Lee Park 311
Toncray's Alley 177
Toncray, Silas T. 216
Topp, Robertson 221, 265, 295
Trail of Tears 4, 133
Trask, Louisa Clark 318
Trask, Thomas Sterne 318, 320–21
Trask, Thomas Sterne Jr. 318
Travellers Rest 17–18, 95, 99, 158–59, 160, 182, 199
Treaty of 1818 113
Treaty of Council House 69
Treaty of New Echota 133
Treaty of Versailles 322
Trezevant, John T. 265
Trigg, Alanson 285
Triune, Tennessee 160
Trollope, Anthony 190, 192
Trollope, Cecilia 190
Trollope, Emily 190
Trollope, Frances 2, 107, 189–93, 195, 292
Trollope, Henry 190, 192
Trollope, Thomas 190
Trollope, Thomas Anthony 189–90
Turner, Nat 204
Twelve Years a Slave 204
T. Woods & Co. 110

Index

U

Uncle Tom's Cabin 194
Underwood, Qunicy K. 107
Union Avenue 97, 106, 293
Union Inn 135
U.S. Constitution 181

V

Van Buren, Martin 136, 221, 257–59, 265
Vance, Arthur (grandson) 302
Vance, Frank (grandson) 302
Vance, Hopefield (grandson) 302
Vance, Lucy (grandaughter) 289
Vance, Robert (grandson) 289, 302
Vance, William Jr. (son-in-law) 289, 300, 312
Vance, William L. 222
Van Pelt, Catherine 319
Van Pelt, Henry 319
Views of Society and Manners in America 138
Vollintine Avenue 97

W

Waldron, William B. 115, 343
Walker, Archibald 222
Walker, David 206
Walton, Augustus Q. 255
War Hawks 26, 27, 44, 258
War of 1812 2, 22, 25, 27, 39, 44, 47–48, 67, 82, 113, 116, 152–53, 171, 173, 183, 258, 299
Washington City 39, 57, 140, 157, 171, 204, 210, 213
Washington, D.C. 29, 42, 112, 139
Washington (enslaved) 208
Washington, George 8, 13, 14, 21, 34, 36, 40, 56, 65, 97, 138–39, 160, 286
Washington, Martha 140
Washington (steamboat) 183
Washita River 215
Water Street 105, 114
Watson, Samuel 278
Wayne, Anthony 40, 323
Weakley County 61, 90
Webb, Arthur 176, 323
Webster, Daniel 201, 257
We Come to Stay (tugboat) 301
Wesley, John 186
Western World and Memphis Banner of the Constitution 110
West Memphis Packet Company 301
West Point 68, 318
Wheatley, Seth 128, 231, 236, 238–39, 242, 244, 283–86
Wheeler, Andrew Jackson 307
Whitby, Camilla Wright 137, 143, 188–89, 194–95, 197, 336
Whitby, Frances 194–95
Whitby, Minerva 307
Whitby, Richeson 188, 194, 290, 307
White House 136, 154–55, 157, 221, 265–68
White, Hugh Lawson 243, 250, 257
White, James 95
Whitemore House 226
White Oak River 94
White's Level 9, 33
Wilkinson, James 173
Williams Jr., Willoughby 283
Willis, Benjamin 113
Wilson, Robert 143
Wilson, Ruby 220
Winchester, Almira (Wynne) (sister) 21
Winchester, Amarante Loiselle (wife) 4, 125, 143, 165–66, 168–71, 173–76, 178, 188, 201, 206, 256, 259, 263–64, 276–77, 287, 289–01, 319, 326, 327
Winchester, Caroline "Betsy Ann" (Shelby) (sister) 21, 268–69, 319
Winchester & Carr 92, 107, 177
Winchester Cemetery 153, 188, 209, 217, 300, 316, 317, 319–22, 334, 345
Winchester, Cynthia (aunt) 151
Winchester, Elizabeth (Vance) (aunt) 150
Winchester, Frances Wright (Vance) (daughter) 144, 178, 276, 289, 302
Winchester, George Washington (brother) 21, 110, 113, 151, 286–87, 315
Winchester, George Washington (uncle) 8, 9, 12, 14, 20, 33, 151
Winchester, Helen Marr (sister) 21, 151
Winchester, James (father) 1–3, 7–10, 12–14, 17–18, 21–22, 25–28, 31–34, 36, 39–41, 43–48, 62–63, 67, 77–78, 81–82, 92–95, 97, 106, 110, 112, 113, 119–20, 144, 150–54, 184–85, 257, 260, 299
Winchester, James Martin (brother) 21, 151
Winchester, Laura (Nelson) (daughter) 178, 264, 276, 289, 301–02
Winchester, Lisida (Organ) (daughter) 179, 263–64, 276
Winchester, Loiselle (son) 179, 264, 276, 301
Winchester, Louisa (daughter) 179, 276, 302, 305, 307–08
Winchester, Louisa Orville (sister) 21, 160, 302, 305, 307–08
Winchester, Lucilius (brother) 21, 82
Winchester, Lucy McLean (wife) 4, 166, 275, 276–77, 279, 289, 297, 300–02, 305, 307–08, 320, 323
Winchester, Lydia (Richards) (aunt) 32, 150

363

Winchester, Malvina Gaines (sister-in-law) 21, 151, 287
Winchester, Maria Eliza (Breedlove) (sister) 21, 22, 43, 47, 152, 263
Winchester, Mary A. McNamara (daughter-in-law) 301
Winchester, Napoleon (brother) 21, 82, 151, 342
Winchester, Richard (uncle) 150
Winchester, Robert Owen (son) 143, 178, 276, 288, 301
Winchester, Selima (daughter) 21, 179, 264, 276, 287–88
Winchester, Stephen (uncle) 22, 62, 290, 334–35
Winchester Street 233
Winchester, Susan Black (mother) 18, 20–21, 28, 151–53, 221, 315, 321
Winchester, Valeria (Richards) (daughter) 179, 264, 276
Winchester, Valerius Publicola "Val" (brother) 21, 82
Winchester, William David (uncle) 8, 150
Wise, Harry A. 159
Wolfe, Tobias 225–26
Wolf, Narcissus 225
Wolf River 54, 56, 61, 86, 91-94, 101, 108–09, 120, 135-137, 142, 143, 177, 210, 219, 224, 226, 292
Woods, D. W. 116
Worcester v. Georgia 133
World War I 311, 322
World War II 322
Worsham Hotel 307
Worsham, James J. 307
Wray, Harriet C. Reinhardt 300
Wray, James Richmond 300
Wright, Frances 2, 125, 136-144, 168, 182, 188-197, 203, 256, 257, 297

Wright, James 137
Wright, Joseph 182

Y

Yellow fever 55, 57, 68, 128, 148, 149, 217, 277, 287, 311
Yoakum, Henderson King 271
Yoakum, Henry 288
Young, Emma J. 319
Young, Emmanuel 215, 219
Young, Gus 136
Young, John Preston 318, 323
Young, Tom 219
Youree, Frank 185

Lithograph by Eugène Robyn of St. Louis, from a daguerreotype by
Yandell A. Carr & Co., Memphis. From *Rainey's Memphis City Directory, 1855*.

About the Author

R. Scott Williams is a seventh-generation Tennessean dedicated to uncovering the forgotten stories of those who helped shape American history and popular culture. In addittition to this one on Marcus Winchester, he is the author of biographies on adventurer Richard Halliburton, pioneering entertainment reporter Odd McIntyre, and American folk hero David Crockett.

With a career spanning influential cultural institutions, Williams has led teams at the Newseum, a Washington, D.C. museum dedicated to journalism and the First Amendment, and at Elvis Presley's Graceland in Memphis. He is currently the CEO of Discovery Park of America in Union City, Tennessee, a museum and heritage park dedicated to inspiring discovery and curiosity in visitors of all ages.

His wife, Michelle, teaches art history at The University of Tennessee at Martin and they are blessed with two adult daughters, Alex and Liv, and a son-in-law, Eric.

Also by R. Scott Williams:

For more information, visit rscottwilliams.info.

www.ingramcontent.com/pod-product-compliance
Lightning Source LLC
Chambersburg PA
CBHW051359070526
44584CB00023B/3216